Kate Lore

The Prophethood of All Believers

James Luther Adams (Photo: George K. Beach)

JAMES LUTHER ADAMS

The *Prophethood of* *All Believers*

Edited and with an Introduction
by George K. Beach

BEACON PRESS · *Boston*

Beacon Press
25 Beacon Street
Boston, Massachusetts 02108

Beacon Press books are published under the auspices of
the Unitarian Universalist Association of Congregations
in North America.

92 91 90 89 88 87 86   8 7 6 5 4 3 2 1

Library of Congress Cataloging in Publication Data

Adams, James Luther, 1901–
  The prophethood of all believers.

  Includes index.
  1. Theology. I. Beach, George K. II. Title.
BR85.A295 1985   230'.8   85-73368
ISBN 0-8070-1602-0

Text design: Dennis Anderson

Grateful acknowledgment is given to reprint "The Posture" from *The Poetry of Robert Frost,* edited by Edward Connery Lathem. Copyright 1939 © 1967, 1969 by Holt, Rinehart and Winston. Reprinted by permission of Henry Holt and Company. The lines from W. H. Auden's "September 1, 1939" and "Musée des Beaux Arts" are reprinted from *W. H. Auden, Selected Poems, New Edition,* by W. H. Auden, edited by Edward Mendelsohn, published by Random House, © 1979. "Merry-Go-Round" by Langston Hughes is reprinted from *Selected Poems of Langston Hughes,* published by Random House, © 1974.

To Paul Johannes Tillich

And a young man ran and told Moses,
"Eldad and Medad are prophesying in the camp."
And Joshua the son of Nun,
the minister of Moses,
one of his chosen men, said,
"My lord Moses, forbid them."
But Moses said to him,
"Are you jealous for my sake?
Would that all the LORD'S people were prophets,
that the LORD would put his spirit upon them!"

Numbers 11: 27–29 *(Revised Standard Version)*

Contents

Part Four: Vocation and Voluntary Associations

Acknowledgments

I would like to acknowledge my gratitude to James Luther Adams for his warm encouragement and help in the making of this book. He has been supportive at every stage of its preparation, leaving me free to shape the book in general design and in specific detail; so too, responsibility for any shortcomings in the editing belongs to me alone.

Dr. Adams recommended the book's title (a phrase of his own invention, we believe) and the inclusion of many of the works that appear in this volume. Some of these works have been previously published; others were selected from Dr. Adams's unpublished manuscripts. An acknowledgment of original publication or an identification of the occasion for which the piece was written is given in a footnote on the first page of each essay. When changes in an original version were made, such as altering language to be gender-inclusive, Dr. Adams reviewed the editorial decisions and often supplied information or suggestions of his own.

I would like also to thank others who have helped carry this project through to completion: Linda Mountel and Elsie Kimbrell for typing manuscripts and attending to other secretarial tasks, Joan Helde for proofreading and preparing the index, Caroline Birdsall and Jeffrey Smith, editors at Beacon Press, and Pam Pokorney, Beacon's production manager, for the exacting care they have given to the preparation of the book for publication. My special thanks are due to my wife, Barbara Kres Beach, for her professional assistance and her personal support throughout the project.

Work on the book was undertaken in 1983 with the financial assistance of the North Shore Unitarian-Universalist Veatch Committee. I would like to thank the committee and others whose generous gifts have made the publication possible: Stephen H. and Dorothy Beach, Peter and Ruth Fleck, John and Muriel Hayward, Spencer and Susan Lavan, Joe and Alice Blair Welsey, Alan W. and Helene N. Wolff.

G.K.B.

Introduction

GEORGE K. BEACH

Robert Frost once said that education is a matter of "hanging around until you catch on." This suggests that once we have a grasp of the subject at hand—once we understand how it works and how it works well—we can begin to teach ourselves, extending and strengthening our grasp. But if the subject is religion, even with many years of "liberal education" behind us, many feel doubtful that it holds anything to "catch on" to. For some, religion is a "Burned-over District," as upstate New York came to be known in the last century after repeated religious revivals. For others, perhaps, there was never a teacher for whom religious learning was an engine of intellectual insight and moral energy. Yet for many James Luther Adams has been such a teacher. It is my hope that this volume will serve as a sourcebook of Adamsean insight and energy, both for those already familiar with the man and his work and for those who may, with its help, make first acquaintance with him.

Through the major part of his long career, Adams has been a professor of religious social ethics, first at Meadville/Lombard Theological School and the Federated Theological Faculty in Chicago, and later at Harvard Divinity School and Andover Newton Theological School in metropolitan Boston. He has influenced clergy of various denominations and, through his many doctoral students, the teaching of social ethics in universities and theological schools.[1] Nor has his teaching been confined to theological students. At Harvard he co-conducted seminars in religion and law at the law school, and on religion and business decisions at the business school.

In a memoir of his former teacher, Frederick S. Carney described the impact that Adams's lectures had on him at the University of Chicago, at a time when he was still undecided about his field of doctoral study.

> I was aware that this man had been an astute and resourceful foe of Nazism, of racial segregation, of big-business paternalism toward labor, and of several other forms of institutionalized evil in modern society. I expected to hear in his lectures such institutional and moral analyses as would illumine and encourage social action. And I was not disappointed. What I was almost wholly unprepared for, however, was the rich texture of theology, philosophy, law, history, literature, music, and art in which ethics was presented.

I

The precise event that stood out for me, then, and still stands out today, was a highly animated and largely spontaneous lecture of forty minutes on, of all things, the religious experience of looking at a Cézanne apple. Imagine that! Teaching ethics by employing a nineteenth-century artist to communicate to his hearers a sense of the metaphysical reality of the world, of the divine mystery that undergirds it, and of the resulting seriousness of the moral life! I decided before that day was over that my doctoral field would be Christian ethics.[2]

In short, Adams is an educator whom several generations of students have found irresistible. Intrigued by his distinctive angle of vision, they have "hung around" his lectures and informal colloquies expecting that they, too, might learn to see what he has seen.

Two notable features of Adams's pedagogical method are exhibited in many of his essays and addresses. The first is his use of striking conceptual formulations of ideas and issues—generalizations which seem, at first blush, to be oversimplifications; for example, the contrast between "prophetic" and "pietistic" religion. Attention having been arrested, qualifications are entered. It is a technique he attributes to George Lyman Kittredge, the Shakespeare scholar under whom he studied at Harvard, namely, "perpetrating a lie, and then qualifying it."

Storytelling is the other often-noted method that Adams uses. He retells, for instance, this story. Kittredge once set out to study a Latin inscription on an ancient church in Rome. Feeling uncertain of his command of Italian, he sought out a knowledgeable monk who might discuss it with him in Latin. The monk whom he found readily agreed to do so—but first, he wanted to know, who was this Latin-speaking American? Did he perhaps intend to enter the cloister? No, Kittredge replied, in fact he was not even Catholic. Eyes widening, the monk asked, was he then a *Protestant*? Yes, a Congregationalist in particular, Kittredge said, "and I hold to its tenets." Well, the monk said, at once curious and agitated, there are after all so many varieties of Protestants! How had he happened to choose *that* one? Kittredge reflected momentarily and then replied that he had perhaps not so much chosen it as inherited it. The Congregational church in his native town on Cape Cod had been his family's church for as long as they had lived there. The monk, too, reflected for several moments, then exclaimed, "You know, I think that's why I'm a Catholic!"[3]

Adams's stories entertain but are always, in my experience, more than entertainment. The foregoing story exemplifies the "shock of recognition" in a form characteristic of his thought: sudden awakening to the historical particularity in which ultimate loyalties are always embedded. Told with precision and animation, such a story distills simple and feeling-laden meanings from the complexity of human experience.

"JLA," as James Luther Adams is commonly known, is an intellectual, a man absorbed in ideas. At the same time, his striking personal qualities mark virtually all of the works in this volume. His thought and personality are so closely intertwined that it is difficult to discuss one without discussing the other.[4] Outgoing and genial, consummate raconteur, he draws freely on his experience beyond the academic world. He enjoys dialogue with "all sorts and conditions" of persons on issues of social or personal significance. Always generous with his time, he has made himself widely available to others. I first heard him speak at a youth conference in 1953. Now in retirement, so called, he receives visitors at his home in Cambridge, Massachusetts, in a continuous stream.

His erudition and powers of recall are legendary. Students have discovered that he is a ready source of bibliographical references in answer to virtually any inquiry. In his writings, allusions to the arts and the social sciences, as well as to theology, abound. His rhetoric also reflects a keen awareness of style. He enjoys an arresting turn of phrase and is capable of biting sarcasm, yet he draws most deeply on his enthusiasms. Appreciation of the work of others is for him both a pedagogical technique and an intellectual strategy: entering into and recreating their thought, incorporating their insights and formulations into his own creative synthesis.

The bibliography of Adams's published writings—essays, addresses, sermons, books, book reviews, and introductions—runs to hundreds of items.[5] Still, the lament is often heard that his writings, being scattered in various books and periodicals, are not readily available. This volume answers a major part of the need. While it excludes academically specialized and highly topical works, it includes works reflecting Adams's theological, historical, cultural, and sociological interests, in its four parts, respectively.

Written over a period of almost five decades, these essays and addresses represent a lifetime of learning. Many of them were composed for particular occasions. Some are quite short—distillations of Adams's special brand of wisdom. They reflect his distinctive viewpoint and, at the same time, the broad scope of his intellectual and ethical concerns. To use Paul Tillich's terms, they reflect an *ultimate* concern rooted in a great breadth of *proximate*—close at hand—concerns. In a remarkable personal tribute, Tillich called attention to these two sides of Adams.

> I even may confess that I feel him as "a thorn in the flesh," when "the flesh" tries to ignore the social implications of the Christian message. He represents in his whole being a warning against a theology that sacrifices the prophetic for the mystical element, though both of them, as he and I agree, are essential for religion generally and Christianity especially.[6]

While identifying the prophetic element as the nerve of Adams's ultimate concern, Tillich said he found "equally astonishing" the breadth of Adams's proximate concerns—"the largeness of interests and involvements in all sides of man's cultural creativity: in the arts as well as in the sciences."

Adams defines theological ethics as "faith seeking understanding in the realm of moral action."[7] His social ethics deals with the way in which religious and moral meanings shape forms of social organization and action, and are in turn shaped by them. His recurrent theme is the critical and creative role of prophetic faith in sustaining free institutions and in seeking a more just social order.

In the three sections that follow I seek to clarify Adams's concept of prophetic faith and to show how it developed through the course of his career. I want also to show how Adams relates philosophic assumptions to social-ethical applications, to the end that we should become "our own teachers" in relating faith and moral action—our ultimate and proximate concerns.

I

Recalling the book of Genesis account of Adam and Eve naming all the flora and fauna, Adams tells the story of how

> they finally sat down in the shade of a tree, thinking with some satisfaction, "Well, we've named them all," when suddenly something came hopping through the grass which they hadn't seen before. "What's that?" said Adam. "I've never seen that before." Eve—she was the really creative figure— seeing this thing hopping around said, "Ah, ha! It looks just like a frog to me." She named it.

Naming, Adams comments, is one of the great theological themes in Jewish thought: "Human beings, who have to achieve self-understanding and communication, have to name things; so in his commandment to name things, God was commanding something absolutely indispensable to human beings if they were going to be human beings."[8] The Genesis story suggests that human beings participate in the act of creation in a way that is essential to their personal and social humanity. The world is not complete until they have created a "humanly habitable" social reality. The process of naming to which Adams, like others, calls attention is a matter not of arbitrary labeling, but of active engagement in the world through initiative and response, will and understanding.

There is, then, a close correlation between philosophical ideas and social-ethical values. Adams's method is rooted in the Platonic dialectic— "the dialogue of the mind with itself" or process of "division" through which the basic forms of reality are marked off from one another. Adams draws contrasts along the perceived cleavages in reality and asserts connective links where things cleave together. Fundamentally, the method is one of naming: calling attention to distinctions among things of a certain kind—diversities within perceived unities—and thus giving them conceptual status. Such namings become ways in which we grasp and articulate a concept of reality.

Adams speaks of the biblical concept of covenant, in particular, as "one of the great 'namings' in theological history."[9] Covenants are solemn promises, voluntarily undertaken, that establish bonds of lasting commitment among the parties to them. In the biblical tradition, then, a "political metaphor" is used to characterize the fundamental relationship between God and humanity. Indeed, "covenant" lays the basis of an ethical and historical conception of religion in all its aspects. Reality as a whole is understood in social terms: The world is constituted by an original agreement or "covenant of being," in the phrase used by Adams. The fundamental nerve of covenant, he notes, is affection, not command or law. God is the One who will be faithful to his promises and who, through steadfast love, enables a like fidelity to take root among persons and communities.

The idea of prophetic faith arises in the context of this religious history. Prophets are those who descry the brokenness of historical covenants and demand their renewal. The prophets of ancient Israel and Judah were not so much prognosticators of future events as proclaimers of divine warning. *If* the people continue to violate the fundamental terms of their covenant with God—the charter that constitutes them as a people—*then* "there is hell to pay." The basic terms of this charter, as we see in the Mosaic Decalogue, were not only religious but also ethical—the requirements of a just community.

The two basic values of the prophetic covenant, justice and love, work together. Justice is rendered creative through compassion and care; creative justice is justice motivated by love rather than by a thirst for retribution.[10] Prophetic moral commitment is rooted in a faith that sees the essential meaning of human life in the struggle to shape and reshape a just and compassionate community. It seeks religious meaning not only in the explicitly "religious" realm but also, even especially, in the so-called "secular" realm.

The theater of prophetic faith is necessarily public and historical, requiring us to look "inward" only after we have looked "outward" to what is happening in the world. Human freedom is always exercised within the possibilities and limitations of a given historical situation. Adams points out that each person must choose what he or she will honor, trust, rely on. In this sense, faith is humanly inescapable. So, too, we are inescapably responsible for taking part in the shaping of the basic conditions of our lives. In Adams's phrase, "We are fated to be free."[11] In this process everyone must make judgments, and the better judgments are those that are overtly and critically examined. Paraphrasing Socrates, he says, "An unexamined faith is not worth having."

Adams often contrasts "prophetism" to "pietism," the latter being the perennially popular form of religion. Pietism, in Adams's lexicon, is the religion of inwardness, of individual virtue, of "peace of mind." The following program note, which he wrote for a church concert, illustrates how sharply he etches the contrast between these two religious orientations:

> The text . . . of Mendelssohn's *Elijah* [includes] the familiar biblical passage about the prophet Elijah's running away from the Lord's call to prophesy against the wickedness of King Ahab, and then in his flight being confronted in turn by a great wind, an earthquake, a fire and a tempest. Yet, the Lord was not in these but in a "still, small voice." In conventional interpretation, the still small voice has been wrongly associated only with the privatized inner life of the individual, a reduction that amounts to a spiritual lobotomy making possible an easy social and political conscience. In the Biblical narrative it possesses radical political import. Elijah's life was in danger because he had condemned the (false) gods of the authoritarian Baal and also because he opposed the queen Jezebel's attempt to import a totalitarian political system in violation of Judah's more democratic ways. The still small voice was urging him to do his duty as a prophet. Elijah was a worthy,

courageous precursor of the great eighth-century political prophets of the Covenant.[12]

As sociologist as well as theologian, Adams calls attention not only to the substantive message of the prophets of ancient Israel and Judah but also to their social standing. Because they were audacious critics of the religious and political establishments of their time, theirs was a precarious position. Like Jesus in a later age, the prophets were notoriously independent and constantly getting into trouble with the authorities. Their message to be delivered at all required their independence from the royal court, the Temple, and the people of wealth. By assuming the freedom to criticize society, the prophets established the principle of the independence of the religious sphere from official control by the state; they effected in their own era the separation of powers that is basic to the tradition of democratic societies. Also like Jesus, the prophets were not simply lone individuals; they, too, had disciples, organized groups. That their writings were preserved and eventually accepted as sacred Scripture is evidence that they formed schools of thought that demanded and in time gained recognition. Thus the prophetic as distinct from the priestly idea of Judaism became institutionalized.

From these historical roots a decisive and, for Adams, authentic form of religious consciousness sprang to life. The prophets speak in the name of the God who above all else seeks justice, mercy, righteousness, faithfulness, and peace. Faith is not primarily right or orthodox belief but fidelity to these transcendent purposes and values in the life of human communities. Great prophets of every human tradition, though they be outsiders, appeal to a covenantal bond, a fundamental law and love through which human community is shaped—and when broken, is reshaped. Being themselves bound by it, they feel compelled to speak out for it.

Radically extending Martin Luther's idea of "the priesthood of all believers," Adams speaks of "the prophethood of all believers."[13] The phrase reflects the fact that he is not simply concerned with social issues or institutions, but with the formation of the individual's *vocation* within the social-ethical covenant. Elijah's "still small voice" recalls the prophet, Adams says, to his vocation—a prophethood that properly belongs to all persons. That the community must recognize and honor this vocation of individuals becomes, in turn, its corporate vocation. Thus an essential purpose and task of groups is to remain open to diverse human perspectives, including the voices of those who have been excluded from the covenant of common well-being and political participation: the dissenters, the poor, the "marginalized" people.

Adams is interested in prophetic faith wherever it appears, including its covertly religious, humanistic, or "secular" forms. He tells this story:

> One night at two o'clock in the morning I was talking with Erich Fromm at Gould Farm [a therapeutic community in which Adams had a long-standing interest]. He used to come visit us there. I said, "I want to ask you a delicate question, a Boswellian question." He said, "Well, go ahead." "I want to ask you, what makes you tick?" He said, "I think I know that. Old Testament Messianism. From the Old Testament I learned that the meaning of history is the struggle of justice against injustice. That's what makes me tick."[14]

Prophets are often accused of being too worldly and political. In fact they are always "political theologians"—the term, Adams points out, that Edmund Burke used to excoriate the nonconforming ministers who spoke well of the political liberties claimed by the French Revolution.[15] They have been branded disbelievers in the established gods. Curiously, prophets have also often been accused of being too otherworldly, making unrealistic demands for radical transformations. They tend, like Jesus, to be messianic proclaimers of an eschatological kingdom.

Jesus' message renewed and intensified the prophetic faith in his own age. The kingdom of God he announced became the "new covenant" of early Christianity—a community of outsiders, the "poor in spirit." It was renewed again in the sixteenth and seventeenth centuries by the groups of the Radical Reformation, from which the Free Church movement first arose. The spirit of prophetic faith is heard again in Thomas Münzer, a leading figure of the Radical Reformation and the Peasants' Revolt of 1525. Adams has briefly characterized Münzer's genius:

> When one suffers, then the Holy Spirit comes in. Revelation appears to us at the point where we realize our limitations, where human nature finds its limits, where God is acting in history. . . . For Münzer grace overcomes nature; the human spirit must be denuded; the Gospel is for "the poor in spirit." Genuine faith is courage for the impossible. It springs from the abyss in one's own heart.[16]

The direct historical antecedents of contemporary liberal religion lie in the ideas and Free Church traditions of the Radical Reformation. Adams holds that for liberal religion to recover its "prophetic genius," it must

recover its sources in this era, preceding the rationalism of the Enlightenment. The emergence of a new historical situation in our time calls forth
new theological and philosophical ideas. Enlightenment liberalism was
rooted in the philosophical idealism and romanticism of the past two
centuries. The neoliberalism that Adams has advocated as more adequate to
the needs of our time is marked by a turn toward philosophical realism and
existentialism. Thus Adams cites the maxim of realism, "Being is older
than value," or recalls Friedrich von Hügel's similar reminder that "oughtness" is rooted in "isness." The imperative mood of the moralist needs to be
grounded in the indicative mood of the ontologist.

Any conception of the nature of reality—a metaphysics or an on-
tology—that does not carry temporality at its heart cannot speak to the
need of our age. Following Whitehead, Adams holds that only that which
partakes of time and space is actual. He writes:

> Alfred North Whitehead was fond of saying that "definition is the soul of
> actuality," by which he meant that particularity and limitedness condition
> every entity, yet that each entity partakes of the soul of being. The view
> recalls the prophetic outlook of the Old Testament. For the prophets, the
> once-happening individuation and scatteredness of human existence, the
> creatureliness of the human being and society, imply that everything finite is
> subject to criticism. At the same time, the particular, the individual, the
> concretely limited, is related to the Creator that transcends the particular,
> the individual, the limited. Here, then, is a positive, if qualified, evaluation
> of individuation. [17]

Adams uses Whitehead's dictum to support the idea that finitude and
particularity are necessary conditions of historical actuality. Paradoxically,
this same particularity enables a finite being to be effectively rooted in "the
soul of being." Everything appears on the stage of history by virtue of both
its separateness and its connectedness, its independence and its dependence, its uniqueness and its commonality. The dynamic interplay of these
seeming contraries, now one predominating and now the other, underlies
the dynamism of history.

These ideas form the metaphysical background of Adams's thought.
Against them his foreground concerns—for an ethics potent enough to
challenge the multiple, interlocking social crises of our age—stand in bold
relief. Because he seeks historically effective ideas, not just abstract or
theoretical truth, he constantly points to the institutional forms that ideas
take in history.

Adams reminds us that justice is achieved in history "not without dust and heat." The phrase, which he has often used, is from a passage in *Areopagitica*, John Milton's impassioned and eloquent argument for freedom from state censorship in publishing. Adams's lifelong devotion to civil liberties is but one point of affinity discernible between him and Milton; a philosophical and moral affinity can also be seen, for example in the same passage of Milton.

> It was from out the rind of one apple tasted, that the knowledge of good and evil as two twins cleaving together leaped forth into the world. And perhaps this is the doom which Adam fell into of knowing good and evil, that is to say of knowing good by evil. . . . I cannot praise a fugitive and cloistered virtue, unexercised and unbreathed, that never sallies forth and sees her adversary, but slinks out of the race, where that immortal garland is to be run for, not without dust and heat.[18]

"Cleaving" means both to divide and to cling together. Milton exploits this doubleness to suggest that knowledge is necessarily impure, partially distorting "the whole truth"; it always mixes together good and evil elements. It follows that any advance of knowledge in history requires the freedom to express and test what is held to be good or true. The testing is not only critical in the negative sense. It is also creative, insofar as any assertion of the good, the true, or the beautiful has "leaped forth into the world" from an original unity of meaning and power. Whatever is powerful and true cleaves—both splits asunder and draws together, both divides and unifies.

Milton thus invokes the biblical imagery of the creation and fall with the same double vision that Adams finds in Whitehead. If the apple is a symbol of the world, then tasting it—an act that requires breaking through the original unity contained by its "rind"—is an image of knowledge. To know, in this sense, is not passively to receive information but actively to partake of reality. Nor can this kind of knowledge rightly be claimed as the sole possession of any individual or group. Thus the quest for knowledge involves increasingly "individuated" voices in a complex and never conflict-free society of voices. It requires the institutionalization of freedom. Authentic social institutions are those that protect and promote the freedom of those who live within their covenants. Human freedom expresses the creative thrust of the spirit—toward definition, toward individuation, toward actualization in history.

To be sure, these activistic conceptions of knowledge and society are in danger of moral overreaching. In the absence of genuine self-criticism or moral humility, the part may claim to represent the whole, and in consequence tragically distort it. Indeed, Adams notes the pervasiveness of demonic distortions that rush in where arrogance and lack of self-criticism prevail. Thus he reminds us again and again that we must acknowledge that we may be mistaken. We partake of freedom not for the sake of self-aggrandizement but to renew the covenantal bond—the original relation of all things to the ultimate source of being and freedom—of which Milton's apple, or Cézanne's, is a visible sign.

e. g. Bush

II

Taking certain words of Jesus as succinct expressions of an authentic faith, W. H. Auden distinguishes the serious from the frivolous in human life.

> The past is not to be taken seriously (*Let the dead bury their dead*) nor the future (*Take no thought for the morrow*), but only the present instant and that, not for its aesthetic emotional content but for its historic decisiveness. (*Now is the appointed time.*)[19]

The central religious issue in life, then, is discernment: being able to recognize the difference between what is serious and what is frivolous. Idolatry, Auden says, is "taking the frivolous seriously."

Like Auden, Adams finds the touchstone of authentic faith in words of Jesus. A pertinent example, in this context, is his frequent appeal to Jesus' principle of discernment, "By their fruits you shall know them." Human beings necessarily believe in something; we are, Adams has said, "incurably religious." Thus the central religious problem is not atheism but idolatry, that is, not the *absence* of faith but *misplaced* faith.

Adams's personal history is a key to understanding his mature religious and intellectual stance. His autobiographical essay, "Taking Time Seriously,"[20] documents certain formative experiences of his life in response to the shifting intellectual, political, and religious currents of the age. Thus it is the story of "the education of JLA," indicating how he came to put the temporality of existence at the center of his theological and ethical thought. The Greek language distinguishes two kinds of time: *kairos*, an opportune or appointed time, and *chronos*, duration or chronological time.[21] An awareness of time as *kairos*, as fraught with "peril and possibility," in Adams's phrase, marks the prophetic consciousness. "Taking time seriously" means taking seriously the fatefulness and opportunity, the judgment and grace, that are inherent in history.

As it happened, the essay was published within a few days of the Nazi invasion of Poland, on the day memorialized by W. H. Auden's poem "September 1, 1939."

> Uncertain and afraid
> As the clever hopes expire
> Of a low dishonest decade . . .
> The unmentionable odour of death
> Offends the September night.[22]

The sense of living in a time of crisis, when great issues confront free institutions, colors many of Adams's writings. The outcome is uncertain in large part, he believes, because the religious institutions fall so far short of fulfilling their prophetic vocation. We live "under the Great Taskmaster's eye," he says, recalling John Milton's term for the God who sets new tasks for each generation. A vocation, Adams has said, is "both gift and task"— both grace and responsibility. How his own sense of vocation took shape during the first decades of his life is told in "Taking Time Seriously."

James Luther Adams was born in Ritzville, Washington, in 1901, to Lella May (Barnett) and James Carey Adams, the latter a farmer and an itinerant Baptist preacher. A large chart on the wall of his father's church made a vivid impression on him as a child. It showed the "whole plan of salvation" in several "dispensations" according to the Scofield Reference Bible. He links this memory to his lifelong interest in theories of the periodization of history—usually in three great ages—from Joachim of Fiore, the twelfth-century theologian and philosopher, to Karl Marx. Such eschatological theories arise in times of crisis, when a new dispensation or age of salvation is urgently expected or sought. Indeed, Adams's earliest childhood memory sounds an eschatological note—his deliverance after being lost in a blinding dust storm.

Eschatology, reflecting on the end of personal or cosmic time, raises many intellectual and religious puzzles. I recall Adams telling the story of his fundamentalist parents' worry, when he was a youth, that he was liable to hellfire, for he had reached the age of reason but had not attested to a personal conversion. Still young Luther (as he was called) resisted their urgent appeals, using against them what he later confessed was cruel logic.

"You say Heaven is perfect bliss and if I'm not saved I'll go to Hell?" "That's

right," they replied. "And you're so concerned because you love me?" "Yes."
"Well, if you love me and you're up in Heaven while I'm down in Hell, how
can that be perfect bliss for you?"

It was his age of reason with a vengeance. Early precocity notwithstanding,
he later responded to the altar call and was "saved."

The literal, cataclysmic eschatology of his fundamentalist upbringing
was cast aside in the course of his education at the University of Minnesota,
a process he calls his "deprovincialization." Today we find it hard to think
of eschatology in terms other than the lurid images of an Armageddon—a
final battle between cosmic forces of good and evil. This apocalyptic
imagery has recently regained currency because of awareness of the threat of
nuclear holocaust. But this secular eschatology—the end of the world by
self-destruction—does *not* signify a final conquest of satanic forces by the
godly and good, as in the Christian myth, but the opposite. Eschatology in
this modern, "demythologized" form is not a way of preserving historical
meaning through a time of troubles, but of abolishing all meaning along
with human history.[23]

Adams sharply distinguishes the mythic idea of "the satanic," evil as
absolute negation, from the prophetic idea of "the demonic," evil as a
perversion or a distortion of what is essentially good. The threat of a nuclear
holocaust, too, must be demythologized; it is not a satanic force independent of human moral control but a demonic distortion of human relatedness
crying out for a change of heart, mind, and will.

Adams transposes eschatology into the language of ethical responsibility
for what Jonathan Schell has called "the fate of the earth." He says, for
instance,

> We are already living in the future in the sense that what we do or fail to do
> will affect the future. Authentic religion, relevant concern for meaning,
> demands eschatological orientation.[24]

Many modern commentators have concluded that Jesus' announcement
that "the kingdom of God is at hand" was simply mistaken. It didn't
happen, they have said, oddly confident that they know precisely what "it"
is. In this way the centrality of eschatological expectation to Jesus' entire
message becomes a stumbling block to comprehension of his contemporary
religious and ethical relevance. Adams invites a reappropriation of Jesus'
message with the eschatological element intact. Doing good to one's friends
is only doing what comes naturally, as Jesus pointed out, but the seeds of

the kingdom of God are present in those who love their enemies, seeking in this way to befriend them and to effect a fundamentally changed situation.[25] The stumbling block remains, but it lies in the "costing commitment" that is required of us to effect significant change in the human situation. The message of an authentic prophet, Adams has said, always points to some personal cost.

On the personal level, then, every morally creative decision is eschatological, entailing a sacrifice of one's old "world" for the sake of a new. Such a decision represents the passage to a new stage of life. On the socio-ethical level, it means deciding to work for new communal bonds, understanding human history as the process through which new communities take root in the world, or else perish.

It may be said that the inward and personal side of eschatology is "conversion," that is, a fundamental change of heart, mind, and will. The personally affective element of religion comes to the fore in Adams's account of "the changes wrought" in himself through the early decades of his life. During his undergraduate years he had abandoned the fundamentalist Christianity of his youth for scientific humanism. Thereafter three major changes, or deepening levels of conversion, emerged.

An authentic conversion, in Adams's thought, is not a shift to a new fixity of belief—the popular idea of being born again. The term *conversion* is here used in Bernard Lonergan's sense of an act of "vertical freedom," the opening of a new "horizon" of understanding. Such an act allows perceptions to emerge that had been obscured by one's previous vantage point. Lonergan's schema of three interlocking levels of conversion—intellectual, moral, and religious—helps clarify Adams's development as he describes it in "Taking Time Seriously."[26]

The first major change in his mature thought came during graduate studies at Harvard under Irving Babbitt, a relationship Adams has called a discipleship. Babbitt's literary humanism opened for him a new intellectual perspective, an appreciation of the way in which basic religious ideas lie at the foundations of both Eastern and Western civilizations. Babbitt taught that personal commitment to ethical standards is essential to a great culture. Adams came to see that a new act of commitment, in a time of cultural crisis, entails "something like conversion." The enthusiasm with which he took up literary humanism, and the lasting effect it had on his interests in education, culture, and the arts, suggest that he experienced at this point in his life an "intellectual conversion."

Adams indicates that, in time, he came to see certain limitations in

Babbitt's vision. "Literary humanism did not, except in the schools, elicit participation in the processes by which a more just social order and even a humanistic education are to be achieved." He now emphasizes the distance between himself and the deeply conservative implications of Babbitt's thought. "An individual psychology of self-culture," he says, does not yet ✓ "take time seriously." But Adams did not simply reject literary humanism; he subsumed it within the larger intellectual horizon that it had opened for him.

Somewhat later Adams underwent a second, more deeply personal "change of heart"—a change involving the *will* over and above the *mind*. This change, as he tells in "Taking Time Seriously," came in the aftermath of singing Bach's *Mass in B Minor* with the Harvard Glee Club at Boston's Symphony Hall. At first exhilarated by the experience, he began to feel like a parasite—feeding on the body of a "costly spiritual heritage" but not contributing to its sustenance or renewal. Aesthetic and intellectual appreciation for Bach had come readily to him; but now, as his words suggest, the relative detachment of feeling and thought yielded to the moment of existential decision, an engagement of the will. The incident, reported with considerable reticence, has undertones of guilt and repentance. At issue was the decision to reorient his vocation in a way that would enable him to make his own social and cultural contribution. The experience suggests what Lonergan calls moral conversion.

The year 1927 brought major new commitments: Jim Adams and Margaret Young, of Salem, Massachusetts, were married, and he was ordained and installed as minister of the Second Church (Unitarian) of Salem. Adams recognized the need for shared devotional disciplines from the time of his early parish ministries in Salem and in Wellesley Hills. The Brothers of the Way, an organization Adams helped found among fellow clergy, worked out a series of personal and interpersonal disciplines that included not only daily prayer and meditation, but also active membership in a voluntary association concerned with controversial issues. He comments, "It was understood that it did not count if the individual were a member of the Library Board unless the librarian was under attack as a Communist."

Adams drew the larger world into his vocational sights from the outset. Also in 1927 he made the first of several trips to Europe, during which he pursued a wide range of opportunities for study and discussion with church leaders and theologians.[27] Again in 1935 he traveled to England, France, and Germany, taking a year to prepare for the theological professorship which he had, by this time, determined to be his calling. To further his understanding of devotional discipline and to cultivate his own spiritual life, he placed himself under the tutelage of an eminent "spiritual director," Father Charles Levassor-Berus, for an extended period in Paris. But "the inward life" could scarcely be kept inward and apart from the world in such a time, certainly not for a man of his temper. "Each week I posed my questions on prayer, and the following week he answered them," Adams recalls. "But I always felt the gap between the cultivation of mental prayer and the bludgeonings of a period of history that was swiftly moving into the storms of our time."[28]

Already in 1927 he had encountered Nazism at a Nuremberg rally, and later through Peter Brunner had been introduced to the anti-Nazi Confessing Church movement. He vividly recalls "the maelstrom of this whole experience in Germany, an experience that brought fearful encounter with the police and a frightening encounter two years later with the Gestapo." The formation in this period of the theological stance that has marked his thought ever since, and his conviction that religious ideas only come alive through engagement in a social and political context, suggest the emergence and consolidation of a "religious conversion" through these experiences.

Adams's long conversations with Rudolf Otto, the noted German scholar of Christian origins, seem to have affected him the most deeply. "In [Otto's] interpretation of Jesus," Adams says, "I saw again the man who took time seriously: 'The kingdom of heaven is at hand.'" At this point in his life, Adams was moving decisively beyond the individualistic and ahistorical ideas of freedom and the moralistic understanding of Jesus that marked the "old" religious liberalism. He did not turn back to the quest for "pure doctrine" as did many others in the wake of Barthian "neo-orthodoxy." His liberalism, though chastened by an enlarged awareness of human evil and the tragic dimension of history, found in these events renewed grounds for his conviction that theological doctrine cannot be lifted above the tides of history. It must emerge in critical and creative response to them.

As various autobiographical writings and comments more amply tell, Nazism provoked a deep sense of spiritual crisis in Adams. In this context Otto's theological insights assumed special importance for him.

What gave focus to the whole experience in Germany was Rudolf Otto's *The Kingdom of God and the Son of Man*. The conception of the kingdom as more than judgment, as redemptive dynamics, as the seed that grows of itself in the struggle against the demonic powers, the Son of Man as suffering servant, the kingdom as both present and future—all of this represented a turning point away from the consistent [or "thoroughgoing"] eschatology of [Albert] Schweitzer. In the course of studying simultaneously the anti-prophetic organic symbolisms of Nazi myth, I, like everyone else, became more vividly aware than hitherto of the role of myth in religion and culture, but more specifically I became aware of the *types* of symbolism.[29]

Adams identifies, then, two types of myth, the historical-dynamic and the cyclic-naturalistic, which he relates respectively to temporal and spatial symbols. The former normally bear positive, prophetic meaning, while the latter are regularly exploited in ways that fragment and segregate life. Nazi symbolism, such as *Lebensraum* and "the master race," is spatial; it is oriented to "blood and soil," sacred races and places. He continues:

But more significant than this sort of typology was the distinction between symbols that relate the concept of the kingdom of God to the inner life or the life of the individual, and [those] that relate the concept of the kingdom of God to institutions. Quite decisive for me was the recognition of the political character of biblical symbolism.

The experience in Germany gave Adams a "shock of recognition" as an American; he has said that at this time he came to see white racism as "our Nazism." Personally, he has said, "the experience of Nazism induced a kind of conversion"—one in which the several aspects of his mature religious position came together.

I did in those days recover a sense of the centrality of the Bible and of the decisive role in history of both the sacramental and the prophetic elements. I mention only in passing the influence of Christian art, and especially of Bach, upon me. In addition, I pressed upon myself the question, "If Fascism should arise in the States, what in your past would constitute a pattern or framework of resistance?" I could give only a feeble answer to the question. My principal political activities had been reading the newspapers and voting. I had preached sermons on the depression or in defense of strikers. Occasionally, I uttered protests against censorship in Boston, but I had *no adequate conception of citizen participation* [emphasis added].[30]

In conversation Adams judges himself still more sharply. He decided, he says, to be "a political eunuch" no longer!

Beginning in the 1940s Adams became deeply involved in Chicago ward politics. He helped organize and was active in the Independent Voters of Illinois (the I.V.I.), first as a means to fight isolationism and later to counter racism and the tide of McCarthyism. In time the I.V.I. developed sufficient political clout to command the respect of the local political establishment. Candidates were promoted, several were elected to local offices and to Congress, and the national Democratic party took note of its grass roots work.[31] Harold Ickes once told Adams that the I.V.I. was producing "the best damn political literature in the country."

On account of these activities the right wing *Chicago Tribune* attempted to smear Adams as a fellow traveler of the Communists. (It is told that rather than ever purchase this paper, he would poke through his neighbors' trash cans in the alley behind the house, sometimes in his bathrobe in the early hours of the morning, looking for a current copy — nor does he deny the story.) He tells with considerable relish of a certain *Tribune* reporter who was assigned to cover the speeches he gave.

> He would come up to talk to me after I made a speech and say complimentary things. But the next day in the paper I was presented as an ass, a bumbler in politics. So one evening I asked him, "Why are you doing this to me? You tell me my speeches are pretty good and then I pick up the paper and you present me as a first-class fool. How come?" "That's my job," he said. "I'm just doing my assignment. I'm to follow you around and write you up this way." So I said to him, "I'd just like to know, what's the difference between you and a whore?" "Well," he said, "we have a good vacation policy and fringe benefits and insurance." He listed that sort of thing. "Oh, I see," I said, "you're not a whore. You're just a very well-paid prostitute!"[32]

The activist then reverts to the professor, to explain the political lessons of his I.V.I. experience. First, Adams asserts, to make an impression on the political machine a group must *demonstrate* its influence. It had to get its people out at election time and prove that it could decide issues and elect candidates. Second, he says, a group had to generate a broad-based appeal. The single-issue people were the "friends" who most frustrated the long-term effort to build an effective political organization. Third, it is very hard to get people to attend meetings and to play their role in the shaping of policy. (Especially the professors, Adams adds: "They'd come around to my office three days before the election, poke their heads in the door and say, 'Say, Jim, whom should I vote for?' I'd throw them out!") While everyone has a contribution to make — he recalls A. D. Lindsay saying — the problem is to get them actually to make it. It is those who stay to the end of the meeting who exercise the influence, since that is when most of the decisions are made. This third lesson leads Adams to recall Robert Michels's "iron law of oligarchy." In any organization, oligarchy tends to set in; the reason, in Adams's words, is that "the members simply will not pay attention, and so the eager beavers take over."

National issues also engaged his energies. With the aid of several colleagues at the University of Chicago, Adams initiated a letter to President Harry S. Truman, dated August 27, 1945. In the name of the covenantal bond of humanity, it issued a prophetic warning and a corresponding ethical demand. Shortly after the atomic bombs were dropped on Hiroshima and Nagasaki and following the Japanese surrender, Adams was approached by Leo Szilard, the noted physicist and friend of Albert Einstein. Adams recalls Szilard as saying, "It is time for religion and science to come together" to warn against the perils of an atomic age. Thereafter Adams, with Professors Charles Hartshorne, Reginald Stephenson, and John A. Wilson, circulated the draft of a letter to the *New York Times*; signatures of sixty professors were soon gathered. It said, in part:

> The atomic bomb accentuates an already desperate need for world unification. . . . Secrecy concerning the atomic bomb is a temporary safeguard against frightful dangers; yet if we attempt, probably vainly, to maintain the secret for long, we thereby reveal and encourage unfaith in the United Nations and appear to initiate a secret armament race, preeminence in which could only be determined by sudden war, presumably catastrophic to both sides but giving a probable advantage to the aggressor or to the country with the most widely dispersed industry and population. On the other hand, if we could secure mutual sharing of information among the United Nations, a new basis of confidence and real security might be attained.
>
> Ought not the government take steps . . . with a view to finding, if possible, a more hopeful and statesmanlike solution than that of mere persistence in secrecy and the effort to maintain our technical lead? Our country has shown its strength in war. It has now to show wisdom in peace, its magnanimity and constructive daring.[33]

The "adequate conception of citizen participation" Adams had sought emerged, then, from his practical experience. From his work in local politics, especially, he drew his convictions regarding the essential and innovative role of voluntary associations in free societies. Their role necessarily entails, he says, "the power of organization and the organization of power." Over the years Adams has helped found, presided over, and otherwise participated in a great variety of organizations. Aware of his reputation for hyperactivity (some would call it his demon), he recalls a conversation he had with an old friend, Charles Hartshorne.[34] When Hartshorne spoke of having slept for eleven hours the night before, Adams said, "Charles, if I slept for eleven hours I'd be uncontrollable." Hartshorne retorted, "What makes you think you're not already?"

III

Adams's work is characterized, as we have seen, by both the complexity of many different interests and the simplicity of one central, guiding interest. Looking back on his intellectual career, he recently observed:

> A thread in my development may be traced from the early fundamentalism to my studies under Irving Babbitt at Harvard through the experience of Nazism on to the study of Tillich. Babbitt, with his emphasis on the "higher will," defends the primacy of will over intellect, and then Tillich does the same. One can trace this heritage primarily from the Bible, for instance early in the idea of the will of God, in Jesus' conception of *metanoia*, in the Pauline war among the members, and in Augustine where the authentic will is love, where "two cities" represent on the one hand the authentic will and on the other the perverted will, and on through Duns Scotus, Luther, and Calvin, and perhaps to Jonathan Edwards. With Tillich, however, autonomy is not to be repressed but is rather to be fulfilled in theonomy. In Irving Babbitt's *Democracy and Leadership* appears an appendix entitled "The Primacy of the Will," a very suggestive though somewhat inadequate presentation.
>
> In any event, I think I now understand why I went from fundamentalism (through "scientific humanism") to Babbitt to Tillich. This thread of development, to be sure, takes on its own special character by reason of my reactions to the world about me. It is significant, by the way, that my first sermon at Meadville Theological School [after returning from Germany in 1936] was on the theme "Conversion." In those days, I was reading and translating German treatises on Augustine, giving attention especially to his psychology, according to which one's attention is conditioned by one's will, what one loves—and not by reason of purely intellectual concern.[35]

Adams's own intellectual and spiritual quest reflects, then, what he has called "the perennial problem of the one and the many." He works now in one direction, drawing out a complex web of ideas and historical connections, and now in the other, drawing ideas together in a unifying concept.

For Adams the quest comes into focus in what Tillich called "the Protestant principle," the principle of prophetic protest against the claim by anything finite to represent the infinite fully or unambiguously. Only by this principle, Adams says, is religion able to "transcend its cultural entanglements at any particular time and offer both criticism and creative direction in personal and social life."[36]

Adams's major contributions in the academic world are his work on the history and theory of voluntary associations, especially with reference to their role in free societies, and his interpretation and transmission of three major theological figures of this century, Ernst Troeltsch, Karl Holl, and Paul Tillich.[37] Essays on voluntary associations and on Troeltsch and Tillich are included in this volume, as are essays on two other thinkers who have significantly influenced him, Friedrich von Hügel and Alfred North Whitehead. An interest in intellectual and social history as well as in philosophical and theological thought characterizes the work of all these thinkers. Adams has drawn deeply on the thought of Tillich and Whitehead, finding in their work a contemporary metaphysical basis for his own constructive position in theology and ethics. Yet his position cannot simply be identified with either. Once asked if he were a "Tillichian" or a "Whiteheadian," Adams replied with a wry smile, "There is always Troeltsch."

Adams's seminars and publications have furthered the renewal of interest in Troeltsch, a liberal German historian and theologian of the early twentieth century. Troeltsch is perhaps best known for his typology of forms of religious organization in Christian history and their distinctive social-ethical ideals, or "social teachings." Although not well known today outside the academic world, his influence is felt wherever the churches seek to create what Lewis Mudge has called "new social forms of faith,"[38] that is, organizational forms that are capable of meeting the challenges arising from rapid social and economic change in the modern world. Attention in recent theologies of liberation to communal forms of participation, consensus formation, and action bears witness to Troeltsch's continuing influence.

Here, too, we recognize the characteristic thrust of Adams's own thought: toward recognition of the close relationship between religious meaning and ethical import. Forms of religious community tend to dictate the forms and motives of religious social action. Such forms become models for the re-formation of the political community itself. This is why institutions, voluntary associations, churches, vocations, professions and professional organizations, families, therapeutic communities, covenants, political metaphors, and the kingdom of God all figure prominently in Adams's thought. His God is "the community-forming power."

The same institutional and historical bent accounts for Adams's interest in Friedrich von Hügel, a contemporary of William James who shared his interest in mysticism. But unlike James, as Adams has shown, von Hügel understood that religious experience is always embedded in historical institutions.[39] Adams cites James's statement, "I am no committee man," confirming his frequently voiced suspicion that those for whom religion is primarily a matter of inward or mystical experience have a "truncated" idea of religion. Their practice reflects their theory: they have little stomach for committees or other essential institutional means of doing "the humdrum work of democracy." Serious religious commitments require historical embodiment; the spirit of prophetic faith seeks to create new social and cultural forms.

Adams cites T. S. Eliot's dictum, "The *spirit* killeth, the *letter* giveth life,"[40] in support of his contention that today, at least, the enemy of authentic religious faith is not "legalism" (excessive devotion to "the letter of the law") but "inwardness" (spirituality without historical and institutional roots). "A purely spiritual religion," he says, "is a purely spurious religion." This characteristic accent of Adams's contrasts sharply with the popular view, which sees mysticism or "religious experience" as the purest form of religion.

While identifying himself with liberal religion, Adams has worked for its social-ethical and theological renewal. His "voluntaristic" philosophical position has developed, in part, as a corrective to the naively optimistic, idealistic, and individualistic tendencies of liberalism. He derides that "humanism" which, having abandoned its theological roots, is reduced to asserting, "It's good to be good." Yet he knows also that philosophical or theological ideas cannot be judged in the abstract, apart from their social and ethical "fruits." Thus Adams notes that humanistic critics of religion have often exhibited greater passion for social justice than have conventionally religious people. He enjoys telling the story of Karl Marx, who, faced with his wife and daughter dressed in their Sunday best for church services, lost all patience and thundered, "If you are so damned much interested in religion, I suggest one Sunday you stay home and read the Old Testament prophets, and you'll see what it is!"[41]

Adams's leadership within his own denomination, the Unitarian Universalist Association, is reflected in the several "intellectual agendas" that he has generated for religious liberals. They call for renewed doctrines of

God, church, and covenant, and for a renewed historical consciousness generally. From the beginning of his career as a parish minister, Adams has been an active religious institutionalist; he has practiced what he preached. But as a young Unitarian minister he soon came to feel deeply uneasy about his adopted denomination. "Religious liberalism . . . appeared to me to represent a cultural lag, the tail end of the laissez-faire philosophy of the nineteenth century." This judgment remains substantially unrevised to this day, a cruel irony for religious liberals who, despite their small numbers, like to think that the world will evolve into something "just like us." Adams writes:

> The element of commitment, of change of heart, of decision, so much emphasized in the Gospels, has been neglected by religious liberalism, and that is the prime source of its enfeeblement. We liberals are largely an uncommitted and therefore a self-frustrating people. Our first task, then, is to restore to liberalism its own dynamic and its own prophetic genius. We need conversion within ourselves.[42]

The chronic theological thinness of liberal religion will be overcome, Adams holds, as it reroots itself in the resources of its historical tradition. Particularly are the Bible and the Radical Reformation of the sixteenth and seventeenth centuries sources of its prophetic genius. The study of history not only thickens one's perception of the present; it also enables one to recover a historical and prophetic conception of religion itself. Such a conception is marked, according to Adams, by three things: interest in groups and social institutions, an eschatological (or future-directed) orientation, and an interpretation of history as marked by successive periods.[43]

I suspect that Adams would agree with Robert Frost's observation, cited at the outset of this introduction. The end of education is to "catch on," to liberate the capacity for continued, self-initiated learning. But he would add that it matters a great deal *what* it is that the learner catches on to. He has suggested that a criterion by which a liberal education can be judged is what it moves the student to do in the public realm. Here again the basic themes of Adams's thought are heard.

> History is made by groups. Groups form parties, industries, trade associations, patriotic associations, sit-in demonstrations, colleges, foundations. The types of group to which we belong largely determine the quality and the relevance of our sensitivities and commitments in the face of the changing

community. Certain groups to which we belong may serve to diffuse identity, or to draw us merely into the realm of the undifferentiated, of the interchangeable person. Other types of group may rigidify and foreclose our sensitivities and commitments. A recent study of the groups to which business and professional men in Denver belong reveals that in the main these groups entrench their members in the narrow class perspectives and the party biases to which they are accustomed and in which they feel particularly comfortable. These men are all college graduates, they have had training in the ability to think, but (judging from the report) their rational and other powers are by their type of group participation truncated and placed in the service of provincial gods. I need not give illustrations of other types of group which define and elicit a wider and deeper kind of sharing of perspective and commitment. Respecting this associational dimension of human existence, we may say of the college as well as of other people, *By their groups shall ye know them.* It is through group participation that sensitivity and commitment to values are given institutional expression; it is through groups that social power is organized. It is through groups that community needs are brought to the focus that affects public policy. It is through groups, for example, that race segregation and race desegregation are promoted. It is through groups that the cultural atmosphere of a community and a nation is created.

The liberal arts college must be tested by the quality of persons and of group participation it elicits. This quality is something that can be observed only long after the student has left the academic grove. For this reason Dorothy Canfield Fisher, the novelist, used to say that the college degree should perhaps be granted only ten years after the customary graduation day, on the basis of the graduate's performance as a citizen, as professional person, as parent. This would constitute a severe test for most of us. The suggestion, however, does accentuate the view that the liberal arts college aims to develop the rational powers of men and women, so that they may become responsible in the criticism and the service of worthy and viable ends shared by a community of free men and women. Hence, the pertinence of the two tests: *By their roots shall ye know them*; and *by their groups shall ye know them.*

Precisely these tests are presupposed in the ancient biblical doctrine of the covenant, a covenant grounded in the faithfulness of God and placing upon the believer the joy and obligations of serving the Lord of history whose power groweth not old, the dayspring on high.[44]

Adams has not attempted to create a theological or an ethical system. Many of his writings are not easily categorized, largely because he works with ideas that draw connections between seemingly disparate things. For all his theological and ethical seriousness, his intellectual curiosity is also playful; it can turn a lunchtime with the television "soaps" or an evening at Wonderland, the dog track in suburban Boston, into sociological research. Or it can turn an evening's informal gathering, such as he and Margaret hosted for Unitarian Universalist theological students and their spouses in Cambridge, into a seminar on the mysteries of Anton Webern's twelve-tone music. The material for these intellectual adventures may be either popular or arcane: He wants to grasp and include it all.

Sometimes, of course, he would plunge in and come up empty-handed. On one such occasion my wife and I went with him to a jazz performance by a group reputed, he had explained in advance, to transform Baroque contrapuntalism into popular idiom. But after listening to the droning, "mellow" sounds at some length, he turned to us and whispered with superlative mock weariness, "There is a certain sameness about it, isn't there?"

It would probably be a mistake to take the foregoing analysis of Adams's "three levels of conversion" too literally, as if they were existentially distinct or temporally successive. Rather they seem to be dimensions of any profound experience. His report on the experience of singing the Bach *Mass in B Minor* had deeply affected me on first reading. When I asked him about its import for himself, he insisted that it had affected him on all three levels—the intellectual, the moral, and the religious. Clearly it was a pivotal experience, not to be reduced merely to the moral question of what he would contribute to this "costly spiritual heritage." It was also an experience of being the recipient of an unaccountable grace, mediated by Bach's music.[45] His frequent references to conversion—*metanoia*, the New Testament Greek term that can be rendered "new-mindedness"—indicates how important the idea has been in his development. Profound changes in a person's life are sometimes not gradual but sudden, marked by "caesura" or by what Jonathan Edwards called "thunderclaps of grace." And yet, despite all protests to the contrary, such breaks with the past also preserve and transform essential elements of one's past.

If moral judgment involves the sense of being cast down, faith can be said to uplift and enable. Although the sharp edge of prophetic social criticism is virtually never absent from his work, Adams speaks of himself as a "theologian of grace." Accordingly, while his judgments can be cutting, he is never narrowly moralistic. While he reminds us that it has always been the prophet's task "to proclaim doom," he reminds us also that the proclamation is conditional. That is, he conveys also the prophet's escape clause, the divine possibilities of mercy, love, grace. Hence Adams has earned the epithet "the smiling prophet."[46]

Music has always been important in his life. He recalls when young "Luther Adams" accompanied hymns on the violin for church services led by his father, and evenings in later years when he and Margaret, a graduate of the New England Conservatory, played duets for violin and piano, especially Mozart and Handel, at home.[47] The human capacity to appreciate music is so profoundly significant, Adams suggests, that it can be called our sixth sense.

Something analagous can be said of religion. In this vein Adams has noted that Max Weber, the eminent German sociologist of religion, spoke of himself as "religiously unmusical."[48] Many people today would say the same of themselves. They may admire the passion for great issues and the expressive power of well-known figures like Martin Luther King Jr. or the artist Corita Kent, or some little-known person of their acquaintance. Still, they feel intellectually or emotionally tone deaf to the religious meanings and motives that enliven such lives. I am told, however, that anyone can learn to sing, and I am similarly convinced that even the religiously unmusical can catch on to what Adams has to teach.

Notes

1. See, for example, the papers relating to some of Adams's basic themes presented by his former students at the James Luther Adams Festival, Andover Newton Theological School, November 14, 1981. They include Donald W. Shriver Jr. on Adams as teacher, Max L. Stackhouse on the concept of vocation in Max Weber, David Little on natural law, M. Gregor Goethals on "public symbols," and Theodore M. Steeman on ethics and the social sciences; published in the *Union Seminary Quarterly Review* 37, no. 3 (1983).

2. Frederick S. Carney, "James Luther Adams: The Christian Actionist as a Man of Culture," *Perkins Review*, Fall 1972, p. 15.

3. Story told in editor's words as he recalls Adams telling it in 1983. Adams has reviewed this and the other recollections of the editor as reported in this Introduction.

4. See George H. Williams, "A Tribute to James Luther Adams," *Godbox* 2, no. 3 (Winter 1968); the essays by George H. Williams and Walter George Muelder, *Andover Newton Quarterly* 17, no. 3 (January 1977); the essays by James D. Hunt and Max L. Stackhouse in *Voluntary Associations: A Study of Groups in Free Societies: Essays in Honor of James Luther Adams*, ed. D. B. Robertson (Richmond, Va.: John Knox Press, 1966); John R. Wilcox, *Taking Time Seriously: James Luther*

Adams (Washington, D.C.: University Press of America, 1978); James D. Hunt, "James Luther Adams and His Demand for an Effective Religious Liberalism" (Ph.D. diss., Syracuse University, 1965).

5. The most complete bibliography of Adams's works to 1977—approximately 450 items—is found in Wilcox, *Taking Time Seriously*, pp. 163–208. Besides this volume, Adams's essays have been collected in two other volumes: *On Being Human Religiously: Selected Essays in Religion and Society*, edited and introduced by Max L. Stackhouse (Boston: Beacon Press, 1976), and *Voluntary Associations: Socio-Cultural Analyses and Theological Interpretation*, edited by J. Ronald Engel (Chicago: Exploration Press, 1986).

6. Paul Tillich, Foreword to *Voluntary Associations*, ed. Robertson, pp. 5–6.

7. James Luther Adams, "Ethics," in *A Handbook of Christian Theology*, ed. Marvin Halverson (New York: Living Age Books, 1958), p. 111.

8. "The Prophetic Covenant," in "Three Lectures," mimeographed from transcription by Alice Blair Wesley, Meadville/Lombard Theological School, January 1977, p. 6.

9. Ibid.

10. See George K. Beach, "Covenantal Ethics," in *The Life of Choice*, ed. Clark Kucheman (Boston: Beacon Press, 1977), pp. 117–18.

11. See "A Faith for the Free," in this volume.

12. Undated program note published by the Arlington Street Church, Unitarian Universalist, Boston, Mass.

13. See "Radical Laicism" and "The Prophethood of All Believers," in this volume. See Num. 11:29; a strikingly similar story appears in Mark 9:38–40, concluding, "For he that is not against us is for us."

14. "Covenant and Congregational Polity," in "Three Lectures," p. 41.

15. See Edmund Burke, *Reflections on the Revolution in France and on the Proceedings in Certain Societies in London Relative to that Event* (1790), ed. Conor Cruise O'Brien (Baltimore: Penguin Books, 1969), p. 93. Adams cites and discusses this passage from Burke in "Law and Love and the 'Good Old Cause,'" in this volume.

16. From the editor's notes on a lecture by Adams, October 1957. Adams sharply dissents, however, from Münzer's justification of violence, e.g., in his "Sermon Before the Princes" (1524). See *Spiritualist and Anabaptist Writings*, ed. George H. Williams (Philadelphia: Westminster Press, 1957), pp. 47–70.

17. "The Uses of Diversity," convocation address, Harvard Divinity School, 1957, pp. 5–6.

18. *Complete Poetry and Selected Prose of John Milton*, Introduction by Cleanth Brooks (New York: The Modern Library, 1950), p. 56. See also "A Little Lower than the Angels," in this volume.

19. W. H. Auden, "Postscript: the Frivolous and the Earnest," in his *The Dyer's Hand and Other Essays* (New York: Vintage Books, 1948), p. 430.

20. In this volume.

28 INTRODUCTION

21. See Paul Tillich, "Kairos," in his *The Protestant Era*, trans. with a concluding essay by James Luther Adams (Chicago: University of Chicago Press, 1948), pp. 32–51.

22. *The Major Poets*, ed. Charles M. Coffin (New York: Harcourt, Brace & Co., 1954), p. 318.

23. Gordon D. Kaufman, "Nuclear Eschatology and the Study of Religion," *Harvard Divinity Bulletin* 13, no. 3 (February–March 1983).

24. See "Pietism and Prophetism: Religion and Social Issues," in this volume.

25. "For if you love only those who love you, what reward have you? Do not even the tax collectors do the same?" (Matt. 5:46).

26. See Bernard Lonergan, *Method in Theology* (New York: Herder and Herder, 1972), pp. 237ff.

27. Adams remembers especially, in England: C. C. J. Webb, the Oxford philosopher of religion; A. D. Lindsay, master of Balliol College, Oxford, and his successors, Geoffrey Nuttall and Christopher Hill; and T. S. Eliot, with whom he had become acquainted at Harvard; in France: Gabriel Marcel and Nicholas Berdayev, the philosophers of religion, and Fr. leBreton, the church historian, in Paris; Albert Schweitzer and Fr. Maurice Nodoncelle, in Strasbourg; in Germany: Martin Niemöller, Karl Barth, Heinrich Frisch, Friedrich Heiler, Rudolf Otto, Peter Brunner—theologians and church leaders; in Switzerland: Karl Jaspers, the philosopher, and Fritz Buri, the theologian. Also in 1927 Adams first encountered the writings of Paul Tillich, who took on increasing significance for Adams in the years following (see note 37).

28. James Luther Adams, "The Evolution of My Social Concern," an address to the American Society for Christian Ethics, 1961, published in *The Unitarian Universalist Christian* 32, nos. 1–2 (Spring–Summer 1977): 14.

29. Ibid., pp. 15–16.

30. Ibid., p. 19.

31. See Leo A. Lerner, "A Reporter Recalling a Chicago Firefighter: Adams in Action (1935–1956)," *Journal of the Liberal Ministry* 6, no. 3 (Fall 1966).

32. Story transcribed from a recorded conversation with Adams, August 1982.

33. "To the President of the United States," draft copy of the letter to gather signatures, from the files of James Luther Adams, dated August 27, 1945.

34. Story told by Linda L. Barnes, "James Luther Adams: Tribute to a 'Smiling Prophet,'" *Harvard Divinity Bulletin*, June–July 1981. Wilcox, *Taking Time Seriously*, lists more than seventy organizational activities of Adams through 1977 in an appendix. Among these, Adams has been an initiator and member of the American Unitarian Association Commission of Appraisal, which brought about denominational reorganization in 1937, a member and president of the American Theological Society, a member and president of the Society for the Arts, Religion, and Contemporary Culture, a member for twenty years and an executive committee

member of the Council on Religion and Law, a founder and president of the Society for the Scientific Study of Religion, and for more than a decade chairperson of the Committee on Church and State of the Civil Liberties Union of Massachusetts.

35. From a letter to George K. Beach, January 6, 1984. On the voluntarist tradition in philosophy, see Adams, "Root Ideas of Human Freedom," in *On Being Human Religiously*, pp. 45ff., and "Freud, Mannheim, and the Liberal Doctrine of Human Being," in this volume.

36. *On Being Human Religiously*, p. 238. Adams notes that Emerson called "the one and the many" *the* problem of philosophy—the problem, in Plato's words, "to find a ground unconditioned and absolute for all that exists conditionally"; see *Sophist* 253.

37. See James Luther Adams, *Paul Tillich's Philosophy of Culture, Science, and Religion* (New York: Harper and Row, 1965; reprint New York: Schocken Books, 1970; reprint, Washington, D.C.: University Press of America, 1982); Tillich, *Protestant Era*; Paul Tillich, *Political Expectation*, introduction by James Luther Adams (New York: Harper and Row, 1971); Paul Tillich, *What Is Religion?* trans. with introduction by James Luther Adams (New York: Harper and Row, 1973). Adams is preparing for publication, with an introduction, a volume of translated essays by Tillich, to be titled *Great Figures*, and is a contributor to and editor of, with Wilhelm Pauck and Roger L. Shinn, *The Thought of Paul Tillich* (New York: Harper and Row, 1985). Ernst Troeltsch, *The Absoluteness of Christianity and the History of Religions*, introduction by James Luther Adams, trans. David Reid (Richmond, Va.: John Knox Press, 1971); Robert J. Rubanowice, *Crisis in Consciousness: The Thought of Ernst Troeltsch*, foreword by James Luther Adams (Tallahassee, Fla.: University of Florida Press, 1982). Adams and Walter F. Bense have prepared three volumes of essays by Ernst Troeltsch for publication by T. and T. Clark, Edinburgh—indicative of the renewed interest in Troeltsch. Also with Bense, Adams is editing five volumes of essays by Karl Holl, an initiator of modern Luther studies and a critic of Troeltsch, two of which have been published to date: *What Did Luther Understand by Religion?* (Philadelphia: Fortress Press, 1977), and *Reconstruction of Morality* (Minneapolis: Augsburg Publishing House, 1979).

38. Lewis S. Mudge, "Searching for Faith's Social Reality," inaugural lecture for Bond Chapel, University of Chicago, May 6, 1976.

39. See James Luther Adams, "Letter from Friedrich von Hügel to William James," *Journal of the American Academy of Religion* 45, no. 4, suppl. (December 1977): 1101–34.

40. See "The Sacred and the Secular: Friedrich von Hügel," in this volume.

41. Adams comments that Marx himself told this in a letter to an old friend; see "The Prophetic Covenant," pp. 2–3.

42. "Root Ideas of Human Freedom," p. 56.

43. "The Prophetic Covenant," pp. 3–4.

44. James Luther Adams, "The Purpose of a Liberal Arts Education," address at the installation of the president of Wagner College, Fall 1961, published in *The Journal of the Liberal Ministry* 11, no. 2 (Spring 1969): 7–8.

45. See "Music as a Means of Grace," in *On Being Human Religiously*, pp. 151–154.

46. See Barnes, "James Luther Adams," n. 34.

47. Music was but one of the personal and social concerns that Margaret and Jim Adams shared. Margaret studied English literature at Radcliffe College and social work at the University of Chicago. In Chicago she devoted considerable effort to the YWCA, including a committee concerned with wages and working conditions of domestic help. She and Jim raised three daughters and welcomed countless students and others to their home through fifty years of marriage. In 1978 Margaret succumbed to cancer. Adams dedicated his major work on Paul Tillich "To Margaret, the beloved."

48. See "The Protestant Ethic and Society: Max Weber," in *On Being Human Religiously*, p. 175.

Part One

The Spirit and Forms
of Prophetic Faith

J AMES LUTHER ADAMS IS A MAN OF APPARENTLY OMNIVOROUS
intellectual appetite. The essays and addresses which he has produced in
a constant stream, unabated even now in his mideighties, reflect his
wide-ranging interests in theology, social and intellectual history, contemporary culture, and sociology. These fields of scholarly interest form,
respectively, the organizational lines along which the works collected in
this book have been divided. The classification is rough, however, since in
his writings Adams characteristically crosses over academic boundaries and
incorporates materials from disparate sources. He has articulated an insight
into the intellectual process that aptly applies to himself: original work is
virtually always a creative synthesis of what has gone before.

Adams's central, moving concern has long been the cultural crisis of the
present age and the capacity of religious institutions to respond to it with
clarity and courage. He is above all a theologian, but one who puts
commitment to social justice at the heart of his religious commitment. The
prophetic faith to which he appeals, while rooted in the biblical prophets, is
not confined to the forms of religious life and thought of any one tradition.
The nerve of this faith is a spirit; it is a keen sense of transcendent meaning,
breaking through and re-creating the old forms of religious and cultural
life. Especially, then, it is a spirit that speaks to an age, like our own, of
crisis and change.

The first essay in this section, "Taking Time Seriously," recalls the
events through which Adams, responding to his own changing perceptions
of the crisis of this century, forged his religious and vocational identity. In
this midlife essay on his spiritual and intellectual journey, virtually the
whole outline of his mature work is visible. The inescapability of the

question, What faith shall be mine?, is treated in the essay which follows, "A Faith for the Free." Here Adams defines three "guiding principles" which shape an authentic, humanly liberating faith.

"Everyone is a theologian, whether conscious or unconscious," Adams asserts in "Prophetic Judgment and Grace," that is, "everyone has some conception of the nature of reality, of the demands of reality, and of those elements of reality that support or threaten meaningful existence." The statement encapsulates his conception of the theological enterprise. First, since faith is humanly inescapable, it is better to be a conscious and critical theologian than one short on self-critical insight. Second, not only professionals but all persons bear responsibility to reflect on the meaning of that on which they ultimately rely; hence Adams's assertion of "the priesthood and the prophethood of all believers." Third, the dynamic and historical character of reality requires that we make decisions; the prophet is one who articulates in timely ways the demands of personal and social transformation. Finally, the theological enterprise requires of us discernment among those things that either threaten or support meaningful human existence.

"The Sacred and the Secular: Friedrich von Hügel" assesses what Adams learned from the great Roman Catholic lay theologian, especially the need to give spiritual ideals worldly form and substance and to ground ethical ideals theologically. "Changing Frontiers of Liberal Religion" spells out an intellectual agenda for religious communities generally and religious liberals particularly, lest they be isolated by sectarianism and caught in a fatal cultural lag.

In "Hidden Evils and Hidden Resources" Adams describes a world in which the various "threats and supports to meaningful existence" are mingled and, as a consequence, obscurely perceived. This being the human condition, he calls the church and its ministry to prophetic insight and response to the ill-perceived and often-shunned sufferings of humanity.

Three troublesome theological issues for liberal theology are the reality of evil, the mediation of judgment and grace, and the religious necessity of religious community. These issues are addressed in the short essays that conclude this section: our need to acknowledge and yet courageously meet gross historical evils, in "A Theological Interpretation of the Holocaust"; the significance of Jesus as a mediator of ultimate meaning, particularly as one whose teachings model a parabolic form of discernment, in "By Their Roots Shall You Know Them"; and the church as a religious community in which equality and solidarity go hand in hand, in "Radical Laicism."

G.K.B.

1 · *Taking Time Seriously*

My earliest recollection goes back to the year 1906 when I was four years old. Our family was kneeling in prayer, all of us burying our heads in pillows. We could scarcely breathe, for our farmhouse was in the path of one of the worst dust storms of a decade in the Pacific Northwest, and we were praying for relief. A few minutes before, blinded by the dust, I had lost my way in the farmyard, and on rejoining the family circle my prayer may well have been one of thanksgiving for having found the path to the house as well as of petition for the quieting of the wind. I was told much later that my father, a Baptist country preacher of premillenarian persuasion, prayed then and there for the Second Coming.

At one time my father was what might be called a circuit rider and I can remember riding behind him on horseback on some of his trips. Later on, I used to take my violin along in order to accompany the hymn singing.

My father was as otherworldly as the head of a family could possibly be. Very often he would tell us after family prayers before retiring at night that we might not see each other again on this earth. Christ might come before morning and we should all meet him in the air. He interpreted the World War as evidence of the approaching end of the present "dispensation." Later on, after he had joined the Plymouth Brethren, he refused on religious principle to vote. He gave up his life insurance policy because he felt it betrayed a lack of faith in God. When he was employed by the American Railway Express Company he refused to join the union on the ground that it was a worldly organization with worldly aims. Indeed, he had taken up railway work because of his decision to follow St. Paul's example and refuse to accept wages for preaching the gospel. In short, my father was a man of principle.

By the age of eleven I knew the whole plan of salvation according to the Scofield Reference Bible, and I testified for it in season and out. I even preached on the street and at the Salvation Army during my earlier years in college. The break came before I left college, but I did not give up religion.

Copyright 1939 Christian Century Foundation. Reprinted by permission from the September 6, 1939, issue of *The Christian Century* 61, no. 36. It was subsequently printed in Adams's *Taking Time Seriously* (Glencoe, Ill.: The Free Press, 1957).

I simply changed my attitude: I decided that it was my mission to attack religion in season and out. I became a "campus radical" and joined with some other quondam fundamentalists to publish an undergraduate free-lance sheet which we smugly called the *Angels' Revolt*. My new law was in the scientific humanism of John Dietrich and my new prophecy was in the anti-Rotarianism of H. L. Mencken.

One of the great surprises of my life came at the end of my senior year in college. I had been taking a course in public speaking and all my speeches had been vicious attacks on religion as I knew it—at least, they had been as vicious as I could make them. The shock came one day when on leaving the classroom I happened to say quite casually to the professor that I did not know what I was going to do after graduation. I was already profitably engaged in business, but I was thoroughly discontented. The professor replied in a flash, "You don't know what you are going to do? Why, I have known for months. Come around and talk to me some day." And then, right there in the presence of my enemies, the fundamentalists, he smote me. "There is no possible doubt about it," he said. "You are going to be a preacher!" Later, I went by night, like Nicodemus, to question this strange counselor, Professor Frank Rarig. Within six weeks the arrangements were complete. I was to attend Harvard Divinity School.

II

The changes that have taken place in me since then have been changes largely characterized by a slow process of deprovincialization, and yet by a process that has found its frame of reference for the most part in the catholic tradition of Christianity. The thread of continuity running through these changes has been an interest in history. Hence, the French proverb that the more human nature changes the more it remains the same, may find some illustration in my own thinking. After all, the expectation of the Second Coming "when time shall be no more" involved at least an otherworldly, negative interest in history. The major change (aside from a difference in attitude toward science and toward the kind of authority the Bible posses-ses) centers around a change of attitude toward, rather than a diminution of interest in, time. Whereas in my youth I felt myself to be a stranger in time, a pilgrim on a foreign strand, now (largely under the influence of Dewey, Whitehead, Tillich, and the Bible) I believe time itself to be of the essence of both God and human being. Whereas formerly I thought of salvation as an escape of the elect from time, I now envisage it as taking place in community and in time, whether here or hereafter.

III

At the beginning of this decade, I was a disciple of Irving Babbitt, the leader of the movement known as literary humanism. As I look back upon this phase of development, it seems to me that there was little at variance between what I took from Babbitt and what I had gained from the theological and historical disciples of the divinity school. Babbitt (along with Paul Elmer More) did for me what he did for hundreds of others. He made the religious ideas of Plato, the Buddha, and Jesus, as well as Christian theology, come alive. He led us back to fundamental ideas, but by a path that seemed new.

Scientific humanism had stressed a faith in education and in progress through science. At the same time it was, when consistent, purely relativistic in its ethics. Literary humanism, to my mind, had a more realistic conception of human nature: It envisaged the central problem of civilization as that of ethical standards and, without being obscurantist, it stressed the necessity of something like conversion, of a change in the will whereby a person would develop inner ethical control and work toward a richly human, universal norm. Through Babbitt's stress on these ideas I came to understand and value Greek and Chinese humanism, the Christian doctrines of sin and grace, and the Christian emphasis on conversion and humility. I also thus acquired a skepticism of the romantic liberal conception of human nature which was later to be so severely scrutinized by "realistic theology."

Yet literary humanism, despite its challenging sense of the past, did not possess a dynamic conception of history. The meaning of history tended to be localized more in the individual than in society. This was, to be sure, a needed emphasis at a time when humanitarianism was equated with Christianity by many of the "social gospelers," and with religion by scientific humanists. But, with the reading of Karl Marx and a study of the Anglo-catholic view of the church and its role in society, I began to look upon literary humanism as more satisfactory as an individual psychology of self-culture than as a social and institutional psychology. Literary humanism did not, except in the schools, elicit participation in the processes by which a more just social order and even a humanistic education are to be achieved.

Moreover, the humanistic interpretations of sin and grace and humility were truncated. As I indicated in my long critique of literary humanism, which appeared in *Hound and Horn* in 1932, these interpretations seemed to me to be only humanistic parodies of Christian theology. Humanism envisaged them in too narrow a frame of reference. It reckoned without its host, "our neighbor the universe." Both scientific and literary humanism had done what Millet did when he first painted *The Sower*. They and he alike left no room on the canvas for the field into which the sower was casting his seed. Like the Millet of the second (and better-known) painting, I felt that the man should be placed in a larger setting so that there might be two principals rather than one: the man *and* the earth upon which he is dependent for the growth of the seed.

It was only later that the full significance of the New Testament idea concerning the seed growing of itself was to be impressed upon me by Rudolf Otto. At that time, Henry Nelson Wieman's definition of God provided a great stimulus. Religion, I came to believe, requires the declarative as well as the imperative mood. It has to do with facts as well as with hopes and demands, facts about human beings, especially about the resources upon which we are dependent for growth and re-creation. I began to appreciate again certain aspects of the Christian doctrines of creation and redemption. Humanism, in eschewing metaphysics, presupposed an unexamined metaphysics, and I decided that an unexamined metaphysics was not worth having.

My gratitude to Irving Babbitt has increased with the years and will probably continue to increase; indeed, I have tried to give expression to it in my contribution to the volume in honor of Babbitt published by some of his students. Nevertheless, I was constrained to go beyond humanism, both scientific and literary. My desire was to find a metaphysics in addition to ethical standards and a meaning in history which would involve them both.

IV

At this time two significant changes took place. One of these changes was brought about through my work as a minister in the liberal church. The other was induced through my reading of Baron Friedrich von Hügel. But before speaking of these developments, I should like to repeal reticence still further by referring to a personal experience.

At the beginning of this decade I was a graduate student of philosophy and comparative literature at Harvard. During this period I became a member of the Harvard Glee Club. Nathan Söderblom has remarked that Bach's *St. Matthew Passion* music should be called the Fifth Evangelist. So was Bach for me. One night after singing with the club in the *Mass in B Minor* under Serge Koussevitzky at Symphony Hall in Boston, a renewed conviction came over me that here in the mass, beginning with the *Kyrie* and proceeding through the *Crucifixus* to the *Agnus Dei* and *Dona nobis pacem*, all that was essential in the human and the divine was expressed. My love of the music awakened in me a profound sense of gratitude to Bach for having displayed as through a prism and in a way that was irresistible for me, the essence of Christianity.

I realize now that this was only the culmination of my *praeparatio evangelica*. For suddenly I wondered if I had a right even to enjoy what Bach had given me. I wondered if I was not a spiritual parasite, one who was willing to trade on the costly spiritual heritage of Christianity, but who was perhaps doing very little to keep that heritage alive. In the language of Kierkegaard, I was forced out of the spectator into the "existential" attitude. This experience as such was, to be sure, not a new one: It was simply a more decisive one. I could now see what Nietzsche meant when, in speaking of the *Passion* music, he said, "Whoever has wholly forgotten Christianity will hear it there again."

V

As an active minister (which I had been from the time of my graduation from Harvard Divinity School in 1927), I began to feel an increasing uneasiness about religious liberalism. It appeared to me to represent a cultural lag, the tail end of the laissez-faire philosophy of the nineteenth century. Its competitive character and its atomistic individualism forced upon me the question of what the theological method of liberalism is and should be, and also of what its religious content actually is. Reinhold Niebuhr, Walter Marshall Horton, and John Bennett had their share in pointing up these questions, if not in raising them. Especially influential at that time was T. S. Eliot's criticism of Babbitt's cosmopolitanism and the strictures of Hermelink and Otto upon so-called universal religion.

Through these writers as well as through personal experience I came to see that religion lives not only by means of universally valid *ideas*, but also through the warmer, more concrete, historical tradition that possesses its sense of community, its prophets and its "acts" of the apostles, its liturgy and literature, its peculiar language and disciplines. "The spirit killeth, the letter giveth life." Not that I doubted the validity of the principle of disciplined freedom. Rather the question was: Is there a liberal church, or are there only aggregates of individuals, each claiming to search the truth—as though none had yet been found? Despite my (still existing) conviction that the empirical method is the proper one for theology,

Anglo-catholicism and Barthianism with their respective emphases on a common faith and a "church theology" served as a challenge.

These questions were the source of great distress to me. I even contemplated giving up the ministry and going into teaching. Indeed, I did later become a full-time instructor in English at Boston University, continuing the while my work as a minister.

Some of the younger Unitarian ministers in New England had organized themselves into a study group for the purpose of working out together a critique of liberalism and also of searching for a remedy. Over a period of years this group (later to be known as the Greenfield Group) read, discussed, and wrote papers on the outstanding theologians of the twentieth century as well as on some of the earlier ones, both Roman Catholic and Protestant. They hammered out together a "church theology" that would enable them as liberals to restate in modern terms the Christian doctrines of God and the human being, of sin and grace, and of the church. Pursuing the implications of their group method, they attempted to set forth the principal disciplines that these doctrines seemed to demand. Nor did they confine their attention to the harmless concerns of academic theology. The necessity of carrying their conclusions over into the work of the church and a year spent studying books like Troeltsch's *Social Teachings of the Christian Churches* helped us, as F. R. Barry would say, to make our Christianity relevant. But many of us felt that we had much to do yet before we learned to take contemporary history seriously.

VI

Although von Hügel did not meet this need for orientation in time, his influence upon me and certain other Unitarian ministers in the Greenfield Group was profound. My own interest in von Hügel I owe, like many another fruit-bearing seed, to Dean Willard Sperry of Harvard Divinity School. Von Hügel's philosophy of critical realism, his emphasis on the role of the body, history, and institutions in religion, his attack (along with Maritain's) on the "pure spirituality" of unhistorical, noninstitutional, nonincarnational religion became determinative for my conception of religion. Much of this side of von Hügel was the more impressive because of the way in which he showed how James Martineau, a Unitarian theologian, had espoused similar views. Through reading von Hügel's *Letters to a Niece* I found a new reality in the devotional life, especially because of his insistence that there should exist a tension between the sacred and the secular, and between Hebraism, Hellenism, and science.

I went on from von Hügel to the reading of certain of the other great spiritual directors of history, and especially of St. Francis of Sales. Several groups of Unitarian ministers at about this time were developing cooperatively certain disciplines for the devotional life. One of our groups (the Brothers of the Way), suspicious of the sort of devotions that aim at a cloistered virtue, included within its disciplines weekly visits of mercy to the needy, a "general" discipline of active participation in some secular organization of socially prophetic significance, and an annual retreat where we participated in discussions of social issues and in the sacraments of silence and of the Lord's Supper.

A sense for the ontological, the historical, and the institutional elements in Christianity was by now deeply formed. Still I only vaguely apprehended the relation of all these things to the history that was in the making. This statement seems to me accurate despite the fact that I had been actively interested in strikes (a minister could not live in Salem, Massachusetts, without having something to do with strikes), despite the fact that I knew something about the lot of the laborer by having worked for six years on the railroad, and despite the fact that one of our groups of Unitarian ministers had for a period used St. Francis of Sales and Karl Marx for daily devotional reading. I was not yet taking time seriously. Von Hügel, like Babbitt, had increased in me a sense of the past which gave perspective to immediate interests, but he had no theology for social salvation.

VII

In 1935 and 1936 I spent almost a year abroad in preparation for coming to teach at the Meadville Theological School in Chicago. Because of my interest in the liturgical movement, I devoted a portion of my time to visiting Benedictine monasteries. But I spent the greater part of the year attending lectures in philosophy and theology in French and Swiss universities. I also became familiar with the writings of a French Protestant religious socialist, André Philip, a professor of law in Lyons and a member of the Chamber of Deputies.

Pursuing still further my interest in the devotional life, I secured through the good offices of Catholic friends in America a spiritual director at the famous seminary of Saint Sulpice in Paris. Two hours a week for a period of three months with one of the finest spirits I have known will not be forgotten. Here I came to know a man for whom the devotional life was far more than a discipline. It was a growing in the grace and knowledge of Christ. He did for me what I should have expected from a Protestant: he acquainted me with a living Christ. Yet the Christ he made vivid for me was not the harbinger of the Kingdom, but rather the obedient servant of God in the inner life and in the personal virtues.

On leaving France I went to live with an old Harvard friend, Peter Brunher, a German, who was professor of theology in a Confessional Front theological school and who had just been released from a concentration camp. Through his aid I became acquainted with Confessional Church leaders in the various sections of Germany. I saw with my own eyes what I had previously not seen even in print. I accompanied one young minister just out of concentration camp on a preaching tour, and I heard him speak out against the government, mincing no words, knowing that very often the secret police were in his audience.

I soon learned, of course, that these Confessional people have little interest in strictly social and political questions, that they are scarcely aware of the fact that their present plight is tied in with the breakdown of capitalism. But I learned at first hand what it means when we say that the struggle in our world is between paganism and Christianity, between nationalism and Christianity. I talked not only with Martin Niemöller but also with his enemies and with leaders in the German Christian and pagan movements. I learned what the existential attitude is in a situation where the options are living options. By hearing it read in the homes of the persecuted, I learned again how the Bible may be more than something to be read as great literature. I learned the meaning of decision and commitment.

Then I went to visit Rudolf Otto, who was in retirement and whom I had the good fortune to see for an hour or two a day throughout the summer. The struggle of the church was never for long out of our conversation. But more important for me were the discussions of his last, and greatest, book, *The Kingdom of God and the Son of Man*. In his interpretation of Jesus I saw again the man who took time seriously: "The kingdom of heaven is at hand." Already it has partially entered into time, it grows of itself by the power of God (here again was the seed growing of itself), it demands repentance, it is an earnest of the sovereignty of God. It is a mystery. Yet the struggle between the divine and the demonic is evident to all who can read the signs of the times.

VIII

Scarcely a better preparation than the reading of André Philip and the time spent with Otto and among the Confessional Church leaders could have been given me for becoming acquainted subsequently in 1936 and again in 1938 with another group, certain students and admirers of Paul Tillich. I had first become familiar with Tillich's point of view when I was in Germany in 1927. For the appreciation of his use of the voluntarist tradition beginning with Duns Scotus and coming down through Jakob Böhme and later Friedrich Schelling, I had been prepared also by previous acquaintance with the writings of Kurt Leese of Hamburg.

In Tillich's writings I now found a binding together of many of the more significant things that had attracted me in the preceding decade. In his theology I was confronted by a prophetic restatement of the ideas of the Kingdom, of the divine and the demonic, of time being fulfilled, of judgment, of sin and grace, all interpreted in the light of the voluntaristic tradition that I had earlier approached through pragmatism as well as through literary humanism. And, what is more important for me, they were interpreted also in relation to the social (and antisocial) realities that constitute present-day history: self-sufficient nationalism, fascism, communism, capitalism, Bible Protestantism, Roman Catholicism, estheticism, intellectualism on the side of virtual resistance to the grace of God acting in history, and a religious socialism theonomously aware of the dialectical nature of God, human being, and history on the other side.

There is much in Tillich that still remains for me obscure and, where understood, unacceptable. His view of Christ as the center of history and his reading of his own philosophy of religion into Reformation theology are to me unconvincing. Yet, it seems to me that American theologians have much to gain from acquiring a greater familiarity with his work, much of which remains untranslated. In Tillich's view of the dialectical nature of reality, of revelation, of God, of the Kingdom, of human nature and history, I find an interpretation and an application of Christian doctrine which are far more relevant to the social and divine forces that determine the destiny of humanity than in any other theologian I happen to know about. Here, if ever, is a theologian who takes time seriously. This aspect of his thought comes best into relief when he is contrasted with Barth. Indeed, Tillich has made the most penetrating criticism of so-called dialectical theology that has yet appeared, namely, that it is not in truth dialectical.

One who takes time seriously, however, must do more than talk about it. He must learn somehow to take time by the forelock. He must learn to act as a Christian and as a citizen through socially effective institutions, to do what E. C. Lindeman has called the humdrum work of democracy. I for one now believe that every Christian should be actively and persistently engaged in the work of at least one secular organization that is exercising a positive influence for the sake of peace and justice against the forces of hate and greed. But even this is, of course, not enough.

The question is whether the churches as corporate bodies can learn to take contemporary history seriously, whether Christianity will act in time, whether it will not as at the beginning be betrayed in its critical moment by those who sit at its table. The danger is, as Stanley Jones has recently warned us, that the church will be more interested in itself than in the Kingdom. Otto Dibelius once inadvertently wrote of the twentieth century as the "century of the church." What has happened since that phrase was coined lends to it an ironic and ominous overtone. This is indeed the century of the church. It is the century in which the church will have to decide unequivocally whether it means business, whether it will play a constructive role in the dynamic process that makes history meaningful. It will have to come to grips with pacifism, nationalism, and capitalism.

This, then, is the change that the decade has wrought in me. Christianity is no longer an optional luxury for me. Salvation does not come through worship and prayer alone, nor through private virtues that camouflage public indolence. Time and history are fraught with judgment and fulfillment. *We* are in the valley of decision. But there is reason for hope, for God will make all his mountains a way.

2 · A Faith for the Free

All men and women are faithful, but not all can distinguish between faiths and separate the good from the evil. Even the great, good words of ancient religion do not always draw upon a full treasury of great and good faith. The words can circulate as a debased currency, a currency that can be used for illicit traffic in credulity.

The very age and the universal appeal of religion make it almost inevitable that its words shall degenerate into a debased coinage, a coinage that sometimes deceives even the elect and that repels those who would prefer moral and intellectual integrity to "piety." Every sharp ear would detect the counterfeit ring of this debased coinage of "faith," this brummagem currency of credulity. With good reason a modern prophet has said, "The beginning of all criticism is the criticism of religion."

Not only religion as ordinarily understood requires this criticism. Religion can disguise itself in protean ways. A new faith can hide behind what appears to be irreligion. The criticism of religion must include the criticism of the faiths that are concealed behind seemingly irreligious words and acts.

What, then, is faith?

To many people the word signifies the acceptance of something that puts a strain on the intelligence. Accordingly, faith is to them a belief in what is not true or in what is by nature not fact but wish.

To others the word *faith* signifies the acceptance of some belief simply because a church, a tradition, a state, a party, demands it. They may recall that St. Ignatius of Loyola once said, "We should always be disposed to believe that that which appears to us to be white is really black, if the hierarchy of the Church so decides." With some justification, then, they hold that faith is a belief in "some nice tenets," a "dear deceit" (as archaic as those phrases suggest), which relieves one of the responsibility of thinking for oneself; it is therefore a positively dangerous thing, a form of bigotry that will brook no questioning or criticism and that dresses itself up as "the cure for modern pride" and as "humble obedience to the will of God."

But conventionally "religious" people have no monopoly on credulity.

This essay originally appeared in *Together We Advance*, ed. Stephen H. Fritchman (Boston: Beacon Press, 1946). Reprinted by permission.

Those who reject the inherited "faith" are sometimes only the victims of a new credulity. Nothing could be more credulous than the belief that faith dies when some traditional belief dies. Our world is full to bursting with faiths, each contending for allegiance. Hitler claimed to teach again the meaning of faith, Mussolini shouted to his disciples, "Believe, follow, and act." "Fascism," he said, "before being a party is a religion." Those who were called to put down the battalions of the brown shirts and the black shirts were asked to show the faith that lies behind freedom.

So the procession of the gods passes over the stage of our world. Human history is not the struggle between religion and irreligion; it is veritably a battle of faiths; a battle of the gods who claim human allegiance.

An Unexamined Faith Is Not Worth Having

Not long ago I heard a German exile tell a story of Nazi horror. As he reached the end of his story he became mute with revulsion and indignation. How could he speak with sufficient contempt of what the Gestapo had done to his friend? Painfully he groped for words, and then, speaking with revived fear of the Gestapo officers who had committed the murder in cold blood, he asked, "Are these men completely without awe, are they completely without faith?" Immediately he answered his own question: "There is," he said, "no such thing as a man completely without faith. What a demonic faith is the faith of the Nazis!" We can readily understand what he meant. The differences among people do not lie in the fact that some have faith and others do not. *They lie only in a difference of faith.* The Gestapo put its confidence in obedience to the Führer, in obedience to the call of "blood and soil." Its victims placed their confidence in something thicker than blood, in something stronger than death or fear of death. Whether or not this particular victim used the word "faith" or any other words from religious tradition, we do not know, but it is evident that he put his confidence in something more powerful and commanding than the Gestapo. It is possible that his was a faith for the free. In any event, such a faith did rise up against the Gestapo.

Fortunately, not many of us have had the experience of confronting Gestapo agents. We have liked to believe that we did not share *their* faith, yet we have all had some part in creating or appeasing Gestapos—and we could do it again. We have also had some part in stopping the Gestapo. In fact, the spirit, if not the brutality, of the Gestapo has to be stopped in ourselves every day, and we are not always successful, either because of our impotence or because of our lack of conviction. The faith of the unfree can raise its ugly head even in a "free" country.

Recently this fact was impressed upon me in an unforgettably vivid way. During the Second World War it was at one time my task to lecture on the Nazi faith to a large group of U.S. Army officers who were preparing for service later in the occupation army in Germany. As I lectured I realized that together with a just resentment against the Nazis I was engendering in the students an orgy of self-righteousness. This self-righteousness, I decided, ought somehow to be checked. Otherwise, I might succeed only in strengthening the morale of a bumptious hundred-percent "Americanism," and that was not the faith we were supposed to be fighting for. Toward the end of the lecture I recapitulated the ideas of the Nazi "faith," stressing the Nazi belief in the superiority of the Teutons and in the inferiority of other "races." I also reminded the officers of similar attitudes to be observed in America, not only among the lunatic and subversive groups but also among respectable Americans in the army of democracy. Then I asked these army officers to pose one or two questions to be answered by each man in his own conscience. First: "Is there any essential difference between your attitude toward the Negro and the Jew, and the Nazi attitude toward other 'races'—not a difference in brutality but a difference in basic philosophy?" "If there is an essential difference," I said, "then the American soldier might logically become a defender of the Four Freedoms, but if there is no essential difference between your race philosophy and that of the Nazis, a second question should be posed: 'What are you fighting for?'"

I blush when I think of some of the responses I received. I was immediately besieged with questions like these: "Do you think we should marry the 'nigger'?" "Aren't Negroes a naturally indolent and dirty race?" "Haven't you been in business, and don't you know that every Jew is a kike?" Questions like these came back to me for over an hour. I simply repeated my question again and again: "How do you distinguish between yourself and a Nazi?" Seldom have I witnessed such agony of spirit in a public place.

Many of these Americans who could not distinguish between themselves and Nazis came from "religious" homes, or they claimed to be representatives (or even leaders) of the American faith. Apparently their faith was quite different from the faith behind the Four Freedoms. On the other hand, many of them no doubt would have disclaimed possessing anything they would call faith, yet all of them, whatever their answers to these questions, spoke the faith that was in them, and for many of them it was a trust in white, gentile supremacy—faith in the blood.

Faith is by no means dead in the world. A devil's plenty of it is loose on the planet. "A man bears beliefs," said Emerson, "as a tree bears apples." He bears beliefs about himself, about his fellows, about his work and his play, about his past, about his future, about human destiny. What he loves, what he serves, what he sacrifices for, what he tolerates, what he fights against—these signify his faith. They show what he places his confidence in.

Right or wrong, our faith must needs express itself and have its consequences for woe or weal. There is no escape. We cannot escape history, whether it be the history around us, the history behind us, or the springs of history within us, for all of these are forces that make history—and we are caught in history. Down among the nerve cells and fibers, up in the brain cells as well as out in the world around us, faith is at work—or, rather, a multitude of faiths is at work.

The question concerning faith is not, Shall I be a person of faith? The proper question is, rather, Which faith is mine? or, better, Which faith should be mine? for, whether a person craves prestige, wealth, security, or amusement, whether a person lives for country, for science, for God, or for plunder, that person is demonstrating a faith, is showing that she or he puts confidence in something.

The faiths of the twentieth century have been as powerful and influential as any that have ever been. They have created its science and its atom bombs, its nationalisms and its internationalisms, its wars and its "peace," its heroisms and its despairs, its Hollywoods and its Broadways, its Wall Streets and its Main Streets, its Gestapos and its undergrounds, its democracies and its fascisms, its socialisms and its communisms, its wealth and its poverty, its securities and its insecurities, its beliefs and its unbeliefs, its questions and its answers.

We must not believe every "pious" man's religion to be what he says it is. He may go to church regularly, he may profess some denominational affiliation, he may repeat his creed regularly, but he may actually give his deepest loyalty to something quite different from these things and from what they represent. Find out what that is and you have found his religion. You will have found his god. It will be the thing he gets most excited about, the thing that most deeply concerns him. But speak against it in the pulpit or the Pullman car, and he may forget what he calls his religion or his god and rush "religiously" to the defense of what really concerns him. What moves him now is more important than his creed or his atheism; it gives meaning and direction to his life, to his struggles, and even to his foibles.

WE ARE FATED TO BE FREE

The fact that every man and woman, whether they will it or not, must put trust in something, is no basis for any particular faith. Rather, the necessity as well as the fact shows only that we humans must *choose*. We cannot escape making a choice, nor can we escape the responsibility for the choices we make, any more than we can escape their consequences. We cannot hide behind someone else's authority or choice. Whenever we delegate a decision to someone else, or to the Bible or a church, we have made a decision. The decision is still our own, and the claim that humility dictates the decision does not make the decision any the less our own.

We cannot escape from freedom and its responsibilities. Every attempt to do so is an act of freedom, an act that must be implicitly repeated at every moment. Freedom is our fate as well as our birthright, and we cannot, even if we wish to, slide back into vegetability. Even the abuse of freedom is a use of freedom. Hence in our kind of world *every* faith is, in a certain sense, a faith of the free, whether it is a faith that takes us with the prodigal son to eat with swine, or a faith that shackles us to a political or an ecclesiastical Führer, or a faith that generates freedom. *We have no choice but to be free in the choice of our faith.*

Just because we are compelled to make a decision and a choice we are compelled to have faith in ourselves. Even those who say they cannot trust their judgments will have to do so to the extent of deciding what they can trust. Indeed, those who claim to be able to identify an infallible authority "above" themselves really claim to be themselves infallible. Such a claim as this presupposes an unwarranted (and credulous) faith in humanity.

Even the less credulous faith that acknowledges human fallibility also requires a faith in humanity. This faith may be a more modest one than that of orthodox belief in infallibility, but it holds that a more reliable object of faith can be found if people are free to learn from each other by mutual criticism, free to discard old error, free to discover new insight, free to judge, free to test. The free person's faith is not merely a faith in oneself: It is a faith in the capacity of sincere persons to find freely together that which is worthy of confidence. John Milton, the great Puritan apostle of freedom, epitomized this faith in discussion in those ringing words that are always quoted when freedom of printing and of speech seems threatened: "Who ever knew truth put to the worse in a free and open encounter?"

The free woman and the free man are not bound to accept a faith "once delivered." Indeed, they see no virtue in accepting a faith simply on the ground that it was determined before their births. In their view, consensus, not compulsion, free and open discussion, not docile obedience, should rule in matters of faith. The denial of the right and duty to discuss one's faith is tantamount to making credulity a work of piety.

The free person does not live by an unexamined faith. To do so is to worship an idol whittled out and made into a fetish. The free person believes with Socrates that the true can be separated from the false only through observation and rational discussion. In this view the faith that cannot be discussed is a form of tyranny.

An unexamined faith is not worth having, for it can be true only by accident. A faith worth having is a faith worth discussing and testing. To believe that a fence of taboo should be built around some formulation is to believe that a person can become God (or his exclusive private secretary) and speak for him. No authority, including the authority of individual conviction, is rightly exempt from discussion and criticism. The faith of the free, if it is to escape the tyranny of the arbitrary, must be available to all, testable by all (and not merely by an elite), valid for all. It is something that is intelligible and justifiable.

THREE TENETS OF A FAITH FOR THE FREE

As creatures fated to be free, as creatures who must make responsible decisions, what may we place our confidence in? What can we have faith in? What should we serve?

1. *The first tenet of the free person's faith is that our ultimate dependence for being and freedom is upon a creative power and upon processes not of our own making.* Our ultimate faith is not in ourselves. We find ourselves historical beings, beings living in nature and history, beings having freedom in nature and in history. The forms that nature and history take possess a certain given, fateful character, and yet they are also fraught with meaningful possibilities.

Within this framework the person finds something dependable and also many things that are not dependable. One thing that is dependable is the order of nature and of history which the sciences are able to describe with varying degrees of precision.

How long the order of nature will continue to support human life is beyond our ken. Probably our earth and our sun will one day cool off and freeze. Moreover, everyone is condemned to what we call death. Whether beyond this death there is a new life is a matter of faith, of a faith that trusts the universe as we have known it. Like one of old we may say to this universe and its ruling power, "Into thy hands I commend my spirit."

Whatever the destiny of the planet or of the individual life, a sustaining meaning is discernible and commanding in the here and now. Anyone who denies this denies that there is anything worth taking seriously or even worth talking about. Every blade of grass, every work of art, every scientific endeavor, every striving for righteousness bears witness to this meaning. Indeed, every frustration or perversion of truth, beauty, or goodness also bears this witness, as the shadow points round to the sun.

One way of characterizing this meaning is to say that through it God is active or is fulfilling himself in nature and history. To be sure, the word *God* is so heavily laden with unacceptable connotations that it is for many people scarcely usable without confusion. It is therefore well for us to indicate briefly what the word signifies here. In considering this definition, however, the reader should remember that among many religious liberals no formulation is definitive and mandatory. Indeed, the word *God* may in the following formulations be replaced by the phrase, "that which ultimately concerns humans," or by the phrase, "that which we should place our confidence in." Perhaps it would be well for the reader to make these substitutions.

God (or that in which we have faith) is the inescapable, commanding reality that sustains and transforms all meaningful existence. It is inescapable, for no one can live without somehow coming to terms with it. It is commanding, for it provides the structure or the process through which existence is maintained and by which any meaningful achievement is realized. (Indeed, every meaning in life is related to this commanding meaning that no one can manipulate and that stands beyond every merely personal preference or whim.) It is transforming, for it breaks through any given achievement, it invades any mind or heart open to it, luring it on to richer or more relevant achievement; it is a self-surpassing reality. God is that reality which works upon us and through us and in accord with which we can achieve truth, beauty, or goodness. It is that creativity which works in nature and history, under certain conditions creating human good in human community. Where these conditions are not met, human good, as sure as the night follows the day, will be frustrated or perverted. True freedom and individual or social health will be impaired. It is only because of this reality that, in Tennyson's words,

. . . Spirit with Spirit can meet—
Closer is He than breathing, and nearer than hands and feet.

The only person who is really an atheist is one who denies that there is any reality that sustains meaning and goodness in the human venture. The true atheist is one who recognizes nothing as validly commanding. It is very difficult to find this sort of atheist, perhaps impossible.

This reality that is dependable and in which we may place our confidence is not, then, ourselves—in it we live and move and have our being—nor is it a mere projection of human wishes; it is a working reality that every person is coerced to live with. In this sense the faith of the free is not free; the human being is not free to work without the sustaining, commanding reality. One is free only to obstruct it or to conform to the conditions it demands for growth. This reality is, then, no human contrivance; it is a reality without which no human good can be realized and without which growth or meaning is impossible. Theists and religious humanists find common ground here. They differ in defining the context in which human existence and human good are to be understood.

The free person's faith is therefore a faith in the giver of being and freedom. Human dignity derives from the fact that to be a person means to participate in the being and freedom of this reality. If we use the terms of historical Christianity we may say, the man and the woman are made in the image of this creative reality. Under its auspices they become themselves creators.

But humanity not only participates in this divinely given being and freedom. Through the abuse of freedom it also perverts and frustrates them. It distorts or petrifies the forms of creation and freedom. Hence free persons cannot properly place their confidence in their own creations; they must depend upon a transforming reality that breaks through encrusted forms of life and thought to create new forms. Free women and men put their faith in a creative reality that is re-creative.

2. *The second tenet of the free person's faith is that the commanding, sustaining, transforming reality finds its richest focus in meaningful human history, in free, cooperative effort for the common good.* In other words, this reality fulfills our life only when people stand in right relation to each other. As historical beings, they come most fully to terms with this reality in the exercise of the freedom that works for justice in the human community. Only what creates freedom in a community of justice is dependable. "Faith is the sister of justice." Only the society that gives every person the opportunity to share in the

process whereby human potentiality is realizable, only the society that creates the social forms of freedom in a community of justice (where all are given their due), only the freedom that respects the divine image and dignity in each person, are dependable. As Lincoln put it, "Those who deny freedom to others deserve it not for themselves, and, under a just God, cannot long retain it."

A faith that is not the sister of justice is bound to bring people to grief. It thwarts creation, a divinely given possibility; it robs them of their birth-right of freedom in an open universe; it robs the community of the spiritual riches latent in its members; it reduces the person to a beast of burden in slavish subservience to a state, a church, or a party—to a god made by human hands. That way lie the grinding rut and tyranny of the Vatican line, the Nuremberg line, and the Moscow line, different though these lines are from each other in their fear and obstruction of freedom.

To try to manipulate or domesticate the integrity of freedom is to rely upon the unreliable—an attempt that ends in reliance upon arbitrary power and upon arbitrary counsels. Sooner or later the arbitary confronts either stagnation from within or eruption both from without and from within. The stars in their courses fight against it.

This faith in the freedom that creates the just community is the faith of the Old Testament prophets. They repudiated the idea that the meaning of life is to be achieved either by exclusive devotion to ritual or by devotion to blood and soil, the idols of the tribe. The "holy" thing in life is the participation in those processes that give body and form to universal justice. Injustice brings judgment and suffering in its train. It is tolerated only at the peril of stability and meaning.

Again and again in the history of our civilization this prophetic idea of the purpose of God in history comes to new birth. Jesus deepened and extended the idea when he proclaimed that the kingdom of God is at hand. The reign of God, the reign of the sustaining, commanding, transforming reality, is the reign of love, a love that fulfills and goes beyond justice, a love that "cares" for the fullest personal good of all. This love is not something that is ultimately created by us or that is even at our disposal. It seizes us and transforms us, bringing us into a new kind of community that provides new channels for love.

Jesus uses the figure of the seed to describe this power. The power of God is like a seed that grows of itself if we will use our freedom to meet the conditions for its growth. It is not only a principle by which life may be guided; it is also a power that transforms life. It is a power we may trust to heal the wounds of life and to create the joy of sharing and of community. This is the power the Christian calls the forgiving, redemptive power of God, a power every person may know and experience whether or not one uses these words to describe it.

Not that it demands no wounds itself. It drew Jesus up Golgotha to a cross. Thus Jesus was not only a martyr dying for his convictions, but also the incarnation of the affirmative power of love transforming life, even in death, and creating a transforming community, a fellowship of free men and women yielding to the tides of the spirit.

This commanding, sustaining, transforming power can, at least for a time, be bottled up in dead words or in frozen instructions. (The cross has been smothered in lilies.) The sustaining, transforming reality can be perverted by willful humans, abusing their freedom, into a power that up to a point supports evil—yet, if humanity could not so abuse its freedom, it would not be free.

In history and in the human heart there are, then, destructive as well as creative powers. These destructive powers are manifest in the social as well as in the individual life, though they are most subtly destructive in the social life where the individual's egotism fights under the camouflage of the "good" of the nation, the race, the church, or the class. These destructive impulses (thoroughly familiar to the psychologist if not to their victims) seem veritably to "possess" people, blinding them, inciting them to greed, damaging the holy gifts God provides. This is precisely the reason for the need of the redemptive, transforming power. Indeed, "pious" folk are often the most in need of the transformation.

3. *The third tenet of the free person's faith is that the achievement of freedom in community requires the power of organization and the organization of power.* The free person will be unfree, will be a victim of tyranny from within or from without, if her or his faith does not assume *form*, in both word and deed. The commanding, transforming reality is a shaping power; it shapes one's beliefs about that reality and when it works through persons it shapes the community of justice and love.

There is no such thing as poetry without poems, art without paintings, architecture without buildings, and there is no such thing as an enduring faith without beliefs. The *living* spirit, says the poet Schiller, creates and molds.

There can be no reliable faith for the free unless there are faith-ful men and women who form the faith into beliefs, who test and criticize the beliefs, and who then transform and transmit the beliefs. This process of forming and transforming the beliefs of the free faith is a process of discussion; it is a cooperative endeavor in which people surrender to the commanding, transforming reality. The only way men and women can reliably form and transform beliefs is through the sharing of tradition and new insights and through the cooperative criticism and testing of tradition and insight. In other words, people must sincerely work with each other in order to give reliable form and expression to faith. This is the only way freedom *from* tyranny can be fulfilled in freedom *with* justice and truth.

Belief in merely individualistic, fissiparous freedom of faith can lead only to vapidity, to a faith in "I know not what," to faith in the arbitrary.

Faith in the knowledge about the commanding, sustaining, transforming reality cannot be "just any faith." If it is to make a difference, if it is to enable us to distinguish between ourselves and Nazis, then it must have a definite, particular form. Religious liberals who say that religious liberalism encourages people merely to think as they please no longer believe there is a commanding reality. They have become "faith-fully" neutral, and this neutrality is only a halfway station (if not already a camouflage) for an unexamined faith, for an unreliable, destructive faith. Neither the vague nor the neutral "faith" can be overcome except in a faith-ful community.

The free church is that community which is committed to determining what is rightly of ultimate concern to persons of free faith. It is a community of the faith-ful and a community of sinners. When alive, it is the community in which men and women are called to seek fulfillment by the surrender of their lives to the control of the commanding, sustaining, transforming reality. It is the community in which women and men are called to recognize and abandon their ever-recurrent reliance upon the unreliable. It is the community in which the living spirit of faith tries to create and mold life-giving, life-transforming beliefs, the community in which persons open themselves to God and each other and to commanding, sustaining, transforming experiences from the past, appropriating, criticizing, and transforming tradition and giving that tradition as well as newborn faith the occasion to become relevant to the needs of a time. These roots of faith grow in the individual as one participates in the worshiping, educating, socially active fellowship of the church. And certainly if they do not grow in the individual they will not grow in the family, if they do not grow in the family they will not grow in the community, and if they do not grow in the community they will not grow in the nation and the world.

Now the idea of forming a community of such a faith is a bold venture. It means that women and men must be willing not only to recognize their frustration of the transforming reality, but also to re-form themselves and their faith. As we have suggested, not every kind of freedom is permissible in this kind of community. Doctrinal tests are not the way to determine the character of the community, but if the community possesses no recognizable form and criterion (except that it offers absolute freedom), then it will be utterly undependable. It will degenerate into faith-ful and ethical neutrality.

An example of this degeneration recently came to light in a prominent congregation. The minister had been preaching vigorously and calling for action against race discrimination. Certain members of the board of trustees in the church did not like this sort of interpretation of our common humanity; apparently they thought that freedom of faith should permit freedom to believe in race discrimination. They called their minister to task and charged him with jeopardizing the principles of a free church. He was wrong, they said, in assuming that the church must stand unambiguously against race discrimination. Some people in the group made this assumption, they admitted, but some did not. Therefore, if the church was to remain a free fellowship, these different ideas about race discrimination should be given equal respect. Otherwise, the freedom of faith would be violated! In effect these "Christians" wanted their church to go the straight and narrow path—between right and wrong. They repudiated the "faith for the free" by trying to conceal injustice behind a simulated ethical neutrality.

A faith that creates no community of faith and a faith that assumes no definite form is not only a protection against any explicit faith, it is probably also a protection for a hidden idolatry of blood or state or economic interest, a protection for some kind of tyranny. It is not the faith of the free. The faith of free persons must tangibly make them free in a community of human dignity and equal justice.

The community of justice and love is not an ethereal fellowship that is *above* the conflicts and turmoils of the world. It is one that takes shape in nature and history, one that requires the achievement of freedom with respect to material resources as well as with respect to spiritual resources. Indeed, the one kind of freedom is not genuine without the other. Freedom requires a body as well as a spirit. We live not by spirit alone. A purely spiritual religion is a purely spurious religion; it is one that exempts its believer from surrender to the sustaining, transforming reality that demands the community of justice and love. This sham spirituality, far more than materialism, is the great enemy of religion.

Now, anything that exists effectively in history must have form, and the creation of a form requires power, not only the power of thought (mentioned above) but also the power of organization and the organization of power. There is no such thing as goodness as such; there is no such thing as a good man or woman as such. There is only the good spouse, the good worker, the good employer, the good churchperson, the good citizen. The decisive forms of goodness in society are institutional forms. No one can properly put faith in merely individual virtue, even though that is a prerequisite for societal virtues. The faith of the free must express itself in societal forms, in the forms of education, in economic and social organization, in political organization. Without these, freedom and justice in community are impossible.

The faith of a church or of a nation is an adequate faith only when it inspires persons to give of their time and energy to shape the various institutions—social, economic, and political—of the common life. A faith in the commanding, sustaining, transforming reality is one that shapes history. Any other faith is thoroughly undependable; it is also impotent. It is not a faith that molds history. It is the "faith" that enables history to crush humanity.

Here we confront a fact that can be ignored only at our peril. The creation of justice in community requires the organization of power. Through the organization of power the free person ties into history; otherwise one cannot achieve freedom *in history*. Injustice in community is a form of power, an abuse of power, and justice is an exercise of just and lawful institutional power.

The kind of freedom that expresses itself only within the family and within the narrow confines of one's daily work is not the faith of the free. It is as lopsided as the other kind of "freedom" that tries to express itself only in larger public affairs and forgets that the health of the body politic depends on the health and faith of its individual members. At best it creates and expresses cloistered virtues of loyalty, honesty, and diligence. This kind of faith can be oblivious of the injustices of the economic and political order; it can be a form of assistance to the powers of evil in public life and consequently also in the private life.

Today we are living in a time of sifting. No mere "return to religion" in the conventional sense will give us the vision or the power to match the demands. "Return to religion" as usually understood restores only the ashes and not the fires of faith. In a time when we must determine whether we will have "One World or None," only a costing commitment to a tough faith in the commanding, sustaining, transforming power of God will even start us on the steep path toward a world in which there will be room for people of free faith. If we can get such a world without a struggle for justice, it will, like an unexamined faith, not be worth having. In fact, we shall not have it for long — for the Lord of history will not fail nor faint till he has set justice in the earth, until he has burst the cruel yoke asunder and given liberty to the captive and to them that are oppressed. This is the Lord of whom it is commanded, Thou shalt love the Lord thy God with all thy heart, and with all thy soul, and with all thy mind, and with all thy strength. Would any other Lord, of any name or no name, be lovable? If the men and women of a free faith do not love *that* commanding, sustaining, transforming reality, what else in heaven or earth could they or should they love? What else could they have faith in?

3 · *Prophetic Judgment and Grace*

I

We had an oral tradition at Harvard Divinity School in my youth. You were likely to get one question almost for sure in the final exam. (I sat before thirteen professors for three hours and they all took turns at me, a little peewee sitting down at one end of that long table.) You would surely be asked to define a prophet. According to the oral tradition you could get away with it if you said, "A prophet is one who proclaims doom."

An authentic prophet is one who prophesies in fashion that does not comfort the people, but actually calls them to make some new sacrifices. That's an authentic prophet, whether one speaks in the name of God or whatever. A great deal of authentic prophetism in the modern world is to be found in nonreligious terms and in nonchurch configurations, often even hostile to the church. The churches themselves have broadly failed in the prophetic function. Therefore a good deal of so-called atheism is itself, from my point of view, theologically significant. It is the working of God in history, and judgment upon the pious. An authentic prophet can and should be a radical critic of spurious piety, of sham spirituality.

One of the great things about the Western tradition, previously biblical and oriented to religious symbols, is that it has had a tradition of prophetic utterance. In certain quarters it has even institutionalized that tradition. After Vatican II we see Roman Catholicism gradually adopting many of these features. John XXIII said—and it was confirmed in the Vatican Council at which I was a Protestant observer and had occasion for discussions of the matter—that it is the obligation of the Catholic Christian to participate in groups concerned with the general welfare, whether or not they are under religious or ecclesiastical auspices. That is a kind of institutionalization of prophetism.

Everyone is a theologian, either conscious or unconscious, in the sense that everyone has some conception of the nature of reality, of the demands of

These impromptu responses by Adams to questions following his lecture "The Prophetic Covenant" at Meadville/Lombard Theological School, January 1977, were transcribed from a tape recording by Alice Blair Wesley.

reality, and of those elements in reality that support or threaten meaningful existence. My own position is one that attempts to restate a doctrine of grace. Human beings are dependent upon realities not of their own making, realities that oftentimes destroy their own makings.

An interpretation of the fundamental qualities of divine power—as a creative, sustaining, community-forming and -transforming power— represents a selection of elements from reality. It is not as though the list of these qualities were a description of the total reality. Total reality lends itself to various selections of elements from the available resources, which are themselves variously defined. With the humanist philosopher William R. Jones, I would say that whatever the theological position, it is one that has to be *chosen*. A theological position claims to be a reading of reality, but this claim can never be properly stated as one objectively sanctioned by reality. Always it has to be chosen.

Awareness of this inherent limitation of all claims should keep us humble in discussing the matter. I think those liberal religious groups now attempting to discuss, to reconceive, to understand anew a doctrine of grace and of the covenant—the basic theological issues that you will find in the historical tradition—are those having a promise of new vitality. When there is this kind of discussion, the covenanting element is not left to be merely a decison about "what we agree upon"; the consensus looks for some kind of theological basis.

III

The major contribution of the left wing of the Reformation, from which religious liberalism derives, was an attempt to break the centralization of ecclesiastical, economic, and political power. These were joined together in a covenant that made dissent impossible. The peril of such restrictive covenants is the centralization of power. As John Adams once said, "Those who are in power have the ready capacity to find that God is behind them, and they are making their sacrifices for the good of all."

We need a better understanding of our historical rootage in terms of covenanting and the history of attacks on what were believed to be the corrupt, restrictive covenants. The covenant idea was, for at least two centuries, the key idea of left wing Protestantism. We are generally the descendants of neo-Calvinism, that is, the democratic qualification of the Calvinist form of covenant. That understanding of our Calvinist background would deepen—give thickness, substance—to our historical sense.

We must also find a theology in attempts at consensus, or at any rate vigorous discussion, of "the covenant of Being." In other words we must try to understand ourselves and our intentions and performance in the liberal churches in terms of some relationship to fundamental reality. That becomes a theological discussion, even if traditional theological language is not used.

A third point concerns society. A major characteristic of our tradition has been that the covenant by and large has been interpreted in terms of the possessing classes, those who have relative power in the community, to the neglect of the deprived. I would say our covenants are in large degree invalid; they represent a special class of people, who are addicted to our churches.

My thesis — my claim — is that there are elements in reality that sustain mutuality. An element of mutuality runs through all of nature, despite the struggle for existence. Anything completely lacking the capacity for mutuality with other persons and other beings is on the way out of existence.

Now there are many ways in which restrictive covenants can have long-lasting power, and maintain themselves by restrictive and very exclusive forms of mutuality. The sustaining power—this capacity for mutuality—is the quality built into reality; we didn't make it that way; it is indispensable. If it is completely lost, one reaches nonexistence. The distinction has been made since the seventeenth century between the demonic and the satanic. The satanic is that which is nonexistent because it has no relationship to the structures of being. The demonic is therefore defined as the perversions of these qualities, but perversions able to maintain themselves for a time. So there is that sustaining quality present in whatever is.

IV

Our tradition has articulated and emphasized the notion, not only of the *priesthood* of all believers, but also of the *prophethood* of all believers. This means especially the capacity and the right to participate in the shaping of the congregation. The prophethood belongs not merely to the clergy: It belongs to the congregation and to the individuals in the congregation. But authentic prophecy does not appear very often within the churches; therefore it had to appear in nonreligious, or even antichurch communities.

But the covenant is a covenant of grace, beyond the prophetic judgment. In my judgment one of the greatest religious seers and intellectuals in the history of humanity was the prophet Hosea. Compare Amos. Amos is the prophet who says, "You've got to do justice or you're gonna get it in the neck." Amos voiced a very salutary doctrine; it put the fear of God into some people. But Hosea says, "Look! If that's the whole story, we're all doomed because we've all been involved in injustice." I would put it this way—Hosea really rejects the Greek idea of nemesis, an idea that is so similar to Amos's at this point: Once violation of the covenant has taken place, then from generation to generation the curse is on you. Hosea says, "Well, we're all lost, then!" I think this is one of the most profound men in the history of mankind, womankind, humankind.

So what does he do? Hosea gives you a metaphor, in this case a domestic metaphor, but *interpreting* the covenant, the political metaphor. Hosea, you will remember, imagines that Yahweh has a faithless bride. She has violated the covenant. Hosea creates this marvelous picture of the groom who has been betrayed. The groom pursues the faithless violator of the covenant and says, "I know what you did! I know what you've done! I understand. I know what you will do. Don't you understand? I love you *nevertheless!*"

I would like to add, here, that I think it is greatly to be lamented that, for instance, the Lutherans and the Lutheran Hour are always solving all problems in terms of forgiveness. I used to say to my classes at Harvard, "I will immediately with great delight give ten dollars to anybody who can come in on a Monday and say the Lutheran Hour did not solve *all* the problems yesterday by saying, 'forgiveness.'" I never had to spend that ten dollars. The idea of forgiveness, taken alone, is another form of idolatry, because forgiveness has to be related, somehow, to the creative maintenance of justice.

This creative principle is heard in Hosea. Hosea is asserting that you have to understand the covenant as providing the occasion, through the remaking of the covenant, for new beginnings. If you have only a doctrine of justice, or nemesis, there cannot be new beginnings. There is just constant suffering from the violations of the past. Hosea is a great anticipator of Henri Bergson, Whitehead, and others who have emphasized the idea of novelty, the possibility of a new event. In human terms this means that we are not caught in the vise of cause and effect, the past determining the present. It is possible to introduce something new: that is the meaning of the idea of forgiveness. Forgiveness means: what has happened—I won't say "whatever," for judgment is not ruled out—what has happened in the past shall not completely determine the future. You can make a new covenant; you can renew the commitment and you can start again.

4 · The Sacred and the Secular: Friedrich von Hügel

Emerson remarks that the farmers in the region of the Catskills do not call particular summits, such as Killington, Camel's Hump, and Saddle Back, mountains, but they refer to them as only "them 'ere rises." They reserve the word *mountain* for the great range.

Baron Friedrich von Hügel among the theologians of our century is in stature and influence more than one of "them 'ere rises." Dean Inge of St. Paul's has called him "one of the deepest thinkers of our day." A reviewer in *The* (London) *Times Literary Supplement* said of him, "Baron von Hügel is, we think, the most powerful apologist for the Roman Church now living." But von Hügel, in spite of the "excessively handsome and resonantly sympathetic" attitude of the writer, felt constrained to express some misgivings. In the next issue of *The Times* he wrote: "A dog who is quietly conscious of being but a dog, and of having long striven just to be a dog, and nothing more or other, may be allowed, perhaps, to feel some perplexity amidst his gratitude upon finding himself first prize among the cats."

Von Hügel was always annoyed by the apologist's mentality, much though he loved the Catholic Church. Indeed, it is partly because of his annoyance at the attitude and method of the apologist that he succeeded in becoming one of the most influential minds of our time even among Protestants. He has been reproached by some members of his own faith because he was not content with exercising a deep and lasting influence on Protestant thinkers, but allowed himself to be influenced in turn by them. With such catholic preparation as was his, it is not surprising that he became, according to the eminent Protestant theologian Friedrich Heiler, "the greatest Roman Catholic lay theologian in history and the greatest in Catholicism since Newman." It must be conceded, however, that Catholic officials would hardly concur in this judgment. In fact, they prefer to "dump von Hügel in foreign ports," that is, they desire that potential converts and nonpracticing Catholics should read him: his connection with

This essay is an abridged version of Adams's contribution to the series "Contemporary Thought Around the World," from *The Christian Register* October 11, 1934. Reprinted by permission of the Unitarian Universalist Association.

the modernist movement in the early part of the century brought upon him the suspicions of the circumspectly orthodox.

Stevenson once said that Robert Burns died of being Robert Burns. And so it might be said that Friedrich von Hügel commands attention because he tried only to be himself in the highest degree, and not an apologist for the Roman Catholic Church.[1] In his letter to *The Times* mentioned above, he indicates in a concrete and striking way the motive of much of his work. "It was in 1883 that a far-sighted friend pressed upon me the religious problem raised by Anthony Trollope's *Autobiography*—that faithful account of a long life, so pure, truthful, modest, laborious, affectionate, and without one trace of hunger after God, the Other or the More. The problem has never left me since then." In a word, von Hügel was anxious to dispose the modern man or woman who feels content with a purely secular or scientific worldview to envisage the self and the environment in a larger context.

But von Hügel was concerned not only about that part of the world that has gone secular. He saw also that organized religion is ever in danger of lagging behind the best thought of the secular-minded world. Here, too, then, he saw a great need, and set for himself the aim "to do all I can to make the old church as inhabitable *intellectually* as ever I can—not because the intellect is the most important thing in religion—it is not; but because the old church already possesses in full the knowledge and the aids to *spirituality,* whilst, for various reasons which would fill a volume, it is much less strong as regards the needs, rights and duties of the mental life."

What Friedrich von Hügel wrote came not only out of his reading, but also out of his life—his work, his friendships, his worship, and, in strict truth, even out of his play.[2] He was no mere system maker. For him life and God were not known until they were experienced as immensely rich, complex, and many-faceted.

"Isness" and "Oughtness"

For von Hügel the first question the mind turning toward religion asks is not, What kind of person ought I to become? but rather, What *is* truth? To the person who says that religion is the quest for the good life, von Hügel would respond, yes, but religion is not forever searching an unfound good or trying to create good. Religion is evidential, it has primarily to do with "Isness" and only secondarily to do with "Oughtness." Before religion can inspire an intelligent desire for what ought to be, it must induce a humble, "costing," teachable interest in, and a "fear, love, and adoration" of what already is. Religion does bring ethical insight; but that ethical insight is not primary. It is derived from the prime insight of religion, an insight into what *is*. Hence it is that religion expresses itself first in the declarative mood and only later in the imperative mood: God *is*.

Religion must, then, in its mature and characteristic form, grow out of an apprehension of reality. That apprehension at its best may be associated with ethical and esthetic experience, but for the religious person it is something revealed. It depends upon human experience only in the sense that it is a human response. But it is a response to something greater than "we little people," a response to something that has an objective existence largely independent of the mind and of the desires of the thinking subject.

> The given-ness of God—everything is given. The moderns say: "Thank goodness we have got rid of the awful position of servant and master" (is it awful?). Canon S——says God needs us to make the world. I must say I never heard Canon S——helped God to make Saturn's rings. It sounds rather fusty somehow to me.

Such an attitude as this does not imply that the inward spiritual experience of the human creature is dispensable. It only means that the point of reference is not simply human. The point of reference is Reality, not the self. God is given. He is not an ideal construction of humanity's. He comments,

> Some people are so fond of ideas. A new idea is a kind of magic to them! I don't care about ideas, I want facts. God is not an idea. He is a fact.

To be sure, we do find it desirable to formulate ideas about God. But an idea about God is not God. It is only a human formula. We should no more identify our idea about God with God than we should identify a physicist's formula for the operation of electrical energy with electricity. The religious reality, like physical reality, may need interpreting, but it is itself given from the beginning. Religious reality, like physical reality, however, is reticent: It does not lend itself to final or satisfactory definition. Huge surpluses of reality avoid our formulas. Just as the physical world is on a level below our minds, so the religious object is above our minds. This reticence of reality suggests to von Hügel the peculiar dilemma of religion, indeed of all attempts to apprehend reality. In religion this dilemma arises out of the fact that the affirmation of the certainty of God is always accompanied in the honest mind with the assurance that we can never comprehend the nature of God. We believe that our knowledge is relevant, but we know that it is incomplete.

> If I can see things through and through, I get uneasy—I feel it's a fake. I know I have left something out, I've made some mistake. . . .
>
> God, our own souls, all the supreme realities and truths, supremely deserving and claiming our assent and practice—are both *incomprehensible* and *indefinitely apprehensible,* and the constant vivid realization of these two qualities, insuperably inherent to all our knowledge and practice of them, is a primary and equal importance for us.

One has always the feeling in reading von Hügel, no matter what the problem, that he has devoted years of painful labor checking his intimations of reality. The whole history of religion, philosophy, ethics, politics, the arts, and the sciences, is constantly drawn upon, not only for confirmation of his guiding principles, but also for possible objections to his findings. He does not knowingly evade any difficulty. The error of overemphasis on Christ in certain types of Christianity, the pathological phenomena of mysticism, the dreadful persecutions perpetrated in the name of religion, Jesus' belief in demons and in the Second Coming, and a host of other ticklish problems for the Catholic Christian are brought into the broad daylight of honest, searching criticism. Suffice to say that von Hügel insists that without a recognition of a real Other, a religious object, there can be no religion, no prayer, no worship. For this reason he says:

> A religion without God does not correspond to the specific religious sense, because no amount of *Oughtness* can be made to take the place of *Isness.*

TENSION BETWEEN THE SACRED AND THE SECULAR

I have said that von Hügel was no mere system maker and that he did not think of himself as an apologist for the Catholic Church. He withdraws himself characteristically from either classification in his attitude toward the problem of evil. Dr. L. P. Jacks once said that when we start to think about this problem, our temptation is to explain evil away and make it seem good. Baron von Hügel never yielded to that temptation. He resolutely affirmed that a sound philosophy can have no explanation of evil. Evil is a "dread reality." The only thing to do with it, he would say, is not to explain it but to overcome it, or, if that is impossible, to endure it.

Among those evils that may be overcome, he wishes to make the modern world particularly aware of two that have long been the objects of derision in the tradition of "devout (or Catholic) humanism." The one is familiar in the literature of all orthodox Christianity as well—it is pride. Of it we shall speak later. The other is more particularly associated with the (classical) humanist strain in Catholicism—the (classical) humanists call it specialism, Baron von Hügel calls it thinness. In his discussion of these two vices and their counteracting virtues, we find a genuine survival of what was best in medieval and Renaissance Christian humanism.

Von Hügel conceives of God as inexhaustibly operative on the many levels of existence and experience. Religion proclaims the divine richness of all life. It follows, then, that the besetting sin of even conscientious and enthusiastic religious people is that they tend to become narrow, lopsided, specialized, thin. Matthew Arnold, noting this narrowness in English religion, spoke of the need for the corrective influence of Hellenism. In von Hügel's view, the religious person should cultivate an all-round interest in the world. The deeper one's sense of the reality of God, the more urgent should be the desire to enrich one's mind and spirit with all that the secular as well as the sacred order has to offer, for everyone has the *religious* obligation of coming to know the many-leveled, many-faceted reality around us in as many ways as are possible, *for oneself.*

> The fact is that the Christian, indeed the man of any religion, who wishes to make and to keep his religion strong, will doubtless have to live it with all he is and has; but that Christians, and indeed religionists of any kind, can not (all of them in the long run) ignore the other activities of man's manifold life, nor simply sacrifice either their religion to these activities or these activities to their religion. God is the God of the body and mind as He is of the soul; of science as He is of faith; of criticism and theory as of fact and reality.

The vitally religious person, then, sets up a tension between the secular and the sacred disciplines. Strictly speaking, a person's activities and duties cannot, of course, be divided into the "religious" and the "secular." And yet, there is a difference between the spirit in which "religious" and "worldly" persons discharge their duties. The religious person discharges his or her duties "to the glory of God," and at its best religion infuses even the ordinary virtues with a "homely heroism." This heroism is no mere conformity to an external standard, but it is an "interior attitude of the soul in the face of all occasions, great or small."

But there is a difference between the religious and the secular besides that represented in the intention of serving God. Some actions (worship and prayer, for instance) are more directly religious than others. Von Hügel holds that it is the duty of the religious person, just because he or she is religious, to "cultivate the more carefully and lovingly, also the interests, the activities, that are not directly religious." His own thorough and highly disciplined study of geology and history exemplifies in his own life this theory of the necessity of "turning to the visible" as a corrective of excess in the other direction. In the less contemplative life, the discipline might well be, as it has often been in the lives of religious people, a heroic devotion to social, industrial, or educational activity. For von Hügel this buckling of one's mind and will down to the objective facts and values of science, history, and sociology constitutes a kind of modern asceticism, a self-obliteration and prostration before the facts and needs of the world. This discipline not only makes life richer, more useful, more flexible, more susceptible to fresh discovery. It may, like strenuous moral self-discipline, prepare the mind for a richer apprehension of the Other, the religious object, God; for the richer the imagination that is brought to the experience of God, the greater the capacity to be informed or inspired with new insights. But perhaps even more important than this enriched apprehension is the effect of the tension upon the whole social context in which vital religion exists: On the one hand, religion is prevented thus from becoming odd, isolated, antiworldly, thin; on the other, the "world" is prevented from becoming dryly secular, respectable, unadventurous, unheroic. That is, the religious ideal is provided with medium or material to work in and upon, and is prevented from becoming irrelevant to the here and now. Thus is spirituality civilized and civilization spiritualized.

THE BODY, HISTORY, AND INSTITUTIONS

For von Hügel, then, the truly religious life is one that does not exclusively love religion, or Christ, or goodness, or truth, or beauty. It is richer than the love of any one of these, richer than even their summation; it is a harmony, an interplay among them.

And yet, although religion does crave the full energy of the well-rounded personality, von Hügel would not allow that there is a private, royal highway for the intellectual or the highbrow. Indeed, the intellectual is ever in danger of losing the essential virtue of religion—humility. In von Hügel's view, the central sin, for the Christian, is pride and self-sufficiency. Hence it is that everyone needs an institution and a community of faith that transcends the human categories of class and intellectual prowess. Else animal vitality, or sophistication, or sheer indifference will kill the conscious need for God.[3]

Whether, then, the individual is absorbed in the full round of enriching experiences that are possible in modern urban life or is on the verge of slipping into the slothful and enervating weariness of acedia, one should so "tend his own soul" as to allow for regular periods of concentration of mind and will upon "the Other and the More." Only this holding our life up to God can develop in us a sense of belonging to God, and save us from the pride of self-sufficiency. Through the contemplation and adoration of God, the inexhaustibly rich "Reality, *the* Reality distinct from the world, which nevertheless springs from, is supported, and is penetrated by him," we gain a humility, a sense of "creatureliness," a consciousness of needing, of depending upon, of serving the God of all being.

But adoration, "creatureliness," humility are not to be purchased by an easy expense of spirit. They need for their enriched development the sense of the past, the standard of a tradition, and the stimulus of an institutional discipline. Writing to his niece of the need for a sense of history in religion, the baron speaks very caustically of the "purely personal religion" divorced from tradition and history.

> History is an enlargement of personal experience, history pressing the past. We must have the closest contact with the past. How poor and thin a thing is all purely personal religion. You must get a larger experience—you gain it by a study of history; the individualistic basis simply doesn't work. . . . Religion to be rich and deep must be historical.

Just as we are dependent upon sense stimuli for our awareness of the reality underlying all experience, just as intelligent progress in the arts, the sciences, and philosophy depends upon an assimilation of the best that has already been thought and done, just as an effective morality requires the institutions of the family, the trades union, and the state, so does the religious spirit need the stimulus, the fellowship, and the standards that exist only in a religious institution where the accumulated experience of the race, both in habit and insight, are available.

Von Hügel, as we have seen, would not have religion isolated from the rest of life, but rather would have it operate as an element of enrichment and tension in all of life. Likewise, he would not have religion itself be simply a matter of pure spirit. Indeed, he holds that materialism is not the most dangerous of the spirit's enemies. Its greatest enemy is "pure spirituality," the illusion that religion does not involve the body and the senses in specific acts of self-discipline and worship.

The sensible always conveys the spiritual: the invisible in the visible. Christ everywhere makes use of the sensible to convey the spiritual, never the spirit alone.

T. S. Eliot has ingeniously stated this objection to a religion of "pure spirituality" in his revision of the familiar verse of Scripture: "The spirit killeth, the letter giveth life." Without specific acts, without the letter, the spirit dies. Just as the poet must accept some convention of poetic form in order to achieve a recognizable beauty of sound and rhythm, so the growing religious spirit must deliberately impose upon itself the conventions of some tradition of religion if it is to achieve the accredited virtues of religion. Without definite times and places for worship, for prayer, for the reading of religious literature, for receiving instruction and giving it, all of these things disappear and the fruits of religion with them.

Obviously, then, in von Hügel's mind, the church is more than a society for research, hunting for an unfound good. It may be this, but it is also a vessel and channel of already extant, positive religious experience and conviction. It makes known the facts of history, the beliefs, the ideals, and the rites that form the nucleus of a religion of sense and spirit, of past and present and future. It reminds us of the slowness and humility of religion in its beginnings and developments, and, most important of all, it establishes through its sense and spirit medium a conviction of our need for our fellow creatures. With all of these aids the soul is enriched and prepared for a joyous response to God and humanity and nature. Thus only may we come to know the God "Who, however dimly *yet directly,* touches our souls and awakens them in and through all those minor stimulations and apprehensions, to that noblest incurable discontent with our own petty self, and to that sense of and thirst for the Infinite and Abiding, which articulates man's deepest requirement and characteristic."

Notes

1. Born in Florence when his father, a statesman, scientist, and world traveler, was Austrian ambassador to Tuscany, he had the opportunity of learning Italian almost as a native language. Following the Revolution of 1859, which overthrew the grand duke of Tuscany, the von Hügel family moved to Brussels, where the father was to be appointed Austrian minister in 1860. Perhaps because his mother was Presbyterian and his father Catholic, Friedrich was tutored there by a Lutheran pastor and the German Catholic historian Alfred von Reumont. From this time he

acquired an intimate knowledge of the sciences, the classics, and the French and German languages. After the Austro-Prussian War of 1866 the family moved to England, and except for numerous short residences on the Continent, von Hügel spent the rest of his life in England. Throughout his life he maintained an active interest in entomology and geology, biblical criticism, literature, history, philosophy, and the arts. He died in 1923 at the age of seventy-three.

2. The reader who is unacquainted with von Hügel's writings should, in order first to discover the man in all his vital integrity, begin with either his *Letters to a Niece* (Chicago: Henry Regnery, 1955), or the lucid and critical study by L. V. Lester-Garland, *The Religious Philosophy of Baron Friedrich von Hügel* (New York: Dutton, 1933). Then the reader will be prepared for a richly rewarding perusal of *Essays and Addresses: Second Series* (London: Dent; New York: Dutton, 1926), *Eternal Life* (Edinburgh: T. and T. Clark, 1912), *The Mystical Element of Religion* (London: Dent; New York: Dutton, 1908), and *Selected Letters 1896–1924*, ed. Bernard Holland (London: J. M. Dent, 1928).

3. [Von Hügel's emphasis on the historical and institutional side of religion, to which Adams here draws attention, is pertinent to continuing interest in William James. More than thirty years after this essay was written, Adams discovered a letter from von Hügel to James, dated May 10, 1909, in the Houghton Library at Harvard University. He notes that "this bulky, hand-written letter had remained for over sixty years tucked into the copy of the von Hügel work"—*The Mystical Element of Religion* (two vols., 1908)—which von Hügel had autographed and sent to James. The letter is appreciative of James's famous work on mysticism, *The Varieties of Religious Experience* (1902), but also critical. The text of the letter, with a detailed introduction by Adams, was published in the *Journal of the American Academy of Religion* 45, no. 4, suppl. (December 1977): 1101–34. An excerpt from the abstract indicates Adams's summary and assessment: "James's exclusive concern for 'the personal and private' in religion, von Huegel asserts, leads him to abandon his inductive, concrete *a posteriori* method and to exhibit a reductive *a priori* conception that neglects corporate religious experience with its institutional influences, disciplines, and responsibilities. Von Huegel shows himself to be closer in all this to Ernst Troeltsch and Reinhold Niebuhr than to James by reason of the latter's failing actually to deal with the varieties of religious experience, instead presenting it as privatized religion, the consequence in part of the one-eyed approach of pietism and psychology, and in part of a narrow conception of psychotherapy." In relation to psychotherapy, see Adams's critique of the pastoral care movement, "Social Ethics and Pastoral Care," in *Pastoral Care in the Liberal Churches*, ed. James Luther Adams and Seward Hiltner (Nashville and New York: Abingdon Press, 1970), pp. 174–220.—Ed.]

4. [Because of his accent on the prophetic and ethical elements of religion, Adams's attitude toward mysticism has often been questioned. His positive but qualified valuation of mysticism is seen, however, in citations from von Hügel such

as the one that concludes this essay, and in the memorandum (recent but undated) that Adams wrote on mysticism in response to an inquiry, here appended. —Ed.]

"Mysticism is a sense and taste of the presence of or union with the ground of meaningful existence and purpose, the ground of everything finite, yet transcending everything finite. It is thus an indispensable *element* of all religion, but it is never properly a separate element. It must willy-nilly obtain in relation to other aspects of religion, sacramental (meaning as mediated—made present—through finite, tangible vessels), and prophetic (meaning as personal, social-ethical demand), whether this relationship is positive or negative.

"When the relationship is negative, mysticism may be indifferent to the sacramental; it may be demonic—identifying the relative with the absolute (tribalism, nationalism, blood and soil, a social or ecclesiastical or scriptural system, an ideology). When it is positive in relation to the sacramental *and* the prophetic, it points beyond and remains critical of all forms (pointing characteristically beyond its own and all conceptualizations). It may relate itself primarily to the personal or individual, thus neglecting and surrendering to institutional power (economic and political), as in much Christian pietism and Buddhism. This is a demonic attachment, as is tribalism. Likewise, exclusive concentration on the social-ethical may be demonic. Nature mysticism can be similarly narrow. When mysticism aims to remain separated it becomes demonic, inflating an "element" into identification with the whole. The hardest knife ill-used doth lose its edge.

"A religion that does not have the mystical element flattens out into mere sacramentalism: participation in socially accepted forms—La Salle Street 'Christians,' or the member of the Church of England who according to the late Bishop Gore holds to the sacraments but does not believe in God. (A person who 'just loves' the liturgy.)

"The Hebrew word *shalom* suggests the criterion for the view set forth here. One meaning of the word is *wholeness*. I can sum up what I have said here through an analogy. Air is indispensable for life but insufficient for nourishment. The mystical element is indispensable for religion but it must be accompanied by, indeed must serve, sacramental and prophetic forces. The authentic mystical element is no anchorite. Let us not to the marriage of true members admit impediments."

5 · *Changing Frontiers of Liberal Religion*

The idea of living on the frontier is a familiar, indeed a characteristic, idea for Americans. But originally the idea comes of ancient biblical lineage. It played a role also in the Reformation, particularly in its left wing, both European and American.

The Israelites gave to the idea its classical religious form. The basic image of the Old Testament is that of a people being led by God into ever new situations, journeying through the wilderness into a Promised Land. The exodus from Egypt was viewed as a divinely given liberation from bondage and as a thrust toward fulfillment, under covenant with the Lord of history. As John Donne would say, this People of God was on pilgrimage; it had made a future engagement with its higher self. This pattern of pilgrimage is characteristically prominent in the eschatological consciousness of the prophets. Essentially the same image, compounded of liberation from bondage and divine promise of newness of life, pervades the New Testament—in Jesus' message of repentance and forgiveness in the face of the newly working Kingdom of God, in Paul's conception of history as rooted in the new life in Christ, in the Epistle to the Hebrews, which expands one of the earliest versions of the image, the migrations of Abraham the man of faith.

In the Old Testament we find also a counterimage, that of the disobedient, the stiff-necked people. The children in the wilderness murmur against God and fall into temptation. Trying vainly to manipulate the Determiner of Destiny, they make a Golden Calf. In this yielding to temptation they give themselves to something unreliable; they adopt the faith of self-worship.

This composite of the liberation from bondage, the thrust of the divine initiative moving toward the fulfillment of human life, and the fall into temptation that distorts the faith in the Lord of history reappears in much later times. Professor George H. Williams of Harvard Divinity School in his anthology *Spiritual and Anabaptist Writers* shows how this total image

This essay is from *The Unitarian Christian*, supplement in pamphlet form, 1957, reprinted by permission. Adams has served as a vice president of the Unitarian Universalist Christian Fellowship for many years.

figures in the thought and action of the Radical Reformation. These left wing reformers interpreted their own innovating movement as a trek through a new wilderness toward the Promised Land. At the same time they saw a threat latent within the new experience of faith: the new faith might be perverted into a means of self-inflation, and its adherents might consequently lose their way. Here again we see the providential, dynamic conception of history, the sense of direction and directedness. We see also the fear of distortion; life on the frontier has its hazards.

Liberal religion by its very nature has aimed to live on the frontier and to break new paths. Moreover, making no claims of infallibility for itself, it has aimed also to be self-critical. But to remain critical is by no means easy. Movement itself can be merely inertia. Terrain that was once a frontier can become simply an old frontier; and an old frontier is no longer a frontier. Strategies that were appropriate for former frontiers may no longer be appropriate for the new situation. Self-appraisal is therefore demanded if we are to recognize the frontiers that are vanishing and if we are to find new strategies for the frontiers that are emerging. It is demanded also if we are to resist the temptation to wander in the wilderness of self-worship.

Three of these vanishing frontiers and three correspondingly new frontiers I would like to consider here. These particular frontiers, offering vistas of opportunity and peril, impinge upon problems connected with (1) the historical criticism and the contemporary relevance of the Bible, (2) the scientific method and the effect of science upon society, and (3) the vocation of true piety.

BIBLICAL CRITICISM AND RELEVANCE

During almost two centuries higher criticism has constituted a major frontier for religious liberalism. Indeed, it is a frontier that was opened up by the liberals. It has rendered the Bible virtually a new book, revealing its various strands and sources, its milieu and its conflicting perspectives, its primitive, priestly, and prophetic elements, its mixture of legend and myth, of miracle and historical events. Out of life on this frontier the modern religious mentality has taken shape. Even today, the higher criticism elicits embarrassment among most adherents of Christianity (and of Judaism); indeed it arouses continuing hostility, for it insists that if truth is to be served, the sacred literature must be studied like any other literature. Sacred literature deserves no special privilege, even though it may require special insight from the interpreter.

This frontier will require exploration as long as human curiosity remains alive and serious. The higher criticism will continue its search for new findings that in turn will require new interpretation and even new methods of interpretation.

Scholars will struggle to unveil presuppositions of their own that lead to misinterpretation of the literature, and particularly to misinterpretation of its inner religious import. They will also continue to struggle against theologically oriented scholars who wish to manipulate or suppress evidence. In these respects, important changes are to be observed in contemporary historical criticism and in hermeneutics. All of this belongs to higher criticism in its exercise of the freedom of inquiry.

But for the religious liberal, historical criticism is no longer a new path. Insofar as it works under the aegis of freedom of inquiry, it is an old frontier. In this sense it is a vanishing frontier. Long ago a different frontier has supervened.

THE FRONTIER OF ULTIMATE QUESTIONS

The frontier that we face here is also an old one in point of time. It rises into view simultaneously with historical criticism. But whereas historical criticism is among religious liberals accepted in principle, this related frontier raises questions of principle on which we have scarcely achieved significant consensus, unless it be that of agreement to disagree. The questions of this frontier are: What comes after historical criticism? What is the biblical faith to us? What of it is ours?

Some deny that these questions point to any important frontier. Biblical faith, they appear to say, is simply a thing of the past, and that's an end of it. They would perhaps go on to say that at most we should concern ourselves with the Bible in order to understand our past. Others would probably say that a contemporary religious fellowship in no substantial way depends upon theological convictions of the sort one finds in the Bible: Liberal religion is sufficiently defined by the desire to promote reason, tolerance, and freedom; at most the Bible is for us a repository of ethical idealism. I know of no proper reason for denying these views a firm place in a free church.

In response to these and similar views one, of course, might argue that it is illiberal and provincial to break off discussion with Protestantism; or that religious liberals today as in the past might be expected to attempt to contribute something to the understanding of the Bible; or that any religious movement in our culture forfeits the possibility of significant self-interpretation and leadership if it refuses to come to terms positively with the classical religious literature of our heritage. For the moment, however, I venture a response of a quite different order, though to be sure it will possess no novelty.

The principles of reason, tolerance, and freedom never stand alone—as if they themselves generated the power for their realization. They presuppose something more. They presuppose that resources are available for the realization of a way of life and a fellowship, indeed of a fellowship that includes much more than reason, tolerance, and freedom. Ultimately, our faith is in these resources, not in the principles. This fact becomes clear, for example, when religious liberals speak of their "faith in man."

It is just here that we move into the frontier marked by the question, What is the biblical faith to us? There are many ways in which the characteristically biblical perspectives can be formulated. I would say that the Bible is most concerned with the resources upon which meaningful existence is ultimately dependent, with the resources that give rise to a community of viable justice and righteousness ("a many-flavored compound" elusive to definition). For the Bible human history is the arena of a struggle between the forces or capacities that make for the development of individual and social integrity and the forces that impede that development. But in the Bible the ultimate resource for this fulfillment is not in humanity, though the human being is created in the image of God and is something more than an object—a creative self. Paradoxically, the integrating forces represent at the same time a divine gift and a divinely given task or vocation for persons. The lines of a Michelangelo sonnet express the transcending dimension of this paradox:

> . . . What leads me on
> Is not in me.

Here the biblical image of which I have spoken earlier, the image of divine liberation from bondage and the divine promise of newness of life, is determinative. The prophets in the very name of the divinely given creative and fulfilling powers oppose every bondage that cramps the human spirit; they understand human fellowship to be inextricably bound up with obedience to and inward fellowship with the divine power that is sovereign over all of life; they believe that history is going somewhere and on the way they see persons as responsible under God for the character and direction of their social existence. For the sake of these convictions the prophets devise dramatic means of communication and agitation that anticipate the modern free press and other modern implementations of public opinion. In Old Testament prophetism our relation to the final resource—to the Lord of history—is intimate and ultimate; and its active thrust is toward the corporate, for salvation is for time and history.

The human vocation can claim no security on the basis of human accomplishment. The only reliable object of faith is the transforming power that creates justice and fellowship among persons. In the creative moments of human experience this power demands sensitive identification with the other, and it makes possible mercy and forgiveness, repentance and new beginning. This wondrous power is not of human devising; it is rather a persuasion in human affairs that comes to us through openness and obedience to that which is intrinsically sovereign and alone reliable.

Jesus in his inwardness, in his love of persons, in the audacity of his liberation from the bondage of mere tradition, in his confidence in the Kingdom that grows of itself in reaction to human response, in his faithfulness to his unique mission, in his eliciting of a new community in the world but not of it—above nation and race and class, embracing the humble and the wise, in his trust in the mysterious mercy of God, has made and makes more readily known and available to us the powers that can release us from self-worship and give us constant renewal of life and love. So persuasively and costingly has he made these powers available that we can understand why most of his followers through the ages have given him a special place and function within the order of being.

What is biblical faith to us? This is not a question that one considers for old times' sake. At bottom it is a question about the meaning of life itself, about the ground and purpose of human fellowship.

Historical criticism and biblical hermeneutics have given us and continue to give us the possibility of new understanding of the biblical faith, and touching a much wider range of issues than are intimated here. Just this treasure offered us by historical criticism provides us with a new frontier. It is the frontier of frontiers, perhaps, because it presses upon us the hardest, the elemental questions. These questions will not leave us alone. We cannot escape the frontier except by building a Golden Calf that will temporarily render us insensitive to the "openings" that began with the exodus and Sinai, with Nazareth and Golgotha.

SCIENCE AND SOCIETY

The story is told that the British scientist Michael Faraday one day received a visit in his laboratory from the statesman William Gladstone. Faraday's investigations at the time had nothing directly to do with anything obviously useful. He was concerned with the purely theoretical questions regarding electromagnetism, a phenomenon little understood then. After being shown the extensive laboratory Gladstone in strictly practical mood asked, "But what good is it all?" Confronted by this utilitarian demand of the practical man, Faraday, instead of explaining the purpose and method of pure science that searches primarily for the sake of theoretical knowledge, accommodated himself to the query and replied, "Some day, Mr. Gladstone, you may be able to tax it."

The two aspects of science, pure and applied, cannot be entirely divorced, for the one leads to the other. But the goals of these two aspects of science are distinct, as the Faraday story illustrates. Indeed, we may say that they represent quite different frontiers in the social enterprise.

There was a time when the promotion of purely theoretical science had to struggle for the freedom to inquire. In part the struggle had to be carried on against the churches. Actually, however, the churches divided forces here. In Britain and the United States the Unitarians, for example, were in the forefront of the defense of the freedom of scientific inquiry. Prior to this, Puritan divines in both countries supported the activities of the British Royal Society. The principal and effective supporters, however, were inevitably the universities (and, subsequently, industry).

There have been setbacks in the course of pure science. The bureaucratization of scientific inquiry necessarily impedes freedom. In the United States it is still easier in certain of the sciences to secure financial aid for practical purposes than for purposes of pure research (we think, for example, of the field of mental health). But on the whole the frontier of pure science has been conquered, at least in the democratic countries where freedom of scientific inquiry is at least in principle protected. In the main, that is an old frontier (though here as elsewhere vigilance is the price of liberty).

The frontier that offers the more stubborn resistance is that of applied science. In the practical realm this frontier has replaced the old frontier of the West. For applied science affects the total society. The blessings of applied science are evident on every hand, for example, in the rise in the standard of living for many and in the phenomenal advance of medical technology. On the other hand, the ravages of technology have been legion. The technological society has done much to dehumanize life, to make human beings into cogs, into a commodity, into "mass man." Already a century ago the protests against this dehumanization began. Since that time other crucial and gigantic problems have come to the fore; for example, the imbalance between productive capacity and purchasing power, an imbalance that leads to depression. The advent of world wars and a cold war have prevented our having to deal more than once with any acute dip in the business cycle. Indeed, today we are perhaps saved from economic crisis by the artificial stimulus to the economic system which issues from the high national budget devoted to the military. Some observers claim that radical disarmament would bring enormous economic crisis. These phenomena are sufficiently familiar to require no emphasis.

What does deserve emphasis is the fact that applied science has forced us into a frontier in which public opinion must play an unprecedented role. For a time we may find it unnecessary to grapple with any acute structural maladjustment in the economic order. But in the sphere of the military we confront a problem the resolution of which we cannot wisely postpone.

Norman Cousins has recently reminded us that the testing of the H-bombs has presented to public opinion a new and immediate responsibility. A widespread threat to human life is upon us not only in the danger of an atomic war but also through the radioactive fallout that results from the testing of the bombs.

Writing from his hospital in Africa, Albert Schweitzer has done the world a great service by issuing his recent Declaration of Conscience regarding the possible harmful effects of radioactive fallout upon the present generation and upon succeeding generations. Dr. Schweitzer urges upon world public opinion and especially upon the great powers the responsibility of reaching an agreement to end the testing of atomic weapons. If we fail in this, he says, we shall commit "a folly in thoughtlessness."

The statements of Willard F. Libby of the Atomic Energy Commission have aimed to be reassuring, but his formulations have been changing. From saying earlier that no dangers are involved in H-bomb testing he now, in response to Dr. Schweitzer's declaration, admits that there is some risk. The geneticist Dr. E. B. Lewis of the California Institute of Technology has found that the incidence of leukemia is increased with exposure to even low-dosed radiation. The geochemist Harrison Brown at California Tech has asserted that "continued testing at the present rate may well result in the death each year from leukemia of nearly 10,000 persons who would not otherwise have died." We know now that radioactive fallout can have deleterious effects also on the skin, the bones, the lung, the thyroid gland, and upon reproductive organs and embryos. A group of biologists under the auspices of the National Academy of Sciences has published an extensive report on the effects of radioactivity on mutations of the genes. Practically all increases of mutation, we are told, are harmful. The biologists' report asserts that in the light of their findings "any additional radioaction is undesirable." In this whole matter there are numerous other signs of apprehension among the scientists, though of course there are also points of disagreement among them.

The final responsibility in these grave matters lies with public opinion and through it with the governments. The principle of the consent of the governed demands that the discussion of these matters be brought increasingly out of the protected and congested atmosphere of military and other governmental restrictions. Just this process is apparently taking place now, most recently as a consequence of Dr. Schweitzer's declaration. In face of the responsibility the public cannot hide behind the experts. In a democratic society the public listens with continuing respect to the experts, or it should do so. But public policy belongs to the people, and no one will emphasize this fact more insistently than the untethered scientific expert. Germans after the Second World War were found criminally responsible for submitting to the military policies of the Nazis. When does criminal responsibility begin for nations continuing to test the H-bombs?

The issue presented by the testing of atomic weapons is only a striking exemplification of the frontier to which technological advance has brought us. It may well be that this immediate issue imposes upon religious liberals, along with our fellow citizens, the responsibility of adopting new means of agitation in the very spirit of the Old Testament prophets. The feeling of anxiety that has now emerged should make us not only breathless but also resolute. Certainly, we must resist the temptation of permitting the military to become our Golden Calf.

THE VOCATION OF TRUE PIETY

This situation fraught with anxiety brings us to an old and ever new frontier. Today the issues have been formulated afresh by existentialism. The word *existentialism* is used so extensively and loosely that it is necessary to specify the meaning one attaches to it. There are many existentialisms. As a starting point let us consider the existentialism of Kierkegaard. This Danish writer of one hundred years ago, who has become a center of interest in our time, was a powerful rebel against elements in the thought of his day which were ostensibly liberal. He saw the philosophical idealist, especially

Hegel, as the framer of a system that could all too neatly domesticate and liquidate the tragedies of history. He saw the typical churchman as a time-server, accommodating himself to the false securities of respectability and dubbing them Christian. In both of these ways, the philosophical and the "religious" or ecclesiastical, the individual was lost in a system that insulated the self from confrontation with reality and from costing decision. As against these systems, Kierkegaard endeavored to uncover the isolated individual, revealing the person as lonely, anxious, guilty. This solitary, anxious individual cannot by any rational or social means find a way out of his or her isolation or lostness in a system. Such a person does not *live* from some objective truth, but from an inwardness that is either in despair (sometimes under the mask of comfort) or in openness to love.

Kierkegaard knew about the higher criticism of the Bible, and he believed that there could be no certainty for faith if one tried to accept and live by the findings of scientific research. Therefore, he recommended a leap of faith, a leap whereby one would jump to contemporaneity with Christ, thereby becoming newly open to love and impelled to the works of love.

It must be recognized that Kierkegaard rightly emphasizes the idea of freedom, of freedom to escape from the deadly conformities of church and of mass society; also that he gives the tepid Christian a lesson in the importance of decision and commitment. Moreover, in his description of the anxious individual, and particularly in his analysis of guilt as it burdens the soul of the individual, Kierkegaard anticipated with great acuteness much that was to be observed later by depth psychology. It will be a long time before we shall fully explore the insights that have come from these sources.

Nevertheless, Kierkegaard (and thus also many of his admirers) failed to grasp adequately the relation between the individual and society. He has promoted something analogous to the individualistic conversions that we in the United States associate with revivalism (Billy Graham today). Kierkegaard's mentality is essentially pietistic in the sense that it tries to find the meaning and vocation of life primarily in the existence of the individual and in the realm of its person-to-person relations, thus relatively ignoring the concern and responsibility for social institutions. He tried to leap out of his own culture and even out beyond the church into immediacy of contact with the Christ of the New Testament. Actually, the Christian in transcending his or her own culture and its institutions should bring a new leverage to bear upon them as such.

In attempting this leap, Kierkegaard came near to repudiating a major concern of biblical faith: beginning with the Old Testament prophets. Biblical faith in principle was a response to the power of God through the creation of new community, whether it was the community of Israel or the community of the Christian fellowship. In his pietistic individualism Kierkegaard was in his way as lopsided as was Karl Marx in his sociologism. In contrast to Kierkegaard, Marx tried to understand history and society purely in terms of social forces and institutions. Thus Kierkegaard and Marx are in complementary ways lopsided. What Marx emphasizes in terms of social texture, Kierkegaard almost entirely ignores. What Kierkegaard stresses in terms of individual inwardness and integrity, Marx ignores. The contrast is that between the yogi and the commissar.

Of the two kinds of lopsidedness U.S. Protestantism on the whole favors the pietistic lopsidedness. This is probably true also for most ex-Protestants (or secularized Protestants). This individualistic pietism, both religious and secular, generally ends just where Kierkegaard in protest took his point of departure; it ends in pious and uncritical attachment to the status quo of the social order. Extremes breed extremes.

One can see the pietist mentality today in certain types of pastoral counseling and psychiatry. In a prevalent type of pastoral counseling the individual is dealt with in abstraction from the political and economic structures. In readily observable ways the kind of counseling and preaching which deals primarily with "how to overcome your worries" has found a comfortable and seemingly helpful way of avoiding the discussion of controversial social issues. A recent national survey of theological education discovered that a major concern of the younger generation of ministers and theological students is with pastoral counseling to the exclusion of the social-ethical, prophetic elements in religion. It is worth noting in this connection that Freud himself tries to understand the individual primarily in terms of categories drawn from family existence and not from the embracing social order. One can readily understand why a leading intellectual weekly has issued a series of articles under the rubric "Must Psychoanalysis Be Reactionary?" One can also understand how it is that a large number of the ostensibly sophisticated Protestant clergy of New York City are today promoting the current pietism of Billy Graham which naively assumes that if the individual is regenerated social problems will automatically take care of themselves.

The freedom and fulfillment of the individual are inextricably connected with the freedom and fulfillment of the groups to which one belongs and with the purposes and methods of these groups. Therefore religious liberals, whether they are Christians or not, recognize that the continuing frontier of our cause is the frontier that combines the search for the salvation of the individual with the search for the salvation of the group. As we have seen, this is the demand that confronts us on the three frontiers we have considered here. It is the vocation of true piety.

6 · *Hidden Evils and Hidden Resources*

The kingdom of heaven is like treasure hidden in a field, which a man found. . . .
Matthew 13:44

You may recall seeing reproductions of the paintings of the Dutch painter Pieter Brueghel the Elder, a scion of the Reformation and the Renaissance, for example, *The Wedding Feast,* a picture of peasants dancing around the tables of the nuptial festivities. Brueghel in his paintings did not, like the painters of southern Europe, depict the aristocracy or beautiful Madonnas; he presented scenes from the lives of common people.

One of the paintings by Brueghel is titled *The Fall of Icarus.* This mythological figure Icarus and his father had been imprisoned on the island of Crete. To enable Icarus to escape, the father made some artificial wings, which he attached to his son with wax. But Icarus flew so close to the sun that the wax melted, and Icarus consequently fell into the Aegean Sea. Prominent in the picture are peasants tilling in the field. This dazzling picture of the peasants dominates the painting, with a beautiful ship sailing out of the harbor. Icarus, who has fallen into the sea, is almost invisible in the lower corner of the picture, and his cry of distress remains unheeded. Normal life is going on steadily and unwittingly all around while Icarus falls and drowns. Writing of all this, W. H. Auden in a poem says:

> Everything turns away quite leisurely from the disaster;
> The ploughman may have heard the splash, the forsaken cry,
> But for him it was not an important failure; the sun shone
> As it had to on the white legs disappearing into the green
> Water; and the expensive delicate ship that must have seen
> Something amazing, a boy falling out of the sky,
> Had somewhere to get to and sailed calmly on.

Here we find suggested a paradigm of the vocation of the church and of the minister—to reveal the hidden, to point to hidden realities of human

This sermon was given at the service of ordination for the Reverend Jon Luopa by the First Church of Worcester, Massachusetts, on September 27, 1981.

suffering, and also, as we shall see, to point to hidden realities that offer release and surcease.

A vocation of the church and the minister, then, is to point to what we would prefer to ignore; to use a cliché, it is to point to what we would like to sweep under the rug. In our concern for our day-to-day interests and obligations, we find ways to ignore the plight of those who are deprived of full participation in the common life, the plight of those who live in poverty of body or of spirit.

This fragmentation of the common life is from one perspective an aspect of our fate, the fate of living in a segregated society. We live in neighborhoods segregated from other neighborhoods in terms of education, occupation, and income, also separated by class and pigmentation, that is, by race. The segregations of sexism cut across all of these boundaries. In all too great a measure the churches are a function, and indeed a protection, of these segregations.

In this situation we of the middle class are tempted, indeed almost fated, to adopt the religion of the successful. This religion of the successful amounts to a systematic concealment of, and separation from, reality—a hiding of the plight of those who in one sense or another live across the tracks. In the end this concealment comes from a failure to identify and to enter into combat with what St. Paul called the principalities and powers of evil. The religion of the successful turns out, then, to be a sham spirituality, a cultivated blindness, for it tends to reduce itself to personal kindliness and philanthropy costing little. Thus it betrays the world with a kiss.

Another of his paintings Pieter Brueghel called *The Blind Leading the Blind,* perhaps a satire on the churches. As has been said, he "penetrated into the vanity of human pretensions." For him the religion of the successful was a symbol of "a lost humankind."

Presupposed here is the biblical message, beginning with the Old Testament prophets who remind us that we are a covenanted people responsible not only for human kindliness but also for the character of our institutions, and especially for seeking justice for the poor at the gate. Something of this may have been in Jesus' mind when he said (according to a new translation), "Be ye all-inclusive as your father in heaven is all-inclusive." The prophetic message places the responsibility upon us all, upon all members of the covenanted church—the responsibility of the prophethood of all believers (and not simply of the minister). This prophethood must accompany the priesthood of all believers, the courage to care for persons in need of fellowship.

The Fall of Icarus, by Pieter Brueghel

Musées Royaux des Beaux-arts, Bruxelles (Used by permission)

Much of this view was abridged in the ordination sermon I heard from the lips of Samuel McChord Crothers of the First Parish in Cambridge at my ordination in Salem over fifty years ago. In this sermon Dr. Crothers said, "Every personal problem is a social problem, every social problem is a personal problem."

In confronting these problems and responsibilities the vocation of the church and the minister is also to point beyond the hidden evils to something else that is hidden—to the spiritual resources for authentic human existence. Here the church does not in the first instance call us to respect our obligations. It points, as Jesus suggests, to "treasure hidden in a field," a gift of grace. The message is not initially in the imperative mood; it is in the declarative mood. It calls attention to realities, to the Kingdom of God which is actually and potentially among us in the sense that it is available to us as individuals and as groups. This is the meaning of the proclamation "The Kingdom of God is at hand." The message asks us to open ourselves to a divine reality that can transform us and bring us into a community of caring. The message calls upon us to learn to say, "et cetera," to recognize that what we are and what we have been do not exhaust reality. For there is seed beneath the snow.

Since we here are in a church edifice we may change the metaphor. Many a church is mounted by a steeple. Standing high above ground, the steeple is subject to wind and storm, to weather both clement and inclement, to severe cold and to severe heat. And in addition, this steeple points upward.

The steeple is also grounded by support from below.

We often hear it said that the roots of a tree reach as deeply into the earth as the branches are high. So we might say that the spiritual roots of the steeple go as deeply into the hidden spiritual resources.

We are aware of the axiom from the New Testament, "By their fruits shall ye know them." Of the believer and of the congregation we may say also, By their roots shall ye know them. They are hidden roots to be sure, but roots that ever give life and newness of life to the faithful, to the transformed and transforming community of faith, which instead of "sailing calmly on," can hear the call of human need. That need is for the community seeking for mercy and justice.

7 · A Theological Interpretation of the Holocaust

In the face of the incomprehensible and fearful mystery, the incredibly bestial mass murder attaching to the Holocaust, we recognize the moral necessity of our remembering the Holocaust and our responsibility for preventing its recurrence. (The word *Holocaust* still falls too easily from our lips.) We are reminded that we require a more adequate conception of human nature than was characteristic of the sweet gloss of old-fashioned liberal religion. The lack in the West of heed to the Holocaust for over a decade may be in part due to nicely reasoned interpretations that confine themselves to the anthropological, the human dimension, interpretations that do not venture to give a theological interpretation. I want here to offer all too briefly a theological perspective, and peradventure to risk eliciting revulsion, or at least to risk posing only new, unresolvable problems. But here goes.

In Dostoyevski's *Crime and Punishment,* the author, a relentless theologian, views freedom as the burden and tragedy of human existence, yet also as a divine gift accompanied by the occasion for responsibility. For human being, as an individual and as a collective phenomenon, no limits to the abuse of freedom are imposed. If any limit is imposed upon human freedom, then it simply is not freedom. Everything is allowed, whether it be Raskolnikov's murdering of the old usurer, or whether (we might add) it be the sufferings of Job, the destruction of Hiroshima and Nagasaki, or the Nazi Holocaust. Guernica must be possible. We should not forget that Dostoyevski at great length studied these social demonries, Raskolnikov writ large.

Every abuse of freedom issues from freedom's deteriorating into self-will, into defiant self-affirmation. Raskolnikov, it will be remembered, commits the crime of murder for the sake of a "higher idea"—he plays the role of superman (as does the Grand Inquisitor). He therefore resorts to coercion. Wasn't the usurer anyway a greedy, inferior, and worthless creature?

But enforced goodness is itself evil, as in every authoritarianism. Compulsion is the Antichrist, for Christ gives liberty of conscience, "the liberty of the glory of the children of God." Moreover, a person obsessed is no

This essay is adapted from Adams's contribution to a symposium on the Holocaust, in *Kairos* 23/24 (Summer/Fall 1981). Reprinted by permission.

longer free, whether one be a Inquisitor or a Communist—or a Nazi. Self-will here becomes compulsion and tyranny. In this view the abuse of freedom is the tragic destiny of humankind—and of God.

One is reminded here of Kierkegaard's view that the power of God is not to be discerned in alleged omnipotence. On the contrary, it is to be recognized in his having given rise to a creature that in freedom can turn against him. For Dostoyevski, the freedom permitted by God is manifest in Raskolnikov's very act of murdering the usurer.

In this brief compass I of course cannot play out the implications of what Pascal called the greatness and the misery of humankind. But perhaps this is not necessary, for the ubiquitous presence of racism, of demonic nationalism, of the brutal tyrannies of communism and of what today in some quarters calls itself "Christian capitalism" are darkness visible to those who have eyes to see, particularly to see the herd quality of callous collective behavior. Hannah Arendt has even suggested that Eichmann was merely an obedient, "bourgeois" cog in a bureaucratic machine. On another level: Did not President Roosevelt refuse to endorse the Wagner-Rogers Child Refugee Bill, which aimed to save some German Jewish children by permitting 10,000 of them to immigrate in 1939–40? The bill died in the congressional judiciary committees. On still another level: What are we to think of the claim of our present secretary of state that the U.S.A. possesses one thing in common with the right wing (murdering) generals in El Salvador—"belief in God"? And what about the treatment of German soldiers in U.S. prison camps over there? All of these phenomena reveal the significance and necessity of organized, responsible dissent in society.

These considerations bring into relief the burden and opportunity of *kairos,* that is, of timely, responsible decision in the public sphere. The Jewish philosopher Hans Jonas, an exile from Nazi Germany, in his Ingersoll Lecture at Harvard Divinity School (1962), has suggested that in making unlimited freedom possible for the human being, God has taken a great risk, has made a wager. Therefore, it is for us to accept the challenge of attempting to vindicate God's wager. In a sense he is betting on us.

This, then, is the ontological, theological meaning of divinely given freedom and responsibility. In the face of Hiroshima and the Holocaust and of humanity's multiform inhumanity among the brothers and sisters of Job, God the Great Wagerer is not powerless, for he offers the mystery of grace, sustaining, renewing, and transforming—the ground of hope. And what was the alternative for God? Either to intervene to limit human freedom or to "condition" freedom in the manner of *A Clockwork Orange.*

8 · By Their Roots Shall You Know Them

In the last line of Shelley's "A Defence of Poetry" we read, "The poets are the unacknowledged legislators of the world." We need to alter this axiom only slightly to make it read, "Poetry is the unacknowledged legislator of the world." You may recall that the principal rhetorical devices of the poet are metaphor and simile. We might say with Shelley that they are the great legislators guiding the mind toward or away from reality, actual or possible. Of course one can readily misfire or get mixed up in using metaphors. I recall that when I was teaching in a department of English in my first teaching job, I warned a student if, in his next theme he did not include an integrative metaphor, a clinching incident from history or fiction, he could expect his theme to be returned to him without grade. He turned in a theme on thrift, and the last line of the last paragraph was this sentence: "And so we see that a young man in his youth should save his money in order to have a nest egg to fall back on in his old age." I wrote on the margin at this point, "I hope that the egg will be a Chinese egg, in order to avoid a colorful splash."

We are all entirely familiar with the New Testament axiom, "By their fruits shall you know them," but since fruits cannot appear without roots, are we not entitled to say also, "By their roots shall you know them"? Hence, the root metaphor of this sermon will be "roots." In exploring our roots as liberals we may be able to achieve our sense of identity, thus answering in part the question, Who are we?

Since most of us Unitarian Universalists are "come-outers" from other denominations or from the streets (as is sometimes said) the task of identifying our roots is not an easy one. Indeed, as a historical denomination we must recognize many roots, for example, our roots in the left wing of the Reformation, in our congregational polity, in the Enlightenment and Romanticism, in the dialogue between religion and science in the nineteenth century. For the present discourse I, for the most part, will leave out of consideration these roots. I want to single out our rootage in the Bible and especially in the teachings of Jesus.

At the outset let us recall that one of the world-historical achievements of

This address was presented for the commencement exercises at the Meadville/Lombard Theological School, Chicago, Illinois, in June 1984.

liberalism was higher criticism of the Bible by scholars, who during recent centuries have developed the methods of analyzing historical texts, tracing sources, or tracing even social-psychological motives for the selection and interpretation of texts. Accordingly, the idea of the absolute inerrancy of every word in Scripture has been widely abandoned. Indeed, some of this historical method has been so enlightening an enterprise that it has been taken up in part by leaders of other world religions.

One of the results of this whole endeavor was the distinction between the religion *of* Jesus and the religion *about* Jesus or between the religious outlook of Jesus himself and the christological doctrines that began to develop almost from the beginning. This distinction became ever clearer as the scholars recognized that much that is in the Gospels could not have come from Jesus. Hence, the texts employed by scholars to identify the religion *of* Jesus represent a much-reduced section of the Gospels. Regarding the religion *about* Jesus, the variety of interpretations available in the Scriptures is evident from the fact that in the New Testament one finds seventy-two different honorific titles given to him.

Now, in this whole matter, I want to refer to the work of a former eminent professor at Meadville, Dr. Clayton R. Bowen, the Frederick Henry Hedge Professor of New Testament Interpretation. I lament that I did not have the privilege of knowing him personally, for I arrived at Meadville two years after his death in 1934. In 1922 Dr. Bowen responded to a request from the American Unitarian Association to prepare a pamphlet. His pamphlet of eighteen pages (which was published in numerous editions) carries the title "Why are Unitarians Disciples of Jesus?" His answer to this question is that Unitarians are his disciples in that they adopt the religion *of* Jesus rather than a creedal statement *about* Jesus. Trinitarianism as a doctrine is not found in the New Testament.

Dr. Bowen speaks of Unitarians as "primitive believers, who go back, as no others do, to the original works of faith." He goes on to say, "I have never seen a creed I can imagine Jesus signing or saying. And somehow I can't hear him getting very far in a statement like the Apostles' Creed which asks him to say, 'I believe in God the Father almighty, maker of heaven and earth (yes, surely!) and in myself, his only Son. . . .' No, I think he would have to stop there." One encounters similar difficulties, Dr. Bowen says, if one reads these creedal formulas into the Beatitudes. "Blessed are the pure in heart, for they shall see the Father, the Son, and the Holy Ghost." "Blessed are the peacemakers, for they shall be called the children of the Blessed Trinity." "No," Dr. Bowen concludes, "This monstrous incongruity will not do. The Father is declared the only true God: that is the unitarianism of Jesus."

What is more important for our purpose is Dr. Bowen's description in his other writings on the religion of Jesus and especially on Jesus' conception of the kingdom or the reign of God. At the beginning of the present century Albert Schweitzer had thrown a bombshell into the whole discussion. Schweitzer, before he went to Africa, made a survey of the more important books of the nineteenth century on the kingdom of God. The bombshell thrown by Schweitzer held that absolutely everything in the Gospels is to be interpreted in the light of Jesus' expectation that the kingdom was to come very soon, bringing a new heaven and a new earth. The kingdom is only for the future, and its ethic only an interim ethic. This view of Schweitzer's had been discussed for over twenty years when Dr. Bowen with audacity published an essay to argue that for Jesus the eschatology was only of secondary interest, in short, that Jesus felt that the reign, the kingdom, of God, was not only to come in the future but was already breaking in, calling for the human response of change of heart, mind, and soul. Men and women, said Dr. Bowen, were to live as if the kingdom were already here. One need not wait for the Messiah. As an expression of this in-breaking power of the kingdom, Jesus went about healing the sick, also carrying the message of hope to the despised and neglected, to tax collectors, to prostitutes, to the downtrodden. Dr. Bowen rejected the merely futuristic view of Schweitzer.

What was Jesus' view of the working of the reign of God? Now we come to a mark of the genius of Jesus, the creator of the great parables, the employer of metaphor and simile. Dr. Bowen did not write extensively on the parables, but he wrote eloquently on Jesus the poet. Indeed, he adopted the idea that the utterances of Jesus in the parables are so expressive of a gifted person that they must be genuinely his and not the inventions of others.

Here, then, we see an independent young man who, faced with a great variety of vague and conflicting conceptions of the kingdom, of the Messiah, and of the Last Things, created parables of stunning simplicity which can be read with understanding by men and women of all times and places. The kingdom is *like unto* a seed that grows of itself, even when people are sleeping, it is like a tiny grain of mustard seed that people took and sowed in the fields, or it is like a pearl of great price sought by a merchant.

Several important things are to be observed here. No appeal is made to scriptural sanction or to supernatural revelation, and no fixed program is offered. Instead, Jesus uses a rational method of analogy appealing to empirical experience self-evident to Jew, gentile, or Samaritan. He selects processes in nature and lifts them up to illumine a gift, a reign that is at hand, available, mysterious, hidden and to become manifest, now in our midst, a creative power not of human making but offering new possibility. Instead of appealing to authorities Jesus says, "He that hath ears to hear, let him hear."

So what do we have here? We have the claim that there is a sovereign, universal moral law, a nonmanipulable reality, worthy alone of ultimate loyalty, and the source of peace and human fulfillment. This by the way is what the Unitarian philosophers Henry Nelson Wieman and Charles Hartshorne and Alfred North Whitehead have called their philosophy or theology of creativity.

In his sayings, stories, and actions Jesus not only gives religious-ethical application to the parables, he also discloses ample evidence of his roots in Hebrew piety (and even in Zoroastrian religion). He had *his roots* there, and thus he turns out himself to possess a cluster of roots. From these roots he derives his convictions that the seed that grows of itself sustains and supports and demands righteousness, a universal moral law informing the conscience and engendering just and merciful community. The response to the seed is the creative power of love. This love is not primarily an emotion, but rather energetic good will. In response to the growing seed all men and women are viewed as equal, indeed, even those who in human eyes appear to be unworthy. These are the fruits of the roots.

More than that, Jesus held that with him a new period in history was beginning *following* upon that of the law and the prophets, a period in which the ceremonial laws of Moses would be transcended and would find their essential meaning and purpose. Because of his special role in the new period, Dr. Bowen asserts, "the personality and word of Jesus together make up the Gospel."

Accordingly, the search for a christology, a conception of the theological significance of Jesus, is inevitable.

The new period would experience birth pangs, for all human institutions were to be challenged: the synagogue, the family, the cultural order. In this direction Jesus insisted that the sabbath was made for humans, not humans for the sabbath, and with small cords drove the money changers out of the Temple. This totalistic perspective regarding the culture appears in the imagery of St. Paul when he asserts that at the Last Day of Judgment Jesus Christ will approach the Father Almighty with all of the redeemed, including the redeemed institutions. The vision of Jesus, then, was not confined to a pietism or individualism that sees the meaning of life only in interpersonal relations.

I once heard the theologian-poet W. H. Auden answer a question about Shelley's dictum. He was asked, "Do you agree that the poets are the unacknowledged legislators of the world?" He pondered for a moment, and then in his typically gruff manner said, "The poet? Certainly not. Who are these legislators? I would say—the secret police." Auden's comment gives us occasion to say that the naturistic image of the seed that grows of itself is not the whole story, nature is also red in tooth and claw.

Jesus believed that a cosmic struggle between the divine and the demonic was underway, a struggle against greed, callousness, intolerance, and injustice. Here the ancient teachings of the Old Testament prophets are evident with a new urgency and a totalistic demand and promise.

For all of those who would accept this challenge Jesus is a vital root, though one of the most eminent of our liberal theologians of the twentieth century, Ernst Troeltsch, often said there may be other roots of this sort in the past or in the future.

The special quality of Jesus' teachings is, however, to be discerned in the parables. By devising these parables Jesus points beyond himself to the gift, the potential reign of the mysterious good that is beyond our comprehension. This mystery is a creative, sustaining, commanding, judging, community-forming and -transforming power that grows not old, ever calling for individual and corporate response.

9 · *Radical Laicism*

"Gentleman, let me remind you, Jesus was not a parson." That is, he was from the laity, the people. This salty maxim was a familiar one to theological students sixty years ago from the lectures of the Unitarian theologian Dean William W. Fenn of Harvard Divinity School.

The word *laity* is one of the most ancient in our heritages. It appeared not only in the Old and the New Testaments but also as far back as in Homer. Later, in Athens, "Hear ye, people" (*laos* in Greek) was the traditional cry of the herald to introduce his announcements or official declarations. Eventually the word acquired in Greece a note of "archaic solemnity."

In ancient Israel the word acquired an explicitly religious meaning in the phrase "the people of God" who had received a call, a special vocation. "Thou art a holy people to the Lord, thy God." In certain passages a distinction is made between the laity and the leaders; but all are bound together by a covenant. New dimensions appear in the New Testament.

Years ago the late Frederick M. Eliot, president of the American Unitarian Association, used to say that we can understand this attribution of holiness to the people, and apply it to ourselves individually and collectively if we recognize that a hand, an imperative hand, is laid upon us, giving us a religious vocation.

In the present discussion I want to stress the vocation of the laity, assuming according to tradition that everyone is a layperson, an idea expressed in the phrase "the priesthood of all believers." We must, however, avoid assigning the "people" of the laity to a special religious sphere, for among us the sharp distinction between a sacred and a secular sphere has rightly broken down.

In principle our orientation, our point of identity, is to powers that are creative and sustaining and transforming, not ultimately of our making but rather gifts. In a sense these powers depend on us to respond. Our vocation is to point to these powers and to respond to them for the sake of freedom and mutuality. Obviously, the laity associated with the churches has no monopoly on awareness of or response to these powers, nor for that matter

An abbreviated form of this essay appeared in the *Unitarian Universalist World* 15: no. 1 (January 15, 1984). Reprinted by permission of the Unitarian Universalist Association.

on naming them. It is salutary to recall that almost a century ago President Charles W. Eliot of Harvard, writing of the Social Gospel of the day, said that the stimulus for it came from outside the churches—that is, from the laity in the world.

Freedom finds meaning only through relatedness to the creative and transforming powers. Here freedom confronts its limits, for the ignoring of these powers and their demands brings oppression. The demands are the hand laid upon us, though freedom would have no meaning if we were not free to turn against them in the idolatry of absolutized segments or special interests. Radical laicism, stemming from the Reformation, has asserted that the creative and transforming powers are accessible to the individual but at the same time call for the covenant of common responsibilities.

Two aspects of radical laicism require special attention: what have been called the "priesthood" and the "prophethood" of all believers.

The priesthood of all believers refers at least to two things. In all religions the priest points to holy things and offers thanks. The priest is also concerned with the care of souls. It is, then, the vocation of the laity to express and to elicit a sense of the sacredness, the holiness, the preciousness, of all gifts of creation, as is done in certain works of art (including liturgy), for example in the composer Paul Winter's *Missa Gaia,* or *Earth Mass,* where even the wolves and the whales join in the praise of God and creation; also in prayer (or meditation) individual and collective, for children as well as adults. It is the vocation of the laity that everyone shall be concerned with interpersonal fellowship in the family, in friendship, in work and play, and particularly in affectional relatedness to those especially in need.

The priesthood of all believers is inextricably related to the prophethood. Either of these without the other is a snare and a deception, a violation of any viable covenant, a corruption of the best which leads to the worst.

The prophethood of believers entails the obligation to share in the analysis, criticism, and transformation of institutions, including the analysis and transformation of the church. It requires the capacity to discern and define the actual world about us and in a timely way to envisage the potentialities latent in it and in the creative and transforming powers, the ultimate resource. Here again worship, prayer, meditation can be crucial. Here we reject the assigning of the liberty of prophesying only to the appointed minister. In Melville's novel *Moby-Dick,* Father Mapple mounts the pulpit by a rope ladder and for the sake of his independence pulls the rope up after him. The liberty of prophesying about social and institutional evils certainly belongs to the minister. But in radical laicism the trained minister should as it were take the congregation along into the pulpit. That congregation brings with it its experience from its various occupations and perspectives and from its associations with others in the church and in the world. Thus the laity relates the church and its message to the world. From the laity and its minister (also a layperson) and from their criticism of the injustices of the world emerge innovation or proposals for innovation, proposals affecting the family and the social, economic, and political structures. (In a free church the liberty of prophesying must make room for dissent, especially by reason of the tyranny that can be imposed by an arrogant majority. "By the bowels of Christ," warned Oliver Cromwell, "remember that you may be mistaken.")

As Charles W. Eliot suggested, this criticism and innovation are in part responsive to criticism and innovation in the world outside the church, the world of the other laity. We think here of the labor, women's suffrage, feminist, antiracist, and social welfare movements. And now we live in a world of terrorism, holocausts, nuclear weaponry, and indifference to poverty and hunger. How shall we not feel what Wilfrid Gibson in the poem "Lament" calls "the heart-break in the heart of things"? A hand is laid upon us.

Part Two

Interpreting the Signs
of the Times

A DAMS HAS OFTEN CALLED ATTENTION TO THE ETHICAL SIGNIFI-
cance of interpretations of history, especially as they bear upon an
understanding of the modern era. In the face of the cultural and political
crises of the twentieth century, the old norms of society fall into question;
in this situation the classical methods of moral theology, such as casuis-
try—the art of fitting specific cases to fixed moral rules—tend to break
down. Adams holds that a directive is discernible in history when events are
seen through the prism of the prophetic covenant—the divine and human
covenant founded on justice and love. His method of moral reflection, then,
is more akin to that of the prophet who "interprets the signs of the times"
(see Matt. 16:3) against the background of the basic moral imperatives of
covenantal faith.

In the first essay in this section, "The Prophethood of All Believers,"
Adams applies the principle of radical laicism to his conception of the basic
task of "the prophetic liberal church." He points to the way theories of
successive periods in history bring into focus the social-ethical demands of
the present age.

In "Law and Love and the 'Good Old Cause'" Adams relates the apparent
loss of nerve among English free church adherents in the face of attacks upon
their political loyalty during the French Revolution, to similar attacks
upon the loyalty of Americans during the Cold War; were the free churches
better aware of their heritage, they would know better how to respond
today. The contemporary liberal church will recover its prophetic dynamism, Adams argues, only as it demythologizes the Enlightenment faith in
progress through an automatic harmony of individually pursued interests.
The essay "Natural Religions and the 'Myth' of the Eighteenth Century"

reappraises the harmonism and rationalism that liberals inherit from the Enlightenment and outlines basic elements of a postmodern theological reconstruction.

The pertinence of modern economics to the organizational principles from which the free churches sprang—the ideas of voluntary association and local self-determination—is assessed in "The Enduring Validity of Congregational Polity." Here Adams also calls to mind a number of his personal associations in Chicago. The sociologist Max Weber spoke of the modern economic corporation as forging an "iron cage" around the lives of men and women; in "From Cage to Covenant" Adams calls upon the churches to confront the economic and social conditions of our age through a renewed understanding of covenant, an idea with many levels of meaning.

Adams has long championed the thought of Ernst Troeltsch, the German scholar who demonstrated the historical connections between the forms of organization and the social teachings of the churches. In "Why the Troeltsch Revival?" he examines the renewed interest in Troeltsch among those who wrestle, as Troeltsch did, with the corrosive relativism that accompanies rapid social change. Rather than retreat into pietism or fundamentalism, Adams holds, we need today to advance into a radicalized historical consciousness.

Adams calls for the liberal churches to become bearers of an historically shaped, prophetic religious consciousness in the essay "Our Responsibility in Society." They will do so, he believes, only as they recover their historical roots in the Radical Reformation of the sixteenth and seventeenth centuries. In "We Wrestle Against Principalities and Powers" he points specifically to racism and nationalism as the besetting social manifestations of what Paul Tillich called "the demonic." The delegitimating of such forces stands, then, at the head of the agenda of those who would forthrightly and effectively interpret the signs of the times.

G.K.B.

10 · The Prophethood of All Believers

One of the more vivid recollections of my youth in a fundamentalist group is the memory of their eager interest in the prophecies of the Bible. These prophecies were believed to encompass almost the entire range of human history. One all-embracing "prophetic" image that looms in my mind is that of an immense chart that adorned the wall of the church auditorium.

This chart depicted the pivotal events of creation and redemption, beginning with the original chaos and proceeding through the six days of creation, the first day of rest, the fall, the various dispensations of Old Testament history on down to the annunciation, the incarnation, the crucifixion, and the resurrection and thence on to the Second Coming of Christ, the Battle of Armageddon, the seven years of tribulation, the thousand-year reign of Christ, the chaining of Satan in hell, the last judgment before the great white throne, and the eternal peace and unquiet of the respective final destinations of all human souls. In short, the epochs of "salvation history" were set forth as "by prophet bards foretold."

Religious liberals are accustomed to emphasize the prophetic task of the church. But we have long ago abandoned the whole idea of predicting the future by means of interpreting the biblical prophecies. In conformity with the findings of modern historical research, we have held that prediction is a secondary and even an unimportant aspect of Old Testament prophecy. Accordingly, we say that the prophets were primarily forthtellers and not foretellers; they proclaimed the action of God in history; they disclosed the meaning of history. We see the prophet as one who stands at the edge of a community's experience and tradition, under the Great Taskmaster's eye, viewing human life from a piercing perspective and bringing an imperative sense of the perennial and inescapable struggle of good against evil, of justice against injustice. In the name of the Holy One the prophet shakes us out of our pride and calls for a change of heart and mind and action. With fear and trembling the prophet announces crisis and demands ethical decision here and now.

This function of prophecy is well symbolized by a visual metaphor that is

This essay originally appeared in *The Christian Register*, 126, no. 3 (March 1947), and was republished in Adams's *Taking Time Seriously* (Glencoe, Ill.: The Free Press, 1957). Reprinted by permission of the Unitarian Universalist Association.

said to appear in a church in Toronto. On the altar in this church there stands a large crucifix on which the figure at first seems to be an importunate question mark, the prophetic question mark that stands over humanity's ways that are not the ways of truth and right. It is the question mark that we would often like to liquidate, for it reminds us of the death-dealing effect of our egotism and our "virtue."

But we fall far short of understanding the full nature of prophecy (and of the prophetic task of the church) if we think of the prophets merely as critics dealing with religious and ethical generalities. In the great ages of prophecy the prophets (whether inside or outside the churches) have been foretellers as well as forthtellers. They have been predicters—proclaimers of doom and judgment, heralds of new fulfillment. They have attempted to interpret the signs of the times and to see into the future. They have stood not only at the edge of their own culture but also before the imminent shape of new and better things to come. At times of impending change and decision, they have seen the crisis as the crisis of an age; they have felt called to foresee the coming of a new epoch. That is, they have been "epochal thinkers." Wherever you find a prophet of world-historical significance you find a foreteller, and you find "epochal thinking." By this kind of prophecy the signs of the times are interpreted as parts of a pattern, of an old pattern in the structure of the society which is passing away or of a new pattern of life which is coming into being. Jeremiah and Isaiah, Jesus and Paul, Augustine and Joachim of Fiore were all epochal thinkers in this sense; they saw themselves as standing between the times, between the epochs.

Prophetic prediction and epochal thinking have played an equally significant role in modern times also. The Radical Reformation of the sixteenth century, the heralds of the Renaissance, the mystical and radically democratic sects of the seventeenth century, the democratic revolutionists of the eighteenth century (including the founders of our own nation), the religious liberals of the same period, evolutionists and scientists, and the proponents of the Social Gospel in the nineteenth century—all were prophet bards foretelling, and struggling for, a new epoch.

Not all of these prophets have appeared within the churches. Indeed, some of the most influential of the epochal thinkers in the nineteenth century prophesied against "religion" as inextricably bound up with the passing epoch and as marked for elimination. Karl Marx, for example, in his attempt to interpret the signs of the times, predicted the end of the age of the bourgeoisie and the advent of a new epoch, the real beginning of history in the age of the classless society. He tried to support this prophecy by means of a "science" of society. The influence of Marx even upon non-Marxist thinking has been a profound one, for he has given to the masses a new concern for the "trend" of history and for epochal thinking. Even the proponents of "free enterprise" (the defenders of an earlier progressivist epochal thinking) have been constrained to defend their outlook in terms of prediction and of a theory of the inexhaustibility and viability of the present age. Friedrich Nietzsche, the great critic of Christian "slave morality" and of Prussianism, demanded, like Marx, that the scientist become a philosopher of culture and of history, a demand that many a scientist in the new atomic age is now beginning to recognize; and he predicted (with shrewd accuracy) the present nihilism of European culture as the consequence of the loss of spiritual vitality. He also heralded the coming of a new human. "Man is something that shall be surpassed." Auguste Comte, an even more influential epochal thinker, took up the theme of the coming "third era" (proclaimed in varying ways before him by Joachim and Lessing and Hegel and Marx) and heralded the "third era" of science, the era that was to replace the ages of theology and metaphysics. Under his influence and under similar influences many social scientists have come to hold that their work should include prediction. Indeed, many would say that the ideal of science is to acquire the sort of knowledge that will provide a basis for prediction. So the social scientists (or at least some of them) have become interpreters of the signs of the times, attempting to discriminate the trends of the time and to describe our present position in the changing epoch. Edward Alsworth Ross of the University of Wisconsin, in considering the prophetic elements in contemporary sociology, has recently asserted, "Insight into the future is, in fact, the 'acid test' of our understanding. . . . From the days of Comte our slogan has been *Voir pour prévoir,* i.e., see in order to foresee."

It is not an exaggeration to say that the "anti-Christian" critics of our culture (such critics as Marx, Nietzsche, and Comte) have done more than the churchpeople to revive prophetism as prediction and as epochal thinking. As forthtellers (that is, as interpreters of the ultimate meaning of life) they could learn much about the religious character of true prophetism, but as foretellers and as epochal thinkers they cannot be ignored. We live in a world of change and as religious liberals we have the obligation to confront the problems posed by our social economy, the problems of depression and unemployment and insecurity which have become characteristic of the present phase of that economy. Only those who have a priestly attachment to the status quo (which moves whether we like it or not) will try to persuade us that we are living in a former stage of our epoch or that new occasions do not teach new duties. This sort of attachment produces the false prophets who say, "Ye shall have peace at this time." They say "unto everyone that walketh after the imagination of his own heart, 'No evil shall come upon you.'"

This spirit of false prophecy has been plainly exhibited of late in the journals that have been commending President Truman for his refusal to predict the future in his address to Congress on the state of the nation (even though he had been charged by Congress to do that very thing). To be sure, they do not say that businesspeople should eschew foresight and planning for the future; but they do give the impression that they believe that national history should simply take its course without benefit of foresight. They seem now to say, "No evil shall come upon you." Then when it is too late to prevent a catastrophe, will they say the catastrophe was not our fault, or that it could not have been prevented even if we had tried? It is no wonder that the United States is rapidly regaining its 1929 reputation of being a "bad economic neighbor."

When we speak of prophecy, of prediction, of epochal thinking, a host of questions comes immediately to mind. Can one predict with accuracy what will happen to the entire economy? Do we know enough to make our predictions more than wild guesses? Should we not confine ourselves to piecemeal predictions? Is it not fanciful and even dangerous to talk about new epochs? Does this talk not lead to utopianism and irresponsible tinkering and experimenting? How does one choose from among the predicters? And how can religious belief contribute to prophetic criticism anyway? These questions demand and deserve answers.

But whatever the answers may be, this much we can say. A church that does not concern itself with the struggle in history for human decency and justice, a church that does not show concern for the shape of things to come, a church that does not attempt to interpret the signs of the times, is not a prophetic church. We have long held to the idea of the *priesthood* of all believers, the idea that all believers have direct access to the ultimate resources of the religious life and that every believer has the responsibility of achieving an explicit faith for free persons. As an element of this radical laicism we need also a firm belief in the *prophethood* of all believers. The prophetic liberal church is not a church in which the prophetic function is assigned merely to the few. The prophetic liberal church is the church in which persons think and work together to interpret the signs of the times in the light of their faith, to make explicit through discussion the epochal thinking that the times demand. The prophetic liberal church is the church in which all members share the common responsibility to attempt to foresee the consequences of human behavior (both individual and institutional), with the intention of making history in place of merely being pushed around by it. Only through the prophetism of all believers can we together foresee doom and mend our common ways.

Hope is a virtue, but only when it is accompanied by prediction and by the daring venture of new decisions, only where the prophethood of all believers creates epochal thinking. If this foresight and this epochal thinking do not emerge from the churches, they will have to come from outside the churches. Humanity can surpass itself only by surpassing itself. Do we as religious liberals have access to the religious resources for this surpassing of the present? If not, the time will come when others will have to say to us what Henry IV said to the tardy Crillon after victory had been won, "Hang yourself, brave Crillon! We fought at Arques, and you were not there."

11 · Law and Love and the "Good Old Cause"

When he was at the Benjamin Gate, a sentry there named Irijah . . . seized Jeremiah the prophet, saying, "You are deserting to the Chaldeans." And Jeremiah said, "It is false; I am not deserting to the Chaldeans." But Irijah would not listen to him, and seized Jeremiah and brought him to the princes. And the princes were enraged at Jeremiah, and they beat him and imprisoned him in the house of Jonathan the secretary, for it had been made a prison.

Jeremiah 37:13–17

Not long ago there appeared in the *Information Bulletin* of the U.S.S.R. an article by a Soviet journalist praising the music of the composer Aram Khachaturian. In the next issue of the *Bulletin* there appeared an article that described the earlier article as, in effect, subversive of the best interests of the Soviet state. This second article was written by Khachaturian himself. Combining self-castigation with a boundless patriotism, the composer asserts that, so far from being worthy of praise, he has been unfaithful to the ideals of the fatherland: The Soviet government had laid down rules of composition for Soviet composers, but he had shamelessly violated them.

What was Khachaturian's crime? "The roads to error are many," the composer writes. "The one which I took . . . endeavored by artificial means to unite simultaneously the eleven-voiced sound of the wind instruments with the voice of an instrument such as the organ. I went to an extreme, and the result was an unnecessary conglomeration of sounds. Instead of upholding the tradition of Russian music, I followed a formalistic path alien to the Soviet artist." As a consequence of this deviation, he says, he was properly censured by the Soviet people (meaning, of course, the Soviet government). He concludes his confession with the bending of the knee: "I hope that my future work will give evidence that I have rightly understood the beneficial criticism of my great people." The superpatriots have cracked the whip, and the composer pipes to their tune.

Political and church history, especially in periods of severe conflict, is replete with zealots bent upon ferreting out those who are subversive of national or ecclesiastical solidarity. The story of the inquisition of the

This essay is based on a sermon delivered at Bond Chapel, University of Chicago; it was published in *The Divinity School News* 17, no. 3 (August 1, 1950). Reprinted by permission.

innocent victims appears not only in the *Information Bulletin* of the U.S.S.R. or in the pages of the *Congressional Record* or in the tomes that record church history. It appears also as the red thread that runs through the Bible. For many of the great men of the Bible were subversive in the sense that they did not identify the will of God with the will of the men who held the reins of power; subversive in the sense that they call "unjust" what the pious called "just"; subversive in that they proclaimed a law that is higher than the lawlessness of the patriots; subversive in the sense that they served a power that is stronger than tribalism.

How familiar a pattern in history, and in our own time, is the one that caught Jeremiah, the pattern that brands nonconformity as treason. Jeremiah was a disturber of conscience: he had condemned the unrighteousness of his own people; in the face of military danger he had predicted the doom of the nation. He had gone even further. Believing that restoration would follow the punishment of the nation, he purchased from his relatives the ancestral home at Anathoth, four miles outside Jerusalem, in territory controlled by the Babylonians, who were laying siege to the city. The tribal patriots were much pleased. They could now call him subversive; they now had a pretext to accuse him of treason, to imprison him and get him out of the way.

There is nothing that assists sheer power as against principle better than hysteria arising out of intense social conflict. Hysteria of this sort frightens whole groups of people into a stampede of suppression; and it frightens many victims into submission.

We can observe this sort of hysteria again and again in the annals of Protestantism. The hysteria has appeared in situations very similar to the one that Jeremiah confronted, and the devices of the modern patriots have been similar to those used against Jeremiah. At certain critical moments in the history of Protestantism the accusations and the suppressions growing out of hysteria have crippled the prophetic and creative forces in both church and state. For example, up until the time of the French Revolution and Napoleon, Nonconformity in England was in many ways a profoundly prophetic movement, providing courageous leadership and support for the extension of freedom and justice. But, during the disturbances in France at the end of the eighteenth century and at the beginning of the nineteenth, many of the dissenting churches were frightened into a socially indifferent pietism from which they have not yet recovered on any broad front. Because of the known republicanism and the Whig background of Nonconformity, the Tories were able to stir up the fears of the country and of the Nonconformist churchpeople against the infiltration of dangerous thoughts into their ranks. In 1792, when Price and Priestley by their support of republicanism brought the Unitarians under attack, the aristocracy and the populace combined against the whole group and called them traitors. Chapels were sacked, congregations dared not meet. Tory politicians and Anglican bishops were not slow to take advantage of the unpopularity of the democratic dissenters, to the detriment of Nonconformity as a whole. George Canning, in his *Anti-Jacobin Magazine*, anticipated the devices familiar to us in the Hearst-McCormick press. In every radical critic of the standing order he saw either "a Dissenter or a former Dissenter or a friend of Dissenters." Writing of this wave of hysteria, Halévy in his *History of England in 1815* reports:

> In the associations recently formed by the Independents and Baptists to organize an itinerant ministry Canning saw a scheme plotted by political societies to preach under the disguise of Christianity, republicanism, Deism, perhaps even Atheism. Bishop Horsley of Rochester, in a famous charge, attacked the Methodists as conscious or unconscious agents of the Atheistic and Jacobin propaganda. What, he asked, was the true character of these religious or apparently religious societies which met every evening in the towns and country villages? of these fanatical and uneducated preachers? "The Jacobins of this country," he says, "the Jacobins I very much fear, are at this moment making a tool of Methodism just as the illuminées of Bavaria make a tool of free-masonry; while the real Methodist, like the real Freemason, is kept in utter ignorance of the wicked enterprise the counterfeit has in hand."

What the bishop was really saying was this: "Don't imagine that those Methodists are holding prayer meeting on Wednesday evenings. They are plotting revolution." In this fashion the "right-thinking patriots" forced many a timid Khachaturian to bend the knee and to renounce "alien" ideas.

Already in 1790 Edmund Burke, in his attack on the Unitarian Richard Price, had criticized those churches that permitted the minister even to discuss political and social-ethical issues. He urged that what he called "political theologians" should be discouraged from proclaiming their views from the pulpit. Here are his words, from *Reflections on the Revolution in France*:

> Politics and the pulpit are terms that have little agreement. No sound ought to be heard in the church but the healing voice of Christian charity. The cause of civil liberty and civil government gains as little as that of religion by

this confusion of duties. . . . Surely the church is a place where one day's truce ought to be allowed to the dissensions and animosities of mankind.

On these principles Burke would prevent the churches from "meddling" with the discussion of human rights.

The barrage of "antisubversive" artillery fire directed at the dissenting churches had the intended effect. British Nonconformity during this period lost much of the democratic dynamic that had characterized its earlier struggle for liberty in church and state. It became a new form of conformity, a conformity to what is euphemistically called "established order." A "no-politics rule," "political quietism," became the servant of conservatism—in the guise of neutrality.

Essentially the same story may be told concerning the American Protestant churches of the time. In the years preceding the American Revolution, many of these churches were in the forefront of the struggle for democracy and for the rule of law in the commonwealth. After the French Revolution, "political theologians" increasingly were frowned upon. An American form of pietism developed in reaction against the allegedly subversive deism and the political theology that were associated in the popular mind with French rationalism, infidelity, and revolution. In many quarters "political quietism" and "loyalty" became synonymous.

In our own day the fear of the Soviet Union and its ideology has again become the tool of the superpatriots. Critics of even undemocratic practices in the United States are accused of going over to the enemy. In the name of "Americanism" every sort of bullying is attempted. Even due process of law is ignored. Hearsay—something inadmissible in a court of law—figures as "evidence." Senator McCarthy under the cloak of senatorial immunity can, with impunity, repudiate the rule of law. Some time ago he announced that he had a long list of Communists in government service. First the list numbered 205, then eighty-one, then fifty-seven, and, finally, one; then it went up again. Week after week the senator has recklessly and irresponsibly accused his victims; people have been "tried" not by law but by the ordeal of headlines.

In apparently legal fashion the attorney general has issued a list of subversive organizations. Yet the organizations branded as "subversive" have had no opportunity to secure a legal hearing. In the minds of many, the "principle" of guilt by association is adopted as a proper basis for the accusation of disloyalty.

One must, to be sure, recognize that, for reasons of security, basic safeguards of the national interest must be established to protect certain key positions in government. But this is no justifiable basis for subjecting government employees to the intimidation and indignity of wild tongues as though these employees were second-class citizens.

Nor is it a justification for subjecting employees in the civil service to illegal scrutiny and control. The first rule adopted by the Civil Service Commission, back in 1884, reads as follows: "No question in any form of application or in any examination shall be so framed as to elicit information concerning the political or religious opinions or affiliations of any applicant; nor shall any enquiry be made concerning such opinions or affiliations, and all disclosures thereof shall be discountenanced." Yet here are some of the questions asked at loyalty examinations: What do you think of the third party formed by Henry Wallace? Is your wife a churchgoer? Do you read many books? Do you believe that Negro blood should be segregated in the Red Cross blood bank? Which newspapers do you read? Would you say that your wife has liberal political viewpoints? (Henry Steele Commager, *New York Times*, magazine section, June 26, 1949).

This sort of heresy-hunting is familiar to every student of church history. In the name of loyalty it serves to proscribe the ideas that the belligerent, bullying forces in the community may not happen to like. In many communities today the belligerent, bullying force is of the sort that can be symbolized by the name of William Randolph Hearst.

The state of California does not by law impose any political test upon its teachers, beyond the oath to support the constitution (required of other state employees). In fact, the state constitution asserts that "no oath, declaration, or test, shall be required as a qualification for any office or public trust." Yet the president and the Board of Regents of the University of California have demanded that every employee in the university shall state under oath (or in a contractual letter) that he or she is not a member of the Communist party or of any other organization that advocates the overthrow of the United States government. Six faculty members have been dismissed because they have refused to say whether or not they are members of the Communist party. The legitimacy of the procedure has not yet been tested at court of law.

It should be noted that the demand imposed by the Board of Regents ignores the fact that a Communist will readily sign the non-Communist oath. Hence the oath provides little, if any, protection against Communists. As the *New York Times* says (editorial, June 26, 1950), the genuine test of loyalty "is not a mouthful of words—it is in the character and personality, the observed teaching, of the faculty member."

Extra-legal or high-handed methods have been adopted also beyond the spheres of government and higher education. One example, from the sphere of the churches, will suffice to illustrate the revival of the pattern of hysteria approved over a century ago by the bishop of Rochester. The minister of a church in Peoria, Illinois, who is said to be an American Legion chaplain, a few months ago demanded that the director of Christian education in the parish should give up her friendship with a nurse who had been discharged from her position as instructor in nursing at a church-sponsored hospital in Peoria. Both women are members of the church served by the minister. The nurse had been discharged from her position at the hospital without notice or explanation. An official of the hospital later asserted that she is a radical and an agitator and thus she could not be kept at the hospital. (She had joined and had been active in the Progressive party.)

In face of the minister's demand that she give up her friendship with her fellow church member, the director replied that her choice of friends was a matter of her own decision; as a consequence, she lost her job (she "resigned"). Subsequently, the nurse has learned from an officer in the Americanism program of the American Legion that she was considered to be either a Communist or a friend of Communists; that it did not make much difference which; that the legion had decided there was not sufficient room in Peoria for both the legion and the Communists and their friends; and that the legion intended to remain in Peoria.

In response to a formal request from the nurse, a denominational commission was appointed to make an investigation of the minister's dismissal of the director of Christian education. The commission reported that "there has been a not unreasonable inference, a very real and injurious malignment of [the director's] character, resulting from the abruptness of her resignation exacted by threat of dismissal, without a reasonable explanation being given both to her and the members of the church; that many of the difficulties might have been avoided if [the executive body of the church] had not erred in failing to recognize its moral, spiritual and legal obligation to grant [the director] the hearing which she rightfully requested." Despite the commission's exhortation to "brotherly kindness," neither of the women has been given a formal hearing by the local church. Instead, a denominational official (it is said) has urged the director to drop the whole matter, since nothing can be done.

We often hear it asserted that a wellspring of modern democracy is the Judeo-Christian conception of the divinely derived dignity of the human being. The assertion can be supported cogently.

But the dignity becomes an airy nothing unless it is protected by the respect for law and by the procedures of legitimate legal institutions. The dignity of the child of God cannot be maintained by a figure of speech. Nor can it be maintained by sentiment, not even by the sentiment of love.

Jeremiah and other Old Testament prophets envisaged the will of God as demanding justice. Like love, justice does not become incarnate through simple proclamation. Justice requires just institutions; just attitudes alone are not sufficient. The ideals of justice promoted by the prophets were plowed into history by the Ezras and the Nehemiahs, by the legalists who defined the rights and duties of the nation and of individuals and who elicited loyalty to the institutions that maintain these rights and duties. The prophets provided the consuming vision of Israel, but the law served to give body to the vision.

Jesus affirmed a love that was not to destroy but to fulfill the law. He repudiated the small matters of the law; but the love he offered presupposed the fundamental law before it could fulfill it or go beyond it. A gospel of charity apart from this law is no longer the gospel of love—it is a pious form of irresponsibility. Love may criticize and attempt to enlarge the conceptions of law and justice, but it does not demand something less than these. According to any conception of love that is fully responsible, not only does the Good Samaritan have the duty of personally assisting the victim of lawlessness; he also has the duty of bringing about the enforcement of the law that stops the thievery.

Modern Protestantism, especially in the Anglo-Saxon countries, began as a protest against tyranny. In making this protest, it demanded a law that would bring tyranny to account. This demand is what John Milton and other radical Protestants of the seventeenth century called the "Good Old Cause." They said the cause was "good because it hath a tendency to the securing of people's just rights, liberties, properties, privileges and immunities against tyranny, arbitrariness and oppression; old because anciently and originally all power was in the people" (*The Good Old Cause Explained* [1659]). From this Protestant support of the Good Old Cause issued our modern democracy, with its principles of the rule of law, of equality before the law, and of the consent of the governed. By this Good Old Cause kings and bishops and superpatriots were brought to book.

But tyranny, the rule of naked power, the rule of the arbitrary, reappears; it assumes new forms. Equality before the law, as we have seen, is today again jeopardized by the hysteria that identifies heretics and traitors by resort to the methods of Senator McCarthy, to the methods of the "Christians" in Peoria—that is, to accusation without duly attested evidence, to arbitrary demand and coercion.

Any Christian or any church that does not oppose these tyrannies assists them. The church that considers the issues here involved to be "controversial" and therefore keeps silent is worse than the Levite that passes by on the other side; it helps the thieves.

This is the kind of aloofness and neutrality of which we are wont to call the Germans guilty. They were responsible for Hitler, we say. Why, then, are we not guilty if we remain silent and impotent in the face of lawlessness? How can we say that we are not guilty for the ravages of hysteria among us?

Is there any doubt that the time has come for American Protestantism to learn again that the Good Old Cause is the cause of Christian love, of love that cherishes law and justice as well as charity and meekness?

12 · Natural Religion and the "Myth" of the Eighteenth Century

To speak of the "myth" of the eighteenth century would only puzzle enlightened persons of that time. In their lexicon, the word *myth* denoted fiction, fancy, and fable; it was the opposite of truth and knowledge. Myth was the natural product of the primitive mind. The vocation of the enlightened person was to free humanity from the myths, "the mass of chimeras, dreams, and absurdities" spawned in the "fabulous ages."

Such a mission was in a sense doomed to failure. For the idea of a mythless person is itself a chimera, a dream, an absurdity. The human being, even the enlightened human being, is by nature a myth-bearing creature. People live by faith. In each culture, in each epoch of a culture, and in each major segment of a culture, this faith expresses itself in what the anthropologist today calls a myth, a group of interrelated ideas or symbols which finds embodiment in the manners, the art, the legal forms, the religious conceptions and disciplines, the value preferences, characteristic of the age. For the contemporary historian of culture, the word *mythos* has again approached its original meaning in Greek, where it signified simply a current narrative, without any implication either of truth or falsehood; it now signifies the symbolic means whereby a culture or an epoch, confronting the demands, the threats, the possibilities of existence, dramatizes its decisive insights and its strongest inclinations. Therefore, we can speak of the Christian myth, the myth of Greek classicism, the myth of the Middle Ages, the myth of the Renaissance, the myth of the eighteenth century. Myth is a universal category in the social existence of humans, whether they be literate or preliterate, religious or secular. There is no such thing as a mythless age.

Even if the myth of a previous age is repudiated ostensibly because it is a fanciful myth, it is repudiated in the name of a faith that expresses itself in a new myth. Thales, perhaps the first man of science in the West, rejected the traditional myths, the stories about anthropomorphic gods. These stories

Adams presented the Harvard University Dudleian Lecture in Andover Chapel of the divinity school on April 18, 1950. It is here reprinted by permission from the *Harvard Divinity Bulletin* XLVIII (1951): 217–32.

could no longer explain existence or reliably direct commitment; they were losing their symbolic power, their numinous quality, their reference to the ultimate. But when Thales asserted that water is the first principle of all things, he was opening the way to a new myth; for him, water was probably a numinous reality, it possessed the power, the sovereignty of a god. As George Grote says, even the later metaphysicians only continued this process of the transformation of myth. "They were concerned to show that the gods and spirits of the old myths were really nothing but primitive versions of the new metaphysical concepts."[1] Sometimes prophetic religion has been interpreted as the conquest of religion over myth. Actually, however, it was the outcome of the conflict of one particular myth with another. The ancient Jewish prophets rejected the myth of ecstatic agrarian polytheism; but they posited a new myth that issued in the notion of the chosen people delivered from bondage for the sake of a world-historical mission, a new myth of Origin and Destiny, of Whence and Whither. So also modern secularism in its conflict with, or indifference to, religion does not eliminate myth; it struggles for a new myth. All such struggles are concerned with the question of what is, or should be, sovereign in human existence. Only a new sovereign myth can displace a myth that is no longer sovereign. The standards, the motives, the ends that give content to the successive myths constitute what Whitehead has called "the driving force of ideas in the history of mankind."

The Myth of a Third Age

The myth of the Enlightenment is a composite myth; it is novel mainly in the combination of its ingredients. These ingredients bear a striking resemblance to elements of previous myths. It is customary to say that the myth of the Enlightenment is Stoic in its love of ecumenical order, or that it stems from the confidence in humanity and human reason of the Renaissance and from its protest against obscurantism, otherworldliness, and authoritarianism. But the myth of the Enlightenment, like that of the Renaissance, holds lineage also from the Middle Ages. Already in the twelfth century an anticipation of the modern spirit appears in the revolutionary vision of the Cistercian abbot Joachim of Fiore. He was the first Christian to make a slogan of the word *reformare*. In protest against the hierarchical domination and the sacramental system of the medieval church, Joachim appealed to what he called the Eternal Gospel. He demanded a reform that would emancipate the Christian community from the conservative Augustinian philosophy of church history which had prevailed for over half a millennium. The Augustinians had deprived the primitive Christian eschatology of its power, by affirming in effect that the kingdom of God was already present in the church. Joachim, whose ideas were taken up by the Franciscan Spirituals, revived the ancient yearning for a new age; he proposed a new theory of the periods or dispensations of history. For Augustine, humanity was living in the last age of history, which had begun with Christ. For Joachim, a new, third era was to come. In his view the doctrine of the Trinity symbolized the periods of history. The age of the Father was from the beginning to Christ; the age of the Son was from Christ down to the appearance of a new monastic order that would introduce new life into church and society. In the coming, third era, the age of the Holy Spirit, there would be no need for authority of the priests; the Spirit would be given to everybody. The Gospel of Christ would be replaced by the Eternal Gospel; filial obedience would issue in a new spiritual freedom.

This hope for a new age of freedom, this myth of the Third Era, reappears in one movement after another in succeeding centuries: in the reform movements of the pre-Reformation period, in the Radical Reformation, in certain branches of the Puritan revolution in England, and in the French and the German Enlightenments. It was taken up by Gotthold Lessing, who interpreted it as the promise of the realization of the essence of the human being in the perennial education of the human race. Joachim's three ages of the world, he says, "were not so empty a speculation after all." The idea of a coming, third era was again transformed by the German philosophical idealists, by Kant, Johann Fichte, Hegel, Schelling; it was adopted also by English and French socialists of the nineteenth century; it imbues both the English and the American revolutions; it may have influenced Comte in his formulation of the three ages of human history: the theological, the metaphysical, and the positivist ages. The idea is to be discerned again in Marx's conception of the three ages, the age of primitive communism, the present age of class struggle, and the coming era of the classless society. It reappears in Nietzsche's theory of the three periods, the Christian, the post-Christian, and the anti-Christian eras.

The eighteenth century believed it was ushering in a new era, the Age of Enlightenment. The heralds of the new era loved light and hated darkness. Indeed, the myth of the Enlightenment may be characterized in terms of what Edward Gibbon called "the vicissitudes of light and darkness."

The negative aspects of the myth are easy to grasp. The Enlightenment entertained a profound distaste for the dark, internecine strifes among the rival interpreters of the Christian myth. This battle of the gods had been no mere battle of the books. In the reformations and counterreformations, in the revolutions and counterrevolutions of the sixteenth and seventeenth centuries, the battle had issued in disastrous, carrion struggle. In almost every country of a divided Christendom the "faith" that prevailed in a region owed its success in large part to the political protection and coercion it could muster.[2]

The Enlightenment was weary of the bickerings and conflicts of the dominating groups that thought of themselves as orthodox. It was no less weary of the "enthusiasm" of the sects—that "full but erroneous belief and persuasion that whatever one does act, or speak, or think is from divine inspiration."[3] It wished to dissolve the myths that had sanctioned arbitrariness and pretentiousness. It wished to do away with belief in the gods of the competing absolutes, also with the capricious God of predestination, and with belief in supernatural interventions in human affairs. It wished to do away with ecclesiastical and biblical legend, with belief in the plenary inspiration of Holy Writ, with witchcraft, with magic, miracle, and mystery. It wished to do away with the theological damnification of humanity expressed in the doctrines of original sin and total depravity.

In the Enlightenment a New Reformation begins its march. Immanuel Kant, in his essay on the *Aufklärung,* has given the classic definition of the spirit of the age and of its principal weapon. "Enlightenment," he says, "is man's release from his self-incurred tutelage. Tutelage is man's inability to make use of his understanding without direction from another. Self-incurred is this tutelage, when its cause lies not in lack of reason but in lack of resolution and courage to use it without direction from another. *Sapere aude!* 'Have the courage to use your own reason'—that is the motto of Enlightenment."[4] The desire for autonomy is the nerve of the myth of the Enlightenment; and its guide is reason, not calculating, utilitarian reason, but substantial reason—in the human mind and in the cosmos.

THE MYTHOS OF LOGOS

The New Reformation moves under the sign of reason rather than of spirit. Its mythos is Logos. The change in mentality marks the emergency of the "modern temper." The Joachite version of the Eternal Gospel had been nonrational, ecstatic, and apocalyptic. So also was the version of much of the Radical Reformation. In England and New England the combat between Puritan and Anglican impelled thoughtful persons to probe for some line of thought which was deeper than the opposing parties had traveled and in terms of which the old antagonism might be reconciled. They devised an "enlightened" version of the Eternal Gospel, a version that aimed to be rational and pedagogical, imbued with enthusiasm only for sobriety and common sense. The dynamic of the chiliasm of the left wing was being rationalized into the dynamic of liberal humanitarianism. Through reason the Enlightenment sought the myth to end all myths, the truly Eternal Gospel, a trustworthy orthodoxy in accord with the nature of things and of humanity.

The myth of the Enlightenment is not to be grasped most readily in formal definitions. It is the expression of a particular type of human temperament; it strives for form and for control through form; it is neoclassical in mood. We sense this mood by listening to the music of Handel or of William Billings, the American composer, by looking at the furniture of Chippendale, at the portraits by Sir Joshua Reynolds and at the gardens of Versailles, or by reading the measured prose of John Tillotson and Gibbon. In both art and manners, we find disciplined respect for balance, symmetry, and proportion, an enthusiasm for moderation. The composer Handel exemplifies this temper when in 1740 he adds a third section to his musical settings for Milton's "L'Allegro" and "Il Penseroso." These first two parts represent "extremes," the moods of gaiety and pensiveness. The added section Handel calls "Il Moderato."

This Augustan temperament did not view itself as merely one among a number of appropriate possibilities. By no means. Like ancient Stoicism it claimed to be in accord with nature; it found its sanction in the character of the cosmos. Two quatrains from the libretto for Handel's "Il Moderato" appeal to this sanction.

> Kindly teach, how blest are they
> Who Nature's equal rules obey;
> Who safely steer two rocks between,
> And prudent keep the golden mean.
> . . .
> Each action will derive new grace
> From order, measure, time, and place;
> Till life the goodly structure rise
> In due proportion to the skies.

According to the eighteenth-century myth, the sovereign reality is not the compulsively neurotic god worshiped by submissive, childish orthodoxy; the cosmos possesses the neoclassical temperament. Logos in the human mind is the *Speculum Mundi,* the mirror of the Logos writ large in a universe governed by law and not by gods who may rescind or circumvent the legal order.

This Logos is a divine gift. In other words, the conception of Logos is a special version of the Judeo-Christian doctrine of creation, of the view that the meaningful, creative goodness is an expression of divine fecundity. This version of the doctrine carries with it the implication that the divine Reason imposes a divine imperative, the demand that persons in society should achieve rational autonomy. God in his benevolence has created an orderly universe, and he expects the human being, with the gift of freedom, to emulate this benevolence by achieving order and benevolence in human relations.

NATURAL RELIGION

Taken altogether, this eighteenth-century doctrine of creation included within its purview not only a doctrine of the human being as a rational creature (with a doctrine of natural law in ethics and jurisprudence) but also a doctrine of providence supporting a faith in a sort of automatic harmony and progress that would ensue if each person would follow reason, indeed would ensue somehow in spite of human fallibility and passion.[5] (Of this doctrine of providence it is not possible or necessary to speak further here; it is, of course, an important ingredient of the drive toward a new era.) The eighteenth-century doctrine of creation implied also a doctrine of natural religion, of a universal religion that could be disclosed if we would discern the laws of creation manifest in the order of nature and in the natural, rational piety of humans in all times and places. The idea of natural religion, along with the doctrine of creation, finds elaborate explication in the sciences of nature and society which develop in the Age of Reason.

The seventeenth and eighteenth centuries are the centuries of the great physicists and mathematicians, and on the principles they outlined arose the sciences of optics, acoustics, chemistry, zoology, geology, physiology, medicine, and psychology. In both England and the United States interest in these sciences was widespread. Theologians and other nonprofessional scientists were members of the Royal Society. Among the Americans, Cotton Mather was a member as was also Chief Justice Paul Dudley, the founder of the Dudleian Lecture. Dudley was "an accomplished naturalist" and submitted a number of papers on natural history to the society. Mather, while paradoxically holding to the Puritan notion of special providences and of divine intervention in the terrestrial realm, set forth in *The Christian*

Philosopher (1721) an elaborate demonstration of the orderliness of the natural universe supported by God's benevolence and apparent to human reason. He treats of everything from light and the stars, through the elements, the minerals, and the vegetables, to the four-footed animals and human beings. This order of nature is an order of reason. Of human reason itself he says it is "a faculty formed by God in the mind of man, enabling him to discern certain maxims of truth, which God himself has established, and to make true inferences from them. In all the dictates of reason there is the voice of God. Whenever any reasonable thing is offered I have God speaking to me."[6]

In his espousal of natural theology (coupled, to be sure, with revealed theology), Mather was but tracing the main lines of the system of creation which had been set forth a generation earlier in the book *The Wisdom of God in Creation* (1691), by John Ray, the father of the science of natural history. Mather was using essentially the arguments that Ray had employed to refute the atheists and to interpret the study of nature as the true "preparative to Divinity." A generation later, President Edward Holyoke of Harvard, in the first of the Dudleian Lectures, would in similar fashion appeal to the cosmological argument as a rational demonstration of the existence of God.

Not only the natural world but also human behavior was subjected to the scrutiny of reason in search of universal laws. The interests of the middle classes accelerated the delineation of theories of the "natural order" of society. Historians and political scientists now undertook a comparison of the legal, political, and general social systems of modern states with those of antiquity and of the newly discovered or rediscovered lands. Even the cultures of preliterate peoples as well as the cultures of the East were gradually brought under methodical survey.

These studies of comparative sociology included the investigation of comparative religion. Already in 1678 Ralph Cudworth, the Cambridge Platonist, had interpreted the thinkers of Greece, Iran, and Egypt as teaching the fundamental theological ideas of Christianity. Shortly before this, Lord Herbert of Cherbury's work *The Ancient Religion of the Gentiles* (published posthumously in 1663) laid down the foundation of the natural religion found in all times; this natural religion could be reduced to five inborn ideas—the existence of God, the need to worship, responsibility for virtuous living, the need of repentance, and a judgment in a future life. Hume's *Natural History of Religion* (1757) was a venture of a different sort. Like the studies made by some of his contemporaries in France, it transferred the interest from philosophical to psychological interpretation; Hume viewed religion as a practical affair having its roots in the satisfaction of human needs. More elaborate than Hume's work was that of Christoph Meiners, the Göttingen scholar of comparative religion. He anticipated what is today called sociology of religion, for he discerned structural relations between religious ideas, cultus, and social organization. His major presupposition is worth quoting as indicative of the Enlightenment's search for the "essence" of natural religion: "All religions may possess as many unique features as they please; it is nevertheless certain that each religion resembles others in many more respects than those wherein it differs from them."[7]

But whether the approach was social-psychological or philosophical, the proponents of natural religion affirmed that it is accessible to us through the use of reason without supernatural aid. Some of them held that the positive Christian revelation itself may be rationally defended, some that it corroborates natural religion, some that it goes beyond natural religion. Rational supernaturalists wished to maintain revealed religion alongside natural religion; they believed the former to be a stronger motive for morality or a more effective expression than the latter. The Christian Deists held that the essence of Christian revelation *is* natural religion; they wished to purge the revelation of irrational elements. The anti-Christian Deists, mostly on the Continent, rejected revelation entirely.

THE CULTURAL SYNTHESIS OF THE ENLIGHTENMENT

Overarching these differences, however, we must discern here a cultural and religious development of great import. Through the concern with natural religion a new era was in fact coming into existence. In the previous period Protestant revealed theology had in wide circles created a disjunction between religion and culture. The medieval synthesis with its system of the sciences had vanished; it had become outmoded. The Enlightenment, retaining and supplementing Renaissance humanism, was attempting to create a new synthesis. The doctrine of natural religion provided the integrating principle for this synthesis. Toward this end, all of the disciplines of eighteenth-century science were employed: the natural sciences, the social sciences of comparative law, comparative sociology, comparative religion, higher criticism, social psychology, philosophical anthropology, and theology. Using Cotton Mather's term, we may say that "the Christian philosopher" was reappearing. It is this new spirit in Protestantism that makes the eighteenth century the watershed between earlier and later

Protestantism. This mentality attempts to restore a vital relation and tension between religion and culture, between religion and science.

We can secure an instructive impression of the dimensions assumed by the doctrine of natural religion if we examine the version of it offered by the Boston theologian Charles Chauncy. A great-grandson of a Puritan president of Harvard and the minister of the First Church in Boston for sixty years (from 1727 to 1787), Chauncy was the major intellectual representative of religious liberalism in mid-century New England and a diligent student of the British defenders of natural religion. Although his most important book, *The Benevolence of Deity* (1784), was not published until late in his career, it was written before the establishment of the Dudleian Lecture in 1751. He was himself the Dudleian lecturer in 1762.

Forty-one years before Kant published the essay from which we have cited his definition of the Enlightenment, Chauncy uses words very similar to those of Kant. They appear in his attack on the "enthusiasm" of the Great Awakening.

> The plain Truth is [that] an *enlightened Mind*, and not *raised Affections*, ought always to be the Guide of those who call themselves Men; and this, in the affairs of Religion, as well as other Things. . . . If we would act up to our Character as Men, or Christians, we must not submit blindfold to the Dictates of others. . . . Nor can we be too solicitous, so far as we are able, to see with our own Eyes, and believe with our own Understandings.[8]

He adds that the enlightened mind will be the guide "where God really works on men's hearts by His Spirit." "The voice of reason is the voice of God."[9] In a postscript to his defense of reason in religion, however, he says: "Only in all our Inquiries of this Nature, let the Word of God be our Rule."[10] Chauncy was not one to reject revelation.

Yet the God whom Chauncy worships is the benevolent deity of the rationalists, a God whose attributes are to be observed in the regular, lawful course of nature. He defines God's benevolence as "a principle disposing and prompting to the communication of happiness." This benevolence is "not . . . displayed to separate individuals but to the whole universe and to the constituent parts." Chauncy accepts the Enlightenment conception of the Chain of Being, an ascending scale constituting a perfect and contiguous whole. Natural evils such as pain, disease, disaster, and death are said to be a kind of discipline in the nature of things. The moral irregularities of persons are actually producing in the long run a tendency toward the greater good of the whole. The unhappiness consequent upon immoral conduct discourages sin. Thus God is not arbitrary or partial in the bestowal of happiness. "He cannot do a benevolent action but within the limitations of reasonable and fit conduct." The activity of God always has a reason. This reason is intelligible to human beings, for they possess intellectual and moral powers similar to those of the deity, though in "lower degree."

Like Lessing, Chauncy believed that "knowledge absolutely communicated would not have been capable of yielding so much happiness as that which is attained to, by proper faculties, in the use of labor and pains." "The capacity of making acquisitions *by our own endeavors,* suitably employed, is the true and only basis of all our moral perfection." The human being has the power of distinguishing between good and evil, and the power of self-determination. The Calvinists, Chauncy asserts, believe this, too. "Their practice in life is a confutation of their faith in theory" and "in metaphysical subtility." Humans are not inherently sinful. "The Bible," he says, "teaches no such thing. It is indeed the invention of man, and not a deduction from the Word of God."

Chauncy's system of thought includes elements that reveal his acceptance of the biblical legend concerning the fall, but he rejects the doctrine of original sin; the sin of Adam and Eve affects their descendants as secondary cause. As human beings we are perfectible. We sin when we "do not act up to our rank." But we can become increasingly happy on the earth, and in heaven all will ultimately be saved.

The creation is thoroughly rational, it is moving toward the fulfillment of a benevolent purpose; the human being needs only to see this purpose with an enlightened mind and to imitate the benevolence of God.

Chauncy's writings contain a good many ideas that are not consistent with the strong deistic strain. In fact, his successor William Emerson asserted that his sermons included much that was "calvinistick." In the general view we have just outlined, however, we see the content of natural religion as it was taking shape in the mind of the minister of the First Church in Boston two hundred years ago.

The Failure of the Myth

The myth of the eighteenth century, we have observed, is a myth of Logos and a myth of creation. The deficiencies as well as the positive values of this myth of the Enlightenment derive from its interpretation of these elements.

In favor of the doctrine of reason as it appears in the idea of natural religion it must be said that the intention to discover universal elements in religion and the effort to create a Protestant synthesis could alone give rise to a kind of religion capable of coming to terms with new insights and new skepticisms drawn from the natural and the social sciences, and from modern philosophy. Apart from this effort the religion of the West would be unable to elicit integrating commitment or to find vital points of contact with secularism and with the myths of other religions and cultures. Any fundamental rejection of this effort can lead only to a resurgence and sanctification of arbitrariness and fanaticism. And the consequences of such a rejection can be even more disastrous today than ever before. The eighteenth century's demand for the universal is the perennially valid intention of its myth of reason.

But the idea of natural religion as envisaged by the eighteenth century is provincial and incomplete. This incompleteness now threatens to prevent any idea of natural religion from remaining an ingredient of a sovereign myth. A myth must possess something more than rational structure in order to become sovereign.

Natural religion, as understood by the Enlightenment, did provide a new sense of the orderly providence of God and of the derived dignity of the rational human being. As Whitehead has observed, "To have faith in the order of nature is to know that in being ourselves we are more than ourselves." Yet, to the degree that the natural religion of the Enlightenment possessed this sense of order and of ultimacy it lacked the sense of intimacy and mystery. This one-sidedness is an expression of the Enlightenment's preference for the neoclassical temperament; it is the consequence of the predominant concern with a reason ever demanding clear and distinct ideas and generally missing the depth and richness that only mythopoetic conceptions can grasp. Pascal, scientist and mathematician, already in the seventeenth century turned away from "the abstract God of the philosophers" to the intimacy and the consuming fire of the God of Abraham, Isaac, and Jacob. The Romantic movement of the later part of the eighteenth century protested against the abstractionism, the coldness, the drive for uniformity in the mentality of the Enlightenment; it rejected the neoclassical in favor of individuality, concreteness, warmth, in favor of spontaneity and intimacy. It had discovered that the myth of reason cuts the throat of imagination and poetry as well as of piety. It may well be that the unwillingness of many of the proponents of natural religion in the eighteenth century to relinquish revealed religion was due not only to their conservatism; by retaining revealed religion and the Protestant love for the Bible, they managed to correct the one-sidedness of rationalistic natural religion. Pascal would have said that they required the order of the heart as well as the order of reason, the order of intuitive as well as of discursive, constructive reason. A sense of intimacy in one's love for nature, for humanity, and for God is as important as the sense of ultimacy. Whitehead was not the first or the last of the philosophers to recognize this twofold demand upon metaphysics and upon piety.

Another element of lopsidedness in the natural religion of the Enlightenment derives also from its rationalism. Whether the natural religion was believed to be derived from the timeless rational essence of human being, or from a contemplation of the majestic orders of nature, or from a selection of the common elements in historical religions, its most marked tendency was antitraditional and nonhistorical. This tendency was mitigated for a time by the middle-of-the-road Protestants who retained historical and biblical elements peculiar to revealed religion, but it has contributed greatly to the current religious illiteracy of many people who call themselves religious liberals. The religion of common sense, if it is a religion rather than a catchword, is a peculiarly debilitating form of provincialism. Adolf Harnack has succinctly characterized the deficiency of this nonhistorical aspect of natural religion. "Distilled religion," he says, "is not religion at all. Like every living plant, religion only grows inside the bark." Any natural religion that loses contact with the historical and the concrete substitutes ideas *about* religion for piety. This nonhistorical kind of religion generally creates a religious vacuum. We know from experience what rushes in all too often to fill the vacuum; namely, the concrete, tangible, historical symbols and disciplines of an archaic, irrational traditionalism or the concrete, tangible sacraments of the substitute religions of secularism.

These defects of rationalistic natural religion are not peculiar to the Enlightenment of the eighteenth century. Other periods of Enlightenment, beginning with that of fifth- and fourth-century B.C. Greece, have revealed the same tendencies. An Enlightenment period seems by nature to be followed by a period of superstitious secularism on the one side and of irrational archaism on the other. Both the secularism and the religious archaism of our time have in varying degrees reverted to the rigidity of the revealed religions that the Enlightenment set out to overcome. The myth of reason, in compensating for its repressions, issues in its opposite; it spawns the myth of unreason.

RECOVERY OF A DOCTRINE OF REDEMPTION

The doctrine of creation as it was expounded in the Enlightenment was not a product of pure reason. Human reason has roots in history. What the Chinese reason finds in creation, what the Greek reason finds, what the

Indian reason finds, depends largely on the basic insights, the "original decisions," of the religious tradition in which it is rooted. Although the doctrine of creation in the eighteenth century made a new appeal for autonomy and although it employed the new, rational disciplines of the natural and social sciences, it presupposed, as we have seen, the more basic insight of the Judeo-Christian doctrine of creation, namely, that nature, including human nature, is a manifestation of the divine creativity. Fashioning these elements into an amalgam, the Enlightenment devised a new formulation for the doctrine of creation.

But the Judeo-Christian myth contains more than a doctrine of creation. It asserts also that nature and humanity are fallen and are in need of redemption. The Enlightenment, understandably, could not accept the doctrines of the fall and of redemption as they had been explicated by the Reformation. But it made little effort to give new theological formulation to these dimensions of existence. Impressed as it was by the benevolence of the Creator manifest in the order of nature and in the mind and freedom of the human being, it gave relatively little attention to the theological problem of sin — or it rationalized it away. To live in accord with nature did not involve redemption from sin; it required rather that through the use of the powers of nature one should imitate the benevolence, the balance, the proportion, the symmetry of God. The natural religion of the eighteenth century thus became a piety for the once-born. It looked to persons to supply their own redemption. It became the religion of self-salvation. This is the perfect recipe for secularism. Worship, grace, prayer, vocation from on high, become superfluous. The self-enclosed "bourgeois man," seemingly in control of himself and progressively gaining control of his environment, is his own god. His knees are frozen. Natural religion becomes merely the religion of success.

The Enlightenment's confidence in nature and reason expresses the optimism that accompanies the success of science and philosophy in the achievement of advancing and ordered knowledge about nature and society, the success of a growing industrial civilization, the success of colonial expansion, the success of the middle class in the Industrial Revolution. On the basis of these successes the Enlightenment made our allegedly secure place in nature and the securities implicit in our rational and moral faculties the occasion for its natural religion. The capacities of human being, not the insecurities, the limitations, the perversities, become the point of contact with the divine.

What the Enlightenment fails to emphasize is the fact that reason and moralism, in their "natural" state, are the instruments of self-interest. The reason of the Enlightenment apparently saw nothing irrational in the degradation and the brutality resulting from the Industrial Revolution; these were among the consequences of middle-class autonomy and benevolence. The need to overcome middle-class "virtue" and strength was not sensed by the Enlightenment. This need can be squarely confronted by a religion of redemption, not by natural religion that meets the divine only in the success of "creation." Actually, the need gave rise to a revolt against natural religion, to a new religion of "enthusiasm" which sought release from the burdens imposed by bourgeois reason. Élie Halévy, the French historian, writing about the English people as they were in 1815, asserts that "for sixty years . . . Methodism had been the one really civilizing influence among the miners, whether in Durham or in Cornwall." He adds that a sudden outburst of religious enthusiasm formed the sole counteraction to the debauchery and degradation of the mining communities. J. L. and Barbara Hammond, who as economic historians are impartial in matters religious, state plainly that Methodism was "the most important event in eighteenth-century England." The new religion of enthusiasm, to be sure, was not entirely alone in the effort for economic and political reform; nor was it by any means single-minded in this effort. The middle-class religion of enlightenment struggled for political liberties, but on the whole it did not even try to emancipate the enslaved worker from economic bondage. It sanctified the material and spiritual possessions of those in control.

The God of costing love is confronted only when we stand as it were at the edge of being and at the edge of our possessions, only when we discover our limits, only when we in guilt cry out of the depths for forgiveness, only when we stand in the extreme situation, as the existentialists call it. A contemporary poet puts his finger on the inadequacy of the natural religion that stands on its securities.

> In order to possess what you do not possess
> You must go by the way of dispossession.[11]

The myth of the Enlightenment is a myth in revolt against the myth of the Reformation, the myth whose nerve is the sense of humanity's blasphemous pride in its possessions and of its need for redeeming grace. The Enlightenment revolted because the Reformation exalted sin and redemption at the expense of reason and creation. But a doctrine of creation without redemption is as perverse as a doctrine of redemption without creation.

The neo-Reformation movement of our day has revived the myth of the Reformation, depreciating reason and creation. This neo-orthodox revolt against liberalism is in some quarters as lopsided as was the Enlightenment revolt against the Reformation. And it takes as much pride in *its* possessions (its *doctrines* of sin and redemption) as did the Enlightenment.

May it not be that the era into which Protestantism is now entering is the era that is possible and necessary only because the myths of both the Enlightenment and the Reformation have been tried and found wanting? If we can understand why both of these myths have reached their limits and why both of them are needful, we may be prepared for a religion that will herald a new age of grace and renewal. Of one thing we may be confident: The Eternal Gospel still belongs to the future.

Notes

1. Quoted by Richard Chase, *Quest for Myth* (Baton Rouge, La.: Louisiana State University Press, 1948), p. 1.

2. Jacob Burckhardt, *Force and Freedom*, ed. J. H. Nichols (New York: Pantheon, 1943), pp. 238–39.

3. Theophilus Evans, *History of Modern Enthusiasm* (London, 1752), p. 5.

4. Immanuel Kant, *Critique of Practical Reason and Other Writings in Moral Philosophy*, trans. and ed. Lewis W. Back (Chicago: University of Chicago Press, 1949), p. 286.

5. A typical expression of the faith in progress is given by Edward Gibbon at the end of the third volume of *The History of the Decline and Fall of the Roman Empire* (Boston, New York: C. T. Brainard, n.d.): "We may therefore acquiesce in the pleasing conclusion that every age of the world has increased, and still increases, the real wealth, the happiness, the knowledge, and perhaps the virtue, of the human race."

6. Cotton Mather, *The Christian Philosopher* (London: Printed for Eman. Matthews, 1721), p. 299.

7. Christoph M. Meiners, *Allgemeine kritische Geschichte der Religionen*, I, 1. Cited by G. van der Leeuw, *Religion in Essence and Manifestation*, trans. J. E. Turner (New York: Macmillan, 1938), p. 690.

8. *Seasonable Thoughts on the State of Religion in New-England* (Boston: printed by Rogers and Fowle, for Samuel Eliot, 1743), pp. 326–27, 424.

9. Charles Chauncy, *Civil Magistrates Must Be Just, Ruling in the Fear of God: A Sermon Preached May 27, 1747, Being the Anniversary of the Election* (Boston: printed by order of the Honourable House of Representatives, 1747), p. 9.

10. *State of Religion in New-England*, p. 424.

11. T. S. Eliot, *Four Quartets* (New York: Harcourt, Brace & Co., 1943), p. 15.

13 · The Enduring Validity of Congregational Polity

What a disappointment it is for Mrs. Adams and me to be unable to attend this gracious occasion of the annual award and to thank you for it right heartily. The honor is deeply appreciated. Almost twenty-five years of our lives have been spent among you at the divinity school and at Meadville/ Lombard Theological School, yielding admired colleagues, lifetime friends, and a rich education. I am especially pleased that in my absence my very old friend and former student, Professor Pitcher, is willing to "pitch" for me. I want also immediately to express my long-felt appreciation for the friendship and the many kind offices of Dean Kitagawa, who also years ago was in my classes and who after my retirement at Harvard Divinity School invited me to serve for several years as professor of theology and religious ethics at the divinity school. I regret that it was not possible for me to accept his invitation to teach again during the current academic year. He is the most efficient and relentlessly thoughtful dean I have known. I regret also to have to report that Mrs. Adams's increasingly ominous condition of health has confirmed Dean Kitagawa's proposal that I should not plan to be with you this evening. Having through the years attended the annual banquet of the Baptist Theological Union and having known especially well the late Howard Goodman, I wish to express again the sense of indebtedness to you which the faculty, the students, and the alumni of the divinity school share.

Immediately I want to express for all of us an appreciation of "Al" Pitcher's work as teacher, scholar, and citizen. For example, he for years has been a creative and dedicated leader in race relations projects in Chicago. Paradoxically, the human relations approach had to be combined with a law and order approach in his work. Speaking of the situation in Hyde Park, an old-timer once said, "From 1952 on it was a schizophrenic experience to

This address was Adams's response to being named Alumnus of the Year of the University of Chicago Divinity School, a citation presented annually by the Baptist Theological Union. Because he was unable to be in Chicago for the presentation, on October 19, 1977, this was read for him by Professor Alvin Pitcher. It subsequently appeared in *Criterion*, a publication of the Divinity School of the University of Chicago, 17, no. 1 (Winter 1978), which has granted permission to publish it here.

127

live here. There was Jesus Christ walking down one side of the street, and Julius Caesar marching along the other." Al Pitcher as leader walked with faith and fortitude on both sides.

It is now over thirty years since I received the doctor's degree from the divinity school, a degree that in part was granted by reason of my dissertation on Paul Tillich, which was published subsequently under the title *Paul Tillich's Philosophy of Culture, Science, and Religion.* It was only through the patient support of the divinity school and the University of Chicago Press that I was able also to produce and publish the translation of Paul Tillich's *The Protestant Era.* One day when Tillich as visitor was to give a public lecture at the divinity school I showed him a passage in one of his German essays which I could not make out. After puzzling over it for a few minutes he said, "I haven't the slightest idea of what I was intending to say. Just skip it in the translation." He then added, "Jim, I have learned one thing from having to speak English. I have learned that it is not necessary to be obscure in order to be profound."

You will be amused, I think, if I tell you briefly a story that was told by Dean Colwell at an informal celebration sponsored by members of the faculty of the divinity school on the occasion of my receiving the doctor's degree. During the course of the evening "Pomp" Colwell told a story about Professor Charles Hartshorne (our neighbor), who was not present, though Mrs. Hartshorne, Dorothy, was there. Dean Colwell told about an afternoon affair when Charles got into an intensive discussion with one of his colleagues. At a certain moment Charles looked down at his hand to discover a lighted cigarette there, whereupon he said, "My God! What is that lighted cigarette doing in my hand? I don't smoke." The laughter was of course hearty, for the group had now heard still another story about the notoriously absent-minded Charles. Dorothy Hartshorne, being annoyed, tried to stop the irreverent laughter, but without immediate success. Finally, she was able to say with earnest indignation, "But Charles doesn't swear either."

Speaking of neighbors, I want especially to mention the late Dean Shailer Mathews, who lived across the street from us on Woodlawn Avenue. Let me say that I first heard Shailer Mathews in Minneapolis when I was an undergraduate of the University of Minnesota. I had been reared in the state of Washington in the home of a premillenarian fundamentalist Baptist preacher who always spoke of Mathews as one who was deceiving the very elect and of the divinity school as a "sinkpot" of modernist corruption. Let me interrupt here to share with you some pioneer-stock humor from this fundamentalist circle, the story about two laymen, a Baptist and a Methodist, who were always arguing over the rite of baptism. The Baptist was proud of his minister, for he had the reputation of being able to prove immersion from any text chosen for a sermon. One week the forthcoming sermon text was announced as, "The voice of the turtle is heard in the meadow." "Now," said the Methodist, "he certainly cannot make out immersion from that text." The Baptist assured him that he could, and laid a bet on it. So they went to the Baptist church together to hear the sermon. In the midst of the sermon the preacher said that in the previous week he had been walking in the woods. On becoming tired he decided to take a rest on a log at the edge of a stream. But when he approached the log he noticed a turtle sitting on the end of it. So he tried to step quietly, in order not to frighten the turtle. But when he sat cautiously on the log the turtle jumped "bap" down into the creek. The preacher thought that if he remained very quiet the turtle might come back, and, sure enough, in a few minutes it crawled up out of the water: "tism, tism, tism." The Methodist lost the bet.

My father could never say anything good about the Northern Baptist Convention. The only magazine I saw in our home was A. C. Gaebelein's *Our Hope*, which frequently excoriated the Chicago Divinity School. At the University of Minnesota I had come under the liberal ministry of Norman Henderson of the University Baptist Church, so when the opportunity arose of my seeing and hearing Shailer Mathews I had been somewhat softened up to hear a modernist. Nevertheless, I was destined for surprise. I was accustomed mainly to Bible-pounding Baptist preachers. To my puzzlement here was an independent, vigorous mind, thoroughly conversant with the intellectual and theological trends of the time, uttering irresistible wit.

For me, then, it was twenty years later a veritable covenant of grace that brought me to be a neighbor of Shailer Mathews after his retirement. He could not share my enthusiasm for the writings of Paul Tillich. "How," he asked, "could any modern scholar say that Jesus Christ is the Center of History?" In any event, our relationship became a warm one, and Mathews often lectured for me when I had to be away from Chicago. Indeed, he told me repeatedly that I must not hesitate to ask him to do this; and, naturally I did not fail to give the students an opportunity to hear him.

I had long before come to admire the dean because of his independence and originality of mind and spirit. In illustration of that mind and spirit I want to repeat a story familiar to some of you. It was said that when he spoke at a certain Baptist convention, fundamentalists carried placards of protest in front of the convention hall. After the dean finished his address, a stalwart fundamentalist stood up and with passion and aggressiveness shouted, "I want to ask you a question, and I want a straight answer. I want only a yea or a nay." "What is your question?" asked the dean. "My question is, Do you or do you not believe that every single word of Scripture is inspired of God, yes or no?" To which the dean responded, "If the letter is greater than the spirit, no. If the spirit is greater than the letter, yes." I may add one other tale, the one about the dean's answer to the question as to whether he believed in the immortality of the soul. The dean responded, "Yes, indeed; everyone should believe in the immortality of the soul. And if it isn't true, we will never know."

Having spoken of Dean Mathews I want to add a word about his son, Robert Mathews, for years professor of law at Ohio State University. Some years ago in Cambridge I read in the *New York Times* an account of Robert Mathews's presidential address in Denver for the American Association of Law Schools in which he lamented the lack of courses on ethics in the law schools, and urged reform of the curriculum. On reading the account of the address I wrote him a "fan letter," expressing appreciation. After an exchange of several letters Professor Mathews wrote to ask me to join with him and some others in petitioning a foundation for a grant to enable an investigation of the subject. He received the grant, and subsequently the study was published. In the course of the correspondence he said that since I was on a divinity school faculty he wondered whether I had known his father, Shailer Mathews. That correspondence has continued for well over a decade, especially because at Harvard Law School for about a decade I (as co-conductor) participated in a seminar on theology and law, a seminar that has recently been revived under the leadership (as before) of Professor Harold Berman of the Harvard Law School, with me assisting.

I wish to say two more things about the divinity school at Chicago. My most precious memories are informed by my appreciation of the openness, freedom, and critical rationality of its spirit. Though it was open-minded, its mind was not open at both ends. I recall an oral preliminary doctoral examination in which the student had presented an attack on natural reason, in a positivistic manner demolishing every claim for the use of reason in religion, and then arguing for the need of a leap of faith. In the judgment of the faculty this student could not show that he was familiar with the discipline of philosophical theology. One of us quoted to him the aphorism of George Santayana, "The sheer necessity of believing something is no ground for the direction of any particular leap of faith." The student was not found acceptable by the faculty committee, and he was required to prepare to undergo the examination again at a later date. It was the firm view of the divinity school faculty that faith involves inquiry.

Something more about this outlook I want to report. Twenty-five years ago a group of social psychologists undertook a research project at the law school of the university, probing into the vocational attitudes of the law students. I knew personally one of these sociologists, and when they were nearing the completion of their study he asked me if they could spend an evening at my home to report something of their findings. I of course was delighted with the prospect and invited some divinity students to come along. In the course of the evening the investigators reported that in the law school they found that on the whole the students knew why they were there and what they wished to accomplish in life. By way of contrast, they said, the students in the divinity school did not seem to know whether they believed in the church or even in God. They were frustrated and anxious, not having achieved an identity. Thereupon I said I could scarcely believe the findings of the investigation at the law school, for it would mean that the law students were not questioning the role of the lawyer in the contemporary world, not asking questions as to the meaning of justice, not questioning the political and economic prejudices of lawyers and law professors. I concluded by saying that the dubious report of the team made out the law students to be a bunch of vegetables. The immediate response was "touché." I was proud then and there that the divinity students bore witness to their understanding of faith as requiring radical inquiry. We continued to be skeptical regarding the "findings" of those psychologists regarding the law students.

I think it may fairly be said that I never got over being a Baptist. Indeed, sometimes when my Unitarian colleagues find my notions to be unacceptable they say, "What more can one expect of him? He's a Baptist, and once a Baptist always a Baptist." Some of them ought to know, for they, too, were reared in the Baptist fold.

There is at least one thing that Unitarians share with the Baptists, and also with the Disciples and the Congregationalists, namely, congregational polity. I have long been intrigued by the study of this polity. I trust that the noncongregationalists here this evening will forgive the appearance of narcissism if I speak now only about the congregational polity. It was born in a protest against "the establishment" of the sixteenth and seventeenth centuries in England and New England. These dissenters could not accept the centralized power of the established church. They wished to place authority in the local congregation and thus to be free of control at the hands of bishops and a hierarchical clergy. They revived the covenant theory of the New Testament, and attempted to model the congregation on the primitive Christian church according to Scripture. And, like those early Christians, they had to suffer persecution as a consequence. In this new, covenanted or gathered church they gave the power to the laity along with the clergy. Every member had the right and the responsibility to participate in the making of social decisions regarding policy and even about eligibility for ordination. That, by the way, is a good definition of power, the capacity to participate in making social decisions. So we may say that congregational polity represented a dispersion of power and responsibility in two senses, an assignment of power to the local congregation as such and also to the members of the congregation as participants who held to the principle of the consent of the governed. This dispersion of power was accompanied by what we may call a separation of powers, for these Baptists and other Independents demanded separation of church and state. They rejected coercive taxation for the support of the churches, for they wanted a self-supporting voluntary church. Instead of a church for the masses they wanted a church for believers only. Here explicit faith, close, neighborly relations among the members, and moral discipline were possible. Literacy was placed at a high premium. Hence, the self-supporting character of the congregation and the reliance upon Scripture made the taking of the collection in church and the reading of the Bible virtual sacraments.

The struggle for freedom to form an independent religious association had to be carried on with much dust and heat, indeed arousing persecution that harried many of these dissenters out of the land. They were viewed as disrupting the unity and stability of the commonwealth. A conservative historian of today has called them "spiritual bolsheviks." The promoters of congregational polity presumed to form a self-governing "corporation," to use the word of Roger Williams. And, we might add, they were very skeptical of all ecclesiastical bureaucrats. This feature of the Baptists became prominent in the Great Awakening in New England. Indeed, the Baptists were so much opposed to centralized power of any sort that the great majority of them opposed the ratification of the federal Constitution of the United States; Isaac Backus was the first of the prominent Baptists to favor ratification.

Now, it has been persuasively argued that it was from those small conventicles that modern democracy was born. Indeed, Lord Acton, a

Roman Catholic historian of a century ago, was among the first to say that democracy as we understand it was born in these small congregations rather than in ancient Greece. But it would not be strictly true to say that these congregations were democratic. They did not consider the congregation to be autonomous. The principle of the consent of the governed was closely related to a doctrine and discipline of the Holy Spirit according to Scripture. For this reason this sort of congregation has been called a pneumatocracy, the rule of the Spirit. Yet, Lord Acton's dictum is justified, for these independent congregations promoted the consent of the governed, the responsibility of each member to participate in shaping policy, the separation of powers between church and state and even between congregations. Viewing the phenomenon as a whole we might say that these Independents promoted a form of localism in face of established, centralized powers of state and church.

Now, the striking thing is that this trend toward localism appeared at the same time in the sphere of economic behavior. Just as these Baptists and their fellow travelers rejected centralized power in the church, they protested also against chartered monopolies at the hands of the monarch. Not long ago I talked with Christopher Hill at Oxford University, the eminent historian of the period, and I asked him if it does not make sense to assume that the people who were promoting free enterprise in business were also members of the small conventicles. We know that many of them were householders and small businesspeople: these churches did not make appeal to the privileged classes or to the people at the lower end of the economic ladder. Christopher Hill immediately agreed with this proposal, saying with some vigor that we need further research on this relation between small business and the small church. One might suppose that Max Weber in his study of the so-called Protestant Ethic would have looked into the type of social organization promoted by these people when they went to church. But he largely ignored that aspect of their behavior, concentrating attention on the work ethic. Nevertheless, we may come to a significant observation here, the striking parallel between the drive toward the free congregation and the drive in favor of free business enterprise.

But then an equally significant and surprising consequence follows. The small congregations had rejected the national covenant, the national church establishment, and the small businesspeople had rejected centralized, government-sponsored corporations and monopolies. The members of the small congregations by reason of their heresy were precluded from full participation in politics; and the small businesspeople belonged to a class of people who did not yet have political power. Both the people of the small churches and the people of small business were in favor of localism. For the sake of brevity I have had to state the thesis in highly simplified form. If it is an oversimplification, I have warned you.

But localism in church and business is not in the nature of things in a position to be concerned for the larger territorial situation. A pietistic attitude of indifference to politics was present. Nor did these people concern themselves with the broader consequences of their economic behavior. They seem to have held that if every individual were pious, honest, and thrifty, the problems of the society at large would take care of themselves—a theory of automatic harmony.

Observe, then, that we have here an anticipation of laissez-faire theory in economics, an anticipation of Adam Smith's conception of reliance upon the free market and competition, efficiency to be rewarded by economic success, and inefficiency to be punished by economic distress. And just as the members of the small churches believed in a sort of automatic harmony under the guidance of the Holy Spirit, so the laissez-faire theory places its faith in "an invisible hand" to guide the economy toward benefits for all.

We have now come into a world that Adam Smith could not foresee, a world in which technology of production, of transportation, of communication, requires bigness. Adam Smith had assumed the smallness of the business corporation, a situation that could not threaten autonomy and freedom of enterprise. There is a sense, then, in which what began as a drive toward localism has more and more become a drive toward enormous national and multinational corporations.

Now, I must come quickly to a conclusion, and with something of a bang. We live now in a society in which both church and industry serve as bulwarks of discrimination in terms of racism and sexism. Although some changes have been taking place in these respects, we are living in a society of restricted covenants. It is not necessary to rehearse the facts about the ill-distribution of wealth, of education, of health services, or about the energy and the ecological crisis, or about our responsibilities in face of the Third World.

If we center attention upon industry (leaving aside the political order), we may say that we have come to the place where the principles initially set forth by the Baptists and the other independents assume a new meaning and demand. Self-government, the participation of the constituency in the shaping of decisions, the repersonalizing of the individual, require application to our economic life in face of the compulsions of the system. Organized dissent within the structure of the corporation is practically nonexistent. For this reason Ralph Nader has proposed that we need a new bill of rights to protect this sort of dissent. Dean Roscoe Pound of Harvard Law School long ago asserted that the demand is upon us to inject morals into law. Dr. Douglas Sturm, one of our graduates, has set forth the thesis that principles of constitutionalism are required in industry as in government.

So where are we? Our spiritual ancestors struck out against the establishment, and we are now under a new establishment, an establishment of giantism. One might say that we need spiritual regeneration. That is something not easy to come by. But we can prepare for grace by supporting the new strategies of a participative democracy. Some attempts are under way in American business, for example, in profit sharing and in extending stock privileges to workers. Much is being attempted in Germany and in Scandinavian countries. In Germany, for example, we see the development of *Mitbestimmung* (codetermination), the placing of workers on the board of trustees of the corporation. The labor unions are now training workers in theories of marketing, investment, and management. The prime minister, Helmut Schmidt, has asserted that this strategy is Germany's major contribution to democracy today.

And what is the function of a divinity school in all this? It is in priestly and prophetic fashion to interpret the signs of the times, to attempt through biblical, historical, sociological, and psychological studies, and through theological disciplines, to show at least in part how in the present situation we may anew respond to the creative, sustaining, judging, forgiving, transforming powers of the Divine Majesty.

14 · From Cage to Covenant

Liberal religion's attitude of mind we generally characterize as a critical stance before mere tradition, impatience with creeds once-for-all delivered, the rejection of coercion in religion, freedom of conscience, open-mindedness, tolerance—the liberation of the human spirit from heteronomous authorities. Beautiful attitudes! But attitudes alone do not make or change history. The road to hell is paved with good attitudes. They require institutional embodiment. Indeed, the liberal attitudes mentioned appeared initially in the seventeenth century in connection with a power struggle undertaken in order to change social structures. This struggle was a revolutionary institutional struggle, a struggle against the cage of centralized power in church and state and economic order.[1]

Congregational polity was the new conception of a covenanted church that gave form to this struggle, a polity separating the church from the state, placing responsibility upon the members (the consent of the governed), and giving rise to a self-governing congregation.

But during the past century our society has been moving in the opposite direction, in the direction of a new centralization of power in mammoth bureaucratic government and industry, the fragmentation of responsibility, retreat into privatized religion—all of this in a world of massive poverty and hunger. In the nineteenth century liberal religion promoted these tendencies by emphasizing an atomistic individualism that in a technological society produced the modern industrial corporation with its oligopoly and with even greater power than the government. A major question today in a world of multinational corporations is how to achieve a separation of powers and consent of the governed, a self-governing society in the midst of corporate structures that are rapidly becoming a new cage. So we have moved from cage to cage.

It may well be that we should consider as our intellectual agenda the devising of a doctrine of the church and a theology or philosophy that has an institutional thrust that deals with these issues, not as though the issues were settled, but rather in recognition that within our liberal churches we

This address was presented to Collegium: An Association for Liberal Religious Studies, at its first convocation, in Chicago, on October 29, 1975. It is reprinted, with permission, from *Kairos*, Winter 1976.

shall see more and more (as we saw in the New Deal) a confrontation, a tension between different social philosophies, the one appealing to the liberalism of an earlier epoch, and the other appealing to a new meaning for consent of the governed.

The latter is a new demand for legitimation, that is, the development of responsible corporate policies. In that connection, *the doctrine of covenant* may be a conception to which we should give systematic consideration, for the sake of the revision of that covenant insofar as it did not in earlier days concern itself with communal responsibility in the economic sphere. Especially important is a reconsideration of that covenant in the light of the remarkable biblical scholarship of the last twenty years regarding covenant.

What are the major ingredients of a covenant? With this, I conclude. Five points:

1. Human beings, individually and collectively, become human by making commitment, by making promises. The human being *as such*, as Martin Buber says, is the promise-making, promise-keeping, the promise-breaking, promise-renewing creature. The human being is the promise maker, the commitment maker.

2. The covenant is a covenant of being. It is a covenant with the creative, sustaining, commanding, judging, transforming powers, which may be interpreted theistically, nontheistically, humanistically. In a religious covenant, the orientation is to something we cannot control but something upon which we depend, even for our freedom. Jonathan Edwards called it the "covenant of being."

3. The covenant is for the individual as well as for the collective. Much of the new scholarship on the Old Testament shows how this is true in regard to the Ten Commandments. The individual as well as the collective is brought into the covenant, the individual is brought out of separateness into covenant. So it is for the individual as well as for the collective. We are responsible not only for individual behavior but also for the character of the society—also for the love and preservation of nature.

4. The covenant responsibility is especially directed toward the deprived. Whether these be people suffering from neglect and injustice or those who are caught in the system that suppresses them—that suppresses their own self-determination—it is the gap between covenant and system, between ideal and behavior, which creates deprivation and which makes it difficult for a topflight executive, for example, to speak out in public regarding his or her dissident convictions.

5. The covenant includes a rule of law, but it is not fundamentally a

legal covenant. It depends on faithfulness, and faithfulness is nerved by loyalty, by love. Violation of the covenant is a violation of trust. What holds the world together, according to this dual covenant then, is trustworthiness, eros, love. Ultimately the ground of faithfulness is the divine or human love that will not let us go. Here we see the theological basis for accountability, by persons and by the church. This may be the fundamental intellectual agenda for today: a *doctrine of the covenant* whether it be given that name or not.

Some such doctrine as this with its decisive element of individual responsibility connected with corporate responsibility is surely high on the agenda if, after having been emancipated from the old cage of domination, we are to cope with the new cage of centralized, bureaucratic power.

Note

1. [In a famous passage at the end of his *The Protestant Ethic and the Spirit of Capitalism*, first published in Germany in 1904–1905, Max Weber refers to the modern system of industrial production as an "iron cage." See Adams's essay "The Protestant Ethic and Society: Max Weber," in his *On Being Human Religiously* (Boston: Beacon Press, 1976), p. 181—Ed.]

15 · Why the Troeltsch Revival?

The word *revival* here is perhaps too strong. But, if a revival has not yet come about, a marked increase of interest in the writings of Ernst Troeltsch (1865–1923) is today evident in many quarters.

In *many* quarters—for Troeltsch, the eminent liberal Christian of Heidelberg and Berlin universities, was not only a theologian and philosopher but also an influential historian, philosopher of history, and sociologist of religion. Moreover, when he was professor in Heidelberg (1894–1914) he was for eight years a member of the upper house of the Grand Duchy of Baden (elected from the university); when he taught in Berlin (1915–23) he was an elected representative in the Prussian Landtag, and for two years he served as parliamentary undersecretary of state in the Prussian Ministry of Public Worship and Education; and in 1921 he was a member of the government in the Weimar Republic. During the early years of the republic he published many articles on current events, among the best of the time. These articles reveal the agonies he suffered in that whole period, beginning with the outbreak of the war in 1914. He feared that Germany under the stress of the postwar conflicts would resort to authoritarianism and "barbarity." He sensed that foul whisperings were abroad.

Possessed of enormous energy, his activities, then, were in the practical as well as the theoretical, scholarly sphere. In his view, theory should be related to practice, thought should issue in action. Despite his busy life in church and government, he became one of the most prolific writers among the major thinkers of the present century. So distinctive and original was his outlook that the several dimensions of his work have given rise to renewed interest in him today in the various spheres, religious and secular, of his concern.[1]

The scope of Troeltsch's labors was perhaps not quite as wide as that of Albert Schweitzer. For example, his activity did not carry him into the Third World or into the field of music. Yet, the impact of his thought is today recognized in wider circles. The recent international conference on Troeltsch's writings held at the University of Lancaster in England in

This essay originally appeared as an introduction to a special issue of the quarterly *The Unitarian Universalist Christian* 29, nos. 1–2 (1974), devoted to the thought of Ernst Troeltsch. Reprinted by permission.

January 1974, is, so far as I know, the first international conference on this subject.

That the conference took place fifty years after Troeltsch's death bespeaks a characteristic feature of the past half century of theological discussion. Troeltsch has been under an eclipse created in part by the neo-Reformation theologians Barth, Gogarten, and Brunner and their sympathizers in Europe and the United States who held that the liberal Christians had lost contact with the authentic Reformation and its doctrine of revelation. For that matter, the International Congress for Free Christianity, with which Troeltsch was affiliated, has been under a cloud during this period, at least from the perspective of the neo-Reformation theologians. Meanwhile, the Troeltschean perspectives have suffered a disadvantage, for some of his best pupils were killed in the First World War.

But the situation has been changing of late. It is sometimes said that we are now entering a post-Barthian period. Such a claim, however, should not be taken to mean that nothing has been learned or that nothing needs to be learned from the neo-Reformation thrust, as if all that liberal Christians need to do now is simply to recover the liberalism of an earlier generation.

The new interest in Troeltsch is largely due to the fact that some of the major insights and questions associated with his name are now seen to require further reflection. These issues, it is felt, have been evaded or have been inadequately dealt with by both the neo-Reformation School and the liberal Christians (including Rudolf Bultmann, the German New Testament scholar who is read widely throughout Christendom). In his introduction to an American reprint (1960) of *The Social Teaching of the Christian Churches*, H. Richard Niebuhr wrote, "There are signs that the eclipse is passing and that in theology as well as in the sociology of religion and in history Troeltsch's methods and convictions will again become effective."

The situation is of course more complex than I have suggested. For example, Wolfhart Pannenberg, the prominent German Lutheran theologian of the younger generation (who would not count himself as of either neo-Reformation or liberal Christian outlook), has told me in conversation that he considers Troeltsch to be the most significant theologian of the twentieth century; and his most recent book gives an appreciative, though critical, treatment of his work. He has said that when he reads Barth he thinks he is reading a Church Father of antiquity, but that when he reads Troeltsch he recognizes that this man was writing only yesterday. For characteristic reasons Pannenberg views Troeltsch in opposition to both Barth and Bultmann. Over forty years ago the Unitarian and Universalist ministers of the Greenfield Group in New England undertook a cooperative study of Troeltsch's work, stimulated in part by the appreciative essays on Troeltsch by Baron Friedrich von Hügel, Paul Tillich, and Francis A. Christie of Meadville Theological School (who published the first essay in the United States on Troeltsch as a sociologist of religion). The American theologian H. Richard Niebuhr, who in 1924 submitted his doctoral dissertation on Troeltsch at Yale, has been a major transmitter of Troeltsch's influence. Recently I have been reminded that my first lecture in 1936 as professor at Meadville dealt with Troeltsch's widely influential conception of the three types of religious association—the church, the sect, and the mystical type. I recall that before that time a group of us ministers had read aloud together large sections of Troeltsch's *The Social Teaching of the Christian Churches*, covering an average of seventeen pages of text a day (along with the lengthy, meaty footnotes).

Within the compass of this brief essay I shall single out three problem areas, but even with respect to these areas I must be highly selective and leave out of consideration wide stretches of territory covered by Troeltsch. These three areas are Troeltsch's view of the appropriate method for studying history (and the conception of the role of history in the religious consciousness), his conception of the significance of Jesus for liberal Christianity, and his articulation of the scope of Christian ethical obligations.

HISTORICAL METHOD AND HISTORICAL CONSCIOUSNESS

The story is told that at a gathering of theologians in 1896 when he was thirty-one Troeltsch, in the midst of his critique of the paper of the day and in face of a scornful comment on his remarks, bluntly proclaimed, "Everything is tottering," whereupon he stamped out of the room, slamming the door behind him. He believed that the theological presuppositions and methods of his colleagues were tottering, indeed had collapsed.

Not long after this he set forth in a now-famous article the thesis that the dogmatic method in theology is at an end and must be replaced by a historical method.[2] Three principles or postulates provide the guidelines for historical method. The first is the principle of criticism. It is no longer possible to understand or accept Christianity in terms of a merely inherited dogma to which appeal may be made in simple deduction. The historical method places every tradition and every received interpretation of history under criticism, also remaining ever open to the discovery of fresh and disturbing fact. But here "in the realm of history there can be only judgments of probability."

The second principle Troeltsch calls the "postulate of analogy." If one cannot find an analogy between present experience and alleged past experience of events, the record of the past events cannot stand as authentic. Indeed, apart from some such analogy we today cannot achieve empathy with the past. "This omnipotence of analogy implies the similarity (in principle) of all historical events." One therefore cannot claim sanction for the Christian faith by appeal to miracle, whether the miracle be an alleged event of history or a miracle in the soul of the believer. The modern historical consciousness must take the same attitude toward religious phenomena as it takes toward other events and experiences in history. "Jewish and Christian history are thus made analogous to all other history."

The third basic concept is that of "correlation" or what has been called *relationism*. All events are interrelated—personal, ideational, and institutional. Unique forces emerge in history, but they "stand in a current and context comprehending the totality of events, where we see everything conditioned by everything else so that there is no point within history which is beyond this correlative involvement and mutual influence." The historian must seek to understand the context within which events of past and present occur, taking into account economic and political as well as intellectual and cultural factors. Accordingly, Christianity must be understood as relative to the culture in which it appears and also to the history of religion as a whole.

Taken together, these features of the modern historical consciousness have brought about the "historicization" of all our thinking. The culture has been shaken out of its naive self-confidence. Every system of value and even religion itself were seen to become merely "historical objects beside other historical objects." The self-evidence of their validity was dissolved. The threat to traditional religion was even greater than that coming from the natural sciences, even though more noise about the latter had been made by certain theologians.

Even before Troeltsch published this essay of 1900 on "historical and dogmatic method in theology," he was under attack. He seemed to deny any absolute claims being made in favor of Christianity. Indeed, his relationism was accused of amounting to historical relativism in which no standards of universal validity remain. Troeltsch rejected this accusation and asserted that it was his intention to combat relativism as the "consequence of an atheistic or a religiously skeptical framework," adding that his aim was to "overcome this relativism through the conception of history as a disclosure of the divine reason."

Subsequently, Troeltsch devoted an enormous amount of energy to historical studies as well as to historiography, and he developed in its fullness a view that had been adumbrated already in the nineteenth century. He adopted a fourth postulate that we may call the principle of individuality. Unlike the processes of nature, the events of history do not repeat themselves; they appear as individual, unique events in succession. Historical method must recognize that every person or movement is rooted in a particular history and context, and that out of this context it relates itself to the unique historical situation in which it finds itself. Christianity emerged and developed in a specific and limited territory, mainly in Western civilization. As a "historical individual" it entered into relation with other elements in the culture to achieve new and unique syntheses in its various regions and epochs. The other world religions have exhibited this same interplay with their respective cultures, these religions and cultures possessing their own individuality. In short, Christianity as a historical individual is one religion among many. The claims Christianity, or any other religion, makes for itself inevitably reflect particular historical traditions and sensitivities. Therefore, no religion can claim to be final or absolute. Here relationism in the light of the principle of individuality becomes a kind of relativism.

It should be emphasized here that Troeltsch asserted again and again that his was not an unlimited relativism. In his view, such a relativism was quite unnecessary. It could end only in an "anarchy of convictions" and a paralysis of the will. Troeltsch during the last fifteen years of his life grappled almost unceasingly with this problem. This effort entailed philosophical considerations some of which are dealt with in his essays. Through the years his formulations of the resolution of the problem took a variety of forms, but we should recall that already in his study *The Separation of Church and State* (1906) he spoke of the bewildering variety of perspectives to be observed in Christian history itself. Viewing this variety as it has appeared in the church type, the sect type, and the mystical type of religious association, he said that truth is unavoidably polymorphous, not monomorphous. He came to the same view with respect to the variety of perspectives in the world religions. "Truth," he wrote again in 1907, "is always polymorphous, never monomorphous; it manifests itself in different forms and kinds, not in different degrees." And at the widely heralded Berlin conference of the International Congress for Free Christianity in 1910, he delivered an address, "The Possibility of a Liberal Christianity." He spoke as a liberal Christian when he said:

We would not need to be disturbed by there being still other circles of light, with other sources of light, within the great divine life of the world, or by the possibility that in future ages, perhaps after new ice ages and in completely new structures, there may arise new circles of light of this sort out of the depths of the divine life. The eternal truth of God has its particular historical form for every circle and for every general stance. Whatever is contained in this particular historical form can never, insofar as it is actually truth, become untruth.[3]

We cannot more than mention here the debate over Troeltsch's alleged historical relativism. But we should observe that already in 1906 and 1907 Troeltsch shocked his contemporaries in Germany by writing articles rejecting foreign missions as traditionally conceived, not because he believed Christian faith is not worth sharing, but rather because of what we have called his theory of relationism. He held that the high religions of the world have informed and affected their respective cultures only by virtue of centuries of interplay with these cultures, and that missionary effort to displace them can be neither justified nor successful. (He took a positive attitude toward Christian missions of educational import among the tribal religions.) At the same time Troeltsch did not conceal his view that Christian ethics has exhibited elements of superiority and of universal appeal not available in the other (non-Judaic) religions. It is not possible to surmise what his views regarding the interrelations between the faiths would be in the new historical situation of the second half of this century. What with his appreciative, though critical, estimate of Marxism he probably would not be surprised to observe the appeal which this substitute religion of social revolution has exercised in the East (in contrast to pietistic Christianity).

THE PROSPECTS OF LIBERAL CHRISTIANITY

In the first pages of his address "The Possibility of a Liberal Christianity," Troeltsch raises the question of whether liberal Christianity is "merely the last echo of a disintegrating Christian piety." Or does it have a future? Is it "inherently viable"? He concedes that the number of those who devote themselves to dealing seriously with these questions is "not very great." In much that he wrote these questions were in the back of his mind, for he recognized that liberal as well as orthodox Christianity was affected by the "historicization" of religion and of all human affairs.

In light of the foregoing account of Troeltsch's conception of the modern historical method and consciousness, I wish now to indicate a "lesson" or two to be gleaned from him by the contemporary religious liberal.

One of Troeltsch's major concerns as a liberal Christian was to warn against the vistas of peril that lie in wait for those who try to shortchange the historical consciousness. Neo-Reformation theology made this attempt, and today it is encountering increasing criticism and frustration by reason of its cavalier by-passing of historical method. Many religious liberals in a different way have shown themselves deficient in historical consciousness.

In his essay "Faith and History," which was published in Germany in the same year as the address of 1910, Troeltsch indicates some of the conditions to be met if liberal Christianity is to remain viable. That essay supports a major presupposition of the address, and it gives amplification to the third principle already referred to, the principle of correlation (or relationism). When Troeltsch asserts that all events and experiences are interrelated, the implication is that the interrelationship may be either destructive or constructive. The constructive thrust depends on a critical and creative relationship between present and past and future, and that in terms of a "concrete content of ideas." Positive and effective relationism depends upon the conviction that "history can be overcome by history," to employ a pregnant formulation that appears at the end of his *Historicism and Its Problems* (1922).

The "concrete content of ideas" informing religion in history is not readily and immediately available, for it "derives never solely from a single subject but is the common work of whole cultural epochs and entire generations." Religious liberalism, if it is to achieve significant individuality and thus to remain viable, cannot afford to squander or to ignore the historical heritage. This prerequisite for significant individuality and viability does not belong alone to religion. It obtains also for other aspects of the culture. A nation that does not achieve identity in terms of its heritage of individuality will almost inevitably move toward an "anarchy of convictions" and even toward loss of moral integrity. Literature and the other arts encounter the same prerequisite. I recall years ago hearing John Galsworthy say in a lecture in Symphony Hall, Boston, that as he surveyed the history of the English novel he could understand it only as a series of vertebrae in a connecting spinal column. Each vertebra possesses its own distinctive quality, but that quality, rightly understood, presupposes and is nourished by the heritage. Wordsworth in his sonnet on the sonnet took a similar view. The sonnet, he said, provides a limiting form from the past which offers stimulus for significant novelty.

We have here no mere traditionalism. Fielding and George Eliot, Dickens and Galsworthy and Virginia Woolf wrote novels; Mozart, Beethoven, and Brahms composed symphonies; Paul and Augustine, Luther and Calvin, Schleiermacher and Troeltsch and Tillich promoted theology; Jesus and Francis, Lilburne and Wesley, Woolman and Parker and Schweitzer exemplified Christian ways of life; but none was a mere traditionalist. All bespeak a living tradition. Using technical Troeltschean vocabulary, we may say that for a historically conscious and viable liberal Christianity all of these figures, along with the scientists, exist in continuing polymorphous correlation.

In Troeltsch's view, then, the "content of ideas" of faith, the common work of whole cultural epochs and entire generations, is the work of outstanding personages.

Faith that is informed by a lively historical consciousness is conscious of a need to gather this whole world of ideas at its point of departure and "to embody it in a paradigmatic figure for the sake of its own self-correction and revivification." In Christianity this paradigmatic figure is "its founding prophet," Jesus, though he in turn presupposes the prophets of the Old Testament. Troeltsch's essay "The Ethics of Jesus" provides a compact account of the central, fructifying "content of ideas."

Informing the ethics of Jesus is the hope for the kingdom of God, a hope that invaded the ancient structures of society and gradually transformed them. The ethics of Jesus generated a tension with the world not only because of its utopian and transforming character but also because of the sense of the divinely given inwardness and potency of the person, and also of the divinely given vocation that forms a new community that persists through history with many variations. And now begins to appear the "correlation" that through criticism and creation effects synthesis with the surrounding culture. (Troeltsch sometimes uses the word *compromise* instead of *synthesis*, for the heavy demand of the Christian ethic had to relate itself, accommodate itself, to current needs and possibilities.)

For a long period in the West the "compromise" took the form of an ethical doctrine of natural law which was transformed from Stoicism, a doctrine that served as a basis for social order. But the doctrine was no longer a merely pagan doctrine; it was related to Christian conceptions of the love of God. Troeltsch's great work *The Social Teaching of the Christian Churches* traces the "compromises" (and perversions) through history. In

Western history he finds that the Christian impulse with its capacity for "compromise" has given rise to only two highly unified social-institutional orders, the Roman Catholic and the Calvinist. Troeltsch was among the first of major scholars, moreover, to delineate the Radical Reformation and to recognize its significance for the rise of Anglo-American Nonconformity and of modern democracy as we know it. With the advent of the Enlightenment and the modern historical consciousness the churches, partly by reason of their resistance to this historical consciousness, confronted an increasing secularism, and with the emergence of the period of capitalism, the society, says Troeltsch, could no longer be called Christian. Viable, liberal Christianity with its new historical consciousness allowed itself to be influenced by the modern mind, but it also came into conflict with the modern world wherever it retained the prophetic spirit.

How, then, can history be overcome by history? Certainly not by forgetting it. Rather, by facing the new historical situation with its evils and its possibilities individuals and groups may give new application to the value insights of the heritage. This means, however, that the heritage must be understood critically and be reevaluated. Indeed, it must be judged and transformed if it is to be given effective and creative relation to the present. Troeltsch viewed history as providing the matrix out of which treasures both new and old are born, but only through sharp criticism and reconception in face of new situations. If liberal Christianity cannot deliberately participate in this process, it is not to remain viable, for it cannot assist the person of today to achieve an identity or individuality that overcomes history by history.

Speaking of orthodoxy's bifurcation of history into sacred and secular, into the dogmatic realm of miracle and the realm of the history of culture, Troeltsch characterized the contemporary religious "dogmatists" as those "who believe that they are able to pluck fruit without having a tree or who, after cutting a small, dry twig from an old trunk, expect fruit to grow from this twig." Religious liberals who have desisted from reflection on the pregnant past have for their part attached themselves to a small, dry twig of contemporaneity, expecting fruit to grow from this twig alone. Noting the similarity between this kind of orthodoxy and a converse type of religious liberalism, one may say with Sainte-Beuve that nothing is so much like a hole as a swelling.

But sometimes religious liberalism's practice is better than its preaching. Ralph Waldo Emerson has the reputation of being an apostle of Romantic individualism completely devoted to immediacy of intuition, for example in the "Divinity School Address" and in the "Essay on Self-Reliance." It is not generally remembered, however, that precisely when he was generating these ideas in his late twenties he composed some verses containing quite different doctrine. It is significant that he inscribed them on the inside cover of the first volume of Milton's prose works.

> How much, preventing God, how much I owe
> To the defenses thou hast round me set:
> Example, custom, fear, occasion slow, —
> These scorned bondmen were my parapet. . . .

This poem he entitled "Grace."

Probing into the *Journals* of this period, G. R. Elliott, the Amherst literary critic, discovered that at this very time "Milton was for Emerson the acme of the great tradition coming down from the Greek classics and the New Testament." But Emerson in effect concealed this admiration from the public, giving the laurel to Romantic Wordsworth.[4] Despite his advocacy of ahistorical, transcendental immediacy, Emerson knew that the deeper self upon which he relied was a self nourished by a venerable heritage.

Goethe put into one pithy sentence Troeltsch's sense of the significance of history for the present and future: "A tradition cannot be inherited, it must be earned." Religious liberalism cannot earn its tradition if it cannot achieve some consensus regarding its paradigmatic figures, some consensus as to what constitutes its classical literature in which at least its leaders find a refreshing, invigorating, healing fountain. Religious liberalism without this sense of a living tradition will only resonate like a violin whose sound box is closed.

THE SCOPE OF ETHICAL OBLIGATION

The contribution of Troeltsch as philosopher of religion, as sociologist of religion, as historian of Christianity, and as theologian cannot be dealt with in this brief essay. His association with his Heidelberg colleague Max Weber, the sociologist, goes far to explain his creativity and his influence in the sphere of sociology of religion.[5] In this connection we should observe that Talcott Parsons of Harvard considers Troeltsch to be "the most eminent sociologically oriented historian of Western Christianity." Of his philosophy of religion one should note that he devoted much of his earlier career to the effort to show that religion, especially in its formative stage, is not to be explained or explained away in the manner of "vulgar Marxism" as simply the result of historical conditioning or as the precipitate of ideological class struggle. He held that it is something *sui generis* that transcends the immediate historical situation. Consequently, it is able to enter creatively into it, bringing about transformation in a thousand ways.

In the lengthy study "The Basic Problems of Ethics," Troeltsch points to a conception of Christian vocation that is more ample than that of being a person of integrity open to rich tradition as he or she faces the future. For Troeltsch, as we have observed, thought should issue in action.

In this connection he distinguishes between subjective and objective obligations. Subjective obligations are those that obtain in the immediate relation between the individual and God, and between the individual and other persons. Objective obligations are those that require institutions for their manifestation. The "subjective rules" spring entirely from the bearing of the subjects (e.g., truthfulness, thoughtfulness, courage; benevolence, justice, loyalty). The "objective values," on the other hand, have to do with the family, the state, society, science, art, religion; and these have to be known by means of history, each possessing its own distinct development. Properly understood, subjective and objective values overlap and intertwine. Neither side can be authentic without the other. Again we see the principle of correlation, the "relationism."

Here Troeltsch made one of his most striking attacks on every piety that contents itself with privatization, segregating institutional questions and obligations to the side as secular or nonreligious. In his view, the effectiveness of any religion, orthodox or liberal, depends upon the capacity of the churches as corporate bodies to come to terms with institutional obligations in the society. At times he seemed to despair of the churches in their corporate behavior, predicting that the hope may lie with a "churchless Christianity," a sort of underground church. He predicted also that in this century the nations would become clustered around great military states, employing technology in massive struggles for power. He also surmised that by reason of increasingly concentrated economic power the common citizen in the democratic societies may lose confidence in the effectiveness of the political rule of one person, one vote. Again he sensed that foul whisperings were abroad. The "correlation" could run amuck. All the more needful is it, then, that history overcome history.

Considering the probing concerns, the alluring sensitivities, and the continuing relevance manifest in the writings of the liberal Christian Ernst Troeltsch, it is not surprising if in some quarters today it is said that we are due for a Troeltsch revival.

Notes

1. For a brief account of Troeltsch's career and of his major writings that have appeared in English translation see the article on Troeltsch by James L. Adams in *Encyclopaedia Britannica*. Important recent works are Wilhelm Pauck, *Harnack and Troeltsch* (New York: Oxford University Press, 1968), and Thomas W. Ogletree, *Christian Faith and History: A Critical Comparison of Ernst Troeltsch and Karl Barth* (Nashville: Abingdon Press, 1965). The work by Ogletree is much more critical of Troeltsch than is Pauck's book (Pauck was a pupil of Troeltsch). On the other hand, Ogletree (since publishing the book) has become more sympathetic to Troeltsch's point of view. This shift from Barth to Troeltsch is not a rare occurrence.

2. "Ueber historische und dogmatische Methoden der Theologie" (1900). *Gesammelte Schriften* (Tübingen: J. C. B. Mohr, 1913), vol. 2, pp. 729–53. The translation here used is by Walter Bense.

3. It has become a cliche repeated during the past two generations for certain critics of Troeltsch to say that he never overcame historical relativism. Regarding his way of dealing with the problem see Pauck, *Harnack and Troeltsch*, pp. 85ff. For Tillich's critique of Troeltsch (with which I do not fully agree) see the discussion in my book, *Paul Tillich's Philosophy of Culture, Science and Religion* (New York: Harper and Row, 1965).

4. "On Emerson's 'Grace' and 'Self-Reliance,'" *New England Quarterly* 2 (1929):100.

5. The author discusses Troeltsch's sociology of religion and his philosophy of religion in *The Journal for the Scientific Study of Religion* 1. no. 1 (1961).

16 · Our Responsibility in Society

I will pour out my Spirit on all flesh.

Joel 2:28, Acts 2:17

Our age is an "age of anxiety," a "time of troubles." None among us has escaped the anxiety, though the troubles have come nearer to some than to others. Well do I remember Dr. van Holk's address at the 1938 conference of the International Association for Religious Freedom at Bentveld, Holland, when he predicted that before another such conference would be held, a world war would probably intervene and that consequently some of us then present would not meet each other again.

The fulfillment of that prediction makes the heart heavy, not only because we lament the sufferings and the casualties it has entailed but also because we know that these sufferings were the consequences of irresponsibility, and indeed partly of our irresponsibility. When we say "our irresponsibility," however, we have in mind not merely the unwise collective decisions of international politics but also what lay behind these decisions: our own personal irresponsibility.

For most of us, personal irresponsibility in these matters is not the result of indolence; it is the consequence of misguided energy and devotion. Of this misguided devotion we find a telling parable in Thomas Mann's novel *Dr. Faustus*. In Mann's hero, or perhaps we should call him the antihero, we may see on a wide canvas the projection of personal irresponsibility. Adrien Leverkuhn, Thomas Mann's Faustus, made a compact with the devil, agreeing that in return for fame as a composer he would sever the bonds of normal affection and social responsibility. The outcome was disaster for Adrien and also for his nation: his disease became endemic.

This sort of compact with Satan, we know, has often been made, and not only by artists who claim to remain "above the battle." Some of us make the compact under the aegis of a pseudo-Protestant doctrine of vocation: we are

This essay is reprinted, by permission, from *Faith and Freedom*, published by the Old Students Association of Manchester College, Oxford, England, editor: Peter B. Godfrey, Vol. VI, Part II (Spring 1953). It also appeared in L. J. van Holk, A. V. Murray, and Adams, *Authority and Freedom* (Delft, Netherlands: W. Gaade, N.V., 1953), and in Adams, *Taking Time Seriously* (Glencoe, Ill.: The Free Press, 1957).

prone to take seriously only the responsibility of doing our own professional or vocational work well. In this fashion we evade a costing responsibility for the social policies of the common life. One can find physicians, lawyers, professors, workers who believe that their public responsibilities consist almost entirely in their vocational activity. Many clergy believe that they can be better parish priests if they keep themselves aloof from the controversies of the marketplace and the civic forum. In a time when the slogan that the customer is always right widely prevails, many men and women renounce vigorous participation in community conflicts on the ground not only that they will otherwise jeopardize the high quality of their own work but also that they will offend their customers or clientele if they take a public stand in favor of unpopular causes. The profile of this sort of underling (to use Dostoyevski's term) appears in a tombstone epitaph that Dean Willard Sperry of Harvard Divinity School tells us he once saw in Scotland:

> Here lies John MacDonald
> Born a man
> Died a grocer.

The Hitlers of any age or community are always grateful for, indeed they rely on, the sins of omission committed by these retreating, uncreative eunuchs. As Thomas Mann's parable suggests, this compact for personal success is scarcely reliable. The compact protects the illusion that we are assuming responsibility when in fact we are only personally "getting ahead."

Response to Reliable Power

The Free Christian's sense of responsibility in society issues from concern for something more reliable than the desire for personal success. It issues from the experience of and the demand for community. For the Free Christian, responsibility is a response to the Deed that was "in the beginning," to the Deed of Agape that gave birth to the Christian community. It begins in the indicative mood and ends in the imperative. It is a response to that divine, self-giving, sacrificial love that creates and continually transforms a community of persons. This response by which community is formed and transformed is the process whereby men and women in obedience, freedom, and fellowship come to know God and to enjoy him. Responsibility is response to a divinely given community-forming power; the early Christians spoke of it as "living in Christ," as God's pouring forth of his spirit.

Irresponsibility is not a lack of response. Nor is it indifference or neutrality. It is a response to unreliable powers. Social irresponsibility is a response that expresses the obverse side of love; it is, in biblical language, the working of the Wrath of God. It issues in distress and distortion; and it injures the "just" as well as the "unjust," the responsible as well as the irresponsible.

In the historical community, in the fate of living together, women and men confront the divine powers that form community and the perverting powers that destroy it. They confront these powers not only in themselves and in individual persons but also in the forces that assume impersonal, institutional form. Indeed, the quality of individual personal existence is partly conditioned by the institutional patterns that constitute the body politic. Thus every personal problem is a social problem and every social problem is a personal problem.

Not that the human being is completely expressed or enclosed in the institutional forms. A person is not merely the precipitate of social-institutional forces, but a creature with roots in immemorial being. Or, to use a characteristically Protestant formulation, the person stands directly before God, ever subject to renewal that depends for its initiative upon some vitality beneath the actual, dated forms of institutional existence. But this extrainstitutional dimension of persons is capable also of expressing a distortion of spirit; it is capable of expressing wrath as well as love.

For both the personal existence and the less personal, institutional existence, love is "the dearest freshness [of] deep down things," the dynamic ground of viable and meaningful community. It is the divine "call" to humanity, the divine initiative issuing a call to freedom and obedience and fellowship. The very meaning of history is to be found in the struggle for community, working toward the fulfillment of humanity and of the divine purpose. In this struggle the only reliable "object" of faith and devotion is Agape, the power of God which reconciles and reunites.

LOVE MADE CONCRETE IN THE NEW COMMUNITY

These words about love, the power of God, freedom and fellowship, are sufficiently familiar among us. But again and again we must ask, What do they mean? We must ask because one of the principal obstructions to the working of the power of God—one of the principal obstructions to response and responsibility—is an enervating devotion to mere abstractions. The adequate answer to the question must be a concrete answer. Responsibility is an incarnational response to the divine power of love, a response not only in personal but also in institutional behavior.

This demand of Agape for institutional expression is to be observed already in the early Christian community. Indeed, we see what the early Christians really meant by love, not only through observing their personal attitudes but also by looking at the kind of community which they believed to be demanded by love, and at the corresponding forms of responsibility involved.

For the most part the members of the primitive church were people who had previously been denied the dignity of responsibility in the shaping of policies of "church" and state. Membership in the Christian church released them from this low estate. To be sure, it would be false to assume that the early church aimed directly to bring about a revolution against this situation in politics; theirs was not in the usual sense a social revolution. Yet, they did institute a revolution. The response of these people to the power of God produced not only a new depth and intimacy in personal relations; it issued also in a new organization, in a church in which social responsibility and skill in administration were required.

This new community's influence in the creation of a sense of responsibility is evident from the very beginning; fishermen, artisans, women, and even slaves working together under the power of the Spirit became leaders or responsibly supported the missionary leaders and teachers. Moreover, the responsibilities assumed extended even beyond the strictly ecclesiastical functions. From the research of scholars we learn that the Christians of the first and second centuries formed charitable organizations and employment bureaus; they devised ways also for giving vocational education to orphans within the church. These practices, we must recognize, were an expression of the unfolding Christian conception of Agape, the concern under God for the good of the self, the other, and the community.

This assumption of responsibility on the part of ordinary people was of no small moment in the total context of antiquity. It acquired world-historical significance, for example, when the Roman Empire "fell." Indeed, these responsible ordinary people cushioned the "fall" and hastened the recovery. Scattered over the Mediterranean world there were hundreds of communities of people accustomed to performing special and skilled functions in social organizations. The recovery of the West from the Visigothic invasions would have required centuries longer than it did, had it not been for the sense of responsibility that had issued from the Christian response to the community-forming power of God. The Free Christianity of our modern devotion, as we shall presently show, owes its origin to essentially this same impulse.

THE INSTITUTIONAL CONSEQUENCES OF BELIEF

A highly significant method for understanding the meaning of responsibility, and even of religious-ethical ideas in general, is illustrated by our account of early Christianity. Charles Peirce, the American logician and the teacher of William James, has proposed that an idea becomes clear only when we determine the habits of behavior that follow from it. We have seen that the meaning of the religious-ethical idea of Agape becomes clear only when we determine the habits, personal and institutional, that followed from it.

On the basis of this method of observation we may state a general principle: The meaning of "God" for human experience, and the meaning of response to the power of God, is to be determined in large part by observing the institutional consequences, the aspects of institutional life which the "believers" wish to retain or to change. Paul, Aquinas, Luther, Münzer, and Roger Williams all use the words *God, Spirit, love.* But these realities and concepts assume quite different meanings for these men, differences that can be discriminated in their various conceptions of the appropriate forms of state, church, family, school, and society, and in the corresponding interpretations of social responsibility.[1]

Christian history exhibits a variety of social and political outlooks that have claimed a Christian sanction. At different times Christians have demanded the rule of the free Spirit of God (pneumatocracy), theocracy, absolute monarchy, constitutional monarchy, sectarian communism, constitutional democracy, democratic religious socialism. Each of these views has been conditioned by profound changes in the climate of opinion and in historical circumstance. Each has claimed to be the will of God. The differences between the conceptions of God become evident in the differing conceptions of society and of social responsibility.

The Free Christian conception of the power of God becomes clear in certain of its major expressions if we recall that initially, in the sixteenth and seventeenth centuries, it entailed a new conception of Spirit and of the church and a new kind of social responsibility within and beyond that church. Indeed these new conceptions in part harked back to the outlook of the early church which we have been considering. Stressing the creative power of God for the formation of the free community, our spiritual ancestors centered attention on the day of Pentecost when the prophecy of Joel was, in their view, fulfilled: "I will pour out my Spirit on all flesh."

From the Joachites of the thirteenth century down through the Anabaptists, the Baptists, and the Dutch Calvinists of the sixteenth century, to the English Independents and other aggressive sects of the seventeenth century, we can trace the development of a group of doctrines and practices that were destined to alter the shape of Protestantism and of modern society: a new spirit of toleration, a revived conception of the Holy Spirit and of the earlier doctrine of the church. Some of these sects were imbued with the Calvinist conception of the sovereignty of God with its demand for the establishment of the holy community. Some of them interpreted the meaning of history in terms of the struggle between different conceptions of church and community; they viewed the major phases of church history as the epochs or dispensations of the struggle between God and Satan. (The very title of the book *The Fall of Christianity*, by the Dutch theologian G. J. Heering, is reminiscent of this view, according to which the loss of the early type of church organization was itself the fall of the church.) These early sects of the modern period, in calling for a return to the primitive church organization, also aimed to be the heralds of a new age; Joachim of Fiore called it the Third Era, the era of the Spirit which would bring with it the Church of the Spirit.[2] In our day this movement, with its subsequent issue, is called the Radical Reformation.

This left wing movement wrought a great social revolution in whose heritage we are still living, a revolution analogous to that wrought by the early Christians. The latter-day revolution was carried out in opposition not only to Roman Catholicism but also to the right wing of the Reformation—orthodox Lutheranism and Calvinism. Authority in the right wing of the Reformation and in Roman Catholicism remained in many essentials the same. The doctrine of justification by faith in Lutheranism and of the sovereignty of God in orthodox Calvinism did not in essence do away with the authoritarian structure of the church. Some writers today even assert that there are analogies between the authoritarianism of Calvinist theocracy and that of Russian communism; we are familiar also with the view that the authoritarian structures of Roman Catholicism and of Russian communism bear analogies (which, to be sure, can be overstated). In this struggle between the left and the right wings we can discern the principal motif of modern history.

RADICAL LAICISM AND THE DISPERSION OF POWER

We of the Free Church tradition should never forget, or permit our contemporaries to forget, that the decisive resistance to authoritarianism in both church and state, and the beginning of modern democracy, appeared first in the church and not in the political order. The churches of the left wing of the Reformation held that the churches of the right wing had effected only half a reformation. They gave to Pentecost a new and extended meaning. They demanded a church in which every member, under the power of the Spirit, would have the privilege and the responsibility of interpreting the Gospel and also of assisting to determine the policy of the church. The new church was to make way for a radical laicism — that is, for the priesthood and the prophethood of all believers. "The Spirit blows where it lists."

Out of this rediscovery of the doctrine of the Spirit came the principles of Independency: local autonomy, free discussion, the rejection of coercion and of the ideal of uniformity, the protection of minorities, the separation of church and state. Power and responsibility were to be dispersed. In a fashion not unlike that of the primitive church, the doctrine of the Spirit became the sanction for a new kind of social organization and of social responsibility. A new church was born, and with it a new age.

Once released, the new spirit poured forth into all areas of society. It could not be kept within the bounds of church life. First, it was carried over into the sphere of the state. The Independents began to say, "If we are responsible to God for the kind of church we have, we are responsible also for the kind of state we have. If it is wrong to be coerced by church authorities, it is wrong to be dominated by political authorities. As children of God, we ought to have a greater share of power and responsibility in the state as well as in the church." By analogy the conception of a new church in a new age was extended to include the demand for a democratic state and society. Thus the democratic state is in part the descendant of the Church of the Spirit.

These principles were not enunciated without dust and heat. Nor did they spring into existence suddenly. They were promoted by certain branches of the left wing in various countries and with differing emphases. Not all of the churches, for example, demanded the separation of church and state.

The movement in Britain has been characterized by no one better than by the Roman Catholic historian Lord Acton. Let me quote his words.

For it is by the sects, including the Independents, that the English added to what was done by Luther and Calvin, and advanced beyond the sixteenth-century ideas.

The power of Independency was not in relation to theology, but to Church government. They did not admit the finality of doctrinal formulas, but awaited the development of truth to come. Each congregation governed itself independently, and every member of the Church participated in its administration. There was consocation, but not subordination. The Church was governed, not by the State or by bishops or by the presbytery, but by the multitude of which it was composed. It was the ideal of local selfgovernment and of democracy. . . .

The political consequences reached far. The supremacy of the people, being accepted in Church government, could not be repudiated in the State. There was a strong prejudice in its favour. "We are not over one another," said Robinson, "but one with another." They inclined not only to liberty, but equality, and rejected the authority of the past and the control of the living by the dead. . . . Persecution was declared to be spiritual murder. All sects alike were to be free, and Catholics, Jews, and Turks as well.[3]

Out of this soil of early Free Church doctrine and experience emerged also the principles of connectionalism and federalism, principles that represent attempts to come to terms with the social necessity of achieving integration as well as with the demand for a dispersion of power and responsibility.

In church, state, and society, then, the aggressive sects provided the institutional patterns for the assumption of initiative and responsibility on the part of all members. Political as well as ecclesiastical authorities were asserted to be responsible to the people, and all were responsible to God. In contrast to the right wing principles of domination and hierarchy, the institutional principles of persuasion and coarchy became the signature of the epoch of the Free Church. The watchword of this new epoch was uttered succinctly by a certain Colonel Rainsborough who in the Army Debates of the Cromwellian period said, "Every English he hath his own contribution to make."

In the course of time the new doctrine of the church was applied also beyond the areas of ecclesiastical and political organization. It worked to dissolve the patterns of domination in family and school as well. In all of these areas the existing authorities were made responsible or responsive to other members of the organization. Eventually the patriarchal family authority began to yield to a more democratic authority — to what we today call a permissive atmosphere. The schoolmaster came to recognize the intrinsic dignity of the pupil.

THE FREE CHURCHES AND THE GROWTH OF DEMOCRACY

But the influence of this new conception of the church and of the responsibility of each person reached even beyond the institutions of church, state, school, and family. This influence is to be observed especially in the emergence of an institution that some historians and political scientists consider to be the characteristic and decisive instrument of the democratic society, namely, the voluntary association. The voluntary organization provides the opportunity for ever wider and wider dispersion of responsibility, for the displacement of hierarchy (though it can never rightly dispense with hierarchy altogether, for that way lies chaos). It stands between the individual and the state, and also between the church and the state; and it is controlled by neither the state nor the church. An essential pattern of the voluntary organization was already present in the church of the voluntary covenant and also in the voluntary business association. The many committees and organizations that exist in the modern community, the organizations that work for social reform, for cooperative production or distribution of goods, for the protection of civil rights, for the protection or extension of suffrage, for the maintenance of professional standards, for the promotion of new legislation, and for a thousand and one other purposes that are pursued by the free citizen in a modern democracy, represent the application of the original Free Church idea to organized efforts that serve to shape the policy of the modern community in politics and in commerce, in social welfare and in leisure-time activity. All of these forms of association, including the modern trade union, are in large part the outgrowth of left wing Protestantism; indeed, they may be characterized as the secularization of the Free Church doctrine of the church.[4] Because of just this process of the secularization of the religious groups, Adolph Lowe, the German sociologist, is able to summarize the British experience in the following way:

> It would be a misinterpretation of the facts if we were to equate English liberalism with an atomistic structure of society. What strikes the observer of this period of English history who compares England with the great continental nations, is not an extreme individualism, but the general tendency to form voluntary associations. From the political parties down to the chapel meetings, public life was actually dominated by self-governing bodies, growing up spontaneously but submitting to the principle of democratic leadership.[5]

The mitigation of hierarchy in favor of coarchy and democratic leadership is to be seen today in one of the major innovations in business enterprise. Increasingly, the modern business executive recognizes that high productivity depends on morale, and that high morale depends on the dispersion of responsibility and initiative. Associated with this tendency is the recent development of group dynamics, the effort to delineate the principles whereby universal participation may be elicited and whereby group morale and "productivity" in group consensus may be increased. These efforts presuppose that the abiding strength and spiritual validity of any group depend on a diversity of interests united by more general purposes, that they depend on the power of every member and group to get a hearing. They offer a dramatic illustration of the axiom enunciated by Colonel Rainsborough and of the conception of human being also expressed by Goethe in his couplet:

> Had Allah meant me for a worm
> In shape of a worm he had formed me.

I have mentioned mainly the English Nonconformists. Obviously, other Protestant churches have contributed to the growth of the conception of social responsibility made explicit in the English Free Church tradition. One could trace a similar lineage of development in the United States' experience. The U.S. Constitution and the Federalist Papers are not understandable apart from the historical background of Free Church doctrine and Free Church pluralism. And as for federalism, where could one better study its provenance than in Swiss Protestantism? One could cite a similarly rich heritage in the Netherlands, showing the ways "spiritualist" doctrines and the conception of religious freedom have exercised their influence.

It is precisely in those countries where the left wing doctrines have not become decisive that one finds even today a persistence of the traditions of domination and obedience. The Soviet Union, Germany, and Italy have grievously suffered from tyranny as a partial consequence of the fact that Free Church conceptions of responsibility and of the dispersion of power were held in check. In these countries democratic tendencies in the national life have been relatively weaker than in the countries of a continuing left wing Protestantism, for the countries of the right wing tend to favor conformity rather than discussion.[6]

The eminent German jurist Otto von Gierke has suggested that the major struggle in Western history since the time of Charlemagne has been the struggle between the rival conceptions of community which we have characterized as those of the right wing and the left wing. On the one side we have what von Gierke calls "the lordly union," the society or group in which authority emanates from the top down; against this, we have the society or group that aims to have authority emanate from the bottom of the social pyramid, from the consensus of the "grass roots." In both types of community we find that conceptions of God, love, human being, are appealed to; but these conceptions take on radically different meanings in terms of the different types of consensus favored. The consensus that appears in "the lordly union" tends to be one imposed by a vicar of God or an equivalent authority; the "grass roots" consensus aims to recognize that the Holy Spirit blows where it lists and that people are more likely to yield to that Spirit when they do not blasphemously intrude their own human chain of command.

THE VOCATION OF SOCIAL RESPONSIBILITY

Now, within this brief and elliptical survey of the left wing of the Reformation, which has exercised its influence in all of the churches represented in our International Association for Religious Freedom, we find the context for the understanding of our responsibility in society. Our responsibility is to maintain the heritage that is ours, the heritage of response to the community-forming Power that we confront in the Gospels and in the Free Churches. This community-forming Power calls us to the affirmation of that abundant love which is not ultimately in our possession but is a holy gift. It is the ground and goal of our vocation.

But this vocation cannot be carried out if we try merely to repeat the behavior of our ancestors. In important respects our historical situation is unique. The struggle between the left wing and the right wing is taking new forms. We live in a time when both the theology and the social principles of the old liberalism are under attack.

Today we confront the neo-Reformation movement in Protestant theology. From this source some of us may find certain theological correctives with respect to the ultimate issues of life as liberals have interpreted them. But this neo-Reformation movement in some circles carries with it such a nostalgia for the "pure doctrine" of the past that it also revives the doctrine of the authoritarian church. An authoritarian church is a danger to the free society as well as to the free church. This fact should make us scrutinize the more carefully the "pure doctrine" that is offered. It should make us aware of the present-day need for a neo-Radical Reformation which will creatively resist the patterns of domination and of rigidly conformist obedience.

In our day we confront also the impersonal forces of a mass society with its technological devices for producing stereotyped opinion. In this mass society the individual is always in danger of becoming lost in the "lonely crowd." One is attacked by a stream of prepared "ideas" and "facts" that issue from the endless transmission belts of radio, movie, and press. These "opinion industries" provide a poor substitute for a community of faith. Insofar as they form community at all, it is for the most part the "community" of support for special interests—the interests of nationalism, racism, and business as usual. In large measure this "community" is an instrument manipulated and exploited by central power groups. In short, it is a form of authoritarianism. It is the modern, anonymous version of the earlier imposed direction from the top in face of which the primitive Christian church and the left wing of the Reformation protested in the name of a more intimate, personal community dependent on individual dignity and responsibility.

But there are even more destructive forces that threaten freedom of the spirit. The great economic dislocations of our time have given the age a neurotic character. These dislocations cannot be corrected by our merely exhorting ourselves and others to individual initiative and responsibility; they require concerted analysis and attack. It may be that these dislocations and the exigencies of international conflict will require even more centralized controls than we are now accustomed to. Thus the growth of the patterns of authority characteristic of the traditional mass church may be an unavoidable fate for our time. All the more, then, is our heritage of the left wing threatened and needed. At the same time we face the danger that the small-group organization will become merely a sanction for large-group irresponsibilities.

The revived neo-orthodoxy, the new mass society manipulated by pressure groups, the increase of planning, the fear of the totalitarianism in the East, taken together with modern vocational specialization, have conspired against our maintaining our heritage in a vital way within even our own churches; and they also have made the more difficult the meeting of our social responsibilities through participation in the policy-shaping activities of the community.

It is just here, then, that we encounter our peculiar responsibility in society, the responsibility to offer a church in which there is an explicit faith in the community-forming power of God, a practice of the disciplines of liberty, an eliciting of the participation of our own membership in creative fellowship. From such a fellowship, concerned to extend the community in which all persons may be encouraged to make their own contribution, our members can meet their social responsibilities by expressing in the other areas of life—in the state, the family, the school, the voluntary association, and industry—the response to the love that will not let us go. This movement of the patterns of responsibility from the church to these other areas of life, as we have seen, has taken place since the very beginning of our Free Christianity. It is our social responsibility to maintain and extend this movement in face of human needs for health and shelter and for a world in which (across the lines of race and class and nation) all may enjoy their God-given dignity and responsibility—for a world in which Everyone can make a contribution. If we do not participate in groups that work deliberately for these ends, we are ourselves irresponsible; we are dominated underlings—mass people in compact with Satan.

Here, then, is the vocation placed upon us by the promise of old, "I will pour out my Spirit on all flesh." For us who bear the heritage of Free Christianity, this promise draws and binds us together. The promise is ultimately not one that we make to ourselves. It is one that we receive in faith. Yet it is also a promise whose fulfillment is contingent upon our response in responsibility.

In our time of troubles the problems are vast in their dimensions. But they were vast also in the birth period of the primitive church and in the birth period of our Free Churches. To cringe in despair of ourselves is to despair of the divine promise. It is to forget that responsibility is response to a Spirit that is *given* to us—to the light that has shone and that still shines in the darkness.

Notes

1. It is questionable whether the method of "motif-research" promoted by the Swedish theologian Anders Nygren (*Agape and Eros*) is adequate. Nygren's method restricts itself to examining verbal doctrinal statements. But such a method overlooks very important and relevant facts. We may not assume that Paul and Luther, for example, employ the term *Agape* with the same meaning simply because they use the same theological terms to describe it. Their conceptions of church and state—in short, their conceptions of social responsibility—must be taken seriously into account if we are to grasp the distinctive elements in their conceptions of Christian love.

2. Unitarians in the U.S. are familiar with this phrase particularly through F. G. Peabody's book of a generation ago, *The Church of the Spirit*. European Christians have been reminded of it by Ernst Benz's remarkable study, *Ecclesia Spiritualis*.

3. John Emerich Edward Dalberg-Acton, *Lectures on Modern History* (London: Macmillan and Co., 1906), p. 200.

4. To be sure, many of these voluntary organizations have appeared within the shadow of the right wing, e.g., of Roman Catholicism, but the Church has sought always to keep them under ecclesiastical control. But not only the authoritarian Church has obstructed the free development of voluntary organization. Political dictatorships have always recognized the voluntary organization to be one of their principal enemies, for it provides the citizen with the opportunity of disseminating "dangerous thoughts" and of promoting social policies inimical to the power of the central authorities. Thomas Hobbes, the St. Simonians, the ultramontane Catholics, Hitler, and Mussolini, all agree that free-floating voluntary associations must be forbidden.

5. Adolph Lowe, *Economics and Sociology* (London: George Allen and Unwin, 1935).

6. One of the hopeful signs for democracy in Germany today appears in the marked advance shown by the "free-religious communities." Representatives of these groups attended the Oxford Congress of the International Association for Religious Freedom. Especially impressive are the Evangelical Academies in Germany, the Netherlands, and Sweden as innovations in the direction of radical laicism.

17 · We Wrestle against Principalities and Powers

We wrestle not against flesh and blood, but against the principalities, against the powers, against the world-rulers of this present darkness, against the spiritual hosts of wickedness in the heavenly places.

Ephesians 6:12

This text makes a special demand upon the understanding of the person of our time. "Principalities and powers," "the world-rulers of this present darkness," "the spiritual hosts of wickedness in the heavenly places": These phrases sound fantastic to the ear of our age. If they are to be understood vividly, they demand of us what Samuel Taylor Coleridge called "a willing suspension of disbelief." We must recognize that in their time they pointed to fearful realities, to powers that corrupt and distort and even destroy order and justice and peace.

These powers were sometimes conceived to be fallen angels in contrast to the benevolent angels like those mentioned in the story of the birth of Jesus. These conceptions are so pervasive in both Old and New Testament that many a theologian of the church has been led to give special attention to a doctrine of angels, to what is called angelology. The section on angelology has therefore sometimes provided a substantial part of the systematic theology of Christian and Jewish theologians from St. Paul to Aquinas to Maimonides to Karl Barth. Indeed, at the beginning of the nineteenth century all freshmen at Yale College were required on Sunday evenings to attend a course of lectures on angelology by the Rev. Timothy Dwight, the president of the college.

ANGELS, PRINCIPALITIES, AND POWERS

Last year in Germany I heard a story that presupposes the venerable tradition that demanded a systematic angelology of any full-fledged theologian. At Hamburg University Professor Helmut Thielicke told me an amusing story about a conversation he had with the quondam Harvard

This sermon was given at the ordination of Dr. Hans Rosenwald by the First Parish in Cambridge, Cambridge, Massachusetts, on June 7, 1964.

165

theologian Paul Tillich. Professor Tillich was lecturing at Hamburg University when his seventieth birthday came, and accordingly Professor and Frau Thielicke arranged a birthday dinner. I must explain that when visiting Professor Thielicke at his home Paul Tillich preferred always to sit in a particular place in the study to be able to see through the window a beautiful tree that stands in the garden. Following the birthday dinner the two scholars enjoyed together a flask of wine in the study. After an hour of conversation Professor Thielicke in jovial mood said to Paul Tillich, "I have always wanted to ask you a question about your theology. You have not yet set forth your doctrine of the angels. Paulus, what is your angelology?" The astonished Tillich replied, "Yes, yes, my angelology? My angelology? I must have a doctrine of the angels." After a brief pause, Tillich continued, "Well, here is my angelology. I say that the Greek gods, those wonderful Greek gods, should be considered the Christian angels." "Now, now, Paulus, surely you would not maintain that. Can you really imagine that Pallas Athene was among those angels who at Bethlehem sang 'Glory to God in the highest' at the birth of Christ?" "Yes, yes, that is difficult to believe, isn't it?" replied Tillich. Then, suddenly pointing out the window, Tillich said, "There they are, the angels, in that tree out there! Don't you hear the angels singing there? They are in the branches of that gorgeous tree." Whereupon Professor Thielicke said, "Paulus, this is verily a miracle. You not only hear, you even *see*, angels in that tree. And this after we have drunk only one flask of wine!" I do not know whether this anecdote will serve to induce in you a certain "willing suspension of disbelief," but I ask you to try.

What about the principalities and the powers? What do these terms mean? In the Old Testament one finds a variety of such conceptions. Paul Tillich, in support of his momentary fantasy, might well have appealed to the passage in Job where we read that the angels, "the sons of God," the morning stars, sang together at the creation of the world. In the Old Testament, generally, the angels were undifferentiated as to function, beyond being messengers of Jehovah. But in the later period of Israel the word *principalities* begins to appear. These principalities are distributed in the world, so that they have the various ethnic peoples of the earth under their jurisdiction.

In postbiblical Judaism one encounters a tropically luxuriant world of supernatural powers and forces, divine and satanic, angelic and demonic, a world of intermediary spirits, whose influence, beneficent or malignant, extends and is experienced over the whole domain of nature and of human life. The more majestic and transcendent the conception of God became, the more the pious mentality required intermediary supernatural entities. These intermediary angelic or demonic beings provided a religious framework for the salient events, the theophanies, of immediate experience. They related the Eternal to the events, the frustrations, the impediments, to the theophanies and the hopes of time. They related the vertical religious dimension to the horizontal. Understood sociologically and theologically, this is the meaning of the luxuriant spirit world of the ancient imagination; and analogs may be found also in other cultures and religions.

JESUS AND PAUL

The spirit world of which I have been speaking was generally taken for granted at the time of Jesus and Paul. After his baptism Jesus was assailed and tempted by the "devil" in the wilderness. In the synagogue at Capernaum Jesus is recognized as speaking with power, with authority; the word for power here is the same word that we encounter in our text from Ephesians which speaks of principalities and powers. Immediately after Jesus' interpreting of the Scripture in the synagogue he demonstrated this power by healing a man of unclean spirit. This unclean spirit, "convulsing him and crying with a loud voice, came out of the man." The Gospels are full of these stories about exorcism at the hands of Jesus and his disciples. Here we encounter a psychological-theological interpretation of mental illness.

Presently Jesus appears in public proclaiming the coming of the Reign or the Kingdom of God. In the Old Testament Psalms and in the Prophets the Reign of God is usually set in relation to the overthrow of the "enemies" of God. And so it is also in the New Testament. In the Lord's Prayer we find the petition, "Lead us not into temptation, but deliver us from the evil one," a recollection of the temptation of Jesus in the wilderness. Jesus viewed the Kingdom of God as carrying on a struggle against an enemy, against invisible powers of darkness. "If I by the Spirit cast out demons, then is the Kingdom of God come unto you. Or how can one enter into the house of the strong man, and spoil his goods, except he first bind the strong man? and then he will spoil his house." In this fashion the power, the *exousia*, which Jesus represents comes to mortal grips with the power, the *exousia*, of the demonic world. Jesus apparently viewed himself as the herald of the power of God which can overcome the principalities and powers, "the world rulers of this present darkness."

Paul, in the face of the elaborate demonology and angelology of the Jewish and the pagan world of his time, employed a whole series of terms. Principalities, powers, dominions, gods, lords, the prince of darkness, the world potentates of the present darkness, the spiritual hosts of wickedness, elemental deities and demons, and all sorts of astral forces come into play. In many circles the belief in these forces gave rise to fatalism, to what Gilbert Murray has called "a loss of nerve." Paul in no sense feels himself to be in bondage to this fatalism. He knows a power that is greater than all of them. He admits the existence of these principalities and powers, but he denies their divinity. "There is none other God but one." The Christian, he asserts, has passed beyond the rule of these principalities and powers. In his view, to be sure, they were responsible ultimately for the crucifixion of Jesus, but by the crucifixion they were undone. Caiaphas, Pilate, and Herod were to blame in the immediate sense for the crucifixion, but behind them were invisible powers, infinitely more dangerous, of whom the visible human "rulers" were merely the agents. By "rulers of this world" Paul appears to mean both the cosmic principalities and powers, and their actual human executives. But, like Jesus, he proclaims a power that is sovereign over all of these principalities. Moreover, Christ in his crucifixion took upon himself in his victory all those who through faith had come to be "in him" and thus shared his experience. And when God is all in all and the triumph of Christ is complete, all of these powers of bondage and decay will be brought under subjection. Paul could sing, "We shall over come—some day." These are the conceptions by which the early Christians were kept from "the commonest sense . . . the sense of men asleep."

Now, the remarkable thing about this whole outlook is that Paul, unlike those before him, attempted to specify the actual working in history of the principalities and powers. In this context he identified the totalitarian state, the closed traditions of the gentiles, the legalism of the over-zealous Pharisees, popular public opinion, the customs of idolatry which brought men and women under the rule of bondage and decay, of hatred and injustice. And, finally, he found the evil principalities and powers to be in the human breast. Not that he believed the human heart or the state or the Jewish law or the demonic powers behind them to be absolutely incorrigible. He seems to have believed that the state and the Mosaic law would through the power of Christ be brought to their authentic fulfillment.

What is especially pertinent for us to observe is that in specifying, in identifying, the principalities and powers and in launching attack on them, he pointed, as did Jesus, to a fundamental purpose of any authentic church.

The true church is a community that is alert to the struggle against the distorting demonries of social and personal existence, and is aware of the availability of a power that can overcome or at least cripple them.

THE DEMONIC IN OUR AGE

Now, if we ask the question, What are the areas today in which these demonic forces take possession of men and women? we do not need to seek far for the answer. The term *demonic* has come into currency again in our own time. Indeed, Paul Tillich is the major theologian who has given currency to that term. It came into vogue especially as a description of the totalitarian state of Nazism. But the word *demonic* is applicable not only to the totalitarian state. Nazism was the expression of a major driving force of modern history, so pervasive a force as to be called "humanity's other religion" — nationalism.

One could nominate other principalities and powers such as the devotion to a technology that cramps and distorts both nature and human nature, and that today infects even the atmosphere in incalculable and unpredictable ways. One could name devotion to an economic system, whether it be Soviet and Chinese or Western, which has brought with it the fragmentation of human personality and cyclical unemployment. One could name the technology of communications which in the United States has bound together the dissemination or distortion or suppression of ideas and the marketing of products. Is it not astonishing that we permit the constant interruption of radio and television programs for the advertising of breakfast cereals, automobiles, and a thousand other gadgets? One is reminded here of William Hazlitt's word that his image of America was that of one long bargain counter. In all of these areas, to be sure, benefits as well as distortion have accrued.

But probably we should at the present juncture of international and national affairs give the first rank of principalities and powers to something closely associated with nationalism, the racism that has spread from the West to almost all parts of the planet.

RACISM

A few years ago I had an experience that brought racism as an aspect of our contemporary existence vividly into focus. I delivered an address in Tokyo to representatives of various religions, and in my address I endeavoured to indicate the bases and the means for bringing about a better understanding and a closer cooperation between the religions. Immediately after the address, in the discussion period, a Buddhist monk stood up to pose a question, and he spoke for fifteen minutes, centering his attention on the destruction of Hiroshima and Nagasaki by atom bomb. He concluded his remarks by asking if the Americans would have destroyed these two Japanese cities, with their civilian victims, if they did not assume that the Japanese people are a subhuman species. He might well have asked the same sort of question about the U.S. soldier who brought home a Japanese skull to be shown as a souvenir of war on the mantle, or about the member of Congress who sent President Roosevelt a letter opener made from the forearm of a Japanese soldier killed in action.[1] Racism, he said, is the religion of the West.

Arnold Toynbee offers strong support for this judgment. In his *Study of History* (volume 1) he has shown how race feeling has become a principality and a power and a dominion, as a consequence of the expansion of Western civilization over the face of the earth since the fifteenth century. He points out that in all the countries of this expansion where white people from Western Europe have settled "cheek by jowl" with representatives of other races, there are three elements in the situation which between them go far toward accounting for the strength and virulence of Western race feeling in our time.

> First, the White people have established an ascendancy over the people of other races with whom they have come to share their new homes. Secondly, these White masters have almost everywhere abused their power in some way and in some degree. Thirdly, they are haunted by a perpetual fear that some day the positions may be reversed; that by weight of superior numbers or by more successful adaptation to the local climate or by ability to survive in a lower level of subsistence or by readiness to do harder physical or intellectual work, the Man of Colour may eventually bring the White Man's ascendancy to an end and perhaps even establish an ascendancy of his own over the White Man. The "first shall be the last, and the last first"; and if ever this comes to pass, the White Man's children must expect to have the sins of the fathers visited on their heads, for, in the consciousness of "under-dog," the past is ever present.[2]

Here we see the destructive drive, the specious power, of the principality of pigment. The more this principality favors the people of one pigment, the more it engenders resentment and resistance at the hands of the people of other pigments.

It would be illuminating if the people of the United States could through the press be brought to consider seriously the changes that have taken place in Cuba, and the reasons for them. The United Fruit Company would figure more in this accounting than is customary in the U.S. press.

Karl Marx's description of the exploitations of capitalism and his predictions regarding the increasing proletarianization of the masses have not been vindicated by the internal developments in the capitalist countries, but his description of exploitation has been strikingly illustrated by colonialism. The profits that the colonialist powers have extracted from the exploited powers (for example, from Cuba) have been enormous.

Arnold Toynbee has suggested that the racism that has been spread through colonialism is largely a Protestant force, a Protestant movement that can be traced from the time when the Bible was put into English, and when the preprophetic tribalism of the Old Testament conception of the Chosen People began to infect the West. The King James version of the Bible, he points out, was published in 1611, and a book called *The New English Canaan*, by Thomas Morton, was published in 1637! (We should observe, however, that the Protestant notion of England as an elect nation antedates the publication of the King James version. It found its classic formulation almost fifty years earlier in John Foxe's *Book of Martyrs*.)

But the demonic possession that is upon us all at the hands of racism is manifest in the fact that over a century after our Emancipation Proclamation our Senate is only now attempting to give full meaning to the Fourteenth Amendment, and even then is caught in the throes of a filibuster that has continued for over seventy days. After over a century of our Protestant missions in Africa, the Africans are now sending to the United States emissaries and supporters of the struggle for human rights. In our own midst the power of this principality of racism is so strong that we can say that it functions in a deterministic way reminiscent of the power attributed to astral bodies in the time of Paul. But I do not need to labor the point at a time when we are all aware of the fact that even though the Civil Rights Bill is passed, we probably have a bad summer ahead of us. More than that, more than a bad summer is ahead, for a new humanity for the Negro will require struggle for a long time to come.

The cost in human suffering that has been paid in the past to this principality of racism is incalculable and in the strict sense it is irredeemable. Resentment, self-hatred, aggression, the hardening of the heart, the sense of deprivation—so goes the catalog of sufferings. What our race discrimination has meant and means has been simply and poignantly symbolized in a poem by Langston Hughes. It presents a little child as he stands before a merry-go-round at a carnival, a child who questions whether he may be permitted to ride the merry-go-round.[3]

> Where is the Jim Crow Section
> On this merry-go-round,
> Mister, 'cause I want a ride?
> Down south where I come from
> White and colored
> Can't sit side by side.
> Down south on the train
> There's a Jim Crow car.
> On the bus we're put in the back. —
> But there ain't no back
> To a merry-go-round!
> Where's the horse
> For a kid that's black?

The passage of the Civil Rights Bill will be a mark of progress against the old principality and power of racism, but it will be simply the beginning of a new phase of the struggle, a new phase in the effort to prepare children to pry open the door into the other America, the affluent America, whose whole way of life is "absolutely foreign to the culture of the ghetto-slums."

We must be open to the change that comes from the source of our origin and our fulfillment. We must be open to the power of the Kingdom of God which, as Jesus taught, is always available.[4] With Paul we must recognize that only if we be not conformed to this world, only if we be transformed by the renewal of our minds, may we "take the helmet of salvation and sword of the Spirit." We wrestle not against flesh and blood, but against principalities and powers.

Notes

1. See *Life* magazine, May 22, 1944, and *Time* magazine, June 26, 1944.

2. Arnold Toynbee, *Study of History*, vol. 1 (London: Humphrey Milford, Oxford University Press, 1935), p. 210.

3. Langston Hughes, "Colored Child at Carnival."

4. "The kingdom of God is available" is a translation proposed by the New Testament scholar Henry J. Cadbury; cf. Mark 1:15, "the kingdom of God is at hand," and Luke 17:21, "the kingdom of God is within you" (Authorized Version).

Part Three

Religion and Culture under Judgment

A DAMS DEFINES THEOLOGICAL ETHICS AS "FAITH SEEKING UNDER-
standing in the realm of moral action" and within this broad field
distinguishes "sacramental" and "prophetic" orientations. The sacramental
sees the divine as already present within the social and natural orders;
despite the positive significance Adams finds in this immanentalist viewpoint, it is deficient in critical distance. The prophetic orientation, Adams
says, sees divine power primarily in personal decision and social change in
behalf of a new community. In prophetic perspective, religion is understood as an aspect of human culture; both alike stand "under judgment."

The pendulum of opinion has swung, in the modern era, between
extremes of optimism and pessimism regarding human nature and the
human prospect. Liberalism in particular has been charged with holding
unsupportably optimistic expectations of humanity, resulting in disillu-
sionment and a new cycle of pessimism, cynicism, and resignation. Adams
calls for a more realistic and, at the same time, a more ethically responsible
conception of the human condition. "Angelism," discussed in the essay "A
Little Lower than the Angels" is the temptation to which religious people
are especially prone. It tries to view human life too purely in spiritual terms
and mistakenly sees "materialism" as the chief enemy of religion. In
"Freud, Mannheim, and the Liberal Doctrine of Human Being," Adams
calls attention to the profound ways in which modern psychology and
sociology have undermined the assumptions of human rationality and
individuality held by classical liberalism.

Adams's thought has characteristically proceeded in dialogue with great
thinkers of the past. Essays on two seminal thinkers of this century, Alfred
North Whitehead and Paul Tillich, are included in this section. In the

process philosophy of Whitehead, Adams finds a metaphysics in which, in contrast to most classical metaphysics, the social and temporal dimensions of reality are central. Without wholly adopting Whiteheadean thought, Adams draws many key ideas from his former teacher, as "The Lure of Persuasion: Some Themes from Whitehead," amply shows.

Paul Tillich, who for several years was Adams's colleague on the faculty of Harvard University, has been his major partner in intellectual dialogue. Tillich was not exaggerating when he said that Adams had studied his thought so thoroughly that he knew more about it than he did himself. In "Tillich and the Spirit of Matthew the Painter" (Matthias Grünewald), Adams calls to mind the prophetic side of Tillich, submerged in his later writings but fully visible in the early writings that Adams translated and first introduced to the English-speaking world. The following essay, "The Need for a New Language," elucidates the way Tillich created a theological language that opens awareness of the "theonomous" dimension of secular culture and makes luminous much in the religious tradition that has grown dull with age and misuse.

A renewed theology, Adams holds, will appropriate a deepened awareness of the psychic and social forces that shape human life. "The Phenomenology of Fragmentation and the Ecology of Dreams" reflects theologically on the interpretation of dreams. Adams sees dreaming as an internal process by which religious meaning breaks through the crust of human consciousness; the seeming irrationality of dreams signifies preconscious levels of meaning, rooted in the experience of psychic and social fragmentation in human life. The essay "In Praise of Sleep" interprets the regenerative role of sleep in human life as a natural form of grace.

The two essays that conclude this section, "Pietism and Prophetism: Religion and Social Issues" and "The Politics of Culture in American Perspective," outline the conceptual framework which Adams brings to bear upon the mass technological culture of today. He asserts a fundamental dichotomy, which churches of every theological hue habitually gloss over, between prophetic and pietistic religious consciousness. The distinction is itself a recognition that religious culture, as much as secular, stands under prophetic judgment.

G.K.B.

18 · A Little Lower than the Angels

What is man, that thou are mindful of him?
And the son of man, that thou visitest him?
For thou hast made him but little lower than the angels.

Psalm 8

Man is neither angel nor brute, and he who would act the angel acts the brute.

Pascal

I cannot praise a fugitive and cloistered virtue.

Milton,
Areopagitica

"What a piece of work is man," Shakespeare exclaimed. The human being has been called a tool-making animal, a laughing animal, a featherless biped, a political animal. Some have deemed it sufficient to say that *homo sapiens* is an animal—with the qualification that ours is perhaps the only species that organizes mass murder of itself. What a piece of work is man, in action how like an angel, says Shakespeare.

Perhaps the strangest definition ever offered is the one given by the psalmist. The human being, he says, is a little lower than the angels. Of course, this definition sheds little light, unless we know what an angel is or is supposed to be. I presume that some of you may be tempted to say that if I enter here into a discussion of that subject, you will have a suggestion for a definition I have not yet mentioned, namely, that human beings are those perverse creatures who, not knowing what they are themselves, imagine and define nonexistent beings. But if by considering what men and women have thought about the nature of the angel we can find any important clue to human nature, perhaps the venture ought to be indulged—at least once in a lifetime. Believe it or not: Today you are to hear a discourse on angels! To be sure, it will turn out to be a discourse on human being. You are a captive audience. Nevertheless, I hope you will willingly go along with me in this excursion into angelology, at least some of the way.

This baccalaureate sermon was given at Franklin and Marshall College, Lancaster, Pennsylvania, on June 7, 1959; in an earlier version it was also presented at Adams's *alma mater*, the University of Minnesota.

In asking you to accompany me on this venture I am disposed to quote a few lines of verse from Robert Frost.

> I'm going out to clean the pasture spring;
> I'll only stop to rake the leaves away
> (And wait to watch the water clear, I may);
> I sh'n't be gone long. —You come too.

We shall consider the angels only long enough to rake the leaves away and wait to watch the water clear. Before we start for the spring, I should remind you that the science of angels, their nature and functions, is one of the more venerable of the theological disciplines. Indeed, it long played a part in the history of higher education in both Europe and the United States. It will be sufficient for our purpose if we consider only one of the systematic angelologies, that of the medieval philosopher and theologian Thomas Aquinas. Nor do we need to go into the question of whether angels actually exist or not. You may or you may not believe they exist. I ask only that you join me in raking the leaves away from this old subject; then after we have watched the water clear, we can peer into the medieval angelology as into a sort of mirror in reverse. We shall see what we are not.

According to Thomas Aquinas, three major attributes characterize the angels: First, they have not bodies; they exist independently of things; they are disembodied spirits or intelligences; consequently, they do not live in history. Second, all of their knowledge is innate; by divine illumination this innate knowledge is given them directly by God at the time of creation. Therefore, the angels cannot reason; they do not *need* to draw conclusions from premises or from experience; they have angelic knowledge by divine fiat. Third, there exist no two angels of the same species; each individual angel constitutes a separate species; every angel is an island unto itself.

By means of these characterizations, the medieval thinker (I am convinced) intended to bring into bold relief what a human being is not, and thus by implication he grasped the more clearly what one is. By this means he emphasized that the human being has a body, lives in history, and ideally can learn from experience, and she or he lives with other members of the same species. This is what the medieval thinkers had in mind when they read that man is a little lower than the angels.

You may say that these are extremely obvious facts, whether there are angels or not. We know that we are dust, that we live in a world of things, that we have a body as well as mind, that we must learn from experience in the body and in the world of things, that physical as well as spiritual needs must be met, that we live in history, that we must somehow maintain or achieve community. But these facts are easily and often forgotten by religious people as well as by people who think of themselves as nonreligious or irreligious. These people speak of the spiritual life as if it were only beyond the material order. Any view of life that overlooks these facts should be called pseudospiritual; indeed, we with Jacques Maritain properly call it angelism, for it is in principle guided by the effort to think of oneself as an angel. Let us consider some of the implications of the fact that the human being is not an angel, that (in the words of the psalmist) man is a little lower than the angels. We can do this if we observe the character of some of our most highly civilized, most spiritual, activities.

One of the most spiritual things we know is music. But music is heard through the ears, and it requires wood and steel and horse hair and catgut and finger technique. Bach is not simply a synonym for heavenly and angelic beauty. That name means also the organ pipes, and the organist with skill down to the fingers and toes, and the sheet of music before him, and the wind that courses through the pipes. More than that, music is the result of human cooperation, and it is composed according to certain socially recognizable forms and rhythms. It takes the form of a sonata or a symphony or an Introit or a mass. Granted, music gives us what we call a spiritual pleasure. Yet it requires a human community for its creation or appreciation, and it requires hands and instruments and ears—and experienced listening and taste.

And what of architecture? Here again we need wood and stone and builders, and we need human cooperation and a humanly created and growing tradition. Anything deserving the name of architecture will fit some recognized style of ordering the materials, Gothic, Greek, Georgian, or modern. These styles are simply names for differing ways of employing matter.

We look at a beautiful painting, and we are perhaps moved to speak of ethereal beauty. Yet, if we go into the artist's studio, we are reminded that the artist is dealing with light and canvas, with line and curve, with brushes and oils. A studio in which an artist is working seldom even suggests the ethereal. Moreover, the artist must work in a recognized or recognizable style. "Styleless pictures no more exist than do wordless thoughts" (André Malraux).

Or we look into the face of an Artur Rubinstein. We see there reflected something that we call spirit. But how did the pianist acquire that spirit?

Through ceaseless disciplining of his fingers, through his fingers manipulating little wooden keys that in turn strike steel wires.

Again, a poet is a blithe spirit who transports us to the very gates of heaven. But the poet uses words that can be made winged words only by means of the tongue, the lips, the throat. These words ordinarily must obey socially accepted rules of syntax in order to communicate meaning, or they must violate these rules in a special way if the poet wishes to frustrate us with meaninglessness. And the meanings refer to things and experiences. The poet must achieve rhythm, a rhythm that has some magical correlation with the heartbeat or with the rhythm of respiration. Poetry is *expression*. Outside Thomas Gray's "Elegy" there are no "mute inglorious Miltons." A mute Milton is simply not a Milton; he is a mute.

But when we turn to consider our life in society we find many people who seemingly forget these facts of the human order, who forget that the human being is a little *lower* than the angels. Religion is thought of as being something wholly spiritual and individual, as lifting us to higher levels of apprehension and enjoyment than are possible in the world of things and of rites and ceremonies. Sometimes this yearning for spirituality resorts to such extravagance as to claim that religion has nothing to do with material concerns, that it is something purely inward and has to do only with the soul. Some people even say that religion needs no external forms or social institutions. Indeed, we are frequently told that outward form only kills religion, that outward forms are mere trappings.

But here again, as with music and poetry and architecture, religion must be seen, touched, voiced, heard, in order to be identified or expressed. A religion that has nothing to do with the body, with the life of the senses, with outward communal forms of expression, does not exist except in the imagination. As Cardinal John Henry Newman put it, religion must express itself in particular acts. It develops in ways similar to the other concerns of life, through social forms, through books, music, the spoken word, spoken prayers, church building, through sacrificial action. To claim to be religious and also not to be interested in these things is like saying that one is interested in poetry but in no specific poems; it is like saying that one believes in government but not in legislatures and ballot boxes, that one is interested in education but not in schools. There is no such thing as poetry apart from poems; there is no such thing as government apart from constitutions or courts or police, no such thing as education without the disciplines of education.

The religion that is purely spiritual is purely nonexistent. We often hear it said that the greatest enemy of religion is materialism. This is by no means true. The greatest enemy of religion is sham spirituality, pure spirituality. It is angelism, an indifference to the needs of the body and especially of the body politic. Religion must be realized in particular acts in order to insure its continuing alive. This is the reason Cardinal Newman asserted that we cannot respect religion and insult its forms of expression. In short, angelism can kill religion.

But I am not especially concerned here to derive a defense of institutional religion from the medieval angelology. The general principles implicit in the human condition have a far-reaching application to the *whole* of our life. The good life must be realized in particular acts in order to exist at all. The angel is already perfect. He is only commanded to maintain his status, else he will descend into the pit with Lucifer, the fallen angel.

We have already observed that Aquinas emphasizes the idea that, unlike the angels, human beings live in a world of time and space and matter: they are compounded of spirit and flesh, their creativity appears when they mold the vitality and concreteness of things into form. An equally striking contrast between the human being and the angel is evident from the fact that whereas according to Aquinas each angel is the sole member of its species, the human being belongs to a species in which there are countless other members. The meaning of existence depends therefore upon the quality of one's relatedness to others. This fact is obvious enough, you may say. Human existence involves a relatedness among persons. But this relatedness of persons is not only immediately interpersonal. Human existence obtains also within a framework of institutions, within the context of suprapersonal forces and patterns. Accordingly, one must estimate a human being in terms of the kind of institutions, the kind of family, the kind of schools, the kind of race relations, the kind of industrial system, the kind of state one promotes. This means that the character of loyalties and ideas is in part determined by the kind of influence exercised upon the institutions in which one lives. There is no such thing as a good person as such. One will be a good person only as a good student in school, as a good husband or wife, a good doctor, a good lawyer, a good citizen, a good churchperson. A person whose quality does not positively express itself in the institutions of family, school, industry, church, and state, is one who is good for nothing. Virtue is not a cloistered thing except among the angels. If we wish to see what the human spirit is, we must look around us at the world of objective spirit. To a large degree we are the institutions we make.

The grim, destructive aspects of the world around us, of the world we have made, help us to understand why John Calvin in preaching on the Eighth Psalm asserted that God created man a little lower than the angels, but that man fell from grace and is now little higher than the devils. We cannot with impunity ignore the fact that we must learn from experience, that we are members of a many-numbered species, that we live in a world of things that must be cooperatively shared and shaped for significant ends that express and fulfill human nature. Probably Pascal had these facts of human life in mind when he asserted that a person who sets out to be an angel will end only in becoming a beast.

Angelism, that is, indifference to the concerns and needs of the body politic and of the common life, produces the loneliness, the alienation, the thingification of the person, the loss of human fellowship which the literature of our day so passionately laments. It makes men and women become antiheroes; it in the end makes them say with the antihero of Sartre's play, "Hell is—other people."

One way we can begin to overcome the angelism among us is to become *personally* acquainted with the actual conditions, with the people around us, and especially with those who are suffering. Then only does deep speak to deep. Then only do we come to *cherish* our common humanity and our common responsibility before God. This cherishing of our common humanity, this responsibility before God, is not an optional luxury. It is the imperative of affirmative religion.

In Chicago some years ago this fact was impressed upon me when in my neighborhood a School for Religious Living was conducted by the local churches and synagogues. One section of this school of citizens was assigned to the task of studying the problem of relief, a problem that always confronts us in some fashion, and today particularly in the area of race relations. At an early meeting of this section, a man describing himself as a "conservative" arose to protest against there being any system of relief at all. He used the familiar argument: "I have worked hard and I have saved my money; but now, along comes the government and takes my money and gives it to these people who won't work." Nonetheless the man was persuaded to work with the committee and to call personally on the people "across the tracks." He visited family after family, saw children without proper food or housing, without shoes; he saw fathers who were ill, saw emaciated mothers trying to maintain something of human dignity in the midst of poverty and degradation. Gradually, his attitude began to change. He was becoming acquainted with some strange fellow creatures of his own species. Finally, one evening at a meeting of the people of our neighborhood, he heard a young mother (whom he had visited) retell her story. She was only thirty-five years old but she looked to be fifty, she was poorly clothed, she had a few teeth left, and she was already hunchbacked from her strenuous life. Suddenly, the conservative became indignant in face of our common failure to conserve human values. He jumped to his feet and almost shouted, "Why do you people stand for this? *I* wouldn't do it. I would steal first. I want to know why you don't have the spunk to start a revolution?" Today these questions are being asked with increasing pungency in the economically less developed countries of the world. That evening a man was converted to human fellowship. He identified himself with the need of others, and thus he overcame his alienation. He got mad about our inhumanity to one another. Let us hope (as Bishop McConnell would say) that he stayed mad. And let us hope that he went on to organize his indignation. The moral is clear. The meaning of life is fulfilled only by those who enter the struggle for justice in history and community. Any other way is the way of loneliness, of alienation from each other, and it leads us to the feeling that "hell is other people," knowing the while that it is in ourselves. For the spirit of affirmative religion, let us then invoke the spirit of Milton when he said:

> I cannot praise a fugitive and cloistered virtue, unexercised and unbreathed, that never sallies forth and sees her adversary, but slinks out of the race, where that immortal garland is to be run for, not without dust and heat. That virtue therefore which is but a youngling in the contemplation of evil, and knows not the utmost that vice promises to her followers, and rejects it, is but a blank virtue, not a pure.

19 · Freud, Mannheim, and the Liberal Doctrine of Human Being

For a long time now liberals have been saying that religious liberalism needs a new doctrine of human being. Some liberals who recognize this need want a restatement of the historic doctrines of liberalism, in terms of contemporary thought. Others hold that we need to explore again those ideas of the Christian tradition which liberalism has to its detriment either lost or perverted. Still others believe that the new insights of biology, psychology, and sociology should now be assimilated, with a view to modifying outmoded liberal doctrines of the past. All three of these points of view are fully justified.

Two significant intellectual movements (for which the names of Sigmund Freud and Karl Mannheim may be taken as symbols) have been carrying on an investigation of the validity of eighteenth- and nineteenth-century rationalistic and idealistic conceptions of human nature and society. Neither movement, to be sure, represents a repudiation of basic confidence in humanity or of the guiding role of reason in human life. But both movements have shown that there is a great deal more in the human psyche than was ever dreamed of by the rationalist philosophers. And this "good deal more" they characterize as the deeper, darker, irrational (and even unconscious) forces, forces that erupt into the human consciousness and into society, bringing in their train both peril and opportunity. It would be wrong, however, to suppose that these movements present wholly new emphases. In general, they may be characterized as a continuation of the voluntarist tradition of U.S. and European thought which reaches back through Dewey, James, Charles Peirce, Marx, Schopenhauer, Friedrich Schelling, Kant, Jakob Böhme, and Luther to Duns Scotus. Indeed, one can trace the line on back through Augustine to the Bible and to early Greek philosophy.

Edwin Ewart Aubrey of the Divinity School in the University of Chicago has recently published a book (*Man's Search for Himself,* 1940) that may be taken as representative of this tendency to supplement the rationalist

This essay was originally published in *The Journal of Liberal Religion* 2, no. 3 (Winter 1941).

approach. This book provides stimulating insights concerning the nature of human nature, insights drawn from a fresh consideration of both contemporary social science and historic Christian theology. Of special interest is Professor Aubrey's discussion of the inadequacies of the old rationalistic liberalism. He holds that "personality is grounded in something which is deeper than reason can penetrate or concepts communicate, which foundation has cosmic status and antedates the emergence of human society." He goes on to say that "such a substructure need not be anti-rational; and, indeed, so far as rational communication can and does enrich community, such a substratum must be congenial to reason." The upshot of this emphasis is that "man in search of himself" will surely go astray unless he recognizes that "the thinking person is much broader than the impoverished 'rational man' of the Enlightenment."

Now, what are the implications of these ideas for the liberal conception of human being? The answer to this question is one of the central needs of our generation, and it will require more than a generation to find it. Nevertheless, it may be well for us to attempt a brief statement of the principal considerations relevant for the new liberal doctrine of human being. Certain of these items could, of course, be stated in theological terms (indeed, this also is a pressing need—a need to which Professor Aubrey has addressed himself), but at the moment we shall restrict ourselves mainly to the language of social psychology.

1. Human nature (and with it existence in general) must be interpreted dialectically. Humans possess a fundamental contradiction in their nature: they are conditioned by inner and outer nonrational forces, and yet through the exercise of freedom they may in some measure transcend this conditioning. The old liberalism in its basically nontragical view of life had a very attenuated awareness of the power of the nonrational and the irrational elements in life and thus also a feeble sense of both the full resources for and the obstacles to the achievement of freedom. Both Mannheim and Freud have increased our awareness in these areas. Especially significant is Mannheim's recent attempt to develop a sociology of knowledge. The presupposition of this attempt is the belief that humans can achieve meaningful freedom only by detecting the ways in which they are biased through social conditioning and interest, and by transcending these "situation-bound tendencies." Hence, the Freudian concept of "rationalization" and the Marxian concept of ideology as refined by Mannheim (a conception long ago set forth in Luther's idea of the "man-made God"), must be employed as constant correctives for (bourgeois or proletarian) complacency and self-

absolutization. Yet, these correctives should not be allowed to destroy the courageous dynamic of what Mannheim calls "utopian" (i.e., progressive) action. Faith in the possibility of achieving human fulfillment and community must be maintained. This leads us to a consideration of the means of fulfillment.

2. The bonds of society are nonrational and imaginative as well as rational, unconscious as well as conscious. The old liberalism attached too great a significance, indeed, it laid too great a burden upon, the rational and conscious intellectual life. A person's whole nature and profoundest loyalties can be expressed only in imaginative, emotive symbols that will release and give direction to the deepest tensions of the human psyche and of society at large. The atomization of our society and the social distances that we now suffer from can only be overcome by means of rationally criticized but deeply affective institutional patterns that bring persons together into creative community. (This, of course, raises the whole problem of leadership, a problem that Mannheim relates to the question of the nature and function of the elites who "manipulate" the symbols.) The atomization of our society is due not only to the perennial combativeness of humans, but also to the increasingly rigid stratification of society into widely separated classes and specializations. This consideration leads us to an aspect of the doctrine of human being which has to do with the particular historical situation in which modern humanity finds itself.

3. The irrational element in human nature manifests itself largely in accordance with the pressures and needs peculiar to a given society or historical situation. One main source of the irrationality of human behavior in our day is the oppression and frustration that issue from concentration of power (and the consequent prostitution of the elites) and from the exclusion of average men and women from voluntary and meaningful participation in the activities appropriate to a free society. The older liberal doctrine of human being was egregiously deficient insofar as its theory of freedom viewed the individual as an atomic datum, choosing goals quite freely and setting out to achieve them. As Eduard Lindeman has pointed out, freedom involves not only freedom from coercion but also "freedom with," freedom to participate in a common institutional life that provides criticism, guidance, and group support. People who are not able or are not permitted to make decisions concerning the basic values and ends of life become less than human and resort to irrational and destructive expedients and expediencies. Freedom presupposes the will to be free, a tolerable minimum of economic security, and dynamic social purpose and responsibility. People who have lost these things very readily surrender their freedom to a

"leader." They set up "substitute goals," such as military glory, racial pride, class pride, escapist eroticism, and ecstatic utopianism.

Thus, no doctrine of human being that purports to analyze behavior or recommend suitable action is adequate that does not take into account the effect the particular structure (the *principia media*) of society at a given period has upon its constituents. This statement has two major implications. First, the ways human nature will act at a given moment are not to be attributed solely either to humanity's original virtue or its original sin. The tensions set up by the general social and spiritual situation largely determine how much of the beast, how much of the automaton, and how much of the divine spark in the human being shall find expression. Second (and consequently), merely general pronouncements concerning human virtue or familial love will do little to relieve tensions and resolve conflict. To be sure, accidental human wants must not be uncritically accepted as final and adequate. That is, ultimate value postulates and loyalty to them are indispensable. But they can be implemented only if we learn how to apply them to the unique historical situation in which we find ourselves. Without explicit knowledge of the conditions under which meaningful social changes take place, these values will have little opportunity for expression, except through some inner "spiritual" opium eating or through a privileged and splendid isolation.

This means that any adequate doctrine of human nature today must include an orientation to the future, different from that of the old liberalism. What Mannheim and thinkers like him suggest is that we are now passing from the old form of laissez-faire, semidemocratic, "individualist" society to a society that will be economically highly developed and that will be politically an *organized* mass democracy. In this new society, a long-term and large-scale planning will be necessary. The present world crisis must be interpreted as the prelude either to a totalitarianism that will crush all individual freedom or to a new kind of society in which the enclaves of freedom will be planned and brought into being in the teeth of an irrationalism that is equally destructive in its tendency, whether it come from the conservatives or from the revolt of the masses. If we cannot combine democratic planning and democratic freedom, then both will go. Thus, the old laissez-faire individualism must be viewed as a transitional phase between a medieval feudal structure of society and a new, planned society. Whether that new society will be free or totalitarian will be determined by the strength or weakness of the liberal faith in humanity and in the creative depths of the cosmos itself.

20 · The Lure of Persuasion: Some Themes from Whitehead

It is a common experience for us readily to remember from the lectures or conversations of eminent persons some anecdotes out of their experience and of their own telling. This kind of recollection is especially prevalent among the pupils of Alfred North Whitehead, a lecturer and conversationalist possessing a notable gift for shaping brilliant aphorism and illustrative narrative.

I recall a story Professor Whitehead told in class one day years ago at Harvard. Speaking of John Maynard Keynes, who had been his classmate at Cambridge University, Professor Whitehead said that when he was a student Keynes announced that as a scholar he did not intend to remain at the university, where he would be obliged to climb the tortuous ladder of academic and administrative advancement. No, after graduation he would go up to London, earn two or three million pounds, and then return to Cambridge and achieve his goal despite the bureaucracy. I shall not forget the triumphant, climactic tone in Professor Whitehead's voice when he concluded the story, saying, in rising inflection, "And, by George, he *did* it." The story illustrates a favorite idea in Whitehead's writings, that significant innovation requires that one shall boldly break through the grooves of conventional routine. A major concern of Whitehead was to grasp the nature of a world in which novelty occurs.

Another characteristic concern of Whitehead was his desire to show the decisive role of "feeling" in human existence and indeed in all actualities— he also calls it "prehension." But feeling is not possible without a physical body. Related to feeling and body, however, is the esthetic dimension or thrust of human striving and appreciation. Let me illustrate in a preliminary way the complex relation between feeling, body, and beauty by summoning a prehension of that sublime sculpture by Michelangelo, the *Pietà* (the deposition of Christ), now in Florence. Here the bent, inert body of Christ is supported vertically under the arms of two figures, Mary Magdalene and Mary the Mother, while a fourth person behind Christ,

This essay was originally published in *The Unitarian Universalist Christian* 30, no. 4 (1975–76). Reprinted by permission.

Nicodemus, dominates the group. Most affecting in sculpture is Michelangelo's depiction of intense and varied feeling in the attitudes of the three living persons to Christ. His body seems to be slipping down, and the Virgin with her eyes closed, transfigured by transcendent rapture, receives him into her arms. Their two heads touch. Mary Magdalene, vigorous and firm, full of vitality, yet dazed in visage, kneels on the other side of the dead body, supporting it with her extended arms. Nicodemus, bearing up the two women, looks down upon the group with quietly meditative, yet sustaining, compassion, the very personification of divine Providence. As Charles de Tornay observes, the whole gestalt resembles a slender cone. In this group of interrelated figures, chiseled out of stone, one senses the stresses and strains of weight and emotion, but also an embracing balance and harmony. It has been said that the cowled, bearded figure of Nicodemus is a portrait of the aged artist himself—and "an expression of his deepened faith." The profound tenderness in the face of Nicodemus may be taken not only as the artist's vision of suffering suffused with love but also as the persistent working of divine grace. When one recalls the lives of the two Marys and of Nicodemus, and the life and death of Christ, this work of imagination in stone conveys the sum and substance of essential human- ity and its possibilities. Feeling, body, and beauty are seen to be indispens- able ingredients not only in the work of art but also in life itself. Novelty, feeling, body, and the tender, divine persuasion—there we have also major elements in Whitehead's vision of meaningful existence.

DIVINE PERSUASION

For Whitehead, persuasion is the authentic energizing power in human affairs, persuasion in the sense of persuasive attraction. More than that, it constitutes the essential relation between God and human being. Although God cannot force human action, he can affect it by the lure of persuasion. So it is that Whitehead affirms the crucial, creative significance of persuasion in the history of religion and civilization. "The creation of civilized order," he says, "is the victory of persuasion over force."

Here Whitehead seems to place himself in a mainstream of Western philosophy. Aristotle's God as the Unmoved Mover energizes the world of potentiality by the power of attraction. But Whitehead does not accept the Aristotelian view, for the Unmoved Mover is insulated from the conflicts and sufferings of humanity. Nor does he think of God as the personification of moral energy; such a view Whitehead finds in the Old Testament—it makes of God a "ruthless moralist." Nor does he accept the idea that God is

Pietà, by Michelangelo
Ŝan Maria del Fiore di Firenze
Alinari/Art Resource (Brogi) 3524 (Used by permission)

a ruler, for this view assigns to God the attributes of Caesar. Most of all he objects to this Caesar God, "the old ferocious God . . ., the Oriental despot, the Pharaoh, the Hitler, with everything to enforce obedience, from infant damnation to eternal punishment"—"an abyss of horror." He holds that the divine is to be associated rather with "the tender elements of the world, which slowly and in quietness operate by love. . . . Love neither rules, nor is it unmoved; also it is a little oblivious to morals." The human being is not driven but rather is lured by the divine persuasion. "If I be lifted up, I shall draw all men unto me." In the light of this view we are to understand Whitehead's statement that "the power of God is the worship he inspires." Worship is "a surrender to the claim for assimilation, urged with the motive force of mutual love."

It is in Plato rather than in Aristotle that Whitehead finds the fountain-head, in the idea that the divine element in the world is to be conceived as a persuasive and not as a coercive agency.

Whitehead views this insight to be one of the greatest intellectual discoveries in the history of religion. In this first phase of development, however, Plato wavers inconsistently between the conception of the divine as persuasive agency and of the divine as the final coercive force. The second phase moves from theory to act, the appeal to the life of Christ as a revelation of the nature of God and of agency in the world.

> The Mother, the Child, and the bare manger; the lowly man, homeless and self-forgetful, with his message of peace, love, and sympathy: the suffering, the agony, the tender words as life ebbed, the final despair: and the whole with the authority of supreme victory.

Here we see the Michelangelo *Pietà* as the summation of this phase.

The third phase was again intellectual—in the formation of early Christian theology by the schools of thought mainly associated with Alexandria and Antioch. These theologians improve upon Plato by asserting "the direct immanence of God in the World generally." In a doctrine of Christ and of the Holy Spirit they look toward giving "a rational account of the role of the persuasive agency of God." But this vision was subsequently submerged in a doctrine of God as the one absolute, omnipotent, omniscient source of all being, his own existence requiring no relations to anything beyond himself. Direct immanence in the world became logically impossible. God became again the absolute despot of tradition. The continuing problem is that of understanding the divine as immanent within the transiency and the striving and suffering of the world; it is that of discerning the religious vision of persuasion as the authentic, driving force of philosophy.

These formulations presuppose and bring to a focus Whitehead's view of the world, human being, and God. Most important is the idea that the world and humanity are in process of development. They are in the making. Moreover, everything in the world is related to everything else. That is, everything somehow influences everything else (though immediately contemporary events may be independent of each other). Expounding this idea, the late Dean Samuel H. Miller was wont to say, "When we live by denials, or by anger, or by love—or by any activity whatsoever—we are changing the universe and changing it at much greater distances than we have any idea of." God exercises influence upon us in many ways, but he is also affected by the ways in which we unpredictably use and abuse our freedom. This process of influencing and of being influenced as it takes place in the world should not be viewed as a ceaseless churning of static ingredients. The components of the world in influencing each other modify each other, and through creativity they give rise to novelty. This process exhibits pervasive structures.

Whitehead views the ongoing process as the life of growing organisms. The world as a whole is an organism, and its component parts are also organisms. Ours is a living universe nerved by creativity. Accordingly, Whitehead calls his total outlook a philosophy of organism. It is also called a philosophy of creativity, a process philosophy, a philosophy of becoming in contrast to a philosophy of being. In this view the concept of "becoming" refers to a more concrete reality than do abstractions about being which tend to reduce the reality to something static. God is not a static, self-contained, and self-centered being; nor is the world or human being something self-contained belonging to a fixed order.

ROOT METAPHORS

In using the concept of organism Whitehead deliberately employs a metaphor, that is, he employs a method of analogy. This is an age-old method, for in much of human thought analogies represent a major means of interpreting the world, human being, and God, a major way of conceptualizing and communicating human experience. For a moment we should examine this method in the context of its history. The use of analogy involves the selection of a concept from one area of experience (e.g., from the realm of mathematics, biology, psychology) and applying it to other areas. Whitehead calls this the method of imaginative construction or rationalization; it is a means whereby rationality is traced through the various aspects or levels of reality. A simple example is the popular use of the term "the fabric of society," a metaphor taken from the structure of textiles. Metaphors are used in this way not only in the natural sciences but also in political and economic theory, in poetry and religion—and metaphysics. A metaphor that dominated the Middle Ages was the concept of hierarchy. Hierarchy in human society was claimed to be in accord with a hierarchy, a great chain, of being. Two and three centuries ago people spoke of the world as a machine. They called even the human being a machine. Darwin gave wide currency to the concept of evolution to describe the origin and development of species. For a century and more thereafter the concept was by analogy applied to the history of culture. It became a great cultural "myth." Scores of books were written to trace the "evolution" of technology, of the arts (for example, music and even the sonata and the symphony), of philosophy, of the Bible and of religion in general. But initially the concept was derived from biology. The principle of analogy figures largely, even inevitably, in religious discourse, for here a concept from some sphere of finite human experience is used to characterize the infinite. In the Bible God is spoken of as *king* and he makes a *covenant* with his people, concepts derived from the sphere of politics. Or he is spoken of as *father* or *mother* or *bridegroom*—domestic metaphors. We may say also that metaphor and simile are the life or substance of poetry. Samuel Taylor Coleridge, the poet and philosopher, spoke of the use of metaphor as the esemplastic power of poets, their capacity to shape diverse elements of experience into a unity. And we should add here that major social philosophies in history take the form of an expanded metaphor—covenant, Kingdom of God, drama (Augustine's Two Cities), organism, machine.

In Whitehead's view a crucial decision for metaphysicians is their *selection* of metaphor. Thus they themselves select the concept of organism from the sphere of biology and modify it in order to apply it to all processes in the cosmos, including of course phenomena of the human level of experience. We shall see presently that Whitehead makes use also of metaphors taken from psychology, concepts such as perception, feeling, and appetition. In his view the metaphor enables one to see parallel structures or unities— elements of order in process—throughout the whole range of reality, in the world of nature and human nature, in the individual human organism and in societies of organisms. Indeed, even the word *society* is a metaphor when it is used to characterize the relations between events in the cosmos, or between cells in the body. With similar metaphorical intention Whitehead on occasion has spoken of a tree as a democracy.

In describing this metaphorical method Whitehead employs an ingenious simile. He says that the method of imaginative rationalization is like the flight of an airplane. "It starts from the ground of particular observation; it makes a flight in the thin air of imaginative generalization; and it again lands for renewed observation rendered acute by rational interpretation." By this kind of "imaginative thought" he finds common, pervasive factors in the world.

In the light of his concern with process Whitehead generally intends to interpret any philosophical metaphor in a dynamic fashion appropriate for a philosophy of becoming, that is, in a way that emphasizes order *and* freedom, the openness of structures to the emergence of novelty. His stress upon process is evident in his interpretation of the concept of "organism." Here we may observe a certain contrast between his use of the concept and the use made by Aristotelians, whose school of thought has been fond of biological metaphors. Aristotle's outlook, however, as interpreted by medieval Jewish and Christian thinkers, became more of a theology of being than a theology of becoming. Whitehead rejects this tendency as it appears in the Aristotelian-Thomist system with its concepts of subject and predicate, essence and existence, substance and accident, matter and form. At the beginning of the present century some Roman Catholic philosophers also began to turn away from this outlook or at least to give a more dynamic interpretation of Aquinas. Later on, Teilhard de Chardin's process philosophy in its thrust, if not in its formulations, may be compared to the process philosophy of Whitehead.

We should note something further here about the antecedents of Whitehead's process philosophy. The interpretation of the world as in constant process reminds one of Heraclitus, the Greek philosopher for whom everything is in flux. This affinity is the more evident if we recall that Heraclitus also sought for structure (*logos*) in the flux. Or one might think of the Hegelian school with its conception of dialectical process, particularly in view of the fact that Hegel also made use of the idea that the process is ever moving toward new syntheses. But Whitehead held that the Hegelian notion of dialectical process is too neat, something imposed in a priori fashion on reality. In the main, however, one should "locate" Whitehead in the line of Charles Darwin and Henri Bergson, author of *Creative Evolution*, a line that includes Lloyd Morgan, S. Alexander, Charles S. Peirce, William James, and John Dewey. (Whitehead's view has been spoken of as

"Bergsonized Platonism.") Indeed, by reason of the wide influence of this line of thought we may say that the idea of process and the idea of creativity are quite characteristic of our age. We cannot pause here to examine the relations between this emphasis in modern thought and the cultural mobility of a technological, urbanizing society with its rapid social change, its radical criticism of mere traditionalism, its use of scientific method, its speed in transportation, its "instant" means of communication, and its increasing interdependence. Actually, however, the philosophical problems with which Whitehead was concerned antedate by centuries the appearance of the technological society.

Another feature of the modern, dynamic cultural situation is of special significance for understanding Whitehead's method. One readily associates the aspects of modern society we have just mentioned with the process of secularization. Although Whitehead's philosophy in its outcome is a religious philosophy, it is in important respects a secular philosophy. Indeed, he speaks of the urgency of secularizing "the concept of God's functions in the world." God is not something "out there"; he must be understood in relation to what goes on here and now in the midst of the creative process. When Whitehead speaks of God, moreover, he does not presuppose some special, esoteric experience. His intention is to appeal to and to interpret common experience. He does not exclude what has been called "religious experience"; but he does not believe it to be indispensable. At the same time he does rely on the sort of intuition which in esemplastic fashion integrates human experience in its richness, its depth, and its diversity.

As a secular philosopher Whitehead aims to speak as a modern person and to modern people. His method, he holds, is fundamentally empirical. "Nothing can be omitted, experience drunk and experience sober . . ., experience intellectual and experience physical, experience religious and experience skeptical. . . ." Also in the name of empiricism he says that "actual entities" (or "actual occasions") are the final real things of which the world is made up. There is no going beyond or behind actual entities "to find anything more real. . . . God is an actual entity."

In employing an empirical method, however, Whitehead seeks rationality or structure in the actual occasions and logical coherence in the formulation of generalizations. Here again we encounter his use of the method of imaginative rationality. But the generalizations must refer back to empirical evidence, though one must grant that empirical evidence is subject to dispute. Moreover, generalizations can go askew and distort the reality. Whitehead therefore aims to avoid the oversimplifications of rationalism.

He was wont to say that if one has a perfectly clear and distinct idea about human experience, one should immediately see a red light of warning that one is getting away from the realities. As a process philosopher he claims no finality for his own outlook. "There are always heights beyond," he says, "which block our vision." He insists that his own conception of the world and God is a speculative interpretation, but that as such it aims to take the facts into account as they are evident in the different spheres of experience. For this reason he reflects upon the findings of the various sciences that explore these different areas of experience. Here one may see some analogy between Whitehead's scope and Paul Tillich's in his *System of the Sciences*.

We have set forth this sketch of the general features and the method of Whitehead's process philosophy in order to grasp within its context his conception of persuasion, a conception that of course is only one of the motifs of his outlook. In order now to approach the theory of persuasion we must look more closely at three aspects of this process philosophy, first at the idea of novelty, second at the conception of human being and the world, and third at the idea of God.

Novelty and Synthesis

"The universe is a creative advance into novelty," Whitehead writes. For him a crucial fact of human experience is the awareness of ever new possibilities. Another way of saying this is that Whitehead takes time seriously. Only in a word of time can novelty appear. This recognition of the element of novelty in the time process involves two or three things that are of special significance in process philosophy. First, the events of the world (and the cosmos) in their interrelations of mutual influence do not repeat themselves. In a world of becoming they are always unique. No two events are identical. Time and change are real. This means that events are successive and not repetitive. We should pause here to observe that this kind of awareness of time and novelty is peculiarly evident in the Bible. The primary rhetoric of the Bible is narrative. It is declarative before it is imperative. Even when it becomes admonition the admonition is generally related to *events*, past, present, or future. "And it came to pass" is a characteristic phrase in the Bible. Events follow one another, ever unfolding something new, something unexpected. We may add here that for Whitehead an analogous process giving birth to novelty takes place in subhuman nature, though the time span for the emergence of novelty is a long one. Novelty takes place, then, in an event-ful world.

A second aspect of novelty is related to the nature of events. Every event has its peculiar character, its thisness, its definiteness. There is no such thing as an event in general, any more than there is such a thing as a poem in general. Accordingly, novelty always has specificity, individuality. An event is *this* event and not *that* one. Moreover, there is a certain freshness about events. Whitehead epitomizes the miraculous glow of this process of individuation in his famous aphorism, "Definition is the *soul* of actuality."

The third aspect of novelty is that the drive toward novelty is a drive toward integration of diverse elements, a drive toward a new unity, a new creative synthesis—again, the esthetic dimension. Not that every novelty achieves integration. Yet, events are not only going on, they are also going somewhere. Insofar as human intention plays a role they take a "route" toward the achievement of a goal. To be sure, the end intended may change in the light of experience. This change itself, however, exhibits novelty.

But significant change is not something easy to come by. Every unit in the cosmos, also every person and group, is rooted in a past that persists in some kind of continuity and indeed with stubbornness and compulsoriness. This "causal efficacy," this efficient causation, is at the same time a staff or comfort and a burden, an impediment, an occasion for frustration. The past has its own laws so to speak; but the actual occasions enjoy some degree of creativity and freedom. That is the mystery of the universe's "creative advance into novelty."

All of these aspects of novelty relate to the process of persuasion and thus also to the process of the divine persuasion. This means of course that novelty must be understood in terms of a conception of God and of human being and the world. It would be very convenient if we could simply examine these conceptions in turn. Actually, however, they so much involve each other that when we speak of the one we are at least by implication suggesting something about the others. But there is a more Whiteheadian reason for this interweaving of the understanding of human being, the world, and God. This reason we have already mentioned in our reference to his method of imaginative rationality. He seeks to understand persuasion (and everything else for that matter) in terms of basic qualities or factors that pervade the entire cosmos and that in a fashion are present in God himself as their chief exemplification.

But there is another reason, a deeper reason, a religious reason, for Whitehead's concern for these pervasive factors. One might say that the reason is that as a metaphysician he wishes to construct a system of thought which will provide an integrated conception of reality. Here the concern may be thought of as a desire for the *explanation* of what life and the world are. But this reason for his interest in persuasion and in its relation to the whole of things does not take the full measure of his concern. It would be more adequate to say that his primary concern is to catch and communicate a religious vision of the meaning of life, indeed to grasp and communicate "a vision of greatness." This vision, he is convinced, has to do with something more than the life of the individual, although at one point he does define religion as what the individual "does with his solitariness." This often-quoted and misunderstood maxim should not be taken out of context. It is followed on the next page by the succinct statement, "Religion is world-loyalty." In short, it is concerned with what individuals and groups do with their solitariness in relationship—with their togetherness. It has to do with the creative process through which human existence in its togetherness moves toward fulfillment in joy and peace. This meaningful togetherness involves the human being as a creature in nature, as a member of the human species, as a pilgrim in time and eternity, and as depending for courage, refreshment, and transformation upon a divine resource and companion. This concern for meaningful togetherness informs his conception of persuasion offering attraction leading to significant novelty. This concern becomes evident in his conception of feeling as the basis of all experience, for one may say that feeling as he defines it is the link that binds the world together but that also manifests differentiation, contrast, and conflict. In a sense it is more important than order, for it can make of order something more than "law and order."

The Emotional Basis of All Experience

We have already referred to Whitehead's philosophy as a process philosophy and as a philosophy of organism, according to which everything is in movement and is also related to everything else in a growing process. Now we must ask the question, What are the ingredient elements in this organic process?

If Whitehead draws upon the sphere of biology for this conception of organic process, he turns to psychology for his root metaphor to describe the ingredient elements or units in the process. He envisages everything in the universe in terms of the "experience of subjects." "Apart from the experience of subjects," he says, "there is nothing, nothing, nothing, bare nothingness." It would be too much to say that in Whitehead's view the universe is made up of selves in the subhuman as well as in the human sphere. It would be more accurate to say that certain aspects of the self are found everywhere, specifically perception or feeling, appetition, and mentality.

In emphasizing the word *feeling* Whitehead appeals to everyday experience. He holds that we have not adequately understood human nature when we have tried to interpret it in terms of merely rational or conscious or visual experience. In experience that is fully alive we come to an emotional, throbbing acquaintance with reality and with others, in contrast to possessing distant knowledge about them, knowledge remotely abstracted from feeling. William James called it "acquaintance with" in contrast to "knowledge about."

Now, in Whitehead's view "feeling" attaches not only to human experience; it belongs to all existence, to all entities—indeed it constitutes some unity in each entity. It is a cosmic phenomenon, alive in atoms, minerals, animals, human beings—and also in God. Whitehead is not the first philosopher to have attempted to conceptualize the unit-entities in terms of feeling. Because of the strangeness of the idea, however, readers may need momentarily to exercise what Coleridge called a willing suspension of disbelief in order to accommodate themselves to this use of the term *feeling* and to grasp in a preliminary way what is meant by it.

This word is perhaps the one that most readily comes to mind when we try to analyze our own immediate experience of ourselves and of surrounding realities. We are at all times "taking in" the world through feeling. Whitehead sees more than this in the process. He says that in the process of grasping and fusing into units the buzzing, blooming confusion coming to us from events, whether internal or external, we are achieving our own individuality. Feeling in this sense is a sort of integration of the data of experience.

This concept of feeling is so to speak "radicalized" by Whitehead when he discerns feeling in all entities in their interrelatedness. At this level there is no suggestion of consciousness or of perception that achieves representational quality. Moreover, the concept is applied only to unit-becomings. Chairs and tables do not "feel" in this sense: they consist of processes whose unit-becomings (molecules, atoms) are sentient.

In adopting this concept of feeling as a universal phenomenon Whitehead has rejected the conventional view that the higher levels of existence are to be understood in terms of the simpler and "lower"; he conceives of all levels, high and low, in terms of the human psyche, in this case in terms of feeling. Thus all entities are subjects having feelings. In accord with this anthropomorphic method—sometimes called pan-psychism—Whitehead reads a basic psychic element into all actualities, organic and inorganic, animate and inanimate (and even divine). This is what he has in mind when he speaks of feeling as generic to all actuality, or when he says, "The basis of all experience is emotional." He does not confine himself, however, to this anthropomorphic method. He sometimes uses the language of physics, and then he speaks of this rudimentary factor in all experience as the transference of energy. We shall see, moreover, that he does not interpret feeling in merely psychological terms.

Whitehead frequently uses the term *prehension* instead of the word *feeling*. The generic element in all experience is the capacity to take hold of or grasp other entities (other "subjects") and thus to be affected by them. We sometimes call this prehending process sensation, but Whitehead views it as richer, and indeed oftentimes vaguer and less conscious, than sensation. As with sensation, however, all feeling in its temporal origin is physical. The human being lives in a body, and through the body is in contact with the rest of the world. Physical experience is emotional. Even our memory of the past is informed by feeling that had its origin in experience related to the body or ultimately to things physical. With these presuppositions Whitehead asserts that the whole cosmos is "an ocean of feelings." It is made up of "units of feeling," units of prehending, droplets of experience. He calls them also actual entities and actual occasions; these throbs of feeling are the ultimate psychic components of the universe. Human beings, like most other subjects in nature, consist of societies of actual entities. The body is a society of these unit-entities.

But of course experience is not confined to physical experience, to bodily feelings. Mentality is also present. "An experience starts as that smelly feeling, and is developed by mentality into the feeling of that smell." Here appears not only feeling but also the *concept* of feeling. These are the two basic kinds of feeling: bodily feelings and conceptual feelings. Conceptual feelings appear by virtue of mentality (something present as structure in all entities); but they are bound up with bodily feelings. Body and mind are inseparable. Every event or occasion has a physical and a mental pole. These feelings require the body, and they may be feelings of the body itself as a datum or they may be feelings of data outside the body, including the feeling of other people's feelings (perhaps the most subtle feeling of all). They may be conscious or preconscious. In a strict sense, be it noted, all of these feelings are of something that is past or that has just passed. In this respect they are vectors from the past into the present. Every occasion carries within it feelings of the past, feelings of past feelings. Here something like memory obtains in all entities or societies of entities. Now we have three psychophysical factors: bodily feelings, conceptual feelings, and memory.

We have been speaking of feelings as they attach to all entities, in order to indicate Whitehead's application of his method of imaginative construction to all reality. What with our concern, however, to understand his conception of persuasion, we should now turn our attention primarily to the human person. Passing beyond the realm of physical and conceptual feelings as just described we encounter certain much more complex feelings experienced by the human person and by human groups. In face of the surrounding world the human person assumes an attitude toward the "events" that the initial feelings report. These events, as we have noted, may be physical objects or they may be other persons and especially the intentions of other persons. One evaluates these data by reacting with positive curiosity, with indifference, with relish, with repulsion, with fear, with anger, or with "mixed feelings." These reactions or attitudes are a different kind of feeling from the physical and conceptual feelings previously described. Whitehead calls this kind of feeling "subjective form." Obviously the subjective form, the reaction of the person to the experience of a datum, will be affected by the fundamental purposes or interests of that person. In Whitehead's terms, the subjective form will be conditioned by the subjective aim, the dominant purpose, of the person. And this subjective aim in turn will be oriented to larger ends or purposes such as truth, goodness, beauty. The prehension of these ends is a different kind of feeling from the ones we have previously mentioned. In this connection Whitehead makes still another distinction, that between positive and negative prehensions. A positive prehension is a feeling that a datum will contribute either intrinsically or instrumentally to the pursuance of the subjective aim of the person. In a positive prehension the datum, whether it be a feeling of someone else's feeling or a feeling for beauty or goodness, will be approved for inclusion in the development of the person. A negative prehension, on the other hand, is the exclusion of that element from the subject's internal constitution.

In reflecting upon basic feelings and upon subjective forms as well as upon subjective aims or purposes, the human person engages in abstraction. The kind of abstraction performed may be simply routine performance, perhaps an expression of a previous decision about these matters. Or it may be a new exercise of freedom; in short, the person may introduce novelty at just this point.

The description summarized here is obviously a highly simplified one. In actuality, the exercise of freedom requires the recognition of alternative possibilities. But prior to this recognition the human person confronts conflicts and contrarieties. These opposites may appear respectively in the various types of feeling, for example, in the person's feeling of another person's feelings or in the experience of one's own subjective reactions. And these feelings in turn will depend on the person's range of experience. If this range is narrow, then the subjective reactions may be relatively narrow or provincial. Presently we shall consider some examples of this sort of experience.

The point to be stressed here again is Whitehead's idea that there is an affective tone in all experience, and also the idea that all feelings depend ultimately on bodily feelings. He expresses those ideas in a striking way by saying that a person usually announces, "I am here," but that what is meant is, "I am here with my body and all its feelings."

Fulfillment and Enjoyment

We have previously noted some of the antecedents to Whitehead's process philosophy. Here we should observe that his emphasis on the role of feeling in human experience is in part due to the influence of the Romantic poets in their revulsion for the reductionism and the dryness of the rationalistic Enlightenment. Accordingly, Whitehead holds that the affective or emotional tone is characteristically attenuated in rationalistic liberalism and also in rationalistic orthodoxy. One might add here that insofar as emotional tone weakens in these types of rationalism, the likelihood is that a more vivid emotional tone is sought elsewhere (either surreptitiously or in a yearning for something more engaging).

What, actually, is the essential drive of a person's feelings regarding self, world, and the possibilities of self and world? It is not quite enough to say that it is a drive toward some sort of integration or unity. Behind this drive is an appetition. This appetition can be observed at all levels of reality and also in various modes (instinctive or reflective). Here Whitehead, as before, selects a feature of human psychic experience, and as in his exploring airplane he discovers it in other levels and areas of reality. In his view the fundamental appetition of the various entities is something given (by God), though the human person has the freedom to play variants on this given subject aim. The fundamental aim is that sort of fulfillment which provides enjoyment, an enjoyment in feeling which accompanies and finds intensification in the achievement of unity or harmony. But this enhancement of enjoyment and fulfillment does not follow from mere simplification of feeling. That way lies routine and boredom, the diminution of feeling.

In formulating the authentic goal of fulfillment Whitehead sets forth one of the unique features of his whole process philosophy of organism. He asserts that the fuller enjoyment issues from the feeling of unity in variety, of harmony or synthesis that embraces contrast. In short, his claim is that the ultimate goal is an esthetic goal. God "is the poet of the world, with tender patience leading it by his vision of truth, beauty and goodness." Human fulfillment issues from *Imitatio Dei*. Even ethics is to be understood in terms of esthetics, of unity in diversity. In this view of ethics as the achievement of unity or harmony embracing contrast one is reminded of the Pascal maxim: Practice opposite virtues and occupy the distance in between. If ethical behavior does not confront and embrace contrast, then life loses its zest and color. Strikingly enough, Whitehead even suggests that a *vivid* sense of the difference between one's actuality and one's unrealized ideals or possibilities generates an intensity of feeling which is esthetic in the sense here defined. This intensity of feeling is powerfully expressed in the Gospels. This view of the esthetic character of experience gives a special significance to novelty in Whitehead's process philosophy. The search of authentic human being is for an open unity, for a harmony that leaves open the way to novelty. The final recourse or criterion for humans is not reason, or traditional belief, or a glorious past, but rather the experience of moving toward a harmony that overcomes or unites diverse or contrasting elements in the world and the self. Here again togetherness takes on a special significance and quality. The attraction toward this goal is the divine persuasion.

In the light of this esthetic philosophy of process we can see that the human being is a creature for whom the enjoyment of zest is a built-in demand. Human dignity resides in the capacity for zest in bringing about new coordinations in personal existence and also in culture. That is, human dignity resides in the capacity to participate in a creative process, in short, in the capacity (as we have seen) to be transformed.

What is presupposed here is that human beings and values live in and through and from each other. We depend on each other's sensitivities and feelings. The sociality of experience comes through the "feeling of feeling," the feeling of our own situation with its possibilities, and also the feeling of other persons' feelings. The creative process, then, demands the continuing transformation of persons moving into significant novelty through creative interchange. This capacity to be transformed belongs not only to individuals but also to groups and societies. It is the nerve of civilization, leading "from force to persuasion."

Transformation requires power, two kinds of power. Both of these kinds of power are inherent in the process of becoming. If the civilizing transformation is to take place, the power to exercise an influence must become effective, but something more than this active power is required. The capacity to be influenced, a capacity to develop and respond to new sensitivities, is requisite. If we are to respond to a Jesus or a Plato or a Beethoven, if we are to respond to a new and liberating idea, or to give an old idea new application, we must be capable of being persuaded. Whitehead, following Plato and Locke, calls this passive power.

This whole process of transformation entails the exercise of freedom. Will and reason as well as feeling have their roles to play. Whitehead takes seriously the common experience that the individual has a significant degree of responsibility and freedom. This freedom becomes manifest, for example, in the way a person perceives and conceptualizes experience and in the internal decision regarding the direction to be taken in thought and action. In the process of exercising freedom the person becomes a self, and achieves self-identity. In this sense we "create ourselves" as we go, to be sure always in relation to others. The quality of the self-identity depends on the route taken. The self and the decision are created together. "What we choose is what we are," says the old hymn. This means that many choices may lead to perversion or deterioration or to mere routine and boredom; or they may lead toward increasing value and enjoyment. As a social being the human person confronts the possibilities of new coordinations and new unities in the midst of contrast. These coordinations fail to appear, however, if we become only defensive with respect to what has already been accomplished. "Advance or decadence are the only choices offered to mankind." "Life refuses to be embalmed alive." "Ideas won't keep. Something must be done with them." These often-quoted sentences from Whitehead bespeak his central conviction that the instant we stop adventuring we become merely routes of routine. We have lost the capacity to be persuaded into novelty.

But now the question must be raised, What does God do in the creative process? We have already given some indication of Whitehead's idea of God. Before we proceed further we must make some preliminary remarks that pertain to both "experience religious and experience skeptical." The person of religious faith, particularly one who accepts traditional formulations, is often prone to assume that God must be conceived in one special way. God must be a supernatural, transcendent being, or a ruler from the outside, or a performer of miracles. Accordingly, believers of this sort hold that any deviation from their preconceptions is to be rejected: it is not God. Skeptics for their part often presuppose a similar definition, and on the basis of this preconception profess disbelief. Partly because of these rigidities Whitehead asserts that "today there is but one dogma in debate: What do you mean by 'God'?" For his part he takes a dim view of the traditional conceptions of theism. Specifically, he finds completely unacceptable the notion that God is perfect and immutable in all respects, an entity already possessing maximal value. For one reason, such a God would be incapable of further enrichment; he would not, indeed he could not, be affected by anything that happens in the world of becoming. He would have one kind of power, the active power to influence the world, but be lacking in passive power, the capacity to be affected. At least, this is the logical position that traditional theism must take. As a consequence, this theism is not able to give theological significance to the world of becoming. Logically, human decision, good or evil, can make no difference to this kind of God. Moreover, by reason of its exclusively active power, the God of theism turns out to be either an imperial ruler or a ruthless moralist. In Whitehead's view this kind of "God-talk" is a "scandalous failure." His effort therefore is to work out a new way of conceiving of God which will grapple with these deficiencies of traditional theism.

It is beyond the scope of the present essay even to adumbrate Whitehead's elaborately worked-out doctrine of God. This would entail the analysis of his conception of the primordial nature of God (the principle of concretion) and the consequent nature. We have indicated some of the major motifs that find systematic articulation in this doctrine of God.

EVALUATIONS OF WHITEHEAD

Obviously, we have in Whitehead's writings one of the major, original achievements of the century in the field of religious philosophy, a richly furnished perspective that will continue his persuasive agency as a great teacher for years to come.

Critiques of Whitehead have been legion, ranging from the claim that in his philosophy God's power is reduced to that of a merely persuasive agent, an alluring ideal, to the claim that his God sees every evil as completely contributory to eventual harmony. These criticisms, I believe, cannot be sustained, though they do point to the need for further clarification at the hands of Whitehead's own method.[1]

More pertinent perhaps is the view that Whitehead's outlook bespeaks the optimism of an earlier period. I would be inclined to agree with those who say that in his philosophy he does not give sufficient recognition to the destructive, demonic forces in human nature and human history. At the same time one must recognize that in many a page of his comments on figures and movements in history and in contemporary life he provides data for a more realistic view than the criticisms attributed to him. An anthology of his observations on the brutalities of history (and of historic religion) would add up to a severe indictment. They can be summed up in such an utterance as this: "Man is a queer combination of delicacy of spirit and a brutality which would disgrace a rat." Whitehead knew of the misery as well as of the grandeur.

Paul Tillich held that Whitehead does not present an adequate conception either of the fall or of the goal of humanity. "Infinite creativity simply goes on and on," says Tillich of both Bergson and Whitehead.[2] That is, every human being's involvement in human alienation is more radical than Whitehead seems to grant. The criticism regarding the lack of a goal presupposes a completely victorious God at the "end of history." In response one must say that Whitehead's conception of freedom and creativity and their ambiguities does not permit him to subscribe to a Christian eschatology of this sort.

Instead of making this Tillichian criticism I would argue that Whitehead's philosophy does not achieve full "seasonal relevance": It does not take seriously into account the gigantic configurations of industrial and financial powers in the world of the twentieth century. These powers have become stronger than the governments, and they call for a more radical institutional analysis and counterstrategy than Whitehead seems to have envisaged. The conceptual apparatus of Whitehead's philosophy of civilization lends itself to recognizing such a situation. Whitehead acknowledged that despite the questionable economics of *Das Kapital* "the success of the book—for it is still with us as a power—can only be accounted for by the magnitude of the evils ushered in by the first phase of the industrial revolution. . . . No one now holds that, apart from some further directing agency, mere individualist competition, of itself and by its own self-righting character, will produce a satisfactory society." But the urgency of the historical situation was apparently not upon him. The sense of the seductive, destructive demonic powers was more present in the consciousness of Tillich, as can be seen in his book of 1932, *The Socialist Decision.* Here one sees the joining of a religious philosophy and economic analysis.

Both Whitehead and Tillich were aware of the fact that no particular religious-philosophical system can be viewed as definitive. Each of these men held that some approach other than their own might serve the achievement of "seasonal relevance." Tillich even recognized that his approach was inadequate in the cultural situation produced by National Socialism.

Whatever the just estimate of process philosophy may be in these respects, Whitehead was aware of the epochal changes upon us.

> We have to estimate what has decayed, and what has survived. My thesis is that a new Reformation is in full progress. It is a re-formation; but whether its issue be fortunate or unfortunate depends largely on the actions of comparatively few men, and notably upon the leaders of the protestant clergy.

He was speaking of the need for religious re-formation. It is we, then, who live in the valley of new decision.

Notes

1. Bernard M. Loomer, in his article "Christian Faith and Process Philosophy," *Journal of Religion*, 29, no. 3 (July 1949), has given substantial treatment to major criticisms from the theological side.

2. *Political Expectation*, trans. and ed. James L. Adams (New York: Harper and Row, 1971), p. 153.

21 · *Tillich and the Spirit of*
Matthew the Painter

In about the year 1515 the painter Matthias Grünewald finished his dramatic polyptych for the altar in the Antonite monastery at Isenheim, near Colmar. This group of nine paintings was intended for the afflicted people cared for by the monks. Each of a number of the paintings refers to a particular disease. The centerpiece of the group is the crucifixion. The crucified Christ here is of disproportionate size compared with the figures of the two Marys and the two St. Johns grouped around him, John the Baptist pointing with long forefinger at the wounds and the humiliation. This towering figure dotted with incandescent spots of blood from the flagellation and emblemed with gangrenous wounds is an almost bludgeoning image of a radical disruption of all meaning. Paul Tillich viewed this crucifixion with its depiction of Christ's horrible wounds as "the most religious of all paintings."

The Isenheim Crucifixion is not a study in naturalistic realism. It is a burning symbolic representation of intense emotional power. In Grünewald's mind it probably was in part a bitter comment on a time that was out of joint. He was apparently close, for example, to the peasants' revolts of the region. Perhaps for this reason he was dismissed as court painter. His compatriot, the sculptor Riemenschneider, was tortured on the rack for his participation in the rebellion. The Isenheim Altar was completed only shortly before the revolt that was condemned by Luther. Tillich spoke of Thomas Münzer, a leader of that revolt, as a "depth sociologist."

The suggestion has been made that the open sores of the Isenheim figure represented, in Grünewald's mystical view, the injustices inflicted by the tyrannical forces of his time. "As you did it to one of the least of these my brethren. . . ." In the painter's Karlsruhe Crucifixion of ten years later, John the Baptist is depicted in the stance of appalled indignation and aggressive protest. Paul Tillich might well have called the Isenheim Crucifixion Grünewald's *Guernica*, though the polyptych in its entirety includes (be-

This essay is excerpted from Adams's review essay on *Paul Tillich: His Life and Thought, vol. 1, Life,* by Wilhelm and Marion Pauck (New York: Harper and Row, 1976). The review was originally published in the *Union Seminary Quarterly Review* 32, no. 1 (Fall 1976).

sides the protest) the dimension of hope, evident in the chalice of the life-giving blood of salvation and in the accompanying Resurrection. It is significant that a reproduction of it hung in his study in the 1920s along with a print of the Expressionist painter Schmidt-Rottluff.

Karl Barth, referring to the Isenheim John the Baptist with the long forefinger, construed him as symbolizing the task of theologians to point not to themselves or to their own system but to the Source of redemption. Tillich saw in this crucifixion an expression of what he was later to call "the existentialist point of view." Without rejecting Barth's interpretation of the John the Baptist of the painting, Tillich viewed it as the imperious presentation of human destructiveness and self-destruction. We may say that the Isenheim Altar, taken in its entirety, was a visualization and symbolization of the thrust of his theology of culture (the topic in 1919 of his "first outstanding public lecture").

In this theology he aimed concretely to identify the wounds inflicted by the demonic, the deceptively creative and deeply destructive forces of his period, and at the same time to discern within the total situation the *kairos* of new possibilities, the propitious moment of concrete decision under "the sustaining and directing creativity of God."

A key word here is *concrete*. The basic intention of Tillich's theology of culture can be missed if one quotes out of context his definition of religion as "being grasped by ultimate concern." In Tillich's view, "One is concerned not *in abstracto*, one is concerned concretely."

In a sharply critical, though appreciative, review (1922) of the famous volume on Martin Luther by Karl Holl, "the father of the Luther-renaissance," Tillich laments Holl's failure to indicate how his findings are to achieve relevance today. For Tillich, "Love is the capacity to listen to the concrete." From early in his career Tillich considered concern *in abstracto*, what he called intellectualism, to be a serious wound in the culture. An early essay of his dealt also with the concept of "the present." His concern to relate ideas to specific realities, psychological and sociological, personal and institutional, was perhaps influenced by the "case-by-case" method of Ernst Troeltsch, one of his major mentors.

All of this means that Tillich's own intellectual development is not to be understood *in abstracto*. More than is the case when considering the average scholar or theologian, one can grasp the nature and import of Tillich's contribution only if one sees the relation between his thought and his life, that is, only if one sees how his outlook grew out of (and interpreted) his participation in the culture of his own time.

Crucifixion, by Matthias Grünewald
Musée d'Unterlinden, Colmar (Photo: O. Zimmermann)

Tillich's life was punctuated by the cleavage of major caesuras or breaks. Tillich the young romantic Prussian of Wilhelminian vintage, also Tillich the conventional German scholar and patriot, came to a major turning point as a consequence of his experience as a chaplain in the First World War. (At this time, we should note in passing, came "his discovery of painting . . . as a reaction to the horror, ugliness and destructiveness of war.") And then again with the rise of Hitler and with Tillich's exile from Nazi Germany, another break appears, indeed, strictly speaking, two breaks. By reason of the shock administered by Hitlerism, Tillich was again compelled to surrender much that he had adhered to in the preceding years. He was also obliged to take residence in a foreign country and to learn a new language. The adjustment to these shifts from one period of culture to another, and from one country to another across the ocean, the first when he was thirty-three and the second when he was forty-eight, confronted him with the necessity and opportunity of seeing the wounds in Western culture in differing circumstances and with broadening perspective. In some measure these changes in circumstance brought about some change in Tillich's centerstance. As a consequence he came to see migration as almost a category of human existence.

The wounds in the culture appeared for Tillich in most acute fashion through his four-year experience as an army chaplain, an experience of monstrous "horror, ugliness, and destruction." Before the war, Tillich had become closely identified with the optimism of classical German idealism. The war experience in the very jaws of darkness brought a fundamental metamorphosis. Immediately after the war he associated himself in Berlin with the religious socialist movement. He soon ran afoul of the Brandenburg consistory by reason of his having given a lecture at a meeting of the Independent Social Democrats, who were to the left of the Social Democratic party. The representative of the consistory called him on the carpet, accusing him of mixing religion and politics and reprimanding him for appearing at a radical socialist gathering. Tillich, for his part, sent to the representative a report of the substance of the lecture. In this report one can find many ideas he was to develop in the succeeding years (see my translation in *Metanoia* 3, no. 3 [September 1971]. During the next decade he published a great deal on religious socialism (as well as some of his fundamental writings on the sciences and on philosophy of religion). His first successful book, *The Religious Situation,* appeared in the middle of the decade, stressing the loss in our era of a spiritual center and giving a fresh statement of his theonomous "belief-ful realism." Just before the Nazis came into power his major work on religious socialism, *Socialist Decision,* appeared. This work is the most elaborate constructive statement of religious socialism available, critically coming to terms with the major sociopolitical forces of the era, with conservative, liberal, fascist, capitalist, and Marxist ideologies. Scarcely was the book published (and suppressed by the Nazis) before the author became an exile.

Thirty years later many critics and also admirers of Tillich began asking, What became of his religious socialism in America? Did he finally abandon it? The questions were asked because in the last decades of his life he seemed to turn his energies in other directions, not only to the preparation of the long-hoped for *Systematic Theology,* but also to existentialism and psychological analysis. Although in collaboration with Reinhold Niebuhr he had in the 1940s supported the Fellowship of Socialist Christians, a decade later he came to feel that "there was little any individual could do to change the course of contemporary history." Niebuhr, of course, did not agree. Tillich wrote that because the schizophrenic state of humanity had given rise to a schizophrenic state of many individuals, he was turning his attention to the latter. It is true that he did not in the 1950s entirely abandon his interest in the Christian-Marxist dialogue, as his publications reveal. Yet, a change of emphasis, another metamorphosis, was taking place. His discussion of religion and health, of guilt and anxiety, generally was presented in abstract terms regarding human nature (which previously he had eschewed) or in terms of the individual psyche. He was living in a time when, as H. Richard Niebuhr pointed out to me in connection with his survey of theological education, excitement over pastoral psychology was crowding social ethics out. Tillich's philosophical-theological framework for the discussion of depth psychology elicited widespread interest. He was sought after on all hands. I recall an evening when I happened in at his apartment and found the living room filled with psychiatrists. Several of them said that they had never dreamed that they would find themselves in such a place. Generally, in his writing in this area relatively little attention was given to the relations between psychotherapy and social-institutional change. In the focus on the individual the concern was with the concrete, but with a truncated concreteness.

In 1963 I put some of these questions to him for the volume *Philosophical Interrogations* (edited by Sydney and Beatrice Rome), asking him to explain the implications of his view that we live now in a "sacred void." In response he said that since World War II "despair and cynicism . . . continue to prevail in the present feeling that contemporary history is almost completely determined by trends and that the chances of breaking the control of those trends is minimal." In a conversation several years before this he said that one reason for discouragement is the fact that the labor movement in America has become the bulwark of self-serving bourgeois power. Referring to his recent Rauschenbusch Lectures, he said in the later conversation: "What we can and must do is to analyze and denounce the structures of destruction in our society and in this way prepare the prophetic spirit which may rise again and show the image of a new 'theonomy.'" The *spirit* of Matthew the painter was still there.

22 · *The Need for a New Language*

Among contemporary theologians no one has more radically questioned prevailing ideas and practices in the Christian churches, especially among Protestants, than Paul Tillich. In this respect he scarcely seems typical. For the theologian is not usually thought of as a disturber. When one hears the word "theologian" one is likely to imagine a professional journeyman comfortably ensconced within the securities of a religious institution. Theologians, it is held, by the very nature of their vocation, are engaged in the devising of means whereby "the faithful" may be exhorted to greater fidelity to tradition. They are not expected to serve as gadflies within the church itself, disturbing, attacking the false or irrelevant in church practice. If a theologian does give this appearance, the observer expects that he will turn out to be merely a more subtle, effective stimulus to institutional morale.

Paul Tillich sets forth his criticism of the church precisely as a theologian. For him, protest is an ineradicable element in Protestantism as such, and the first task of the theologian is to proclaim the protest. In his role as disturber within the church Tillich does not, of course, stand alone. Karl Barth, for example, especially in his earliest writings and in his attack upon the "German Christians" of the Third Reich, has secured a reputation as such a disturber. But by the time his second major work was published, Barth's disturbance had quieted down and he had returned to a new form of confessionalism.

Paul Tillich, on the other hand, is acutely aware not only that present-day Protestantism is moribund but also that it is moribund partly because the language of tradition can in our day have little effect upon the believers and still less upon those outside the churches. He holds that the Protestantism to which we are accustomed has almost exhausted itself by becoming

This essay is the first chapter of Adams's book, *Paul Tillich's Philosophy of Culture, Science, and Religion,* originally published by Harper and Row in 1965 and republished by the University Press of America in 1982. In the chapter which follows in the book, Adams deals with various basic concepts of Tillich's "new language" of theology, many of which Adams has himself adopted: spatialization, the present, fate and freedom, depth, the Unconditioned, meaning, spirit, threat and support to existence, cleavage of existence, kairos, theonomy, Gestalt of grace, the demonic.

identified with the dominant powers of the environment—that is, with a convulsive nationalism and with bourgeois interests. Hence, he believes that a radical protest against the churches is necessary if Protestantism is to fulfill its vocation for our time; indeed, he is convinced that for a long time to come protest must take priority.[1] This protest must include a rejection of outdated terminology and it must issue in the creation of the word that speaks to our present condition, to the distressed condition of our particular time and of our particular churches. Emerson said that if one should cut Montaigne's words they would bleed. Tillich's view is that cutting into conventional religious language is almost like dissecting a corpse. He says that "we no longer have words in which the powerfulness of the word pulsates." But protest against dead words is not enough: Protestant protest must result in Protestant realization, in the word that releases new vitality. New life demands new words—first to slay death and then to summon daring novelty.

The more encrusted the habits of the mass of churchpeople and the more rigid the sense of authority attaching to conventional terminology, the more daring will the innovation seem. Innovation with respect to religious language frequently elicits even a sense of shock among the faithful, with the consequence that they make little serious attempt to understand new terms. Indeed, Tillich confesses that in his own life, "the immemorial experience of mankind that new knowledge can be won only through breaking a taboo and that all autonomous thinking is accompanied by a sense of guilt, has been a fundamental experience." The positive effect of this sense of taboo has meant for Tillich that "every step in theological, ethical, and political criticism encountered inhibitions which often could be overcome only after conflicts lasting for years."[2]

If Tillich's attitude toward the language of tradition differs from the attitude of Barth, it offers striking comparison with that of the young Schleiermacher. When Schleiermacher over a century and a half ago summoned "the cultured despisers of religion" and undertook in the *Addresses* to show them the indispensability and inevitableness of religion, he felt he owed his audience an explanation for the fact that his language was not the language of the theologian. After "confessing" to his hearers that he is a theologian by profession, he says,

> It is a willing confession, but my language would not have betrayed me, nor should the "eulogies" of my colleagues in the profession; what I desire lies so far out of their orbit and would little resemble what they wish to see and

hear. . . . I am aware that in all I have to say to you I fully disown my profession, and why should I not therefore confess it like any other misdemeanor?

With greater cause than Schleiermacher, Tillich might well say this of his own language, for, as one of his European critics has observed, "his writings delight the reader in a remarkably untheological, secular way."[3] It is no doubt partially for this reason that Tillich has been sometimes spoken of as an apostle to the Gentiles.

Barth, who says he would be "especially pleased" if his commentary *The Epistle to the Romans* should stray into the hands of some who are not theologians, finds it necessary to beg the indulgence of such nontheological readers because they may find his writings difficult to read. In response to his critics who urge that "simplicity is the mark of divinity" he says, "I could not make the book more easily intelligible than the subject itself allows. If I be not mistaken, we theologians serve the layman best when we refuse to have him especially in mind, and when we simply live of our own."[4]

The explanation of the difference between Tillich and Barth here is to be found in the former's conviction that the words of the theologian should be words that speak to our time. In his view, the theologian must not be content with proclamation of the "Word of God" once delivered; he must accept the responsibility and challenge of apologetics. Strict adherence to an "established," "holy" language constitutes a "legalism of the word." Hence Tillich in many of his writings has made a deliberate effort to express himself in "an untheological, profane way." His *Religious Situation* and scores of his magazine articles published in Germany and America reveal the intent and the effectiveness of this effort.

The affinity between Tillich and Schleiermacher in their search for a new language is by no means a coincidence. They share a similar intellectual parentage. In certain fundamental ways Tillich, like Schleiermacher, stems from the great trunk of German classical philosophy. Without giving systematic attention to further comparisons between Tillich and Schleiermacher, we should here at the outset recall some of the outstanding features of German classical philosophy, viewing it particularly as the background of much of Tillich's work.

The major thrust of German classical philosophy derives in part from the Renaissance, but (more than the Renaissance) it presupposes in a positive way the Christian traditions of theology and philosophy. The German classical school is often spoken of as speculative, but in addition to being speculative in the popular sense, these philosophers were speculative in the generic sense of the term. They aimed to "look" (*speculare*) at the world in a new way, and yet in doing so to penetrate anew the meaning of certain old ways. For our purpose it is especially useful to observe what this school was opposed to and what they viewed as their own positive effort.

On the one hand the German classical school of Kant, Fichte, Schleiermacher, Schelling, and Hegel turned against the Enlightenment with its secularizing, skeptical rationalism which issued in a positivism that did away with the infinite, and also against the authoritarianism of the Age of the Despots. These philosophers in varying ways attempted to "establish" the infinite without the use of finite categories; they also attempted to grasp the fundamental qualities of human freedom. In their rejection of finite categories for understanding the human being's relation to the infinite, these philosophers expressed a characteristic concern of the Romantic movement. They responded to the Faustian impulse, the striving in restless movement toward the infinite (*Unendlichkeitsstreben*), though the "movement" aimed also to relate the infinite to the finite. On the other hand the German classical philosophers were opposed to the supernaturalism of Christian rationalistic orthodoxy and also to the disjunction between theology and philosophy and between religion and culture.

With respect to these various motifs, the German classical school was by no means a unitary movement. Nor is it to be simply identified with philosophical idealism. Indeed, one branch of the classical school (represented especially by the later Schelling), the branch to which Tillich mainly belongs, radically qualified the philosophical idealism of the earlier developments. Indeed, in the writings of Schelling and Kierkegaard, and also of Feuerbach and Marx, one can see the beginnings of modern existentialism. At the same time these later developments can be understood only in relation to the earlier idealism. As against the earlier idealism we find here the assertion that "being is finite, existence is self-contradictory, and life is ambiguous."

Taking into account the positive and negative aspects of the classical school and viewing it as a broad religious and cultural movement, we may say that German classical philosophy represents, among other things, a *diastasis* (separation) from the Enlightenment and from Christian rationalistic orthodoxy with its supernaturalism. It represents also an effort in the direction of synthesis between historic religious and Christian insight and a new, critical and constructive philosophical theology, a theology that, as with Schleiermacher, aims to explicate distinctive Christian elements and at the same time to recognize some positive relation between Christian faith and religiousness in general.

In the effort to overcome the debilitating disjunction between religion and culture the German classical school attempts to take into account and to give a religious interpretation of all spheres of culture—the sciences, the arts, politics, and even play. Tillich has often pointed out that it is no accident that this effort of German classical philosophy was promoted by men who in many instances were sons of Protestant ministers and who were also disciplined in the *Paideia* of the German humanistic *Gymnasium* with its curriculum of classical studies. (Tillich himself had this combination of upbringing and education.) The dichotomy between secular skepticism and traditional faith played a smaller role in Germany than in France and England. In the German classical school a critical attitude toward the Enlightenment and toward Christian orthodoxy was combined with a positive, creative thrust in the direction of reconceiving the relations between theology and philosophy and between religion and culture. This outlook conditions both the ultimate orientation and the breadth of concerns of the German classical philosophers, and it also lies behind their search for a new language. In all of these respects Tillich must be considered a scion of the German classical stock. As we shall observe, however, Tillich's outlook is not confined to these perspectives, and thus it is not oriented merely to idealism or existentialism.

The average reader today will probably view the thrust of the German classical philosophy to be somehow alien to American traditions. The American philosophical tradition is generally thought of as empirical (in the line from Bacon through Locke and Hume) rather than as bearing affinity to the German classical school. Yet, there are strains that are more or less directly connected with that school.

Familiarity in the United States with German philosophy and theology considerably antedates the period of the classical school in Germany. The interest in German literature and philosophy, however, gained markedly at the end of the eighteenth century, largely under the influence of the formidable Salem clergyman-scholar, William Bentley (1759–1819). This is a topic with which the present writer would be pleased to deal at length, for his first parish ministry was in the church in Salem, Massachusetts, of which Dr. Bentley was minister from 1783 until his death in 1819. In Bentley's column, beginning in 1794 in the *Salem Gazette* and from 1800 to 1819 in the semi-weekly *Impartial Register*, he provided a "Summary" of news and of what at the time was deemed noteworthy in the theology and philosophy, the natural sciences, the literature and art of Germany. Bentley's learning with respect to German scholarship gave rise in America to the first general scholarly interest in the subject.

Henry A. Pochmann in his copious work on *German Culture in America: Philosophical and Literary Influences, 1600–1900 (1957)* has fully documented the familiarity in the United States with the writings of the German classical school, showing the growing influence of the school in the nineteenth century and down to the First World War. With varying degrees of understanding all of the major and many of the minor philosophical and theological figures in Germany were known, especially among the Transcendentalists (who, by the way, did not relish this name which was imposed upon them). An explicitly Hegelian movement was established in St. Louis, and in the periodical of this group, *The Journal of Speculative Philosophy* (1867–93), translations and treatments of Kant, Fichte, Schelling, and Hegel appeared. The motto of this magazine was taken from Novalis: "Philosophy can bake no bread, but it can give us God, Freedom and Immortality." In 1873–74 Francis Bowen at Harvard introduced the first collegiate course in German philosophy. In 1884 the Harvard Unitarian theologian Charles Carroll Everett published a critical exposition entitled *Fichte's Science of Knowledge;* this work of Fichte, we shall see, is fundamental for an understanding of Tillich's philosophy of science. But many translations, as we have observed, were available before this. In 1847 the Unitarian theologian Frederick Henry Hedge, later to be professor of German at Harvard, edited and published a very large volume of translations. James Elliott Cabot, who heard Schelling's lectures in Berlin in 1841, immediately sent to Emerson a manuscript translation of Schelling's *Of Human Freedom*, a writing of considerable significance for Tillich—a writing in which Schelling broke through the previous essentialist idealism to an existentialist dialectic. In the twentieth century German classical philosophy has found distinguished representatives in Josiah Royce and William Ernest Hocking, and also in Borden P. Bowne and Edgar Brightman. John Dewey from his early days lived in the foothills of German idealism.

It is not expedient or necessary to try to characterize the tendencies emanating in America from German classical philosophy. It will suffice to say that in general the role of this philosophy in the nineteenth century in America was quite similar to the role played in Germany. Moreover, in the effort to interpret religious and Christian ideas in relation to the various spheres of culture the Americans, like the Germans of the classical school, recognized the need for a new language.

In Tillich's opinion, the traditional language of theology, despite any value it may possess for the expert, tends to create a gulf not only between the church and the world but also between the theologian and the layperson. This traditional language often obscures and even perverts the essential and relevant message of the church, whether it is directed to the churchperson or to the outsider. Because of it the characteristic doctrines of Christianity as well as the liturgy and preaching in the churches are at present largely ineffective. The characteristic doctrines of the Reformation, for example, doctrines that "four centuries ago split the European continent asunder and aroused savage and bloody wars," are now "so strange to the modern man that there is scarcely any way available for making them intelligible."[5] By trying again and again to impose as law the religious language of earlier generations, the churches are defeating their own proper ends. Our intellectual and social situation is different from that out of which previous ecclesiastical formulations were born. Our age has lost "the presuppositions that the Middle Ages and the Reformation had in common: those of the certainty of God, and with it the certainty of truth and meaning."[6] Modern men and women have experienced autonomy and they will not surrender it, at least not for long; and it includes a certain sense of autonomy with respect to modes of expression.

Our intellectual and social situation is different also from the situations in which the traditional liturgical language of the church originated. The liturgies of the churches have little to do with our contemporary society, whether we think of the traditional liturgy or of that which has supposedly undergone "liturgical reform." If there is to be any advance in the direction of making liturgy relevant to the common life, Tillich believes it "must be brought to light not with the 'long arm' of the antiquarian but rather with the 'cutting edge' of contemporaneity."[7] It requires "a new understanding of natural and everyday processes in their transcendent meaning."

The same situation obtains with respect to "the word of the preacher, whether it be spoken in the church or out of it, and also . . . the hymns. . . ." Some preachers wrongly imagine that ecclesiastical and biblical language are devices that will of themselves be sufficient. But Tillich, with his acute sense of the gulf between the church and the world, holds that "insofar as our understanding of the words of the Bible requires us to separate ourselves from the here-and-now, from our own contemporaneity, they are not the Word of God." The test of a realistic faith is the objectively powerful word.

Among "the faithful," the traditional language often serves to develop a mentality that is closed to criticism as well as to new light, a mentality that is unconcerned about either the irrelevance or the ineffectiveness of the churches. Indeed, the indifference of "the world"—and even of the luke-warm within the churches—often elicits among churchpeople only "a spirit of ill-tempered *hybris*."

> Instead of meeting the challenge to speak to the contemporary condition of their hearers, many representatives of the church prefer a sort of intoxicated renunciation of success or effectiveness, a renunciation that is in the end self-destructive. But even the message of the Bible can give no justification for repealing contemporaneity.[8]

In this passage Tillich is thinking especially of the Barthian opposition to any human attempt to give the Word of God contemporaneity, but the implications are also of general import. "The Word of God," he says, "is any reality by means of which the eternal breaks with unconditioned power into our contemporaneity."[9] It is not a question any longer of "a direct proclamation of the religious truths as they are given in the Bible and the tradition, for all of these things are torn down into the general chaos of doubt and questioning."[10] By ignoring these facts, the churches are actually accelerating and deepening the crisis of modern religion and civilization.[11] They are arousing positive hostility to the message and work of the churches not only among the educated but also among the oppressed groups who are seeking a new meaning in life. "Until the appointed representatives of the Protestant message understand this, their work in the widest circles, and especially among the working classes, will be utterly hopeless."[12] Any attempt to proclaim a religious message without taking this situation into account constitutes culpable blindness. Tillich concludes that we have here "the most urgent need of the church today in the proclaiming of its message: its language is remote from contemporary life and yet it makes a demand upon that life."[13] The churches cannot reasonably expect to make any positive impact upon that life if they are ignorant of it or if they are out of direct touch with it. The chasm represented by the differences in language is, of course, only the linguistic reflection of a chasm in life. The one cannot be closed without closing the other, but we must first find the relevant words that "pulsate with the powerfulness of the word."

The problem is more difficult when we remember that the cohesion of a religious community demands continuity of linguistic usage along with novelty introduced for the sake of achieving contemporaneity. In this connection, it should be emphasized that despite his severely critical attitude toward traditional language, Tillich recognizes the significance of "objective constructions like the confessions of a church, the meaning of which transcends subjective belief or doubt, and which are thus able to support communities in which all tendencies of doubt, criticism and certainty are admitted, provided only that the confessional foundation of the community is given general recognition."[14] Tillich's attitude toward the deficiencies of traditional language should, therefore, not be interpreted as favoring an abandonment of all church confessions or of the historic doctrines of the church. He does not propose that a general chaos of fresh thought and language be introduced into church life. As a theologian he hopes rather to give new relevance to the basic faith of the church, to give its doctrines, wherever possible, the living meaning implicit and latent within them. He neither wishes nor expects the new language of a particular theologian to replace the more slowly changing language of the community. As a matter of fact, Tillich's attitude is similar to that of most creative theologians. They have spoken, as it were, in tongues, but they have not aimed to become ventriloquists for the community. We must bear these considerations in mind in our whole discussion of Tillich's criticism of the traditional language of the churches. Otherwise, we shall fail to understand his true meaning and wrongly suppose that he wishes to replace a fetishism for traditional language with a fetishism for novelty. Such a replacement would, of course, be impossible of achievement. And even if it were possible to achieve, it would be psychologically and sociologically self-defeating. As Tillich puts it, "Realization in worship, sermon, and instruction assumes forms that can be imparted. Ecclesiastical reality, the reality of the personal religious life, yes, even the prophetic word itself assumes a sacramental foundation, an abundance from which they live."[15] The demand for novelty must not be interpreted as incompatible with these other aspects of a continuing church fellowship. On the other hand, the latter considerations must not blind one to the imperative character of the demand for novelty.

The church in its rigid adherence to traditional language always appeals to divine sanctions in order to justify itself. But however convincing these sanctions may be, the churches that employ them often actually ignore the fact that the intellectual situation has changed. They ignore the fact also that language is a temporal, cultural creation. A vocabulary that in some different situation in the past served as an effective means of communication is now a strange idiom, a sort of fossil preserved because of the falsely pious notion that it is a sacrosanct ark of the covenant to be touched by human hands only on pain of spiritual death. Stubborn adherence to the language of the fathers generally brings about a degeneration into a quasi-priesthood of Scriptures and "sound doctrine." It may be added that this consequence attaches also to much liberal reinterpretation of traditional language, for the reinterpretation often has as little effect as the original. Thus both the liberal and the orthodox churches communicate something that breeds death or false life. And in the outcome the traditional language, in its resistance to any disturbance of creature comfort, must for its continuing viability depend upon an appeal to "conventional, mediocre theology as a protection against a better, though unconventional, theology."[16]

It would be wrong to suppose that, in Tillich's view, the need for disturbance in the church arises merely from its predicament of being tongue-tied. The predicament is, as we have observed, only one aspect of a larger embarrassment, one due to the fact that Protestantism in its present form is reaching its limit. Protestantism is not now adequately equipped to meet the demands of the historical situation. The powerful motives that were effective in certain earlier periods of Christianity are no longer really functioning. It is to no purpose merely to repeat the old ideas in their frayed forms. Nor will it be possible to leap over the gulf between Protestantism and its lost provinces by simply resuming its connection with the Reformation or with some other period regarded as normative.[17]

Protestantism by its very essence and through its inheritance of the substance of Christianity possesses a basis for coping with the situation. Before God, Protestantism must protest against all false securities and undertake a new realization relevant to the present historical situation. If the churches wish to reach people, they must "discover anew the reality which was apprehended in earlier times and which is in essence the same today, and then present it in quite new terms." Only then can they "understand that reality on the basis of what the old words intended."[18] Only then can they break through the "academically petrified problems" and achieve an immediate knowledge of essential reality. "Religious knowledge is knowledge of reality." It is "not primarily the unfolding of a tradition; it is rather a turning towards reality,"[19] "a penetrating in an ultimate sense into what happens day by day, in labor and industry, in marriage and friendship, in ordinary social intercourse and recreation, in meditation and quiet, and even in sleep."[20]

In this respect, certain secular philosophers of our day are exhibiting more nearly the right attitude than are some theologians. In fact, Tillich's own attempt to discover anew the powerful experiences that lay behind the old religious symbols—now so largely powerless—is, in many ways, similar in purpose, for example, to Martin Heidegger's attempt to discern the original experiences from which the leading conceptions of philosophy have been created. Tillich says:

> Something very tragic tends to happen in all periods of man's spiritual life: truths, once deep and powerful, discovered by the great geniuses with profound suffering and incredible labor, become shallow and superficial when used in daily conversation. How can this happen? It can happen and it unavoidably happens, because there is no depth without the way to depth. Truth without the way to truth is dead; and if it is still used, in detachment, it contributes only to the surface of things.[21]

These words come very near to expressing the sentiments of the existential philosopher Heidegger, though Tillich does not agree with Heidegger's atheistic position.

Other secular philosophies and movements today exhibit the same desire to approach reality directly and to break through the encrustations of impotent traditional conceptions. Thus they confirm and strengthen what is really at issue in theology itself: a penetration unhampered by the restraints of traditional ways of posing problems and concepts. . . . Our attachment should be to the things themselves and not to mere authority."[22] They also demonstrate that no group holds a monopoly on the ability to penetrate reality. This fact leads Tillich to adopt a positive attitude toward secularism in so far as it uncovers depths of being and of history inaccessible to merely traditional ways of thinking and speaking.

Theology must find a new approach to reality. The old method of authority, which appeals to Scripture or church doctrines, breaks down because unavoidable conflicts arise between dogmatic materials and scientific treatment, with the result that either science is mutilated by authority or authority is undermined by science. In face of this situation Tillich agrees with the modern person who believes that the days of authoritarianism and supernaturalism are numbered; science is here to stay.

Since the time of Schleiermacher, an attempt has been made to devise a second approach by combining his psychological method with modern psychology, sociology, and history of religions. But however important its contributions, Tillich holds that this method is also to be criticized. It "remains enclosed in the subjectivity of religious consciousness and never attains an immediate grasp of the contents intended in the religious act, for it is improper to try to define the referent in terms of the act instead of defining the act in terms of the referent." [23]

His criticism of the second method suggests a third way of approaching reality, the path which Tillich wishes to follow. He calls it the immediate approach through "phenomenological intuition." In this approach, he says, "we turn neither to the authorities nor to religious consciousness, but immediately to the whole of reality, and endeavor to uncover that level of reality which is intended by the religious act." [24] This path is to be distinguished especially from that of rationalism, for it is not possible to reach the substance of religion without experience of the religious act itself. Rationalism not only fails to penetrate the depth of the religious act; it also ends by negating the substance of religion.

As we have already indicated, the significant thing to observe is that Tillich attempts in much of his writing to set forth his conception of religion and of reality without resort to the language of tradition. Indeed, in one of the most important expositions of his religious position, the essay entitled "Belief-ful Realism," he sets forth his ideas without making use of conventional "religious" symbols at all. [25] The method of phenomenological intuition insists that the real basis of theological thought is human existence itself and not certain sacrosanct words that have been fixed by the crust of habit or by the traditions of the schools. The methods of the schools derive concepts from concepts instead of from objects. Thus the paradox, the tension, the vitality, the depth and wonder of life are rationalized and lost. Tillich believes that these methods can and must be put aside if the living, concrete, real power of religious symbols is to be allowed to spring forth. The new method must attempt to discover things directly without terminological prejudice.

To be sure, perils attend all attempts to clarify vision or to introduce new language into religious discussions, the perils of the eccentric and the esoteric. But the present theological situation demands that such risks be taken. "Without daring, even frustrated daring, the impasse of the present theology cannot be resolved." [26] The spirit and the intention with which Tillich ventures to escape this impasse can best be indicated by his own characteristic words, words that again reveal the undogmatic theologian:

This unusual method, in which scarcely a word of the religious tradition is used, and for which a painstaking and sensitive intuition of the things nearest to us, the most living things and therefore the most difficult to observe, is demanded—this method is intended only as an attempt that will

be followed by other and better ones, so that we may see with *our own* eyes
and name with *our own* words that which is not bound to any time or any eye
or any word.[27]

What we must see and what we must name is, in the words of the poet,
nothing less than "the grandeur of God," the living majesty in "the dearest
freshness deep down things." This dearest freshness has been seared with
trade, smeared with toil and with the worn-out words which the generations have pressed upon it.

> The world is charged with the grandeur of God.
>   It will flame out, like shining from shook foil;
>   It gathers to a greatness, like the ooze of oil
> Crushed. Why do men then now not reck his rod?
> Generations have trod, have trod, have trod;
>   And all is seared with trade; bleared, smeared with toil;
>   And wears man's smudge and shares man's smell: the soil
> Is bare now, nor can foot feel, being shod.
>
> And for all this, nature is never spent;
>   There lives the dearest freshness deep down things;
> And though the last lights off the black West went
>   Oh, morning, at the brown brink eastward, springs—
> Because the Holy Ghost over the bent
>   World broods with warm breast and with ah! bright wings.[28]

Now, the demand for seeing and naming anew the grandeur of God
would seem, at least at first blush, to be no cause for disturbance in the
churches, or in the "world" either, for that matter. Have not the poets and
the liturgies of the ages again and again seen anew and named the grandeur
of God? The answer is that they have, but that all too often the seeing and
naming anew have caused no disturbance and have brought no new vitality.
If one proposes "to penetrate in an ultimate sense what happens day by day
in labor and industry, in marriage and friendship" and in all the important
concerns of the common life, one proposes to discover anew something that
is seldom suggested, even to the average believer, by the phrase "the
grandeur of God." In Tillich's view, to be sure, the embarrassment of
present-day civilization and of present-day Christianity must be interpreted
in the end as the result of a loss of the sense of the majesty of God. But in
order to interpret the embarrassment after that fashion, one would have to

give the phrase a meaning it does not often possess in ordinary parlance. The word "God" has in many quarters lost its potency and become a trivial breath of tepid air, suitable only for the hollow men of limbo. For many people, in fact, the word represents only a fantasy, a nonentity. For the unbeliever it suggests, and for many believers it provides, an escape from reality rather than a penetration of it. Somehow the believers (as well as the unbelievers) have failed to penetrate in an ultimate sense what happens day by day. Belief in the grandeur of God, as ordinarily understood, is not enough.

These observations only give the greater plausibility to Tillich's claim that we need to discover and name something anew. It may well be that even the word "God" has been so much bleared and seared that it is, for wide circles of men, not even potential with greatness. At least, Tillich's own writings would seem to indicate that he believes this is the case, for he has been veritably ascetic in his sparing use of the word. Indeed, certain theologians in Germany some years ago charged him with being an atheist. Early in his career (in 1926) the clergy in Saxony protested against his appointment to the chair of philosophy in Dresden. This protest was made because of his prominent work among the religious socialists and the unbelievers. The fact that he was known as a religious socialist convinced some conservative Christians that he is surely an atheist. And who would be so bold as to say that knowledge of the same fact would not elicit a similar reaction from many Christians and believers in God in other countries? It would appear that for some people there are matters of much greater moment than "God" or "the grandeur of God." If we could discover what these things are we would have discovered what God really is for these "believers." Evidently the question is: Which God really has the grandeur?

Now, Tillich's writings "delight the reader in a remarkably untheological, profane way" just because he wishes to get behind both religion and irreligion, behind theology and "anti-theology," to penetrate in an ultimate sense into what happens day by day in labor and industry, in war and "peace," in church and culture. For the fulfillment of this end he poses again and again the question: What is man's ultimate concern? Or rather, what should it be? As we have indicated, he believes that the actual ultimate concerns of persons—and of churches—are to be discovered by penetrating their very embarrassments; if one can discover what has caused the embarrassment one may discover what the ultimate concerns have been and also what they should be. In order to accomplish this purpose, he wishes to ascertain anew the dearest freshness deep down things and to remove again the blight that old and uncouth words have wrought upon it.

Notes

1. *Religiöse Verwirklichung* (Berlin: Furche, 1930), p. 44 and note 2. Hereafter abbreviated *Rel. Verw.*

2. *Interpretation of History,* trans. Rasetzki and Talmey (New York: Charles Scribner's Sons, 1936), p. 23.

3. Erica Küppers, "Zur Religionsphilosophie Paul Tillichs," *Zwischen den Zeiten,* IX (1931), 123. The passage from Schleiermacher, cited above, is quoted in this article. Translations from German writings, unless otherwise noted, are by the present writer.

4. Karl Barth, *Epistle to the Romans,* trans. Edwyn C. Hoskyns (London: Oxford University Press, 1933), p. 5.

5. *Rel. Verw.* pp. 30–31.

6. "Rechtfertigung und Zweifel," *Vorträge der Theologischen Konferenz zu Giessen,* No. 39. (Giessen: Töpelmann, 1924), p. 20.

7. *Rel. Verw.,* p. 85.

8. Ibid.

9. Ibid.

10. Ibid., p. 38.

11. Ibid., p. 188.

12. Ibid., pp. 38 and 275, note 20. Here contemporary literature on the proletariat is cited to show the great distance of the workers from the church.

13. Ibid., p. 85.

14. *Interpretation of History,* pp. 18–19. These sentiments reflect Tillich's orientation to the church situation in Europe in 1936.

15. Ibid., p. 27.

16. *Protestantisches Prinzip und proletarische Situation* (Bonn: Cohen, 1931), p. 24.

17. *Rel. Verw.,* p. 47. Protestantism may not "on any point attribute a sort of classical status to the period of the Reformation in a normative sense. It is of the essence of Protestantism that there can be no classical period for it."

18. Ibid., p. 31.

19. Ibid., p. 58.

20. Ibid., p. 61.

21. "Depth," *Christendom,* IX (1944), 319.

22. *Rel. Verw.,* p. 23.

23. Ibid., p. 128.

24. Ibid., p. 129.

25. Cf. Tillich's discussion of the ability of some poets to use words that "are both symbolic and precise" and that "nevertheless penetrate into the deepest levels of existence." Cf. *Rel. Verw.,* p. 109 and note 17.

26. *Interpretation of History*, p. 284.

27. *Rel. Verw.*, p. 141.

28. "God's Grandeur," *Poems of Gerard Hopkins*, with Notes by Robert Bridges (London: Humphrey Milford, 2nd ed., 1931), p. 26.

23 · The Phenomenology of Fragmentation and the Ecology of Dreams

I

Human beings are dreaming, myth-bearing creatures, and our myths are our bane as well as our blessing; they are harbingers of damnation as well as of salvation, of disease as well as of healing, of the demonic as well as of the daimonic, of abject pessimism as well as of indomitable optimism. Every functioning myth is susceptible to the appearance of these polarities. They are latent in the morphology of every dream as they are latent in each of the elements of a viable myth—in the numinous, the cosmic, the social-institutional, and the psychological element, as Joseph Campbell says.

This latent polarity may be observed on many levels. It may be viewed as the metaphysical heritage (and guilt) of finitude—as Anaximander puts it, everything creative in history carries within it a destructive element simply by reason of its inspirited partialness; or it may be seen as the manifestation of the divine-and-demonic nonrational rootedness of all dreams, in Jakob Böhme's phrase; or it may be perceived as the divinely given potentiality of freedom—the majesty of God is present in Raskolnikov's freedom to murder in Dostoyevski's tale.

Latent also in the character of myth is what David Miller calls "the process of fragmentation." This process, however, does not lead to the disappearance of myth but rather to new and distorted myth. When the gods depart, the half-gods arrive. Nietzsche suggests in psychological terms the tragic nature of the process of fragmentation. In order to become effective in history, he says, a thing must be loved for more than it is worth. (Nothing succeeds like excess.) Yet, it thereby becomes a monstrous *Unding* destroying its own context. Demonic fragmentation substitutes the part for the whole.

With the Industrial Revolution the ancient myth of the Occident—a historical, eschatological myth of hope—has been fragmented, bifurcating and spatializing the inner and the outer worlds. On the outer (institutional) side the fragment concentrates its effort on utilitarian goals, eventually

This address was presented at the Annual Congress of Fellows, the Society for the Arts, Religion, and Contemporary Culture, at the Whitney Museum, New York City, on February 26, 1972.

promoting bureaucratization and the concentration of corporate power economic and political, thus imprisoning the human being in a cage, as Max Weber holds. This myth of "progress," a descendant of earlier dreams of the millennium, has been accompanied and supported by the myths of positivism and scientism, antimetaphysical myths cut off from the transcendent. On the inner side, "religion" becomes a fragment: instead of maintaining the prophetic wholeness of its initial eschatological and institutional thrust, it retreats to the realm of a spurious and uncreative privatization. Separated from each other (that is, spatialized), both the inner and the outer fragment become demonic, with the consequence that neither of them fructifies or corrects the other.

II

Two similarly fragmented myths are struggling for birth today. Both of them are seeking liberation from the "objectified," spatialized worlds of self and society by sinking roots "deep down in the spring" of new creativity. The one myth is a new dream of interiorization and spontaneity to replace a dead, merely conformist and repressive privatization—the psychological, ahistorical and apolitical road to depth, sometimes more Oriental in modality than Occidental ("Consciousness III," encounter groups, psychedelic experience, individualistic existentialism). The other is a new dream of institutionalization, a protest driving toward social transformation—the sociological, historical road from the depths of society, "depth sociology." This myth is promoted especially by oppressed minorities and their fellow travelers—ethnic groups, women's liberation, the protest against the depersonalization engendered by the welfare state. Both of these myths are truncated.[1] (These differentiations are of course typological.)

We confine attention here mainly to the truncated quality of the myth of interiorization as a new dream of privatization. Here the psyche leaves the world of history (the world of economic and political powers and institutions) to its own devices and eschatologies, restricting its concern to the immediate, spontaneous personal and interpersonal sphere, and not reckoning with social-ethical obligations in face of the suprapersonal power structures and the injustices of the social-institutional sphere. The myth is the dream of escape from history. It is often claimed that there is nothing inherent in this myth that prevents its moving creatively into the other sphere; yet one seldom sees actual movement in this direction. Meanwhile, the myth presupposes that however meaningless the social-institutional order may be, it will go on supporting the myth. By and large this myth is the indoor luxury of members of the middle classes who enjoy material comfort. Thus it is a dream belonging to a particular power group, and it functions as ideology in the Marxist sense of that term. In general, the myth favors the perspectives of psychology, either ignoring sociological structures altogether or attempting to interpret them in merely psychological terms—the demonry or imperialism of *Innerlichkeit*.[2]

The dream so enunciated is the illusory dream of pietism, whether religious or secular. It is the more deceptive because it seems to be a recovery of and response to the numinous sacred; but in reality its numen is truncated. Eventually, this narcissistic interiorization is impotent in face of social crisis. Hence, it tempts the Lord of history by inviting upon itself a numinously fearful Judgment.

This does not mean, however, that from the myth of interiorization we can learn nothing about the human condition today. We can learn from fragmented myths as we can learn from sectarian movements. Certainly, authentic interiorization precedes or accompanies authentic institutionalization. (Moreover, the cultivation of a simpler life-style than that of a consumer's paradise has much to recommend it; and the communes may presage something valid for the future, in the direction taken toward the extended family.)

The pietistic dream, which at best is only half authentic, is described in a complex, paradoxical way by Karl Marx in the introduction to his *Critique of Hegel's Philosophy of Right* (1844). Here he speaks of German history since the Reformation as a "dream history" (*Traumgeschichte*), though he asserts also that in principle the Reformation was the "prehistory" of a social revolution to come in the future.

III

According to Marx, the two great representatives of this prehistory were Hegel and Luther. In his view, Luther's theology deserves to be called revolutionary—up to the point when it showed its ambiguous quality. In insisting on free access to God and the Bible, and in insisting on the inwardness of faith, Luther emancipated people from dependence on Rome. "He liberated men from outward religiosity because he made religiosity an inward affair." By means of this thrust, however, he served also to emancipate the princes and then to enhance their new, privileged status and that of the upper middle classes in the towns. Yet, Marx adds, "if Protestantism is not the true solution, it was the true formulation of the problem."[3] The Reformation points beyond itself, he says, to the emancipation of people not only from the bonds of Rome but also from the bonds that Luther forged to replace them. In pointing beyond itself the Reformation constitutes "the prehistory of Revolution." In its actuality, however, history since the Reformation (as we have already indicated) has been a "dream history," for in its emphasis on *Innerlichkeit* it has allowed religion to become a *verselbständiges Bewusstsein,* an insulated consciousness unaware of its connection with the actual world of power relations, and unaware of the demand to transform the world. The separation of the self from society is "false consciousness," a frustrating, illusory dream.

A similar false consciousness emerges, we may say, when society or self or both are separated from the cosmos, "our neighbor the universe," or when the numinous is recognized only in relation to the self or to society. Kierkegaard's subjective pietism (or Bultmann's or Heidegger's) is as lopsided as the objectivism of "vulgar Marxism." Something is missing in the roots. Neither of these has penetrated deeply enough into the spring.

No one of course may properly hold that the development of a viable myth is a simple or clear matter. Yet, we may say that a principal thing that is missing is an ecology among the roots and among the fruits. For how can anything have meaning if everything does not? Or, as Calvin would ask, how can anything be viable if it is not rooted in "the God who is the fountain of *all* livingness"—that is, if it is not rooted in grace?

John Bunyan has epitomized what we may call an ecology of grace: "Christians," he says, "are like the several flowers in the garden, that have upon each of them the dew of heaven, which, being shaken with the wind, they let fall their dew at each other's roots, whereby they are jointly nourished, and become nourished of each other." This ecology of grace must obtain for the several elements of myth as well as for persons. The alternative is the myth of demonic fragmentation, the Achilles' heel of sectarian myth. Yet, sectarian myth is indispensable. Its viability can be measured by its power to contribute to "synthesis," to bringing together the paradoxical and contradictory elements that belong to the viable myth of any age.

What is called for is interiorization wedded to creative social protest and institutionalization.[4] The phrase "black is beautiful" and the women's consciousness movement are expressions of the recognized need for psychological and institutional transformation. If the individual is not enabled with others to take responsibility for his or her own historical role, he or she will live on in a "dream history" that reinforces his or her fragmentations.

When all is said and done, however, the demands of a viable myth must be pushed one step further. In actuality, they are counsels of perfection that are not approachable apart from the mystery of grace. They in no sense presuppose that persons can deliberately control or recover the sacred, or can deliberately produce the viable myth. Women and men can earnestly prepare to receive the viable myth as a transcendent gift of grace, but only in hope, that is, in dynamic eschatological tension with the principalities and powers of the world. No one knows this quality of hope better than the artist who in nourishing the creative act contemplates the eschatological victory.

Notes

1. The question may be raised: Which of these myths informs the revolt of youth today? In some instances the revolt appears to belong to the first, in others to the second myth. Regarding the first we ask: Is the privatism of the youth's myth essentially a descendant of the bourgeois privatism? Is the alternative life-style simply another way of refusing or failing to cope with the institutional realities, a protest nerved by despair? Regarding the second type of revolt a more positive evaluation is required.

2. Compare T. W. Adorno, "Sociology and Psychology," *New Left Review* 46 (November–December 1967).

3. Note that Marx is not content with the characterization of religion as "the opiate of the people," a formulation that appears earlier in this same essay.

4. Cf. Ernst Troeltsch, *Politische Ethik und Christentum* (Göttengen; 1904). In this study Troeltsch identifies two motifs that appear throughout history in the political philosophies that have claimed Christian sanction: reliance upon the spontaneity, inwardness, and integrity of the individual and reliance upon the nourishing, guiding, restraining sacraments and institutions. In his view each political philosophy may be characterized in terms of the way in which these two motifs are combined. At one end of the spectrum is spiritual anarchism, and at the other is a monolithic structure leaving little room for individual freedom or for inwardness.

24 · In Praise of Sleep

I

Paul *must* have been a saint. While he was preaching late into the evening a young man, Eutychus, sitting in a window, sank into a deep sleep, fell from the third story, and was "taken up dead." Despite his chagrin as a marathon preacher, Paul hastened immediately to the side of Eutychus, and revived him (Acts 20:6–12).

I am reminded of an incident of milder pattern in the early eighteenth century when Dr. Robert South, the eminent court preacher in London, interrupted his sermon to awaken the prime minister and warn him that if he did not moderate his snoring he might awaken his majesty, the king.

By way of contrast we recall that in ancient times sleeping in church was a hallowed practice. For a long stretch of pagan history sleeping in church, so to speak, was viewed as an act of piety; indeed, as a form of dream therapy it was given a technical name—"incubation." This word denotes the practice among the Greeks and Romans of sleeping within the precincts of a temple for the purpose of receiving a vision, a portent of the future, or relief from disease or pain. Ancient inscriptions record priestly prayers giving thanks to God (under countless names) for revealing himself during the sleep of the worshiper.

Sleep (with its dreams) has been interpreted under countless names— from a supernatural source of revelation and healing to the work of a demon to a biological-psychological fountain of refreshment—and also of terror. The psalmist does not offer a theology of sleep when he utters his prayer, "God's gifts come to his loved ones, as they sleep," but he acknowledges that sleep is worthy of praise and thanks to God. Verily, a pasture spring!

Sleep occupies a substantial portion of our lives. Out of the four score years and ten of an ample life, more than a score is spent in sleep. Is it possible perhaps to find a religious interpretation, a theological understanding, of sleep, and even of dreams? Perhaps we should with Robert Frost go out and try "to clear the pasture spring; . . . to rake the leaves away (and wait to watch the water clear . . .)."

One of the leaves that must be raked away is the notion that the praise of

This essay originally appeared in the Summer 1977 issue of *Kairos* and subsequently in *The Right Time: The Best of Kairos*, edited by David B. Parke (Boston: Skinner House, 1982), from which it is here reprinted, with permission.

sleep is the praise of sloth. To be sure, sleep can become slothful. In a conversation years ago in Strasbourg Albert Schweitzer said when I asked him about his ascetic sleeping habits, that many people tire themselves out by indulging in too much sleep; some of them, he said, are drunk with sleep. So said the man who in his early manhood worked all day studying medicine and then most of the night practicing the organ in preparation for his lesson in the morning. But sleep has its rights, and in its own right it is not sloth.

In the present century more scientific research has been devoted to the study of sleep than ever before. We read of the activity of the left hemisphere of the brain in the waking hours, and of the activity of the right hemisphere in the sleeping and dreaming hours, of rapid eye movement (REM) in dreams, and of four or five stages in sleep, many of these findings being disclosed by the electroencephalograph (EEG). We learn that dreams punctuate our sleep four or five times each night, that we cannot in health get along without them, indeed that we must eventually make up in dreams for any continued interruption of them. The literature has become enormous. In proceeding from Roscher to Freud and Jung and Fromm to Kleitman and others the studies have led from the couch to the laboratory.

In the midst of these findings and theories we can only suggest in a preliminary fashion one possible way of achieving a religious interpretation of sleep and dreams. First, then, we must ask, What constitutes a religious interpretation?

One of the most striking things about dreams, according to Erich Fromm, is "the similarity between the products of our creativeness during sleep and the oldest creations of man—the myths." The myths are concerned even with the difference between waking and sleeping. One of the most familiar is what turns out to be the alternation between attachment and detachment. This dialectic is to be observed in the interpretation of meditation and prayer, and also of mystical experience. For Buddhism deep sleep is a path to detachment, a symbol and anticipation of Nirvana. A similar dialectic between sleeping and waking appears in the notion of return from the tensions of the day mind to a lost unity latent in the night mind. Concerning sleep itself the myth of Oedipus has been the stock in trade of the Freudians. The dimensions of the lost unity, the cleavage in the psyche, and the overcoming of the cleavage, are emphasized in the oldest myth generally familiar to us, the biblical myth of creation, fall, and redemption; a myth that can refer to elements of sleep as well as to our waking life.

Let me be extremely brief as I recapitulate these elements by saying that they point to the basic supports and threats of meaningful human existence. "Creation" refers not only to the initial creation of the world in six days but also to the original innocence and balance of perfect mutuality in the myth of the Garden of Eden. It refers to the covenant of being, in nature and the human person—primordial creativity or "original virtue" in contrast to "original sin." The "fall" is the fateful disturbance of "creation" and of mutuality, the separation from the original unity, the breaking of the covenant of being, through the use and abuse of freedom. The psyche turns against itself and others, and surrenders to a destructive, demonic aggressiveness (or despair) violating mutuality. "Redemption" is not return to the innocence of "creation" but rather the overcoming of cleavage in a new and richer unity. This threefold pattern appears in the Bible, in early Christianity, in the Middle Ages, in the Reformation, and even in Marxism. In some instances it becomes the basis of a philosophy or theology of history.

II

Underlying the whole enterprise of being human are support and threat. But the support is primary, the indispensable dynamic of creative mutuality. Where this element of "creation" is completely absent, where the "fall" is complete and absolute, existence is no longer possible. Here, then, we find the religious intepretation of the human enterprise. The support is ultimately a "gift" (grace), the threat is a lurking temptation and insinuation. The sustaining, creative, commanding, judging, transforming, integrating power is a divine power, ultimately not of human making. The merely aggressive, self-serving, idolatrous perverter of freedom and mutuality is a demonic power that through excess can cause people and even whole communities to become "possessed." Yet, even this power depends in its way upon the support of being.

In the space remaining I want to speak of three forms of sleep or dreaming. The reader will readily discern a host of omissions in our movement toward a theology of sleep, of this "second course of the cosmos."

In the first category, "creation," one must recognize considerable variety. We think first of the idyllic dreams of innocent simplicity, the Edenic dreams of the lost unity of "original creation" when the morning stars sang together, airy sanguine scenes of childhood or of previous enjoyment of family or friendship—seen as perfect mutuality filtered through the gold dust of memory. A note of sadness can invade these dreams. We think of Milton's sonnet on dreaming of his deceased wife.

> But O, as to embrace me she inclined,
> I waked; she fled; and day brought back my night.

Among the dreams of "creation" are the dreams that bring us momentarily before the wonders of creation, also the dreams of sheer delight in play. Coleridge is the master of those who put into music these playful phantoms.

> A damsel with a dulcimer
> In a vision once I saw;
> It was an Abyssinian maid,
> And on her dulcimer she played,
> Singing of Mount Abora.

All of these types of dreaming innocence may be compensatory, serving as a relief from "the briers of the working-day world"—release from the jangling, tiring daytime experience of tension within the person or group in face of other persons or groups and of nature.

In contrast to these intimations of original creation are the dreams of conflict, of frustration, of fear and terror. At the simplest level we dream of hunting for an object that cannot be found, or we go on a journey whose destination eludes us. A dream that I have recurrently is that of finding myself in the pulpit before a congregation, without a manuscript or notes, an agonizing dream. Recalling Franz Kafka's K (in *The Castle*) plodding laboriously in a snowbank and completely without success, one might suggest that this kind of dream is a token of the yearning and self-seeking worship of the bitch goddess Success—the striving for imperious status. This appetite is a universal wolf.

But what of nightmares that elicit pain, fear, and even terror? One may not ignore the possible reflections here of something pathological in the person or the group, something requiring disciplined daytime therapies. The theories of nightmare are legion. One possibility of interpretation has often occurred to me, an observation regarding the uses of adversity.

> Which, like the toad, ugly and venomous
> Wears yet a precious jewel in his head.

A nightmare may be a compensatory dream, a fleeting awareness of dangers and even of forthcoming catastrophe, the sort of thing we like to ignore or gloss over in our daytime mind—tragedy, fatal illness, or death; world war, holocaust, ecological crisis. Dreams under the category of the "fall" bespeak the unresolved or even unresolvable conflicts within the psyche or the society, the loss of creativity and mutuality issuing in pain or fear or even terror. This kind of sleep is exhausting, enervating. It may be that the slings and arrows of fortune in our depersonalizing technological mass society are placing an unprecedented and even insupportable burden on our sleep as well as on our waking life.

One of the characteristic features of dreams is what may be called their diachronic character (if we may draw an analogy from the vocabulary of structuralism). They appear in a narrow, purely linear, one-track series of "events"; their intensity can be in part the consequence of the exclusion of the context that belongs to daytime life, also the consequence of the absence of comparison and contrast, and of critical reflection. Mature human experience is synchronic; it is multidimensional and contextual, it seeks integration or synthesis of contrasting elements.

"Redemptive" sleep seems to approach this quality of integrating movement. It is a parallel subterranean process. Repose enables us to digest what we have taken in in our hunting. Facing a difficult decision, we want to "sleep on it." Carlyle once said of Tennyson, "Alfred always carries a piece of chaos in his waistcoat pocket, turning it into cosmos." This is a process that takes place in redemptive sleep. For this reason the specialist Friedrich Kekulé has said, "Let us learn how to dream, and then perhaps we will discover the truth."

Most of the dreams studied, however, seem to be unpleasant. Sleep and dreams may remain primarily under the rubric of the "fall," denoting a touch of nature that makes the whole world kin. Yet, through a leap in the conscience they can remind us of the sleeplessness and bad dreams of others—for example, of the deprived who know not where they shall find food and clothing for the children, of the deprived who remain at the bottom of the pecking orders of "normal" daytime existence. This sense of judgment upon us is already in the prophetic vestibule of redemption, a harbinger of a new demand for human mutuality—for justice and love.

Recognizing these dimensions of sleep and of theological reflection on sleep, we become aware of the necessity of preparing for grace through meditation and prayer (including prophetic prayer), in order that sleep may become one of nature's chief nourishers at life's feast. For even though the whole person is not active in sleep, or at least not in the fashion of the daytime, a sort of work can go on in sleep, a providential, divinely therapeutic work that is not of our own doing or deliberate intention and that lures us on toward integrity and authentic mutuality. From this therapy of redemptive sleep we may sense anew what Job affirmed in the face of pain and loss: "I know that my Redeemer liveth."

25 · Pietism and Prophetism: Religion and Social Issues

I. Presuppositions

"Man is incurably religious" (Sabatier). In general, there is no such thing as a nonreligious person. All persons have some conception of the meaning of life; they live for meaning, for participation in that which is held to be significant—the fitting relation between the part and the whole, according to Wilhelm Dilthey, between surface and depth, between the transient and the permanent, between the human being and the ground and resource of meaning. From this perspective atheism is only a limiting concept: the atheist is one who claims that nothing has meaning, including atheism. There are three types of religion:

1. Explicit or overt religion: concern for the interconnection and unity of meaning and for the transcending source, ground, resource ("signals of transcendence") within and beyond the human being, expressed through conscious participation in a historical community (the church) possessing doctrine and discipline, and a consequent vocation in the world.

2. Implicit or covert religion: something is de facto accepted as the center of life and the ultimate source of meaning, but this ultimate ground is not consciously or deliberately identified and venerated as such.

3. Secular religion: concern for the interconnection and unity of meaning but without explicit orientation to an ultimate source and resource (culture). In our day secular religion appears within the church as well as outside it. All three types of religion may find expression in integrating loyalties. These loyalties may be fragmented (spatialized) or inconsistent (polytheism). But if meaning or significance is completely lacking, then despair, emptiness, anomie ensue. But even despair, emptiness, and anomie bespeak a hidden concern for meaning. The demand for meaning is inescapable. In a broad sense religion may issue in confidence in the reality and possibility of meaning, or it may issue in a sense of separation from

This highly compact essay was written as a study paper on the topic "religion, politics, economics, and social issues" for study and discussion at the Twentieth Congress of the International Association for Religious Freedom, held in Boston, Massachusetts, July 1969. Reprinted by permission.

meaning—in alienation. In the "high" religions, confidence and sense of alienation (estrangement, sin) belong paradoxically together.

> Whither shall I flee from thy presence?
> If I ascend to heaven, thou art there!
> If I make my bed in Sheol, thou art there!
> —Psalm 139

II. PIETISM AND PROPHETISM

The history of religion is marked by differentiations with respect to scope of meaning and also of responsibility. Pietism tends to "locate" meaning (religious significance and responsibility) in the immediate relation between the person and God and between person and person. In this spatialized piety economic and political structures do not receive direct attention: The pietist assumes that if inwardness (*Innerlichkeit*) is authentic, then institutional (suprapersonal) problems will take care of themselves. All we need is men and women of character or of mature personality, it is said. Freudianism is a secularized form of this spatialized piety. Much of contemporary existentialism, theological and secular, is pietistic and spatialized in this sense.

Prophetic religion with its political metaphors (covenant, Kingdom of God) views the scope of meaning, the scope of the sovereignty of God (the meaning-reality), to be of wider jurisdiction. God is the Lord of history, that is, of collective and institutional as well as of individual and interpersonal existence. People under covenant are responsible not only for individual and interpersonal behavior but also for the character of the society and its institutions. Marxism as a secularized or substitute religion bears some affinity to the institutional concerns of prophetic religion. In ignoring the personal and interior dimension, however, Marxism is as lopsided as the pietism that ignores the institutional dimension. Both subjective and objective virtues (Ernst Troeltsch)—virtues that are personal or interpersonal and virtues that require institutional manifestation—are required. Religious responsibility thus includes corporate responsibility (church, voluntary association, education, business, government). Prophetic religion demands both interiorization and institutionalization; it also demands both a specialized vocation (in the family and on the job) and a generalized vocation to promote the striving for a just and free society. Such terms as "the responsible society," "the responsible corporation," "the responsible voluntary association," point to the interpretation of religion as transcending mere individualism.

III. POWER

This conception of individual and corporate responsibility in the institutional spheres of economic and political structures involves the conception of power. Power as such is not evil, except when it is arbitrary, merely coercive force. Sociologically understood, power is the capacity to participate in the shaping of social decisions. The mere privatization of piety represents by default a surrender of this kind of power. It can be an organized form of irresponsibility—or pious impotence. On the other hand, participation in social power when it is not accompanied by individual piety and integrity can lead to deterioration and corruption of the commonwealth. Authentic religion therefore requires both interiorization and institutionalization.

IV. THE PRESENT SITUATION AND THE FUTURE

In a period of planetary agglomerations and conflicts of power, a period of population explosion, implosion, and diversification, religion more than ever is in danger of surrender to truncated and particularist loyalties, i.e., to demonic loyalties. On the other hand, some people in the face of agglomerations of power (of the military-industrial complex for example) arrive at the conviction that the conventional procedures of democratic, pluralistic society cannot significantly affect the dominant structures of power. Some of these people prefer conscientious privatization, giving up the collective structures and ethos as hopelessly beyond repair or reform. Others, especially the youth, undertake civil disobedience, a protest against a specific policy or law, toward the end of changing this policy or law.

Still others adopt an aggressive, systemic rejection of the social "order," and they struggle for radical transformation of economic and political structures. In their view the institutions of society have become, in Paul Goodman's words, "dangerous to life and liberty—the social compact is dissolved, it has lost its justification." This outlook is to be observed in the student rebellions in Europe and Asia and the Americas, and also in certain segments of the black power movement. In a totalitarian society systemic rejection may take the form of resistance (*Widerstand*). In Western societies today this systemic rejection assumes the form of demand for revolution and of resort to violence, in protest against the "violence" of the establishment and for the sake of radical transformation. The Christian-Marxist (or postrevolutionary neo-Marxist) dialogue is significant here, for it offers the promise of exploring these perspectives—on the one side individualism has often been irresponsible, on the other it has been crushed at the hands of communism. All of these perspectives call for new reflection concerning the nature and role of privatization and interiorization, for reexamination of the means of social criticism and transformation. In the end they call for reconsideration of the doctrine of human being and society and of "the signals of transcendence" which point to the nature of reality itself as source and resource of meaningful existence.

In our megalopolitan, technological society, with its nuclear power, mass media of communication, military-industrial complex, powerful special interest economic and political pressure groups, widespread poverty and dehumanization, both individual and corporate responsibilities must be reconceived (particularly in face of outmoded conceptions of democracy) if religion is to fulfill its vocation—to promote the kind of participation that possesses the wisdom, the audacity and power to risk new social decision. Both present and future are at stake. Indeed, we are already living in the future in the sense that what we do or fail to do will affect the future. Authentic religion, relevant concern for meaning, demands eschatological orientation. But hope, alas, can become a form of cheap grace, unless we recognize that we live in the valley of decision that extracts the high price of sacrificial participation.

To be sure, the final ends of humanity are hidden. Yet, the Kingdom of God is always at hand—"it is always available," in the translation of Joel Cadbury.

26 · The Politics of Culture in American Perspective

Max Weber once suggested that the Old Testament prophets in their independence and criticism of the monarchy and the society were an anticipation of the modern free press. An important difference, however, obtains between the Old Testament prophet and the modern free press. The prophet presupposes a religious vocation, the demand of the Lord of history for a society of justice and mercy combined with a demand for individual piety — corporate and individual integrity under the Great Taskmaster's eye. The priest maintains the traditional fabric of society; the prophet holds up a higher and universal standard that sanctions dissent looking toward social change. Here we have a religious ground for the "autonomy of culture" and also a ground for the "politics of culture," though the term "theonomy of culture" would be more appropriate for the religious perspective. These conceptions were persistently promoted by the late Dr. Umberto Campagnolo, the secretary general of the Société européenne de culture.

In Anglo-American society the prophetic exercise of dissent and the prophetic demand for corporate and individual integrity find their origin in the Radical Reformation of the sixteenth and seventeenth centuries. Here emerged the conviction that the autonomy of culture requires a separation of powers (implicit also in Old Testament prophetism and in the modern free press). The Radical Reformation, in face of the centralization of political, economic, and ecclesiastical power, asserted the right of freedom of association, the right to form religious associations without license from the monarch or the established church. This demand for freedom of association was viewed as heretical. In general, the word *heresy* took its meaning from the Greek word meaning "to choose." The heretical groups were considered blasphemous, for in face of established authority they

This essay first appeared in *The Politics of Culture*, a biannual publication of the Société européenne de culture, vol. 1, issue 1, ed. Nigel Foxall and Bart Landheer (The Hague: Martinus Nijhoff, January 1978); pp. 17–20. Adams contributed articles to *Comprendre*, the yearbook of the society, and for several years served, with Lewis Mumford, as its international vice president. Reprinted by permission.

presumed to demand the right to choose; hence, they were viewed as subversive of the stability of society.

The demand for freedom of religious association carried with it the claim to form a church in which every member had the right and the responsibility to participate in the shaping of policy—a radical self-determination. This democratic conception soon began to appear in the economic and political realms. James I had predicted: Today they are attacking the bishops, tomorrow they will be attacking me. His prediction was correct. By analogy the free church became the model for a democratic state and eventually the sanction for the extension of the suffrage. Just as minority views were to be protected in the free church, so they were to be protected and even listened to in the state. Before the seventeenth century the radical dissenters were hanged or beheaded; after the seventeenth century the political dissenters became a "loyal opposition" and occupied the opposition benches in Parliament with the opportunity to become the party in power. The dissenters of this loyal opposition were not only tolerated, they were also supported financially by the government—as we say in English, they were placed on expense account. Moreover, the demand for freedom of religious association was soon followed by the demand for freedom of other associations. Voluntary associations became agencies of criticism and innovation. Here we see the advent of the modern pluralist society, the dispersion of power and responsibility. Coercion of opinion was in principle outlawed. Eventually came the demand for a written constitution to define and protect rights of freedom and dissent within an embracing, though open, framework. Shakespeare might have called it "union in partition"; Daniel Webster called it "liberty and union."

It was on this soil that the modern conception of human rights, and especially of the right of self-determination and dissent, grew. President Carter's (Baptist) concern for human rights presupposes in part this historical background, supplemented by the Bill of Rights of the U.S. Constitution. At a recent state dinner in Washington Prime Minister Giulio Andreotti of Italy spoke eloquently of this background of President Carter's stress on human rights.

We see in these developments not only the division of powers and the sanction of dissent. We see also that the autonomy of culture was not viewed as merely the free-wheeling of the individual or the free association; it was viewed as requiring institutional framework, as requiring the organization of power and the power of organization. Equally important was the demand for the freedom of the arts and sciences.

In the brief compass of the present essay these developments have been oversimplified. They did not take place without dust and heat or without counterrevolutionary thrusts. But the thread that gives continuity to the developments is the thread of self-determination.

We now live in a mass, technological society made up of great concentrations of power which attempt to control the means of communication and livelihood, a society that in some ways resembles the type of society against which the Radical Reformation initially protested. Freedom of association, or rather the greedy abuse of it, has issued in crude nationalism, imperialism, exploitive colonialism, and multinational corporations that are largely unaccountable, indeed are stronger than many of the "sovereign" states.

The deprived within these states, and also the Third World in certain quarters, are in process of seeking self-determination. The rivalry of the great nation-states has promoted new forms of tribalism, now facing ecological crisis and the threat of annihilation as the outcome of an armament race for nuclear power.

John Milton, the poet of left wing Puritanism who held the Christian to be "a self-governing agent," gives us in *Samson Agonistes* the warning of the imprisoned Samson "eyeless in Gaza";

> Suffices that to me strength is my bane,
> And proves the source of all my miseries. . . .
> O dark, dark, dark, amid the blaze of noon.

The politics of culture can be effective only if it supports institutional agencies that aim to correct the forms of tribalism, of elitism, of discrimination in terms of sex, race, and class. It therefore calls for participation in the shaping of social policy; it calls for the *engagées* and also for the *enragées*. Else we shall be fed with wormwood and be given water of gall to drink. Those who are not "engaged" are by default the supporters of injustice and suppression and even of tyranny in face of the new despotisms.

The Société européenne de culture aims in this situation to serve as an ecumenical congruence of West and East, dedicated to seek for a world combining independence and interdependence, combining both corporate and individual responsibility.

Part Four

Vocation and Voluntary Associations

A N AUTHENTIC RELIGIOUS COMMUNITY, ADAMS HOLDS, IS ONE THAT weaves a network of human relationships to overcome the spatial, racial, economic, and other forms of segregation that mark—and mar— communal life. Hence the title of the short sermon that begins this section, "Fishing with Nets," signifies a basic conception of the vocation of the church and its ministry. "Vocation" connotes the religious sense of calling or mission; in various contexts Adams applies the term to the professions, to the human being as such, and to human associations.

Study of the role of voluntary associations in the formation and continuous reformation of democratic societies is widely recognized as Adams's most distinctive contribution to social ethics. The basic personal discipline of social ethics is active participation in associations that work for social justice, a theme Adams spells out in "The Indispensable Discipline of Social Responsibility: Voluntary Associations." Associations may serve the narrow self-interest of groups; they may be guardians of "restrictive covenants." They may also be agencies of social redemption, insofar as they seek to create more inclusive and just covenants of social, political, and economic order.

The covenant of a democracy is rooted in religious liberty, in Adams's view. A basic purpose of the principle of the separation of church and state, reflected in the essay "Good Fences Make Good Neighbors" is to protect the autonomy of the prophetic religious voice.

To an activist like Adams, good intentions are not good enough. In the debate between the "ethics of conscience" and the "ethics of consequences," he is predominantly on the side of consequences. That is, social responsibility is a matter of being accountable for the consequences of one's actions, above and beyond the conscientiousness or purity of one's motives. Power, both as a theological and sociological concept, is central in Adams's social ethics; in the title of the essay "Blessed Are the Powerful," he boldly ventures a "new beatitude." Law, for example, is an expression of social power. While religious thought has often set law in opposition to love, Adams insists upon the essential role of law as a curb against arbitrary political power.

Conflict is inherent in the human condition, Adams believes, so long as injustice lasts. His essay "The Shock of Recognition: The Black Revolution and Greek Tragedy" brings this complex conviction to bear upon a complex phenomenon, the black power movement. Adams sees it as a fundamentally just response to American racism, even though, in the last analysis, power is truly "blessed" only as it serves such transcendent values as love and peace.

The themes of marriage, family, and aging reflect Adams's interests in the formation and malformation of other forms of human association. In "Aging: A Theological Interpretation," he points to the depersonalizing impact on family life of economic conditions that isolate the nuclear family and segregate the elderly. His reflection on the psychic, sexual, and social meanings of marriage in "Thou Shalt Not Commit Adultery" takes covenant as the central term for interpreting the marriage bond and its violation.

We participate by nature and by conscious decision in what Adams calls the covenant of being. In "Shalom: The Ministry of Wholeness," he refers to the struggle for racial justice in professional baseball and a stabile by Alexander Calder in his interpretation of the conflicting spiritual forces in human life and the quest for *shalom*, the peace of personal and communal wholeness. His is finally an irenic spirit. Covenants are broken, often with tragic consequences, as a result of the failure of moral good will. But since they are rooted in the very nature of human being, they are also reparable through forgiveness and renewed will.

The final essay in this section, "The Ecology of World Religions and Peace," envisions a fundamental unity of purpose amid the diversity of voices with which the great religions of the world speak. To address the world prophetically in the cause of peace, he suggests, the religions must themselves work together, as an ecological system does, planting the seeds and nurturing the vision of world peace.

The Postscript, "The Church That Is Free," is an analogue to William Ellery Channing's ringing lines on the free mind: "I call that mind free . . ." Adams affirms the basic liberal theme of spiritual freedom, yet not in the context of an individualistic moral idealism but in a corporate commitment to prophetic faith, the essential vocation of voluntary associations.

Adams's "Prayer of Dedication" for the ordination of Alice B. Lane at the First Church of Christ (Unitarian) in Lancaster, Massachusetts, on May 27, 1984, reflects his basic convictions regarding the vocation of the church and its ministry. It is also a work wrought with beauty and power, here reprinted from *The Unitarian Universalist Christian* 39 nos. 3–4 (1984):

O thou ancient of days, the great mover of the globe whereon we speed through space and time, thou who art higher than our highest thought, the ground of all that gives us breath and life, we know thee also as nearer to us than breathing, as both intimate and ultimate, as more deeply moving in the contrite heart than in the paths of suns and stars, as more powerfully creative in love and justice than in the might of atoms.

We are grateful that thou hast gathered us into this fellowship of faith, calling us to search and to proclaim knowledge of thy truth and to enter into a covenant with thee and with each other of faithfulness to that truth and its responsibilities both individual and collective. We are grateful for this covenant which has been entered into by men and women of diverse times, places, and traditions.

In thy presence we acknowledge ourselves for what we are—creatures of vision, of blindness, and of perverted vision, stumbling creatures of love and fear and hate. We acknowledge that the cleavages and injustices of our world spring from our indifference and impotence and irresponsibility. In thy presence we know that nothing can be truth for any of us which is not a part of the common life and good of all.

From the covenant opened up for us by Jesus we acknowledge the calling that thou has given us in the priesthood and the prophethood of all believers. Today we acknowledge the indispensable place of scholarship in this calling. Remembering the command that we love thee with heart and soul and mind and strength we in this hour of dedication acknowledge that mind cannot work alone, that to become love of thee it requires also heart and soul and strength. We rejoice that the love and sharing in this community are being strengthened by the gifts and devotion of our sister, Alice Lane, whom we have known with her family in affection now for many fruitful years.

We invoke thy blessing, O GOD. Breathe upon us thy Holy Spirit that the dayspring from on high may visit us day by day to give thy light to them that sit in darkness and in the shadow of death, to preach the gospel to the poor, to heal the broken-hearted and to proclaim the release of all who are captive to sin and death. AMEN.

G.K.B.

27 · *Fishing with Nets*

Miguel de Unamuno, the Spanish philosopher, poet, and novelist, tells of a conversation he had with a young philosophical anarchist, not the kind carrying bombs but one believing in radical individualism, in going his own way, or as we say today, doing his own thing. The young man said, "I am an individualist. I never ride in a car if I can help it. I ride on a bicycle so that I may go my own way." Unamuno responded, "I suppose, then, that you do not ride your bicycle on the road. You pedal across field and hill avoiding every path where anyone else has ever been. And, by the way, who made your bicycle? Did you make it? And if so, where did you get the parts?" In this fashion Unamuno dissolved this fellow's claim to be a radical individualist.

All of us encounter and travel certain paths that have been trod. We may of course make new paths or express some individuality within the path in which we find ourselves. Today we are celebrating the ordination of a minister. That is a special path that involves all of us, and not merely the minister, Judy Deutsch. So the question is, What is the path she is entering and that we have entered, a path in which she has already trod vigorously? In other words, what is the vocation of the minister and of the church?

In answering that question I have decided to adopt a conventional path by speaking on a text, a biblical text in the Gospel of Matthew on which hundreds of ordination sermons have been delivered.

> As Jesus walked by the Sea of Galilee, he saw two brothers, Simon who is called Peter and Andrew, his brother, casting a net into the sea, for they were fishermen. And he said to them, "Follow me, and I will make you fishers of men" (Matt. 4:18–19).

Consequently, I was planning to entitle this sermon of ordination "Fishers of Men." On second thought, however, I did not see how I could manage characterizing a woman minister as a fisher of men. In fact not only men are sinners and in need of salvation. Then I got to thinking about how people fished in those days. They did not fish with a pole, a sinker, and bait,

This sermon was delivered at the ordination of Judy Deutsch by the First Parish Church Of Sudbury, Sudbury Center, Massachusetts, on October 4, 1981.

catching fish one by one. Indeed, the passage says that after Jesus told them to follow him, they cast their nets aside. So the theme of this sermon turned out to be "Fishing with Nets." It was going to ride not on a bicycle but on a metaphor.

The metaphor of a net or network immediately brings to mind the fact that traditionally our churches have been grounded in a covenant binding us together in a fellowship of persons recognizing a common responsibility not only for the authenticity of the local fellowship but also for the character of our community and society. The vocation of the minister and of the fellowship, then, is to create, to maintain, to develop, to deepen, to enrich the priesthood and prophethood of all believers.

But this enterprise of maintaining the network is itself not to be understood as simply a human enterprise. It is a response to a divinely given creative power, a sustaining power, a community-transforming power. This power is ultimately not of our own making, it lays down its conditions, it cannot be manipulated with impunity, and it points to a sustaining meaning, a goal for our existence together. Since it is all of these things it should be called divine. Wherever this power is working God is at work.

Our first impulse here today is one of celebration and of gratitude that we are here together in the covenant of remaining responsive to the sustaining, transforming power that creates the network of community, indeed that enables us to listen to each other, to recognize each other's needs, and to recognize and respond to the needs of those beyond our locale.

But there are many things that separate us from true community. The late Dean Sperry of Harvard Divinity School used to tell the story of his first evening at the graduate school in Yale. For his dinner he went to the Common Room, and at the table he found a stranger sitting by his side. In order to lubricate conversation he said to the fellow student, "My field is New Testament Greek, what is yours?" The stranger replied, "My field is mathematics." Thereupon the conversation ended.

Two summers ago a large group of scientists around the world met for a conference at the Massachusetts Institute of Technology. They lamented not only the separation of the sciences from the humanities; they lamented the specializations that prevent their own intercommunication; most of all, they lamented the separation of the scientists from the public and its concerns in this nuclear and computer age. These are the segregations of specialization.

But there are other kinds of segregation. These are the segregations of neighborhood, neighborhoods that are separated in terms of education,

income, occupation, taste, and race. This kind of neighborhood can be a
highly organized form of separation or segregation, breeding hostility and
resentment. The New England town meeting has enjoyed the reputation of
being the seedbed of U.S. democratic integrity. One of my doctoral
students therefore decided several years ago to study the meetings of a town
near here, a prestigious Boston suburb proud of its tradition of town
meeting. After careful research he found that the meeting could be certain
of the largest attendance if the agenda included the continuing effort to
prevent blacks from residing in that town.

The most dangerous form of segregation is, I suppose, nationality, the
separations caused by the tension between nations. So pervasive has been
nationalism in the modern period that it has been called the modern
person's "other religion." For this religion millions of martyrs have died.
The latest polls indicate that a majority of people in the United States assert
that they assume that war is on the agenda for the near future.

One could therefore say that religion, whether it be the religion of
nationalism or the religion of the churches, is primarily a territorial
religion, basic commitments being rooted in a segregated territorial space.
We are accustomed to the word *geopolitics*. Related to this is the new word
geotheology. Geotheology is a study of the ways in which we are affected by
the place in which we happen to find ourselves. Let me say here that Judy
Deutsch during the past year or two has been very much involved in an
effort in the direction of forming a coalition between Roman Catholics,
Jews, Protestants, and ethnics, whites, blacks, Hispanics, concerned with
religion and economic justice. Here we see the outreach of a network
beyond nationality.

Anatole France years ago told the story of a young man from a small town
in the provinces in France who visited a relative in Paris who showed him,
the country boy, around. In the course of the tour they visited the Chamber
of Deputies, where they found an intensive, heated debate under way. The
provincial could not follow the debate, and when the two visitors got out on
the street the young fellow asked what the argument was all about. The
Parisian replied, "They were discussing the cost of the First World War."
"And what did they decide?" "They decided that the cost was 23 trillion
francs." "And what about the men and women who were killed?" "Oh, they
were included." In short, we may say that the need for network is a far-flung
need, a matter of life and death. That reflection gives us a sense of the
importance of the vocation of the minister and the congregation of a
religious fellowship. And the process begins close to home.

Some years ago I was a member of the Board of Trustees of the First Unitarian Church in Chicago. A member of the board often complained about the minister's preaching too many sermons on race relations. He often said that academics of course know little of the world of reality. One evening at a meeting of the board he opened up again. So the question was put to him, "Do you want the minister to preach sermons that conform to what you have been saying about 'kikes' and blacks?" "No," he replied, "I just want the church to be more realistic." Then the barrage opened, "Will you tell us what is the purpose of a church anyway?" "I'm no theologian. I don't know." "But you have ideas, you are a member here, a member of the Board of Trustees, and you are helping to make decisions here. Go ahead, tell us the purpose of the church. We can't go on unless we have some understanding of what we are up to here." The questioning continued, and items on the agenda for the evening were ignored.

At about one o'clock in the morning our friend became so fatigued that the Holy Spirit took charge. And our friend gave a remarkable statement regarding the nature of our fellowship. He said, "The purpose of the church is. . . . Well, the purpose is to get hold of people like me and change them."

Someone, a former evangelical, suggested that we should adjourn the meeting, but not before we sang, "Amazing grace . . . how sweet the sound. I once was lost but now am found, was blind but now I see."

There is the vocation of the minister and the church, to form a network of fellowship that alone is reliable because it is responsive to a sustaining, commanding, judging, and transforming power.

28 · The Indispensable Discipline of Social Responsibility: Voluntary Associations

In 1927 in the city of Nuremberg, six years before the National Socialists came into power, I was watching a Sunday parade on the occasion of the annual mass rally of the Nazis. Thousands of youth, as a sign of their vigor and patriotism, had walked from various parts of Germany to attend the mass meeting of the party. As I watched the parade, which lasted for four hours and which was punctuated by trumpet and drum corps made up of hundreds of Nazis, I asked some people on the sidelines to explain to me the meaning of the swastika, which decorated many of the banners. Before very long I found myself engaged in a heated argument. Suddenly someone seized me from behind and pulled me by the elbows out of the group with which I was arguing. In the firm grip of someone whom I could barely see I was forced through the crowd and propelled down a side street and up into a dead-end alley. As this happened I assure you my palpitation rose quite perceptibly. I was beginning to feel Nazism existentially. At the end of the alley my uninvited host swung me around quickly, and he shouted at me in German, "You fool. Don't you know? In Germany today when you are watching a parade, you either keep your mouth shut, or you get your head bashed in." I thought he was going to bash it in right there. But then his face changed into a friendly smile, and he said, "If you had continued that argument for five minutes longer, those fellows would have beaten you up." "Why did you decide to help me?" I asked. He replied, "I am an anti-Nazi. As I saw you there, getting into trouble, I thought of the times when in New York City as a sailor of the German merchant marine I received a wonderful hospitality. And I said to myself, "Here is your chance to repay that hospitality.' So I grabbed you, and here we are. I am inviting you home to Sunday dinner."

This man turned out to be an unemployed worker. His home was a tenement apartment in the slums. To reach it, we climbed three flights up a

Adams presented this address at the University of Padua in 1962, following the Second Vatican Council, where he was a Protestant observer. It was published in *The Journal of the Liberal Ministry* 6, no. 2 (1966). Reprinted with permission of the Unitarian Universalist Ministers Association.

staircase that was falling apart, and he ushered me into a barren room where his wife and three small children greeted their unexpected American guest in astonishment. We had the Sunday meal together, a dinner of greasy dumplings and of small beer drunk from a common jug. Within a period of two hours I learned vividly of the economic distress out of which Nazism was born. From this trade-union worker I learned also that one organization after the other that refused to bow to the Nazis was being threatened with compulsion. The totalitarian process had begun. Freedom of association was being abolished. "You keep your mouth shut, and you conform, or you get your head bashed in." A decade later in Germany I was to see at first hand the belated resistance of the churches to this attack upon freedom of speech and freedom of association.

At this juncture I had to confront a rather embarrassing question. I had to ask myself, What in your typical behavior as an American citizen have you done that would help to prevent the rise of authoritarian government in your own country? What disciplines of democracy (except voting) have you habitually undertaken with other people which could serve in any way directly to affect public policy? More bluntly stated: I asked myself, What precisely is the difference between you and a political idiot?

FREEDOM OF ASSOCIATION

Immediately after the Second World War the Swiss theologian Karl Barth made a speaking tour in Germany, and in his talks he stressed the idea that every conscientious German citizen should now participate actively in voluntary associations committed to the task of making democracy work. I do not know whether Karl Barth as a professor in Germany practiced his own preaching when Nazism was on the rise. But in giving his admonition to the Germans after the war, he pointed to a characteristic feature of any democratic society, namely, freedom of association.

Every totalitarian theory rejects just this freedom. Indeed, the rejection of freedom of association, the rejection of the freedom to form groups that attempt democratically to affect public policy, can serve as the beginning of a definition of totalitarianism. We are familiar with the fulminations against freedom of association by Hobbes and Rousseau. Hobbes the totalitarian warns against "the great number of corporations which are as it were many lesser commonwealths in the body of a greater, like worms in the entrails of a natural man." The late Senator Joseph McCarthy worked in the spirit of Hobbes when he tried to smother freedom of association.

As against Hobbes the theorists of democracy have asserted that only through the exercise of freedom of association can consent of the governed become effective; only through the exercise of freedom of association can the citizen in a democracy participate in the process that gives shape to public opinion and to public policy. For this reason we may speak of the voluntary association as a distinctive and indispensable institution of democratic society.

How shall we define voluntary association? Speaking of the situation in the United States of over a hundred years ago, the Frenchman Alexis de Tocqueville observed that "in no country in the world has the principle of association been more successfully used, or applied to a greater multitude of objects, than in America. . . . Wherever, at the head of some new undertaking, you see the government in France, or a man of rank in England, in the United States you will be sure to find an association." De Tocqueville gives the classical description of the multitude of associations in the United States at that time, associations for libraries, hospitals, fire prevention, and for political and philanthropic purposes. One could sum up de Tocqueville's description of the United States at that time by saying that where two or three Americans are gathered together you may be sure that a committee is being formed. We have been "a nation of joiners."

Any healthy democratic society is a multigroup society. One finds in it business corporations, religious associations, trade unions, educational associations, recreational, philanthropic, protective, and political associations, and innumerable social clubs. These associations are, or claim to be, voluntary; they presuppose freedom on the part of the individual to be or not to be a member, to join or withdraw, or to consort with others to form a new association. By way of contrast the state and the family, for example, are as associations involuntary, and in some countries the church also is virtually involuntary. All persons willy-nilly are born into a particular state and a particular family. It is not a matter of choice whether they will belong to these two associations. In this sense they are involuntary. There are other associations, to be sure, that are difficult to classify under either category, voluntary or involuntary. Taken together, these associations, involuntary and voluntary, represent the institutional articulation of the pluralistic society.

The Historical Roots of Voluntary Associations

The appearance of the voluntary association in Western society did not come without a struggle. The initial demand for voluntary association came from the churches of the Radical Reformation, especially the aggressive sects of left wing Puritanism. These churches insisted that religion, in order to be a matter of choice, must be free from state control. Therefore they demanded the separation of church and state. This struggle for freedom of religious association continued for over two centuries. It was accompanied or followed by a struggle for freedom of economic association, for freedom to establish political parties, for freedom of workers to form unions, and for freedom to institute reforms in society. Not all voluntary associations, to be sure, are concerned with public policy. Some associations are simply social clubs, others promote hobbies, and still others are merely status groups. Considering the voluntary association that is concerned with social policy, for example with securing civil liberties or better housing, or with overcoming racial discrimination, we may say that this sort of association stands between the individual and the state and provides the instrumentality for achieving consensus within a group, and for implementing this consensus through either political or nonpolitical means. This sort of association provides the opportunity for discussion, for assembling neglected facts, and for scrutinizing and overcoming mere propaganda.

The voluntary association at its best offers an institutional framework within which the give and take of discussion may be promoted, an institutional framework within which a given consensus or practice may be brought under criticism and be subjected to change. It offers a means for bringing a variety of perspectives into interplay. It offers the means of breaking through old social structures in order to meet new needs. It is a means of dispersing power, in the sense that power is the capacity to participate in making social decisions. It is the training ground of the skills that are required for viable social existence in a democracy. In short, the voluntary association is a means for the institutionalizing of gradual revolution. The process often takes place through the entry into political history of groups hitherto hidden, silent, or suppressed. Here we think of the emergence of the middle class, of the professions, the blacks, and women— and today we see it on a continental scale in the "basic communities" of Latin America.

I have spoken of the fact that freedom of association was fought for by the churches of the left wing of the Reformation. Any adequate treatment of free association demands theological interpretation. Such a treatment would show how the doctrine of the covenant in old and New England was employed to sanction the priesthood and prophethood of all believers, and thus to express religious and social responsibility. By covenant people responded to God's community-forming power. But the prime example of the institutionalization of a doctrine of the covenant is to be found much earlier in Western history. The primitive Christian church illustrates many of the features of a voluntary association which I have mentioned. In one sense, to be sure, the primitive church was not a voluntary association as ordinarily conceived. It was believed to have come into existence through the work of God and not through the acts of persons. Nor was it directly concerned with public policy as such, except that by its very existence it bespoke the demand for freedom of association. Yet the primitive church illustrates the dispersion of power and responsibility, and it illustrates also the breaking through of old social structures toward the end of creating new structures. The primitive church broke through the bonds of the ethnic religion of Judaism: Jew, Greek, Roman, and German could be members. Moreover, the membership of the primitive church came from all classes of society, but especially from the lower classes (including slaves). The church also gave a new status to women. Besides all this, the primitive church gave the common people the opportunity to learn the skills required for effective social organization. The common people who were members had to learn the skills of preaching and teaching, of administration, of missionizing, and also of dispensing charity. The emergence of the primitive church represents, then, one of the great innovative movements of history, a great social revolution. Probably the recovery of the West after the fall of Rome took place with greater speed because of the thousands of people who had been trained in skills that could be employed outside as well as inside the church organization. Here was an enormous dispersion of the capacity to participate in the making of social decision, and in response to a transcendent purpose.

By the time the church had come into its medieval form, however, a great change had taken place in its internal structure. Indeed, certain branches of the Reformation represented a protest against the monolithic power structure of the church, and they carried through this protest by appeal to the model of the primitive church. So we see movement back and forth from one kind of social structure to another.

Thus an association originally intended to disperse power and responsibility undergoes changes moving in the opposite direction, that is, in the direction of concentration of power. In the earliest essay in America on the structure of voluntary associations William Ellery Channing, the Boston Unitarian clergyman, pointed to this danger. The voluntary association, so far from serving as an instrument of freedom, may end in becoming a new instrument of tyranny and conformism. Channing could speak with experience in these matters, for a number of the great reformist associations of the early nineteenth century were organized in his study.

"The Iron Law of Oligarchy"

Robert Michels, the Italian sociologist, has given a memorable account of the internal shift of power that can take place in an association. His view is that in any organization the "eager beavers" can take advantage of the indolence of the average member. By this means they gain control of the organization. This process he describes as the operation of "the iron law of oligarchy."

We can observe the iron law of oligarchy as it operates in the great pressure groups of today. A few years ago some sociologists studied the centralized bureaucracy of the American Medical Association. They found a goodly number of physicians who said that they felt that the A.M.A. through its policies was damaging the image of the physician in the United States today. On being asked why they did not do something to change the structure and the policies of the bureaucracy, some of them gave the answer, "I trained to be a doctor, and I want to practice medicine. In order to break the bureaucracy of the A.M.A., I and many of my colleagues would have to spend much more time than we can afford." It is a striking fact that the large business corporation functions by reducing the role of the shareholder. The average small shareholder surrenders power by signing a proxy to the representative of the managers. This sort of phenomenon belongs to the pathology of associations, and we could find ample illustration of it by examining colleges and churches.

But the pathology does not end with the functioning of the iron law of oligarchy within associations. It can be observed also in the functioning of the great pressure groups as they affect public policy. Legislation regarding the pressure groups has corrected some of the evils. But the role of the special interest pressure group today presents us with a major problem of the democratic society: The power of the pressure group is exercised through collusion with other pressure groups. The lobbyist of the wool growers' association in face of some legislation he wishes to impede goes to the representative of the copper producers' association and says, "I know that you are not interested pro or con in this bit of legislation, but if you will join us now, we shall give you assistance when you need it in a similar situation." In a society where the principle of freedom of association obtains, one to be sure must recognize the legitimate freedom of the pressure groups. Besides this, we must recognize they do not always enter into collusion. In some measure the great special interest pressure groups function as countervailing powers that neutralize each other. This neutralization, however, does not appear when, for example, the issue has to do with the distribution of the tax burden. Here the ordinary citizen gets shortchanged.

Two Types of Associations

This whole situation points to a major requirement for a viable and authentic democratic society. One can roughly classify the great voluntary associations concerned with public policy. The one type of association is called the special interest group. Here the association is judged by its capacity to ring up money on the cash register of the member. These special interest groups became very influential already at the end of the nineteenth century in the U.S.A. Henry Demarest Lloyd pointed out this changing character of American society. Speaking of the great concentrations of business power and of the large special interest pressure groups at the end of the century he said that the letters "U.S.A." had come to mean the "United Syndicates of America."

The other type of association is the sort that directly aims to promote the general welfare. The member of the association does not expect to make personal gain through the association. For example, the average member of the American Civil Liberties Union seldom makes a personal gain from participation in the organization. Members spend their time and money to support the effort to redefine the nature of civil liberties in a changing society, and also to defend those whose liberties are violated or threatened.

In some of the larger associations or pressure groups the broad constituency of the membership makes it possible for us to say that the gain of the members is a gain also for many nonmembers. For example, the civil rights movement with its many associations that aim to promote the liberty of the blacks will in the long run increase the productivity of the entire nation and it will also extend the rights of other underprivileged groups. The award of the Nobel Prize for peace to Martin Luther King Jr. served to recognize the contribution of civil rights organizations to the whole democratic society and even to the forces of emancipation in the world at large.

In face of these two types of association we can say that the health of democracy depends on the capacity of general welfare associations to function as countervailing powers against the narrower purposes of the special interest associations.

Now, I would like to make three brief observations with regard to this demand. First, let me mention the findings of some recent studies of college graduates. These studies indicate that insofar as they are concerned with public policy, most college graduates in the United States are affiliated with special interest groups. Moreover, they give little attention or time to participation in the organizations; they simply pay their dues and expect the bureaucracy to look after their interests. Now, a second observation. A minister in Denver has published an elaborate study of the associational behavior of the members of his middle-class church. He shows that even the associations of philanthropic character to which his church members belong serve mainly to bring together birds of a feather, that is, to bring together people possessing the same economic and political prejudices. So far from extending the range of community across ethnic and class lines, these associations serve to keep the classes and races separate. A third observation: Mirra Komarovsky has studied the associational behavior of the residents of Manhattan. She has found that apart from membership in the church the citizens of Manhattan do not on the average belong to even one association concerned with public policy. She asserts that we have here a good definition of the mass person. Regardless of whether one is "educated" or not, one is a mass person who does not participate in associations concerned with the public benefit. Being only on the receiving end of the mass media of communications, in the world of public policy such a person is a political eunuch.

Human sinfulness expresses itself, then, in the indifference of the average citizen who is so impotent, so idiotic in the sense of that word's Greek root (that is, privatized), as not to exercise freedom of association for the sake of the general welfare and for the sake of becoming a responsible self.

Ernst Troeltsch has made a distinction that is of prime significance here. He distinguishes between what he calls subjective and objective virtues. Subjective virtues are virtues that can be exhibited in immediate person-to-person relations. Objective virtues require an institution for their expression. Thus, from the larger human perspective we can say that the isolated good man or woman is a chimera. There is no such thing as a "good person" as such. There is only the good father or the good mother, the good physician or the good plumber, the good churchperson, the good citizen. The good person of the subjective virtues, to be sure, provides the personal integrity of the individual; without it the viable society is not possible. But from the point of view of the *institutional* commonwealth the merely good individual is good for nothing. Moreover, the narrow range of responsibility of the man or woman who confines attention merely to family and job serves to dehumanize the self.

At the outset I spoke of the experience in pre-Nazi Germany when a man told me, "You either keep your mouth shut, or you get your head bashed in." In the democratic society the nonparticipating citizens bash their own heads in. The living democratic society requires the disciplines of discussion and common action for the determination of policy. The differences between persons are determined by the quality and direction of their participation. In this sense we may understand the New Testament word, "By their fruits shall you know them"; but to this word we should add the admonition, By their groups shall you know them.

29 · *Good Fences Make Good Neighbors*

Be not righteous overmuch.

Ecclesiastes 7:16

In the old days at Harvard, earlier in this century, the former Appleton Chapel was located on this spot where we are at this moment. At the worship services that much larger chapel was filled with hundreds of students. The reason for this is simple. Attendance was required.

In those days the doors were locked when the bells stopped ringing. No late students could enter the chapel. The monitors then stood in their several places to record the absentees.

On the occasion when required attendance was formally abolished at the instigation of the university preacher, Professor Francis Greenwood Peabody, he said in his address that he had been studying compulsory attendance at chapel in various parts of the commonwealth, including the state penitentiary in Concord. The only difference he could find, he said, between chapel services at Harvard and those at the Concord penitentiary was that in Concord the monitors carried guns, an appropriate symbol for coercion. For some years the Yale Chapel retained the practice of required attendance. I recall that Dean Willard Sperry of Harvard Divinity School reported that when he was guest preacher at Yale he could not from the pulpit see the faces of the students. In protest against compulsory attendance they hid themselves behind their newspapers, and the preacher could see only an expansive patchwork quilt of unfolded newspapers. Subsequently, Yale Chapel also abolished the practice. We may say that the abolition of required attendance means that religion and compulsion are by nature incompatible.

An analogous issue today confronts the U.S. public in the much broader contest of national policy. In face of a Supreme Court decision prohibiting public prayers in the schools, the president of the United States has recommended to Congress the passage of an amendment to the Constitu-

Adams presented this sermon at Appleton Chapel, in Harvard University's Memorial Church, Cambridge, Massachusetts, in 1984. His abstract states: "President Reagan's proposed amendment harks back to the authoritarian stance of the Roman Emperor Constantine of the fourth century."

tion permitting officially sanctioned prayer in public schools. Defending his proposal, the president has said that ancient Greece and Rome declined when they began to abandon their gods, and that the Supreme Court's ban on organized school prayer for the past two decades has "diminished the importance of religion . . . and morality." He of course does not call for the recovery of belief in the gods of ancient Greece and Rome. But, surprisingly enough, he does call for the revival of something that belongs to an earlier epoch. He is calling for the revival of a compulsory feature of the authoritarian government of the Roman Emperor Constantine in the fourth century. In this policy the magistrate with the support of the church had the right and duty to maintain the faith and to wield the secular arm on behalf of God and country. This practice obtained for almost 1,500 years.

The abandonment of this Constantinian policy did not come easily even in the revolutionary American colonies. James Madison, eventually the supporter of the First Amendment with its freedom of religion clauses, did not at first call for a bill of rights. At one time he favored even the governmental declaration of days of prayer and fasting. In supporting the First Amendment, however, he wished to prevent the government from inhibiting freedom of conscience and to prevent the majority's oppressing a minority.

Although the president's proposal was rejected yesterday by the U.S. Senate, we may assume that the demand for an amendment is likely to continue. We may recall that the president drew vigorous applause last month at a Republican party rally in Iowa when he urged that "the God who loves us" be welcomed back into the children's classrooms after having been "expelled," as he said, by the Supreme Court.

A White House official asserted this week that the prayers used by the teachers would reflect "consensus" within the community, and that this "consensus" could mean the views of the majority. The school could provide arrangements for the minority to meet outside the classroom. If the minority felt a "stigma" by reason of their nonparticipation, this would not be a significant stigma for a small child to listen to a prayer from a religion other than his or her own or to be removed from the classroom, so that the majority could pray. The White House press office said that the youngsters who wish not to participate would feel less pressure than many of the pressures they experience in everyday life. It is surprising that so many senators voted yesterday in favor of the president's proposed amendment. The motion did not carry, for a two-thirds majority is required. The forty-four Senators, however, in supporting the First Amendment and the

Supreme Court's interpretation, showed perhaps that they recognize the religious wisdom and humility of not being righteous overmuch, indeed the wisdom of the axiom, Good fences make good neighbors. This axiom is exemplified when the government restrains itself by renouncing the spurious Constantinian claims in order to respect freedom of conscience.

30 · Blessed Are the Powerful

We live in a time when almost everyone is acutely conscious of the struggle for power that is going on, in the international theater and also on the home front. Indeed, over wide stretches of the earth revolutionary forces are at work in various ways. Some places, to be sure, remain in a happy state of innocence, but this happiness may soon pass. Our situation today is fraught with danger, readily evident in the appearance of the "confrontation politics" that rejects normal political methods. One of our sages, a seasoned commentator on the political scene, noting the importunate demands for reform, questions whether popular democracy as we know and cherish it is capable of bringing about the changes required in a technological age. There are many paradoxes in the situation.

Ordinarily, the churches and theological seminaries are not expected to concern themselves with struggles for power. What is the world coming to, the pious will ask, if churches and seminaries turn aside from their true vocation to join in the struggles of power politics? It is therefore significant, it is even a sign of audacity, that the opening convocation of the Boston Theological Institute focuses attention on the problem of power.

The word is highly ambiguous, for power can take a great variety of forms. In some circles, power has a very bad reputation. Everyone is familiar with Lord Acton's maxim, "Power tends to corrupt, and absolute power corrupts absolutely." Acton apparently aims to be somewhat ambiguous: Power *tends* to corrupt. Henry Adams is more blunt when he says, "Power is poison." A contemporary American political analyst who aims to reflect a theological perspective says that "man is born a slave, but everywhere he wants to be a master." Somewhat similar was the view of Jacob Burckhardt, the eminent Swiss historian who formulated a basic axiom of his philosophy of history in these words: "Power is not a stability but a lust, and *ipso facto* insatiable; therefore, unhappy in itself and doomed to make others unhappy." Looking back at the period of the Reformation and the

This address was delivered at the inaugural convocation of the Boston Theological Institute in 1968, and was subsequently published in *The Christian Century*, vol. 86, no. 25 (June 18, 1969), copyright 1969 Christian Century Foundation. Reprinted by permission.

Protestant-Catholic struggle, Burckhardt concludes that the confession that became dominant in any region of Europe was the one that possessed the strongest battalions. This view reminds me of a definition I heard recently at a church conference on black power: "Power is not something to be shared. It is something you have to take away from others."

Yet "power" has not always been defined as simply synonymous with coercion or corruption. In the history of religion and thus also of Christianity, it is a venerable concept. God is addressed as the Lord Almighty. In its extended version, the Lord's Prayer concludes with the words, "Thine is the kingdom, and the power and the glory." And the Gospel is said to be the power of God for salvation.

I

Obviously, if one is to speak of power, everything depends on how one defines it. Generically, power is ability, capacity, to get things done, and as such is essential to any person or society and also to God. On the human scene it may be the ability to dominate, to communicate, to manipulate, to play the piano; or it may be the capacity simply to go on existing. Plato said the first quality of anything is that it has power. Reality is power. One of the most familiar definitions asserts that power is the ability to exercise influence. Max Weber spoke of power as the ability to issue a command that must be obeyed, and he added that it might take the indirect form of manipulation. He overlooked Plato's definition of the passive dimension of power: the capacity to be influenced. Plato hints that an essential difference among people is that between their susceptibility to good or evil influence.

But if power as such is evil, then impotence could appear to be divine. Yet God, we are told, is perfect in power. Kierkegaard would say that this perfection of God's power is to be seen in his giving the human being the power to turn against him; for communion with God is not possible if no alternative exists. Here we approach the paradox contained in the dialectic between divine and human power. Human freedom is a gift from God. From a religious perspective, both God and the human being would be impotent but for this grace of freedom.

Much more than this must be said, however, if we are to consider the nature of God's power and the human response. A familiar way of stating the fundamental insight of biblical faith is to say that it is the faith that informs a historical religion which views the human being as a historical, social creature, and that it aims to be confident in the ultimately reliable power. Thus it is a faith that defines and fulfills the destiny of the person as an individual and in community. In a rudimentary fashion, this faith is expressed in Exodus: God is a dynamic power that liberates from slavery — has brought a people out of Egypt and guided it across the Red Sea and the wilderness. "With thy hand thou hast redeemed; thou hast guided them in thy power." This power makes a covenant of faithfulness with a people (and eventually also with individuals); it requires of them that they pursue righteousness and mercy. Because this power is based on affection as much as on law, unfaithfulness is more than violation of law; it is betrayal of affection and trust.

The Old Testament prophets see unfaithfulness not only in idolatry but also in the separation that breeds injustice and destroys community. Sin begins in the human heart and finds social expression in class separation, in neglect of the poor, in the pursuit of vengeance instead of mercy. The sins specified by the prophets turn out to be the sort of thing that appears in today's newspaper, especially in the black press. Indeed, one historian has said that the Old Testament prophets anticipate the modern free press.

The Old Testament conception of the most reliable power, the divine community-forming power, is remarkable. It contains the element of command and at the same time the idea that we are free to respond or not to respond; and it envisions a power that becomes manifest in a community that struggles for righteousness, for justice and mercy. Much of this concept is summed up in Micah's words: "I am full of power in the Holy Spirit, full of judgment and might to declare unto Jacob his transgression, and to Israel its sin."

This conception of the power attributed to God served not only as a standard for and a criterion of all other powers; it also became the basis of hope for the future — so much so that it was projected into the future in the form of an expected Messiah. To be sure, there were nationalist as well as universal ingredients in the idea of the Messiah.

II

It is, of course, not easy to characterize precisely the changes that come with the advent of Jesus and of Christianity. In principle, the nationalist element is eliminated and the messianic kingdom is viewed as already breaking in and also as to come later with power. A new eon is already here in actuality, yet the historical process is brought under radical eschatological judgment and tension. The intermediary powers in the world which make for separation and strife and idolatry among people are viewed as demonic. To himself and to his followers, Jesus is the spearhead of the divine power, breaking into history and pointing beyond history, bringing healing to men and women, calling them into a new covenant of righteousness—a covenant that in the outcome formed a new universal community.

We can agree that this new kingdom movement was not a social reform movement. But a look at the character of the new community they thought was demanded shows us what the early Christians believed to be the truly authentic, the truly ultimate reliable power. In this community economic status, social rank, racial origin, were all subordinated to a broader, transcending, and transforming power. At the same time, the individual was brought into more intimate relationship both with God and with the other members of the fellowship. The direct response to the Holy Spirit gave rise to new problems of organization, for this responsiveness brought into existence a charismatic community under charismatic leadership. Yet it is not possible to interpret the ethic of the new community under any single rubric—for example, under the rubric of spirit to the exclusion of law, or of otherworldliness to the exclusion of this-worldly concerns, or of consistent eschatology to the exclusion of concern and responsibility for the present. Nor can that community be interpreted as being either politically conservative or apolitical. Time was required for it to explore the implications of its confrontation with the dynamics, the power of the kingdom. Actually, the fact that the data regarding this community can be laid hold of in a variety of ways lends it perennial freshness. The many pertinent perspectives reflect the richness of motifs that become available here, and explain why early Christianity is seen as one of the great innovative moments in history, bringing forth treasures new and old.

Especially striking is the fact that here is a community independent of the state, a community freeing itself from idolatrous intermediary powers, promoting and exemplifying a heightened sense of responsibility, not only to and for itself but also to and for the individual—witness its concern to care for the weak and the elderly, slaves and widows. Some early Christian parishes even undertook to provide vocational education for orphans; others formed credit unions. What we see here, then, is a dispersion of power in the sense of dispersion of opportunity to assume responsibility.

Not the least of the latent functions of these new communities was to give and undergo training in the skills of organization and reconciliation. In short, it is not enough to say that a new spirit, a new ethos, here came to birth. That spirit, that ethos found practical and indeed institutional expression precisely among people who previously had been denied opportunities to participate. The new sense of hope cannot be understood merely in terms of eschatological expectation; it was engendered and sustained by the common experience of freedom in Christ, which took shape in new expressions of a covenanted community. In other words, the hope stimulated and was supported by social participation.

In that day, however, the possibility of political participation was practically nil for the Christian or for anyone—a fact that probably explains in part the largely apolitical character of the early Christian ethos and the Pauline admonition to be subject to the governing authorities. How different it is with us. In a democratic society Christians participate in government—at least in the sense that, as citizens, they have the opportunity and the responsibility to share in shaping the nation's policy.

It is therefore understandable that the ecumenical discussion, and specifically the Zagorsk Consultation held in preparation for the recent World Council Assembly in Uppsala, has turned attention to a redefinition of power and of Christian responsibility with respect to power. Quite properly, Zagorsk recognized a variety of methods of dealing with Scripture and of "doing" social ethics; at the same time, it was able to agree on a definition of power—one more or less familiar to us from other, sociological sources—as "conscious and active participation in the decision-making processes of society" which make for justice and "for more meaning for human life in society." The Zagorsk statement applies this criterion not only to the domestic situation in the Western countries, but also to those regions of the world that, in relation to the West, "have not." It even articulates a theory of revolution to justify the effort to change the locus of power in certain countries, to the end of enabling "participation of the masses in the making of decisions." Thus it asserts that Christians "can be free both to accept and to criticize the revolutionary trends in the world."

In the main, however, the Zagorsk statement is a summons to the Christian to shoulder responsibility for promoting justice. It calls for "participation of the masses in the making of decisions." Who are the masses? They are not only the anonymous, readily replaceable man and woman of the labor market. They are also those who do *not* participate in the decision-making processes that affect the community. They are especially the blacks upon whom impotence has been imposed; the alienated people who have not been permitted to have their say in public and institutional undertakings that affect their own way of life.

III

In face of the alienated, of the marginal men and women and children, power must be newly defined: as a creative, innovative relationship between those who have the freedom to participate in making social decisions and those who do not have that freedom. Obviously, the Christian cannot be content with philanthropy, for philanthropy may be a means of keeping others powerless; nor can one be content with simple majority rule. Conventional philanthropy and majority rule can be a means of still further alienating the marginal people, and thus increasing their self-hatred and resentment. There is a good deal of evidence to show that the deeper the sense of alienation the greater the sense of hopelessness, and the more likely the resort to violence. In this context, the people with power engender the violence. One theological tradition has called this process the wrath of God, the strange work of God's love. The Old Testament calls it hardening of the heart.

The Boston Theological Institute comes into being at a time in our nation's history when resentment is growing not only among the powerless but also among the powerful. On the part of the latter, the resentment is a reaction to the demands and the chaotic apocalyptic of the powerless—a reaction that cannot or will not distinguish between the melodrama and the genuine drama of protest. Thus resentment on both sides is every day splitting the nation further apart and is showing itself to be a distinctly dangerous and destructive force. We must recognize that the polarization, the opening to the right, which is appearing among us is supported by large numbers of church people. And the consequence is less and less rationality and mutual understanding, more and more appeal to spurious notions of "law and order." It is precisely these "law and order" people who are demonstrating the weakness of their strength, the sterility of their power.

Commenting on the student revolt in Europe today, the Tübingen New Testament scholar Ernst Käseman recently asserted that the rebels are revealing "what is rotten among us." "When they kicked up a row," Käseman said, "people thought only of the police club. These people did not shriek when they became aware of the millions who are perishing, but they have suddenly found their voice again, and they sing the old song of 'authority and order,' and one now faces new citizen terrors."

The question now before us is whether our churches and theological schools can summon the power to bring about conversations between the powerful and the powerless, to moderate polarization and to encourage self-determination on the part of the alienated. Perhaps the best contribution to society theological schools could make would be for them to demonstrate to the community, and especially to the churches, their capacity to respond to student demand. The challenge facing these schools is typical of what is going on all around us, and creative response to it requires something more than change of procedures: it requires profound changes in theological education. For theological education is not on a pedestal outside, it is part and parcel of our society.

IV

At this juncture, it is highly important that we recall that progress in the authentic use of power has been marked by the inclusion of the marginal people in the systems of power. In the early modern period, the middle class and then the working class were the marginal men and women, and successively they were allowed to acquire power. Unfortunately, the labor movement, like the previous middle-class movement, gradually took on the spirit of exclusion. But just as language is constantly enriched and enlivened from below, so society can be constantly enriched and enlivened by the marginal people with their highly creative potential. Let us hearken to the Exodus theme as expressed in the black spiritual, "Way down in Egypt land . . . Let my people go."

The authenticity of power, however, is determined not alone by the freedom of all individuals and all groups to participate in the making of social decisions, but also by the quality and purpose of their participation. The authenticity of power is determined by the ends it serves and the means it uses. The truly powerful are those who serve large purposes and can accomplish them. This kind of fulfillment requires "power with," not "power over"; it requires love.

The tensions that surround us today can be a source of strength; they provide the occasion for the renewing, community-forming power of God to work. Among women and men this power becomes manifest as they grope for new solutions. Authentic power is a gift to human being, issuing from response to the divine power. To them who have the power to hear, the saving Word of reconciliation will be given. From them who have not this power, even what they have will be taken away. Authentic power is neither poison nor insatiable lust, neither coercion nor corruption born of pride. It is the power that can exhibit the imagination of bold invention, that can respond to the ultimate power that shapes new communion with God and new community among men and women.

It is in this sense that we venture to make a beatitude: Blessed are the powerful. Blessed are the powerful who acknowledge that their power is a gift that imposes ever new responsibilities and offers ever new though costing joys. Blessed are the powerful who acknowledge that authentic power is the capacity to respond to the covenant, the capacity to secure the performance of binding obligations.

31 · *The Shock of Recognition: The Black Revolution and Greek Tragedy*

One of the striking and characteristic features of the language of the Bible is the large amount of seeming hyperbole employed, principally to expose the sins of persons, their greed, their mendacity, their idolatry. "You that put far away the evil day, and cause the seat of violence to come near; that lie upon beds of ivory, and stretch themselves upon their couches. . . ." "Woe unto you hypocrites, you whited sepulchres."

But what seems at first blush to be hyperbole may in reality be something else. In the moment of crisis and of sober judgment the prophetic rhetoric of condemnation can become thoroughly appropriate. Indeed, it can serve as a reality test, for it reminds us of our participation in the cruelties of history and also of the inhumanity of many of our personal relationships. It reminds us of the vast difference between our perception of ourselves and reality. The reason it strikes us as hyperbole is that we easily accommodate ourselves to spurious normality. We speak of the cross as the authentic symbol of Christianity, and then we proceed to smother it in lilies.

This stress on the contrast between truth and appearance, between reality and perception, constitutes perhaps the essential value of hyperbole. It gives us the shock of recognition. It exposes the untruth in what we consider normal common sense.

I

Nothing in our day has made more readily visible the appropriateness of hyperbole than the Black Revolution. Nor has anything done more than the cry for black power to make whites aware of the difference between our perception of ourselves and reality. How paradoxical is that concept, that very phrase *black power*. It is the cry of a group that whites have viewed as fellow citizens or fellow Christians, yet have made largely powerless. The demand for black power is a cry of protest against impotence, against impotence that has been imposed.

This essay originally appeared in the English journal *Faith and Freedom* (Oxford) 21, pt. 3 (1968). It is here reprinted in the abridged version published in the *Harvard Divinity School Bulletin*, new series, Vol. I/3 (Spring 1968): 9–12. Reprinted by permission.

Whites are sometimes inclined to think of black power as merely the expression of hatred for whites. But it is not fundamentally that. It is primarily a rejection of a regnant image and self-image. It is not so much an expression of hatred for whites as it is a renunciation of self-depreciation, an assertion of human dignity.

The Black Revolution is primarily a movement of people who are not ashamed to be black and who are expressing a sense of self-worth. They are making a new frontal attack on subjection and poverty, at the same time calling for new opportunities for blacks in education, jobs, housing, and health. They are making an assault also on the word *Negro* because "Negro is a slave word" given to them by whites. For this thrust in the name of human dignity, whites should be grateful.

At the Black Caucus of the National New Politics Convention held in Chicago, September 1967, one of the leaders said, "For too long we have worried about what white people thought about us and wanted from us to make us worthy of their company. We need to tell Whitey that we are no longer dependent upon his approval. We will make our own choices, our own decisions, and our own value system." This theme was dominant in the three-day meeting. Accordingly, the Black Caucus of the New Politics parley decided not to admit white reporters or television representatives. "We don't need their news coverage and their distorted interpretations of what is happening here," they said. The delegates simply did not care whether the white public approved or disapproved.

A few weeks after the Black Caucus in Chicago a similar caucus was formed at a national conference of Unitarians and Universalists. This conference in New York City, assembled to consider "Unitarianism and the Black Rebellion," turned out to be a bifurcated assembly, with most of the black Unitarians meeting separately. On the final day of the meeting the Black Caucus appeared at the general assembly, presented a list of demands regarding denominational policy with respect to the blacks, and insisted that its resolutions be approved immediately and without discussion.

This was shock treatment. A stormy session ensued. The white and black liberals wanted to discuss the resolutions. In the midst of near chaos a member of the Black Caucus, an attractive woman, dressed in tasteful, conventional style, was aroused to such a peak of indignation by liberals who wanted "to go on *talking* for another century" that she left her seat and swayed in rhythm up and down the aisle, shouting hot words. To express disagreement a member of the audience placed her hand on the woman's arm, holding her back. And what was the response of the black? With fire flashing from her eyes as well as from her words, she shouted, "Don't you understand? I don't speak *liberalese*. Don't you understand? I don't speak *Unitarianese*." Events such as this bespeak a shock of recognition, a rapid change in the perception of certain blacks and whites regarding themselves and each other.

Katherine Whitehouse, in her column in the London *Observer*, recently gave an amusing illustration of the quick change of presupposition possible in another controversial situation. The article deals with the problem of birth control and appears under the title "Suffer *How Many* Little Children?" The author tells of a priest who on his rounds in a maternity hospital called on a mother who had just given birth to her eleventh child. The mother was in despair because of this latest addition to her family. In consoling her the priest stressed the duties of holy motherhood, the blessings of a Christian family, ideals symbolized by the Virgin Mary, the Queen of all mothers. As he was on the point of telling her that the Lord would provide, the mother interrupted, "But Father, I am not a Catholic." Thereupon the priest blurted out, "Holy Mother of God, why all those eleven children then? What are you, a sex maniac or something?" Suddenly he revealed the ambiguity of his own presuppositions. He experienced a shock of recognition, that the issues at stake are not what he had been in the habit of saying they are. For whites and also for many blacks the Black Revolution is inducing such a shock of recognition. Whitney Young of the Urban League, no promoter of riots, has said that by reason of the riots whites have come to recognize that blacks do exist. Ralph Ellison's Invisible Man of 1952 is now above ground, if only we can see him and also see ourselves as he sees us.

II

The term "shock of recognition" is very old. In ancient Greek tragedy a crucial point in the plot comes with what is called the recognition scene, and from it follows a reversal of attitude on the part of the tragic hero. The reversal issues from the central character's acquiring knowledge about herself or himself that was somehow previously withheld. With this recognition—the acquiring of new knowledge—the whole course of action in the play is changed. In *Oedipus Rex*, for example, the king has been seeking the one whose crime has brought on a national calamity; he intends to find this criminal and banish him from the realm. But at the moment of recognition he discovers that he himself is the criminal, that he has killed and supplanted his father and married his mother. By this recognition his attitude is reversed and the whole situation is changed.

Greek tragedy, it will be recalled, was connected with a religious festival, with worship. At its origin and apex it was imbued with an all-pervading presence of a "divine breath of life." On these solemn occasions the high point of religious insight was the recognition scene. According to Aristotle, the scene induced an awesome, cathartic experience impelling the viewer to say, "Oh, *I* may be like that! I may be just the opposite of what I think I am."

Something like this recognition is taking place today among many whites as well as among blacks. For whites, however, the reversal of attitude is not the only thing that is significant. Something even more disturbing emerges in the consciousness, indeed in the conscience. Aristotle, commenting on the poignancy of tragedy, shows that the recognition and the reversal are connected with the special relationship obtaining between the persons in the tragedy. "All human action," he says, "takes place either between friends or between enemies, or between people who are indifferent to each other. If an enemy kills or wishes to kill an enemy, that will not produce any commiseration. When a stranger kills a stranger, that scarcely touches us any further as long as it does not excite any strife in the soul of him who performs the action. But when these things happen between people whose birth or affection binds them together in interest, as when a husband kills or is ready to kill his wife, a mother her children, a brother his sister, it is that which is marvelously suited to tragedy." In short, tragedy issues from betrayal, betrayal of family, friendship, or nation. The recognition scene that is emerging in American culture recapitulates this tragic conception, for the people who have been the victims of white supremacy are bound together with us as our fellow citizens and many of them as our fellow churchpersons.

Moreover, they have been oppressed for three centuries; their ancestors were brought to these shores as slaves before the arrival of the *Mayflower*. This consideration of a long history of oppression and of the slow pace of improvement brings us to another dimension of Greek tragedy. The recognition scene is the culmination of a succession of evils tracing itself to "the dark backward and abysm of time." The nemesis comes from time immemorial, and it continues into the future.

We of the twentieth century must see another analogy, the similarity between the situation in America today and that of ex-Nazi Germany. In the period just after World War II the Germans were told by the Americans and others that they must come to terms with their own Nazi past. In German literature a striking concept was given wide currency, the concept of "an unconquered past." Those who wished to promote an honest, candid recognition of the character of Nazism and of the German guilt insisted that there could be no health in Germany until that past was conquered, until Germans recognized their guilt and did something about it. In face of the Black Revolution Americans are likewise asked to have done with rationalization and to recognize our "unconquered past." We are asked to recognize the inner meaning of this succession of evil and its continuing presence.

One of the most striking analyses of the Detroit riots of last summer found expression in the conference held immediately afterward by black and white leaders in Detroit who had been promoting one of the best programs of social welfare in the nation. When this group of shocked and disappointed leaders, black and white, came together immediately after the riot, they sat for a long time, shaking their heads at each other, saying, "We had the best program in the country, and the city has spent millions of dollars. Why should this have happened to us?" And then came the answer: One thing money cannot buy is the sense of respect and worth that belongs to human beings; we have been cursed by our philanthropy. Again, the shock of recognition.

III

The shock brings with it searching questions: Is the brainwashed American majority obsessed with an inner psychological need to view blacks as less than persons? Is this a "trained incapacity" in white Americans? Blacks answer these questions with a stentorian yes. And for this reason black power is creating in many quarters a new state of mind. Its leaders are saying that white power must be countered by black power. They do not, it is true, represent the sentiments of all blacks, nor do they have a consistent attitude or program. Why expect them to? Yet the main thrust of their appeal is a call to recognize that the blacks must be allowed to develop sufficient power to achieve self-determination. To do this blacks must accept segregation and voluntarily remain segregated. Black power thus calls for the necessity to recognize a new type of American pluralism. In this effort to achieve self-determination blacks can find appropriate support in the workbook published by the Office of Economic Opportunity: "One of the major problems of the poor is that they are not in a position to influence the policies and procedures of the organizations responsible for their welfare." Black power therefore intends to gain a power that can stand up to white power. This surely could have been expected. As the chair of the New York City Commission on Human Rights has said, "There's nothing new at all in blocs of Americans uniting to determine their own destinies."

Nevertheless, many whites say that black power is simply racism in reverse. At the same time, the report of the National Advisory Commission on Civil Disorders brings into the spotlight the root cause of the present injustices: white race prejudice. Racism, racism, who has it not? White racism is not to be overcome merely through kindly sentiments. White race prejudice is an economic power. Why are less than 10 percent of nonwhites in the skilled craft unions? Why is the percentage of blacks unemployed in the nation twice that of whites? Why are 25 to 30 percent of blacks sixteen to twenty-one years old unemployed? The only way blacks can achieve self-determination is through gaining economic control over their own homes, businesses, and banks. Again, for whites to accept this requires a shock of recognition.

But the recognition scene that is upon us requires that we see more than the demand for social change. Black power is getting tough. The recognition scene is bringing into the open the toughness that has been required of blacks if they were to survive the oppression of the ghetto. This toughness can be annoying to whites. It can also be instructive. It can show them at last what it means to face effective power. In the past the whites have been able to take these possibilities in stride. Now the question is: How much punishment do whites require in order to be educated? How much power are they willing to share—and to use for radical social change—without coercion?

In Greek tragedy, the shock of recognition is accompanied by a reversal that brings only destruction. And the destruction does not end with a culminating episode—with the catastrophe for Oedipus and Jocasta. It goes on and on: Their descendants generation after generation are the victims of fate, dooming them to destruction. Retribution, unrelenting retribution, is the watchword of Greek tragedy. Is this the last word that can be said?

The Bible does not accept retribution as the last word. It holds for the possibility of something radically new. In face of injustice and retribution the Old Testament prophets speak of the divine call to persons to "turn again" to the Lord of history. Jesus preaches the gospel of the kingdom. The time is fulfilled. Repent ye. Change heart and mind. And the Book of

Revelation, speaking for the divine power, the only reliable power, says: And he that sat upon the throne said, Behold I make all things new.

I know of no more striking reversal in our day than that which came to the Black Muslim Malcolm X, a man whose name at one time caused shudders among whites and among many blacks.

Malcolm X decided to go to Mecca. There, he came to a complete change of mind and perception. When he returned to New York, reporters asked him about a letter he had written home regarding the new vision of humanity he had gained from Muslims. In response to the reports he said:

> Yes, I wrote that letter from Mecca. You are asking me, didn't you say that now you accept white men as brothers? Well, my answer is that in the Moslem world I saw, I felt and I wrote home how my thinking was broadened. Just as I wrote, I shared true, brotherly love with many white-complexioned Moslems who never gave a single thought to the race or to the complexion of another Moslem. My pilgrimage broadened my scope. It blessed me with a new insight. In two weeks in the Holy Land I saw what I never had seen in 39 years here in America: I saw all races, all colours — blue-eyed blondes to black-skinned Africans — in true brotherhood, in unity, living as one, worshipping as one, no segregationists, no liberals. They would not have known how to interpret the meaning of those words. In the past, yes, I have made sweeping indictments of all white people. I never will be guilty of that again, as I know now that some white people are truly sincere; that some truly are capable of being brotherly toward a black man. The true Islam has shown me that a blanket indictment of all white people is as wrong as when whites make a blanket indictment against blacks. Yes, I have been convinced that some American whites do want to help cure the rampant racism which is on the path to destroy this country.[1]

We are in a period of American history when a new emancipation, a new conquering of our past, is on the agenda. The questions before us are not hyperbole. Shall we promote only nemesis? Shall we only cause the seat of violence to come nearer? What is to be done? Perhaps it is time for whites to accept the recognition scene — to recognize that blacks are genuine inheritors of the ancient (and American) vision that persons should be free to choose, free to express, and free to fulfill their own humanity.

Note

1. *The Autobiography of Malcolm X* (New York: Grove Press, 1966), p. 362.

32 · Aging: A Theological Interpretation

At my back I always hear
Time's winged chariot hurrying near.

Andrew Marvell,
"To a Coy Mistress" (1681)

In this stanza the poet reminds his beloved that "had we but world enough and time," her reluctance to respond to him would not be a serious matter. But they are finite beings subject to Time, and there is no time for tarrying.

These two lines remind us that at every moment we are aging. The poem as a whole, however, lends itself to a broader interpretation than that suggested by its title. Indulging the poetic license of religious allegory, we may say that every person, from childhood onward, is in pursuit of a coy "mistress." Her name is "the meaning of life"; and decision regarding this meaning is ultimately a religious decision. Time is always hurrying near, leaping beside and past us, and one must try and take its meaning by the forelock.

Aging and meaning—the meaning of aging. That is our theme. We shall consider first certain broad aspects of time and aging in our "time" (and particularly in the middle class), then the theology of aging, and finally the vocation of all human persons with respect to the aged and the vocation of the aged themselves. We shall try to understand the meaning of aging in terms of space as well as of time. Persons and events—and aging—appear in time and of course also *somewhere,* that is, in space, in a place.

REASONS FOR THE CURRENT INTEREST IN AGING

The aging process has been studied by scientists of all kinds, also by historians and welfare workers, perhaps still more often by the philosophers. In the twentieth century the subject has attracted so much attention that it has become a specialty of its own called gerontology, a specialty involving biological, psychological, and sociological studies; and theologians have not been far behind.

This essay originally appeared in *The Unitarian Universalist Christian* 28, nos. 2–3 (1973). Reprinted by permission.

The marked increase of the proportion of the aged in the general population is a major factor giving rise to this new discipline in research and reflection. To grasp the magnitude of the increase one need only compare, or rather contrast, the average longevity of today with that of the past. Life expectancy in the Roman Empire was twenty-three years; in 1850 in New England it was forty years; in the U.S.A. in 1900 it was forty-seven years; and today it is seventy. In the United States today one of every ten persons is at least sixty-five years old. Almost half of them are great-grandparents; and one of every three people who are sixty years old has an aging parent. The increase in the number of the aged has been largely the consequence of advances in medical technology. Moreover, in a "service economy" it has brought about the proliferation of a great variety of social agencies and other organizations concerned with the needs of the aged. Even selected sections (or spaces) of the United States have become the haven of the aged. Here time and space intersect in a new way. Theological education is more and more turning attention to the needs and resources of this age group. No experienced politician is unaware of them. I recall participating in a political rally twenty years ago when as a speaker I was interrupted by a retired man who boisterously came down the aisle and mounted the platform, demanding that I "take a stand" on the Townsend Plan. Legislation and social security for the aged and the retired have become the order of the day. Pension funds represent a major segment of investment in the national economy. All of these changes affect the occupation of spaces or places by people and organizations.

RELATIVE ASPECTS OF THE QUESTION

Certain features of the aging process are universal, but other features belong to a particular time and place. A person in embattled military service will the more readily hear the winged chariot hurrying near, as will the person afflicted with a terminal illness. Here importunate Death is felt to be in the driver's seat.

In more normal circumstances the character of the aging process differs considerably from culture to culture (and also from class to class) as does the "image" of the aged. In one culture the aged may be held in high esteem; they may even possess an authority approaching the status of reverence. In another culture the middle years may enjoy greater authority and esteem. Where the younger age groups are in high esteem, the older people may even attempt to camouflage their age.

The "service industries" for the older groups in the United States have become a lucrative business, catering especially to women. Some people seem to identify aging with not-aging. Many older women in the middle class would consider themselves deprived citizens if in order to save money they were obliged to wash their own hair. (That statement is not intended as a moralistic judgment; it is simply an observation regarding a familiar aspect of the current urban economy. After all, a woman is considered to be on the way "over the hill" by her late thirties.) The older men, by way of contrast, are not expected to increase their use of the tonsorial and cosmetic "arts." The age-group industries are by no means recent in the history of "civilization." In ancient Rome a sizable industry catered to the demand for gladiatorial costumes and daggers for children, just as cowboy equipment is available in most countries of the West today. A child on the playground today can be brought to mental distress and even to pathological emotional disturbance if the parents do not allow her or him to purchase a new, regnant style of sweater or jean. A generation ago a young entrepreneur by the name of Gilbert earned a fortune after he convinced the department store managers of the potential market for teen-age costume. All of these features of the common life reflect differentiations of status and style which belong to the various age groups at a particular time and place.

In the differentiations of age-group status we encounter a phenomenon familiar to the cultural anthropologist. A fundamental "task" for any culture is to define the age limits and the status of each age group. These differentiations, of course, are related to the biological life cycle, but the definition of *status* is largely determined by custom and consensus; the definitions vary considerably from culture to culture, and they can differ in different periods of a given culture. In simpler societies the "rites of passage" reflect a fairly explicit demarcation between childhood and youth, between youth and adulthood, and between adulthood and old age. In industrial society—"the open society"—the definitions of the age groups are more flexible, that is, they are subject to change and also to ambiguity. In the Elizabethan period in England "maturity" was reached in the early twenties. In our time (in the middle classes) college and professional education come somewhat later in life, as does maturity as we define it. This later dating of maturity is related to the fact that today many youth are economically dependent upon the parents for a much longer time than youth were in the Elizabethan period, indeed even than was the case in the nineteenth century. An analogous change of definition of age groups is to be seen in the later dating today of the *beginning* of the period of old age or retirement. Changes of this sort bring about disagreements and tensions. I recall a comment made to me by an eminent Italian scholar and playwright who after exile from fascist Italy had become a professor in an American university. At a farewell party for him on his (forced) retirement at the age of 66, he said with passionate resentment in his voice, "I consider the U.S.A. to be a fascist country; it compels me to retire just when I am at the peak of my powers."

ASCRIBED STATUS AND ACHIEVED STATUS

By reason of the inescapable relation to the biological age of the individual, the definition of age status has only a limited relation to the achievements of the individual, that is, to the *"achieved* status." Therefore, one's age grouping is spoken of as "ascribed status." Ascribed status attaches to a person simply because of age or sex or race or class. To persons who are black, a certain status is ascribed; to those eighty years of age, a special status is ascribed. The terms *wop* and *gook* in vulgar parlance are vernacular characterizations of ascribed status. It is often said that the ascriptions of the class system in Britain are roughly equivalent in brutality and stupidity to the race discriminations (or ascriptions) of the U.S.A. The ascriptions of the class system in Britain have been a frequent preoccupation of English writers from *Pygmalion* to *Look Back in Anger* to the film *The Hireling,* the winner of the Cannes Film Festival Grand Prize of 1973.

In contrast to ascribed status, achieved status is attached to persons because of their accomplishments. This emphasis on achievement instead of on age, race, sex, or class makes a strong appeal to the ethical norms of equality and justice. Thus the black liberation movement and the women's liberation movement today are attempting to reduce the significance of ascribed status and to increase the significance and recognition of achieved status. The workers' movement, now well over a century old, was partly motivated by the desire to escape the class inferiority that previously attached to the worker. In all of these liberation movements the ideal of autonomy or self-determination has played a large role.

The movement away from ascribed to achieved status is by no means confined to modern history. In his now famous book *Ancient Law* (1861), Sir Henry Maine over a century ago drew the contrast between early societies in which social relations are dominated by (ascribed) status, "a condition of society in which all relations of Persons are summed up in the relations of Family," and "progressive" (or complex) societies in which social relations are predominantly determined by contract, "the free agreement of individuals," a social system exemplified by the complex Roman society during the time of Justinian (527–65). He concluded that in this sense "the movement in progressive societies has been movement from Status to Contract," that is, from ascribed status to contract. Many objections have been raised to Maine's formulations in his history of ancient law. In the context of our discussion here we may say that his way of defining progress did not recognize that contract, "the free agreement of individuals," also bespeaks a status. Yet, he does show that in "progressive" societies the struggle against ascribed status is a perennial one. In this sense there is contention today over the definition of the ascribed status of old age, a tension between ascribed status conditioned by biological age on the one hand and achieved status oriented to freedom and individuality on the other. Yet, nothing can erase the biological factor of aging, nothing can stop the winged chariot from hurrying near. Some sort of ascribed status in terms of aging will therefore remain. What counts most here, however, is not a merely objective fact of biology; what counts most is *what people believe* you to be by reason of age. The same situation obtains with respect to sex and race. What counts most is not what you really are but what people believe you to be.

New Spatial Relations

We could go on now to consider the effects upon the aged of other factors, such as the effect of life in the metropolis (where anonymity rather than neighborliness is characteristic) or the effect of technology and the division of labor and specialization. These factors have brought about new spatial relations, new boundaries, new mobility, new separations, among the population in a territory. Places of work, places of recreation, places for "services," places of residence for class and ethnic groups, become segregated. Many of these factors tend to reduce the range of shared values. Moreover, in the mass society the mass media of communication tend to dilute or trivialize the values. All of these segregations involve new consumptions of time and space.

An enormous change has taken place in Western culture with regard to the spaces occupied by the family. This change is to be observed especially in the appearance of the nuclear family, an extreme variant of the conjugal family patterns. The rural family of even recent generations was a large family living at the same location, so to speak "under the same roof." Grandparents (the spouses of orientation), along with an unmarried uncle or aunt, lived at "the home place" along with the father and mother (the family of procreation) and the children. Largely as a consequence of industrialization and urbanization the grandparents and other relatives now live apart from the family of procreation, especially in the middle classes. (Some of them are confined in nursing homes or mental institutions.) In part this shift of location has been the expression of a new freedom, the freedom in space of the nuclear family from the other relatives, and the freedom in space of the grandparents and other relatives from the locus of the nuclear family. Through this spatial segregation the autonomy of the nuclear family and the autonomy of the grandparents have been increased. The "in-laws" cannot so readily intrude, nor do they bear the broader responsibilities of the earlier, extended family. With the increase of longevity the desire for autonomy has been intensified. In earlier days the older couple with its shorter life expectancy could the more readily tolerate living under the same roof with the nuclear family, and the nuclear family could the more readily tolerate the constant presence of the grandparents and other relatives. It has been argued that if the aged remained in the restricted space of the contemporary urban family, they would not for the most part be able to survive to old age. The slings and arrows of propinquity would be fatal for them. The length of time for aging would be reduced as a consequence of the cramped space. One is reminded here (by analogy) of the prediction of a marked increase in emotional stress and even of delinquency and crime if the total population in the United States were doubled. Adequate time for aging, then, requires that appropriate space be available.

Consequences for the Nuclear Family

The new spatial relationships obtaining today for the members of the kinship group have brought about a striking difference in interpersonal communion and in the transmission of cultural values, especially in the urban, nuclear family.

In the extended family (say, on the farm) the intimate interpersonal relationships involved a larger number of people than appear in the nuclear family. Thus a greater variety of temperaments was available to the children, and affection was in wider commonalty spread. If we use technical psychological language here, we may say that the extended family provided dispersed cathexis (a wide connectedness of affection with other people), and that the nuclear family offers hypercathexis, that is, intensified emotional relatedness to a smaller number of people. The mental and emotional "landscape" within which one lives makes a world of difference. I can recall that when on the farm I was scheduled for punishment for misdemeanors, my grandmother could be depended upon successfully to mitigate the vigor of my father. Viewing the situation of the extended family as a whole, we can say that more channels for the transmission of value preferences and cultural sensitivities were immediately available. In this matter I can vividly recall two of my grandparents. My grandfather was a delightful raconteur, and I listened to him eagerly while father and mother were busy. My grandmother, in her youth a schoolteacher, was a stickler for grammar, correct spelling, and precise vocabulary and syntax. Besides, she sang old folksongs from the South. "Go tell Aunt Patsie, the old gray goose is dead." And so it went in the extended family. Let us say that Aunt Mary loved poetry, and Uncle George was a Socialist. The father might suggest to the children that George was a crank and should not be taken seriously. But around behind the barn Uncle George expostulated on the evils of capitalism and the "antics" of the revivalist preacher. Aunt Mary in her love for poetry was also not to be taken seriously. What good was that poetry? Both the Uncle George and the Aunt Mary of the extended family represented a gentle criticism of (and complement to) the "establishment." In the nuclear family these channels of sensitivity and stimulus are radically reduced. Meanwhile, more and more of the functions of the extended family have been taken over by extradomestic institutions (including television). Thus the organizations of the youth culture are spatially segregated, giving the youth a greater freedom but also subjecting them to the vise of conformism. For conscientious parents the responsibility for the transmission of values to the children has become a source of frustration, especially in face of the competing agencies.

All of these features and other similar ones indicate the consequences of the spatial segregation of the nuclear family from the grandparents and other relatives. In some measure, the strength of the family as a "reference group" has been diminished: the family does not provide the effective touchstone that was formerly available in the extended family. The grandparents for their part have been somewhat deprived of a cultural function. When the younger generation of the family become procreative, the older generation moves to a new location where they make less of a contribution to the cultural ethos and solidarity of the family. Moreover, the new location offers them not only a new freedom but also a new isolation for the aging process. The children, for their part, can no longer intimately observe the aging process or apprehend its whimsy, its wisdom, its mellowing. The deprivation experienced by the children becomes acutely evident on the untimely death of a parent. In the extended family the gap in cathexis was (so to speak) "compensated" by the remaining, larger family. In the nuclear family spouses of procreation are also brought into a new and difficult situation. The psychic burden upon them at times become unbearable in the education of the children. Moreover, the hypercathexis in the relationships between the spouses can become a liability. A contemporary psychologist, taking into account also the deceptions and false expectations of romantic love, asserts that the married couple is often either excessively happy or excessively unhappy. The great increase in the incidence of divorce cannot be understood apart from all these changes.

Such are the ambiguous consequences, the positive and negative values, attaching to the structure of the nuclear family. As we have observed, all of these features can be understood as the consequence of the curious intersections of time and space and aging brought about by the advent of the nuclear family. In important respects the changes we have described have altered the actual and potential meaning of aging, for these changes alter the mental and emotional "landscape." Thus we have seen some of the implications for our period (in time) of the maxim, Persons and events (and aging) appear in time and somewhere, that is, in a particular time and space.

RELIGIOUS MEANING AND THE DOCTRINE OF CREATION

On hearing the phrase "the theology of aging" the reader at first blush may be perplexed and even incredulous. Do you mean to suggest, one may ask, that there can be a theology of "youthing" or of being middle-aged? What is the meaning of theology in this context?

Theology deals with meaning, with the meaning of life, with its nature and its resources, its perversions, its possibilities. It aims to deal with ultimate issues, with the perspectives in terms of which radical questions can be asked regarding life and its religious meaning. And what is the meaning of "religious meaning"?

The meaning of life is to be found in relatedness to a frame of reference. Religious meaning is relatedness to the ultimate source and resource—to God; and therefore it is a relatedness to that which brings all of our believing and thinking and striving under question. To recognize this relationship or to refuse to recognize it is a part of human freedom. God's power in this relationship is one that leaves us free. God's divinity rests in his power to give rise to a creature who is free to turn against him. At the same time the consequences of a person's action cannot be in one's control; thus human freedom is limited by the demand for justice. A person's relation to God, however, is not fundamentally a legal relationship. It is based rather on love and loyalty. Indeed, love gives a special quality to justice, ever and again breaking open our moralistic, self-serving interpretations. This love is directed ultimately to the Creator and not to the creature, as Augustine never tired of saying. Here we see the transcendent dimension of this frame of reference for meaning.

It is striking to recall that Max Weber, a sociologist who considered himself to be "religiously unmusical" (that is, an unbeliever), saw crucial significance in the Old Testament doctrine of creation, for in making the distinction between Creator and creature it provided a sanction for radical criticism of the creature. The world of human relations and of societal forms is not sacrosanct; it is a world that is subject to radical criticism and change. This attitude toward the world of creatures may be directed also against the definitions of status (both ascribed and achieved) which are a part of the social system.

But before we further examine these statuses we should consider another aspect of the doctrine of creation, a doctrine that points to the continuing divine creativity and not to an initial act of creation in the dark backward and abysm of time. The doctrine of creation historically has placed a strongly positive evaluation on the human creature (as well as upon the order of nature): all humans are created in the image of God. They have a share in the divinely given creativity, and in this they acquire a derived dignity. To be sure, we in our freedom can pervert this dignity, and we can violate the dignity of others. Channing protested against this violation when in face of military custom he cried, "What! Flog a man?" The doctrine of creation, as suggested, is also a doctrine of re-creation, or re-creativity. We can turn from our deviant behavior. The Old Testament prophets often speak of "turning" again to the Creator. They apply this doctrine not only to the individual but also to the nation, that is, to collective existence. We are responsible not only for individual behavior but also for collective, institutional behavior. The New Testament also speaks of turning, the change of heart-mind-soul ("repentance") in response to and in love for the Creator and Re-creator.

The foregoing exposition is a cramped, adumbrated statement of a doctrine of creation, fall, and re-creation. But it may suffice as a point of departure for a "theology of aging."

ASSESSING STATUS THEOLOGICALLY

In the light of a doctrine of creation we must say that the definitions of status (ascribed and achieved) are cultural, finite creations—they are the "doings" of creatures—and as such they are subject to criticism. This attitude applies to both the ideal and the actual patterns of status. Certain aspects of ascribed status deserve criticism and evaluation here in the light of a doctrine of creation. (The reader can supply analogous criticisms of achieved status.)

The definitions of status in our society favor the younger age groups to the value-detriment of the aged and the aging process. In principle, however, every age group possesses its own unique quality and dignity. Each stage of individual development offers unique experience and opportunity. Certain experiences are possible only in youth—for example, the sense of the wide-openness of the future. There comes a time, however, when the individual may say, "Nevermore." Certain options—for example, career options—may no longer be open. Simone de Beauvoir at the age of fifty catalogs the things she will never do again: lie in the hay, slide on morning snow, win a first lover. But other experiences are possible only in fruited old age: the contemplation of satisfactions and beauties of long ago, the cherishing of *old* friendships, the exploration of opportunities previously unheeded (partly because of other importunate obligations), and also the meeting of the adversity of ill health (or of waning powers) with serenity and dignity. In the conjugal relationship the love of the couple for each other in middle life or in old age can possess unique qualities. To appreciate this uniqueness is something that requires thought and new sensitivity. A theology of aging asserts, then, that each age group (and each person) has its own inimitable rendezvous with the coy mistress, the meaning of life.

A major detriment caused by the derogation of the oldest group is the damage it inflicts upon the self-image of the aged. This derogation often operates as a self-fulfilling prophecy. The older person, perhaps in resignation, behaves according to the limited expectations contained in the ascribed status. In face of this derogated status with its restricted expectations we should adopt the Channing protest, "What! *Flog* a man!" The theology of aging demands that the ascribed status of the aging person be elevated in the name of freedom and justice.

Ascribed status produces injustice in still another way. It militates against the recognition of achievements and also of potentiality. This derogation is deleterious for all age groups. The older person of low achievement sometimes "puts down" the youth of higher quality simply by reason of the latter's age.

Ascribed statuses generally become stereotypes that produce a blindness to the actual person cabined within the status. The dignity of the person as such is thereby violated. More than that, the actual concrete person is hidden from us by the stereotype. (The stereotype can even hide us from ourselves.) We see here a fundamental deficiency of all such classifications. No person can be crammed without remainder into a category of this sort. No "status" exhausts the person. An eminent experimental psychologist, Franz Alexander, has shown that empirical psychology was impeded for nearly a half century by the almost fanatical interest of the taxonomists to classify psychological types. The "classifiers" had stopped studying real people. The theology of the person as well as the theology of aging demands that we as persons come to know others as persons. It is said that someone pointed out to Hegel that the facts of the actual history of the United States did not fit into his philosophy of history: and Hegel replied, "So much the worse for the facts." The prejudging of human persons according to a stereotype is an old and familiar way of separating us from reality: "Can any good thing come out of Nazareth?"

Existentialism has the merit of having drawn attention to the deceptions and falsehood issuing from abstractions. Many of the younger generation today have been protesting against the gulf between human beings caused by the "system." Several years ago I served on an ad hoc panel at Harvard to discuss the state of mind at that time of undergraduates at Harvard and Radcliffe. A Harvard psychiatrist on the panel reported that the typical student, feeling the loneliness of his or her subjectivity, wanted nothing more earnestly than to achieve total intimacy with another person. (Some of the encounter groups have pushed this view so much as seemingly to reject all privacy, certainly a violation of the person—and all in the name of personhood.) In the course of the discussion I asked the question, "Do these undergraduates mention one book or author more frequently than any other?" The psychiatrist replied, "That is an easy question to answer. Practically all of them esteem Martin Buber's *I and Thou*." It is precisely the I-Thou relation that ascriptive classifications can smother, except perhaps among the aged themselves. Buber's classic book we might take as a superb introduction to a fundamental dimension of the theology of aging. In its theological orientation it is reminiscent of the Reformation claim that every person stands immediately before God, that is, before the creative and re-creative forces that provide both the gift and the task of vocation. We should add, however, that there are other dimensions to authentic creativity. I think especially of the social-institutional dimension that calls for commitment and vocation to work for a society of justice and mercy—the dimension explored in other writings of Buber (which the Harvard and Radcliffe students apparently ignored).

REQUIREMENTS OF A VOCATION WITH RESPECT TO AGING

With respect to the individuality of the aged *person* we can discern a vocation for all adult age groups and also for the churches. This is the vocation to open up ways in which depersonalization (engendered in a multitude of ways in our megalopolitan society) may be overcome or at least mitigated. Clearly, new forms of education for the life cycle and for the aging process are required. This kind of education is incumbent upon us all, an education of the imagination. Pascal has reminded us that imagination is the mistress of humanity. This mistress is akin to the coy mistress mentioned earlier—the meaning of life in its various stages. It may be that one day this kind of imagination will turn attention to the plight of the aged among the underprivileged.

Adequate education with respect to the aging process should include also education regarding what is already going on in this area. Thirty or forty years ago the attention was directed to child development, and much has been accomplished. Today the aged, including the great-grandparents, are finding new forms of expression despite all ascriptions. As Dr. Bernice Neugarten of the University of Chicago says: "The old rocking chair for grandma is empty. She is versatile, inventful. Don't bring your mending to grandma. She is going to college, or she is writing a book. . . . Grandma goes to work, and mother stays at home." In some quarters we see organizations of the elderly working in coalition with youth organizations and with the black liberation and the women's liberation movements, and with other social reform movements. One can see also that some of the youth are finding among the older age groups assistance in recovering ethnic identification. Some of the aged are becoming foster parents or foster grandparents. Others are entering courses in adult education, thus associating with younger age groups and also learning the disciplines of leisure. Others are becoming senior business advisers. Still others are learning paraprofessional skills.

The possible new roles for the aged in the life of the church are gradually gaining a certain recognition, as is to be observed among us in the efforts of creative programs on aging, such as those of the Benevolent Fraternity (Unitarian Universalist) in Boston. Through imaginative devices the aged can give to the rest of the parish a sense of the past and new visions for the future. They can also carry on community efforts under the aegis of the parish. In a parish in which I was minister several decades ago we brought the aged into the church school to share with the young their reminiscences of the past or their enjoyment of new skills and new experiences. This practice is now being adopted in some of the public schools.

All of these developments are already on the scene. It is the vocation of us all to learn about and to promote integration of the aged into community life in defiance of the stereotypes of ascribed status.

Professor Neugarten has reported that older people engaged in these diversified activities, instrumental as well as expressive, are not as lonely as the elderly are often said to be. These people, to be sure, are middle class and even super middle class, and they are mostly whites. (The blacks and certain other ethnic groups suffer more severely from the slings and arrows of ascribed status.) Then, too, these people belong to the younger old people rather than to the older old people, say beyond eighty years of age. But even among the older elders, as Morton Lieberman (also of the University of Chicago) has observed, an aggressive and even a cantankerous attitude has survival value. Those who have been deceived into trying to "grow old graciously" die younger. Again we see how the self-image of the elderly (as of all people) affects their life-style. In general, we should say that the vocation of all age groups in face of the aged should be that of encouraging a variety of life-styles, indeed also innovation of life-style. We all learn new tastes in the arts, in furniture and architecture and clothing. Why not also in growing old? The older, upper tenth of the population may be able the better to appreciate the image of God in human being if they are asked to contribute expressively and instrumentally to the richness and diversity of life. A major enemy to all this is idolatry and voluntary servitude before the false gods of conventionally defined status. Faith in God and in life's possibilities should give rise to a creative and re-creative character trait. To engender this faith and this character trait we need in the coming years to improve the education (and the textbooks) regarding the life cycle, in order that young and old may strive for the achievement of "effective living space."

But what is to be done about the segregation and restriction of "life-space" we have seen in the diminution of the family unit? Here again experiment and innovation must be placed on the agenda. Indeed, they are already there in some quarters. We may cite here two significant innovations.

First, the "intentional communities" where young and old are brought together for new enjoyment of each other in new communion. Some of these "intentional communities" are promoting political and social action for the sake of the common good. Others are rendering some new service to the community around them. In their ethos they illustrate what Plato had in mind when he said that authentic fellowship grows from transcending goals and not from merely private interest in each other. Fellowship, accordingly, is a by-product of significant commitment. That is the religious meaning of aging, the vocation of the servants and lovers of God.

Second, we cite the new experiments in architecture, new styles and forms of construction that permit the older and the younger age groups, the nuclear family and the other relatives, to live in proximity to each other, yet also to preserve independence and privacy. The "Newtowns" in England and Europe are experimenting with just these innovations toward the end of making physical living quarters flexible in size for a growing or a diminishing nuclear or extended family. In Columbia, Maryland, single-family homes are scattered through the community interspersed with higher-density housing for the older age groups. A minibus system makes available transportation for the very young and for the aged. The older groups receive assistance from the younger families in the care and upkeep of their living quarters.

One can readily see that both of these types of innovation are providing "effective life-space" for both young and old, thus overcoming in part the segregations we have observed in the urban economy. The aging process for both young and old is thereby finding new spaces that are in symbiotic interplay.

What, then, is the meaning of aging? It is stated in classical terms in the Westminster Catechism. The chief end of humans is to know God and to enjoy him. This "chief end" obtains for young and old, for black and white, for rich and poor. But it must be pursued in collaboration. The old adage "cooperate or perish" points to grace as well as to judgment. "Had we but world enough and time" there would be time for tarrying.

33 · "Thou Shalt Not Commit Adultery"

In a memorable short story, "The Darling," Anton Chekhov depicts a woman who successively becomes the wife of several husbands who, one after the other, die or disappear. One of these husbands is the manager of an open-air theater, another is a lumber merchant, and still another is a veterinary surgeon. In each of these marriages the woman of the story completely identified herself with the interests and also with the vocation of her husband. If the husband is absorbed in the problems of managing a theater, "the Darling" engenders a limitless enthusiasm for the details of theater management. When the husband is a timber merchant, she acquires the conviction that the production of lumber is the most important calling possible for a human being; and so on. As a consequence, each of the husbands calls her "a darling." Chekhov, for his part, makes her appear to be a chameleon, possessing no intrinsic mark of her own, though he says also that "she was always fond of some one, and could not exist without loving."

After reading his story, Tolstoy wrote a sharp and perceptive criticism of it. Chekhov, he says, completely misses the heart of the matter. He should not have been content to mock at this woman. Indeed, Tolstoy concludes that Chekhov, "like Balaam, intended to curse, but the god of poetry forbade him, and commanded him to bless. And he did bless, and unconsciously clothed this sweet creature in . . . exquisite radiance."

I do not mention this story here especially because of the point that Tolstoy drives home. Something is to be said of course for the insights of both Chekhov and Tolstoy in the story and the criticism. Of special interest apart from these insights, however, is a striking observation that represents the unarticulated premise of the story. The marriage bond, like all personal relations, is a relationship between unique individuals. Each of the husbands and also the wife of the story possess special qualities and limitations

In 1966 Adams and other members of the faculty of Harvard Divinity School agreed to the joint discipline of writing sermons on each of the Ten Commandments. The seventh was assigned to Professor Adams, who presented the sermon, here reprinted, at Andover Chapel of the divinity school. In 1978 it was published by the Unitarian Universalist Association in the Study Guide for James Luther Adams's *On Being Human Religiously*, Judy Deutsch, ed. Copyright © 1978. Boston: Unitarian Universalist Association. Used by permission.

the like of which constitute in some fashion the uniqueness of every human being. Human persons are not like peas in a pod. Each has her or his own individuality. Yet, each individual is also a person. These facts become especially evident in marriage; they give to marriage many of its peculiar opportunities and responsibilities, and many of its special problems.

Today in this sermon, one of a series on the Ten Commandments by members of the faculty, it is my assignment to consider the Seventh Commandment, "Neither shalt thou commit adultery." I want to consider only three related aspects of the covenant of marriage—the unique role of individuality in the bond between husband and wife, the sexual union as a special nexus of the bond between persons, and the covenant of marriage as part of a larger covenant.

I

The marriage bond is a bond of love between unique individuals. This "individualistic" aspect of the human condition bespeaks a metaphysical condition, and it possesses also a theological significance of wide pertinence. We often overlook this aspect of marriage because we forget what we take simply for granted.

In our cultural tradition, the individuality of the person is deemed to be so fundamental that ordinarily we have difficulty imagining as plausible any alternative perception or evaluation of it. To be sure, a variety of perceptions and evaluations can be found in our own culture, but ordinarily the spectrum is not so wide in its range as to include the denial of the reality or value of individuality. We do not, like the Buddhist for example, reject the principle of individuation so radically as to consider individuality to be an illusion. Yet something similiar to this view is not completely alien to our tradition. In the dark backward abysm of the Western tradition, we can encounter a radically negative evaluation of individuality. We may find it instructive to consider briefly this older view.

The pre-Socratic philosopher Anaximander, reflecting on what we might call the metaphysics of individuation, sees little but tragedy in the pervasive presence of differentiation in the world. He sees nothing but frustrating, destructive limitation in individuality. From his perspective, life is nothing but conflict between differentiated individuals. To be is to be limited, to be separated from that which is whole and boundless, the *apeiron*. Human existence as such is therefore tragic. It is tragic because finite entities in their finitude, in their limitedness, enter inevitably into conflict with each other; and then as a retribution for their injustice they are finally drawn back into the abyss of "the boundless." According to this view, individuality places upon all of us a guilt, not a guilt for which we personally are responsible, but rather a metaphysical guilt. To be is to be demonic, and it is to be guilty. Creation is fall. Existence is nothing but a becoming and a passing away. Passing away is better in principle than becoming. Accordingly, Anaximander speaks of "things perishing into that from which they have their birth, for they pay to one another the penalty of their injustice according to the order of time." Is it any wonder that Nietzsche spoke of the period to which this philosophy belongs as the tragic age of Greek thought?

The contrast between this radically tragic view and the biblical view is fairly clear. In the Bible, finitude as such is not evil: it comes from the hand of God. It stands within the divine economy. This presupposition determines the very nature of creaturehood. The finite creature, the individual or the group, sinfully and demonically tries to become like God, but finiteness is not in itself a metaphysical sin giving cause for guilt. Everything depends upon what we in our freedom do with our individuality. If we abuse our freedom, the remedy is not the destruction of individuality. It is not the punishment of return to undifferentiated being. Salvation does not abrogate individuality but rather calls for "turning," for the restoration of fellowship with God.

Observe, then, the assessment placed upon individuality. Whitehead has given a striking philosophical statement of the essence of the matter. "Definition," he says, "is the soul of actuality." Individuality is not only an inexpugnable reality; it is even the *soul* of actuality. In the spirit of Kierkegaard we may say that for the biblical mentality, individuality is a category. That is, one cannot think of God or human being without thinking in terms of individuality. God himself possesses individuality; he is not the boundless, the *apeiron*. He is thought of in personal terms; he has a character, he is a righteous God. Moreover, he enters into covenant with a particular people. Here again individuality is decisive—this people, if it is to be faithful, is to be a peculiar people. God, who possesses a special character and purpose, enters into relation with a people, and with individuals, bringing them out of loneliness and into a bond of faithfulness, indeed into a new community that looks toward universality. By means of the covenant they are "defined." They are given a soul and a purpose in community.

What has been said here about individuality and community has a special bearing on the relations between partners in a marriage covenant.

Love that issues in a marriage covenant is love between two persons who possess universal qualities that constitute the structure of personality but who possess also the unique qualities of individuals. It is pertinent to recall here that Richard Rodgers says that in his musicals every love song was written, indeed "had to be written for a specific character and scene"; they are not love songs just for anybody. Among men and women one finds an infinite variety of differentiations. The similarities and differences between these partners provide the occasion for both affinities and tension. They become, therefore, the occasion for companionship and estrangement, for spontaneity and discipline, for joy and suffering, for adjustment and sharing. Informing all of these similarities and differences is the differentiation of the sexes. Male and female created he them.

II

Belonging to the order of creation, sexuality—in the biblical view—is of course in essence good. At the same time it is like the other human individuations of which we have been speaking: it is ambiguous. Without it, life could not continue, and in its proper use it brings about a union between man and woman which provides a gracious and unique fulfillment. On the other hand, it is subject to an infinite variety of distortions and frustrations. Besides all this, sexuality represents one of the major differentiations of human (and of almost all biological) existences. Certain of these differentiations of sexuality necessarily obtain in all times and places, but in addition to exhibiting these universal aspects of biological differentiation, sexuality lends itself to an enormous variety of definitions, for example, with respect to masculine and feminine roles that vary greatly. These and other differentiations give to human life fascinating qualities and degrees of individuality.

For our consideration here, the crucial question is the character and significance of the sexual union that belongs to marriage. This question is crucial, particularly in face of the commandment, "Thou shalt not commit adultery." When we consider this ancient commandment as a commandment we must recall that, like the other commandments of the ten, it is not merely legal imperative. Nor are they designed to enable us merely "to have a happy time of it" in the human adventure. By the covenant they are grounded in faithfulness and devotion; they are grounded in a relationship and not in a law. They are based upon trust and gratitude toward God for his gracious covenant, a trust and gratitude that determine not only our relation to God but also our relation to nature and the community. In marriage they condition especially the relations between husband and wife and family, but these relations extend to wider spheres. Adultery, then, is a breaking of a larger covenant as well as of the marriage bond.

The definition of adultery, however, has varied greatly in different times and places. According to the custom of ancient Israel, for example, any woman who out of wedlock consorted with a man other than her husband was an adulteress. But the husband's consorting with a bondmaid or even with a single woman was not considered to be adultery. For the man, adultery was confined to cohabitation with the wife or the bethrothed of another.

In later times, the definition of adultery has become broader than it was in ancient Israel. But this is not the only, perhaps not the most significant, difference with respect to relations between man and woman. A contemporary social scientist has characterized our time as one in which all adults in a special way are "permanently available" as potential marriage partners, whatever their current age or marital status. We live in a time when there is high mobility; a high degree of anonymity is possible; women have gone out of the home to work in industry, to enter into professional careers, and to engage in business. These and other factors, such as the concept of incompatibility, have given rise to new conceptions of "freedom." It is therefore important for Christians to be mindful of a religious conception of marriage and of sexual union.

St. Paul sees this relationship in a peculiarly profound way. In his view, sexual intercourse brings man and woman into a relationship that makes one body. His use of the term *body* instead of *flesh* shows in a unique way how he understands the significance of sexual union. He sees the sexual union as a uniting of nature and spirit. The "body" is not simply the physical organism; it is the total self. Intercourse is therefore much more than a physical act that takes place as it were on the periphery of personal experience. It involves and affects the whole man and the whole woman in the very center of their beings.

Here we see the individuality of each drawn into a broader, richer "individuality" of union. Each becomes "opened" to the other, and each becomes united to the other—a dynamic union for which the word *ecstasy* in its philosophical as well as in its emotional meaning is a peculiarly apt expression. And in a new way each becomes also a vessel of divine, transforming power. The union can be viewed, then, as bringing about an ontological change.

The intercourse that makes two people into one body is imbued with the love of the one for the other. It is without its proper meaning unless it consummates love in its various dimensions, and unless it expresses the recognition of the ontological change in the man and the woman and in their relation to each other, a change that gives rise to a special vocation of togetherness under God.

Adultery is a denial of this ontological change and a demise of the new vocation. This denial can issue from a variety of motives. It can be a form of discontent with the self or of discontent with the other. It can issue from a chaotic desire for variety. As such it is a form of acedia similar to the slothfulness of noonday which Cassian attributed to the monk who in a wandering of spirit and in loss of self-discipline yearns for a different monastery where, he imagines, true piety is properly appreciated. Sometimes, the talk is of incompatibility, and the latter surely can and does obtain. The ambiguity of the marriage relationship was stated succinctly by the Britisher who on hearing that large numbers of people in the United States are becoming divorced by reason of incompatibility, exclaimed, "But I thought that was the purpose of marriage." This comment serves to remind us of an extremely important aspect of marriage and also of friendship—the role of contrast in the relations between individuals.

Marriage brings together two people possessing special individualities with particular qualities and limitations. Acceptance of the limitations of the self and of the other, besides appreciation of the positive qualities of each, is an implication of the covenant. The vocation, the opportunities and the perils, of the marriage covenant reside in a special way precisely in the particularity (and even in the limitations) of the partners of the covenant.

Here I would like to draw an analogy, granting that it is imperfect. The artist in selecting material is attracted by its peculiar qualities and possibilities: at the same time, however, the artist must recognize and adjust to the limitations of the material. If the wood or stone possess a particular grain, the artist takes the grain into account, adjusts to it—creatively. The work of art acquires its attractive quality partly as a consequence of the artist's reverence for the material. Wordsworth, writing about the sonnet form, sees in its confines something like "the convent's narrow room."

> . . . 'twas pastime to be bound
> within the Sonnet's scanty plot of ground.

The beauty of a particular poem depends upon the poet's respect for the unique form of the sonnet.

Marriage is not dissimilar in its opportunities and demands. It is the enduring occasion, the vocation, to find meaningful and responsible fulfillment in the peculiar, individual qualities and limitations of the other and the self; that is, in the uniting of individuality and universality in marital union and companionship. From this individuality of union and companionship issues not only the family with its joys and responsibilities but also the courage to confront tragedy. From it issues also the courage to meet the tensions and responsibilities to the community. Marked failure or frustration in this vocation can justify separation and divorce. To deny this is to promote lovelessness in the name of covenant. But adultery is not the remedy, for it does not carry with it the possibility of meaningful vocation, the possibility of the responsible fulfillment of the whole personality of either partner in the adultery.

In saying these things, however, we must recognize a broad responsibility that lies upon us all. The dignity of individuality and also of the marriage covenant can scarcely be maintained in the ghettos that are the siamese twin of the contemporary urban, middle-class community or of suburbia. These inhuman conditions that militate against covenant-faithfulness are a part of *us*. They are in part the consequence of our "restrictive covenants." It is a strange fact that the word *covenant* today is most familiar in that notorious phrase. Here we encounter again the broad, universal implications of authentic covenant.

III

Marriage, we have recognized, is a bond within the context of a larger covenant, of a covenant of the community of faith under God. To violate the covenant of marriage through the act of adultery is to break not only a covenant between husband and wife but also their covenant with the community. One cannot consider adultery a merely private action. It has consequences not only for the unfaithful one and for the spouse and members of the immediate family who suffer from the unfaithfulness. It bears consequences also in the community at large. By the power of evil example it can make faithfulness more difficult for others in the community.

Here let me again cite an analogy, this time from the realm of personal relations rather than from that of art. In a parish I served in my youth a prominent member in despair attempted to commit suicide. By chance, however, he was discovered before it was too late, and he was restored. But he vehemently resented having been frustrated in his attempt. He argued that he had every justification for committing suicide. Because of the widespread depression he had lost his position as an executive. He had been unable to secure any employment, and he asserted that by reason of his frustration and unhappiness, he was only a burden to his family. He claimed that insurance would give his family economic security, and he insisted that everyone would be better off if he were "out of the way." He had properly met his responsibilities, he said, and he should be free to end his life. Why had others interfered? I was an old friend of his as well as the minister of the parish, and I argued with him to the best of my powers. But to no avail. In the midst of these discussions I called on Dr. Richard Cabot of the Harvard Faculty, and appealed for assistance. Dr. Cabot immediately said that my friend had by no means met his responsibilities. Every suicide, he said, offers new temptations to others considering suicide, making it more difficult for them to resist the temptation. I then resumed the argument with my friend. In the end he yielded by recognizing with conviction that he had been wrong in believing he had been fully responsible, and particularly by recognizing that his suicide, if successful, would have weakened the texture and health of the community.

The covenant of marriage is not merely a family covenant. It is a circle within, and integrally related to, the concentric circles of the larger communities of participation and responsibility. If it were not, it would be the enemy of justice and peace, a restrictive covenant.

Ultimately of course the covenant of marriage, like the covenant of the community of faith, is not rooted in a sense of responsibility under a stern god of duty. It is rooted in a love that is stronger than passion, stronger than the slings and arrows of fortune.

These dimensions of covenant are often recognized most poignantly when the loved one is taken by death. They find expression in words of homage and faithfulness spoken by a widow who had just lost her husband of many years. Remembering his prophetic act when he first became aware of his fatal illness, she used the word that is the title of the Chekhov story, "He had come to me directly and placed his lover's hand on my shoulder. He had said good-by to me in his own way and reassured me that his spirit would always be at my side. 'My darling' was all I could say. . . . How unbelievable that you are gone. I say 'Hello Darling' to the night sky, the moon, the stars; to the daylight creating a vivid brilliance; and to the sunset so various in beauty, stirring in me the wish to touch that distance and fathom it. . . . I am the emblem of a love affair that was important because it saw, and felt, and held great beauty. Through sickness and health, for richer for poorer, there remained always a magic bond."

The covenant of marriage is rooted in the affection, the magic bond, that holds the world together. It is rooted in the covenant of being itself.

34 · Shalom: The Ministry of Wholeness

Everyone deals falsely; they have healed the wounds of my people lightly, saying, "Peace, Peace," when there is no peace.

Jeremiah 6:14

And when he was come near, he beheld the city, and wept over it, saying, if thou hadst known, even thou, at least in this thy day, the things which belong unto thy peace; but now they are hid from thine eyes.

Luke 19:41−42

Shalom, the word for peace, is probably the Hebrew word most familiar to gentiles. In Yiddish the word is pronounced "sholem," and in its most popular usage, it is the equivalent of "hello" or "goodbye." The question has been raised as to why the same word may be used for both "hello" and "goodbye." The Israelis say it is "because we have so many problems that half the time we don't know whether we are going or coming." In the form *shalom aleichem* the term means, as you know, "Peace be with you."

In the Scripture, however, the term is more than a salutation, it also means more than the absence of war. It is a profoundly religious term, used to describe material and spiritual well-being, cognate with heal, healthy, hale, whole. Sometimes God is spoken of as Shalom. In both the Old and the New Testament it is sometimes synonymous with "the messianic kingdom of God." For the ancient prophets the word refers not only to the health or wholeness of the individual but also to the health of the society, to the people as a corporate body under covenant. Sometimes the idea of corporate personality is implied, as though the society is a person capable of health or ill health. The word *shalom,* then, possesses a striking breadth and depth of meaning, the *wholeness* of authentic human life, God's intention for human being and community. Shalom is holistic. Nothing is secular and beyond scrutiny. All is sacred. Just this is contained in the words from Jeremiah, "My people . . . saying, 'Peace, peace,' when there is no peace."

The full force of the word *shalom* became electrically alive in the Nazi

This essay is based on the sermon which Adams delivered at the service of ordination of Geoffrey Gilbert Drutchas, at the Medford, Massachusetts, Unitarian Universalist Church, August 8, 1982.

period in Germany where the common greeting imposed upon the nation was the words "Heil Hitler." A Christian professor of Old Testament at Marburg University paraphrased Jeremiah's words to read, "My people say, 'Heil, Heil,' and they know not what they mean." This paraphrase of a Jewish prophet was calculated to bring scorn upon the anti-Semitism of the Nazis, and it did so; all over Germany, especially in Christian anti-Nazi groups, the professor's translation was quoted. The memory of the Jew Jeremiah was still alive, although the Old Testament was no longer read in pro-Nazi churches and the photograph of Hitler the Jew-hater was placed on the altar in some churches. In this situation Jeremiah might justly excoriate those who deal falsely by attempting to "heal the wound of my people lightly" by daubing a gloss over the wound to peace, to wholeness. In the view of Jeremiah, the society thereby remains a suffering patient.

What, then, is wholeness? It is concern for the whole as well as for the parts, the recognition that no individual, no congregation, may consider itself an isolated entity. Not only the health of the individual but also the covenant of the commonwealth is the responsibility of all. Wholeness can exist only where justice and mercy are freely sought after. The integrity of the individual is bound up with the integrity of the society. Shalom is holistic. For Jeremiah and the great prophets the lack of wholeness was seen especially in the neglect of the needy at the gate. The needy are an inextricable part of us and of the whole. We deal falsely when we gloss over the wound. Indeed, we deal falsely when we ignore the fact that our problems and goals are not only personal (they are that of course) but are also institutional. At this moment I recall that Samuel McChord Crothers in the sermon he gave at my ordination over fifty years ago in Salem carried this refrain: Every personal problem is a social problem, every social problem is a personal problem.

It is noteworthy that in some churches today in Central and South America one of the remarkable movements is that of liberation theology, liberation from the imprisonment of classism, racism, and sexism. In the view of these Catholics and Protestants we cannot be whole persons in unjust institutions. In such institutions the self is fragmented and distorted—human potential is stifled. The liberation movement tries to take seriously Jesus' words when he wept, "If thou hadst known, even thou, at least in this thy day, the things which belong to thy peace! but now they are hidden from thine eyes."

Here we must distinguish between serious commitment to social change and the entertainment of noble attitudes. Kindly and seemingly generous attitudes do not suffice to achieve wholeness. Mere attitude can be a form of treachery protecting institutional prejudice and injustice. In the 1960s black leaders often spoke caustically of "beautiful attitudes" that leave institutions unchanged, institutions with their built-in racism. Institutional change, not beautiful attitude, is required.

One could illustrate this truism from life in the church, in the business office, in colleges and universities, in trade unions, in labor-management relations, in the local community, in government, and in international affairs. In the international sphere we witness today the demand for a nuclear freeze. One may illustrate the truism also in the time-honored subordination of women and of other minority groups.

Today I want to illustrate the truism that the achievement of justice requires institutional change in an area about which we generally hear little in the church—the area of professional sport. I want to speak of the fairly recent breakdown of the color barrier, in the struggle for peace and wholeness, in major league baseball. You may be surprised to learn that in its initial stage the struggle was religiously motivated.

The story of this struggle is set forth eloquently and in great detail by Harvey Frommer in his recently published book, *Rickey and Robinson*. Here this skilled sports writer shows how two men's planning and strategy were required to overcome deep-seated prejudice.

Branch Rickey, years later to be the manager of the Brooklyn Dodgers, a Methodist and a graduate of Ohio Wesleyan University, observed again and again how blacks were maltreated in the small-league baseball teams, and were forced to accept injustice silently. He resolved to end this, at least in baseball. For this and other reasons he invented the farm system. By this means he was able to discover all sorts of talent, including hitherto hidden black talent—that of the needy at the gate. For years he kept a detailed record of all these previously neglected players, recording not only their baseball skills but also their habits and character. For a major leaguer he sought first of all for a first-rate ballplayer. It would not be sufficient to find a nice black fellow, a "good guy" easily likable. He must be absolutely superior as a ballplayer. In addition, he wanted a fighter, but a special kind of fighter—one who would not fight back.

On an appointed day in a memorable encounter at baseball headquarters in Brooklyn, Rickey put Jackie through a grueling test. He contrived to imagine a variety of scenes in which Jackie would be humiliated at the hands of other players, white players, at the hands of managers and coaches, and of people in the bleachers and on the street or in restaurants. In each instance Rickey stressed the idea that Jackie must never fight back, never even talk back. He should concentrate on showing his skill in baseball. If he fought back, even only in words, he would do just what the racists hoped for. He would be immediately trapped into a fist-fight. He might even trigger a riot, and as a consequence bring to an end that "foolish and mad" attempt to bring blacks into the major baseball leagues.

For this purpose, then, Rickey selected a supreme ballplayer, Jackie Robinson, who happened also to be a Methodist and a graduate of his own college. As Harvey Frommer says, Rickey for his part

> had been a country schoolteacher, earned three college degrees, played and coached collegiate baseball and football, played professional baseball and football, lectured extensively on behalf of Prohibition, and been a college instructor (in Latin), an athletic director, and a lawyer. He had come through two bouts with tuberculosis. An abstemious Sabbath-observing Methodist whose vilest expletive was "Judas Priest," he was primed to enter the rough-and-tumble world of major-league baseball. The sport would never be the same.

The dialogue in the office ended with Rickey's asking Jackie, a fellow Methodist, to read several passages about Jesus' teachings from Giovanni Papini's *Life of Christ,* passages about turning the other cheek and about violence. After reading the passages, Jackie closed the book gently and handed it back to Rickey. "I understand," he said. The compact was made—not to fight back.

I do not need to rehearse here the signs of extraordinary courage and persistence displayed by Jackie through the following years when the humiliations predicted by Rickey were suffered, including even physical injuries deliberately inflicted by white players. It is significant that Rickey was able to persuade black organizations not to parade in honor of Jackie's victories on the field. He feared that such demonstrations would incite to riot. Ups and downs of controversy were on the agenda for both Rickey and Robinson. But in the end they broke the color line in baseball. Eventually, Jackie landed in the Hall of Fame, and years later (last week in fact), the U.S. Postal Service issued a stamp featuring Jackie Robinson. Together these two men had set at liberty those who were oppressed, bringing release to the powerless.

This, of course, does not mean that the overall struggle has ended. Last week, for example, K.K.K. signs were found chalked on the lockers of black policemen in Cambridge, and less violent forms of discrimination are still widely respectable, including those newly permitted by the Supreme Court. But it does mean that basic changes take place slowly and primarily through group action, through organizations and movements within and outside the church supported by skill, courage, and persistence. These are organizations that go beyond philanthropy in the struggle for integrity and wholeness. Here the individual must choose to become involved, pledged, *engagê*.

Social struggle is, of course, only one aspect of the search for integrity and wholeness. As the present moment and in this place we are aware of the centrality of worship, prayer, and meditation, of religious education, the disciplines of individual fulfillment, the joy of meaningful fellowship, of play, of the appreciation of science and the arts. None of these can be entirely separated from the social struggle for its risks and responsibilities.

I have just spoken of play and the arts. It has occurred to me that the discussion here so far today has employed language, communication through the ear. Two centuries ago the distinction was made between ear-people and eye-people. Would it be possible to contrive a visual image, an icon that projects for us the nature of shalom, of peace and wholeness, in a way that is appropriate for our religious faith, appropriate for the recognition of individual conscience in an open and free community? Can we find an image for a community that strives for unity in diversity, a visual image that takes into account a concern for the powerless in our society, an image that can communicate to the eye what language cannot do through the ear?

To my surprise there has come to mind a visual image from the work of a contemporary American artist, Alexander Calder, who is famous for his mobiles. How shall we in words describe a mobile? Everyone has seen one. A mobile is a light, abstract construction usually suspended from the ceiling. It is made up of little pieces of metal subtly poised and deployed in space and delicately held in balance by a web of thin wires. The entire mobile is sensitive to gentle breezes that stir it into movement. Each little piece of metal possesses its individuality, sometimes enhanced by color; yet, all of the pieces taken together form a unity, a community, a covenant of being composing a whole. Individuality of the members, relatedness of each to each and to all, organic wholeness, and all in movement and in perfect balance and tension. Why not call it shalom?

This mobile, we may say, is an artist's ideal image, a composite icon of dynamic fulfillment individual and social—the transcending harmony of the kingdom of God. In this image the powerless have a place in which they

Black Beast, stabile by Alexander Calder
(Photo: Pedro E. Guerrero)

possess the power of self-determination in community. Moreover, when you disturb a mobile by touching it, it veers out of balance but then returns to equilibrium drawn thither by gravity, the integrating power of the divine.

I know not what Alexander Calder would have said to my calling one of his mobiles an image of the kingdom of God susceptible to the tides, the wind, of the spirit—to my saying as in a parable, "The kingdom of heaven is like unto—a mobile." He might have pleaded, "God save me from pulpit homilies." But could not Jeremiah yearning for shalom, and Jesus weeping over Jerusalem, see in it an ideal image nourished by hope? The image, to be sure is an ideal, it is not an image of "the real world," but it suggests how that world lives when it is creating a viable world of wholeness.

One or two things, however, are lacking in a Calder mobile if it is taken as an image of fulfillment: There is no hint here that in the enjoyment of fulfillment there always shall have been suffering and struggle against evil. The Calder image reminds one of the tendency of some churches to smother the cross in the lilies of Easter.

Calder, however, is by no means unaware of evil, as can be observed in his stabile entitled *Black Beast,* a strange monster. Here we see four large but thin plates of iron intersecting at extreme angles, with the suggestion of heads and legs attached to torsos, the very opposite of wholeness.

The church as a community of faith and hope is entrusted in a special way with the ministry of wholeness for the individual and the society, for each member individually and all together. The church is, then, the messenger of hope for the kingdom which through God's grace is always "at hand," available.

35 · The Ecology of World Religions and Peace

For centuries it has been known that the cultivated fig tree will bear fruit only if the caprifig, a wild fig, is growing in the vicinity and now we know why this is so. The caprifig gives lodging to a small wasp that pollinates the cultivated fig, thus stimulating it to mature and become edible. The process is called caprification, and it represents the working of an ecosystem that brings separate organisms into mutual relationship. Without this ecosystem they would remain in disjunction.

The significance of the World Conference on Religion and Peace consists of its participants recognizing that the religions must try to form a new working relationship if they are to contribute effectively to world peace. This new interrelationship must in turn achieve dynamic interaction with the other ecosystems of nature and society.

The goal of the new ecosystem is certainly not the homogenizing of the religions. The authentic goal is twofold: (1) that through interaction and in face of the problems of peace, each religion will be stimulated to become aware of the best that is in it, and to make it effectively available, and (2) that out of the mutual influence of the religions the disjunctions that now prevail within and between them and society may be recognized and in some degree overcome. The most debilitating and destructive schisms are due to the arrogance and provincialism of the religions.

A new cooperative system cannot succeed unless it can in some measure overcome these and other disjunctions such as the dualism between body and spirit, inner and outer life, the personal and the institutional, spirituality and economic-political obligations, science and religion, the immanent and the transcendent, and utopianism and realism. The existence of these extremes reveals that religion (which ostensibly aims to provide reconciliation and healing) shares most of the ruptures to which persons and society are subject and which bespeak the unjust distribution of natural and human resources. A crucial test, then, of the new cooperation between the religions will be the quality and degree of concern for the injustice, abject depen-

This essay is reprinted with the permission of Kosei Publishing Company from *Dharma World*, September 1978, Vol. 5, copyright 1978.

dency, poverty, racism, and egregious nationalism that disrupt our social structures and thus promote war.

Wherever people are striving to overcome these disjunctions a divine power is at work. Faith in that power brings confidence that the resources for healing and reconciliation are available to all persons, and especially to those committed to humility and charity and audacity. This faith arises from and serves the divine ecology.

Postscript: The Church That Is Free

I call that church free which enters into covenant with the ground of freedom, that sustaining, judging, transforming power not made with hands. It protests against the idolatry of any human claim to absolute truth or authority. This covenant is the charter and joy of worship in the beauty of holiness.

I call that church free which in covenant with that divine community-forming power brings the individual, even the unacceptable, into a caring, trusting fellowship that protects and nourishes his or her integrity and spiritual freedom. Its goal is the prophethood and the priesthood of all believers — the one for the liberty of prophesying, the other for the ministry of healing. It therefore protests against the infringement of autonomy or participation, whether it be in the church, the state, the family, the daily work (or the lack of it), or in other social spheres.

I call that church free which liberates from bondage to the principalities and powers of the world, whether churchly or secular, and which promotes the continuing reformation of its own and other institutions. It protests against routine conformity or thoughtless nonconformity that lead to deformity of mind and heart and community.

I call that church free which in charity promotes freedom in fellowship, seeking unity in diversity. This unity is a potential gift, sought through devotion to the transforming power of creative interchange in generous dialogue. But it will remain unity in diversity.

I call that church free which responds in responsibility to the Spirit that bloweth where it listeth. The tide of the Spirit finds utterance ever and again through a minority. It invites and engenders liberation from repression and exploitation, whether of nation or economic system, of race or sex or class. It bursts through rigid, cramping inheritance, giving rise to new language, to new forms of cooperation, to new and broader fellowship. The church of the Spirit is a pilgrim church on adventure.

I call that church free which is not bound to the present, which cowers

This statement was written by Adams for presentation in a service at the First and Second Church of Boston, on May 25, 1975, marking the sesquicentennial of the founding of the American Unitarian Association.

not before the vaunted spirit of the times. It earns and creates a tradition binding together past, present, and future in a living tether, in a continuing covenant and identity, bringing forth treasures both new and old. God speaks, he has also spoken.

I call that church free which is not imprisoned in itself or in a sect. In loyalty to its own historic character and norms, it is open to insight and conscience from every source. The church that would be free yearns to belong to the church universal, catholic and invisible.

But the church is never wholly free: It tolerates injustice, special privilege, and indifference to suffering, as though it were not accountable to a tribunal higher than the world's. It passes by on the other side, thus breaking the covenant. In the midst of this unfreedom the congregation comes together to adore that which is holy, to confess its own brokenness, and to renew the covenant.

I call that church free which does not cringe in despair, but casting off fear is lured by the divine persuasion to respond in hope to the light that has shone and that still shines in the darkness.

Index

Abraham, 71, 122
Acton, Lord John Emerich Dalberg, 132–33, (quoted) 157–58, 267
Adam and Eve, 4, 10
Adams, Henry, 267
Adams, James Luther: academic contributions, 21–22; assessments of, 4, 26n4; childhood and youth, 12, 26, 33, 128–29, 287; conception of prophetic faith, 4–11; formative influences on, 14–17, 28n27, 33–42, 255–56; marriage and family, 15, 30n47; organizational activities, 28n34; personal and intellectual development, 11–20; as political activist, 17–20; publications, 3, 27n5, 29n37; as teacher, 1–3, 26, 38, 39, 88; thought of, 4–11, 31, 97, 173, 247; *Paul Tillich's Philosophy of Culture, Science and Religion,* 128
Adams, John, 58
Adams, Margaret Young, 15, 25, 26, 29–30n47
Adorno, T. W., 232n2
Adultery, 295, 298–303
Agape, 152, 153, 154, 163n1
Agape and Eros (Nygren), 163n1
Age of Reason, 117
Aging: cultural variations, 282–83; meaning of, 294; social status and, 283, 284–85; theology of, 281–94
Alexander, Franz, 291
Alexander, Samuel, 192
Alienation, 180, 181
American Civil Liberties Union, 261
American Legion, 109
American Medical Association, 260
American Unitarian Association, 89, 93, 313
American Unitarian Association Commission of Appraisal, 28n34
Amos, 60
Anabaptists, 156
Anaximander, 228, 296–97
Ancient Law (Maine), 284–85
Ancient Religion of the Gentiles (Lord Herbert of Cherbury), 118
Andover Newton Theological School, 1, 26
Andreotti, Giulio, 244
Angelism, 173, 177, 179, 180
Angelology, 165, 166, 175–76
Anglo-catholicism, 38

Anti-Semitism, of Nazis, 305
Apologetic theology, 61, 214
Aquinas, Thomas, 155, 176, 179
Architecture, and family, 294
Arendt, Hannah, 87
Areopagitica (Milton), quoted, 10, 175, 181
Aristotle, 187, 277
Arnold, Matthew, 65
Associational behavior, 262
Associations, 260, 261–62
Atheism, 11, 50, 57, 239
Atomic Energy Commission, 77
Aubrey, Edwin Ewart, 182–83
Auden, W. H., 11, 92; "Musée des Beaux Arts," 82; "September 1, 1939," 12
Augustine, 20, 100, 182, 289
Authoritarianism, 86; of church, 156
Autobiography (Trollope), 62

Babbitt, Irving, 14, 20, 35, 36
Bach, J. S., 15, 25, 36, 37
Backus, Isaac, 132
Baptists, 129, 131–34, 156
Baptist Theological Union, 127
Barry, F. R., 38
Barth, Karl, 41, 140, 207, 212, 214, 256
Barthianism, 38
"Basic Problems of Ethics, The" (Troeltsch), 149
Beauvoir, Simone de, 290
Beethoven, L. v., 202
Beliefs, 52, 53; institutional consequences of, 155
Benevolence of Deity, The (Chauncy), 120
Benevolent Fraternity (Unitarian Universalist), 292
Bennett, John, 37
Bentley, William, 216–17
Benz, Ernst, 164n2
Bergson, Henri, 60, 192, 204
Berman, Harold, 130
Bible, 20, 23, 40, 93, 122, 132, 165, 182, 194, 279; influence on Adams, 34; creation and, 297; higher criticism, 72, 79, 89, 119; and historical religion, 17; language of, 274; meaning of, 73–75; *shalom* in, 304; Unitarian Universalist roots in, 23, 88–92

315

Ray, John, 118
Realism, 9, 38, 209
Reality, God as ultimate, 49, 52, 53, 85, 91, 116
Redemption, 36, 123–24, 237
Reflections on the Revolution in France (Burke), 106
Reformation, of institutions, 313
Reformation, the, 94, 124, 230–31, 291; left wing of, 58, 88, 116, 157–62, 258. *See also* Radical Reformation
Relativism, 98
Religion: and culture, 173, 229, 241; historical tradition in, 37, 67, 123; material and spiritual, 178–79; mystical element of, 70n4; prophetic element, 80, 83; sacramental and prophetic, 70n4; and science, 88; three types of, 239; and Whitehead, 196; world religions, 248. *See also* Prophetic religion
Religious liberalism, 53, 58, 145, 148; Adams's critique of, 16, 22, 23, 37; historical heritage (Troeltsch), 145; conception of human nature in, 182–85; in 18th-century New England, 120. *See also* Liberal religion
Religious Situation, The (Tillich), 209, 214
Religious socialism, Tillich and, 209–10
Responsibility: communal, 137; corporate and individual, 151–52, 240, 245; and covenant, 83, 137; as response to God, 180, 313; social, 78, 152, 161, 163n1, 255, 270, 271
Retribution, 279
Revelation, 119, 120, 122, 123
Revivalism, 79
Reynolds, Sir Joshua, 116
Rickey, Branch, 306–7
Rickey and Robinson (Frommer), 306–7
Riemenschneider, Tilman, 206
Robinson, Jackie, 306–7
Roman Catholicism, 156, 164n3; modernism in, 62; von Hügel and, 61
Roman Empire, 154
Romanticism, 9, 122, 200, 215
Rome, Sydney and Beatrice, 210
Roosevelt, Franklin D., 87
Ross, Edward Alsworth, 101
Rousseau, Jean Jacques, 256
Royal Society (British), 76, 117
Royce, Josiah, 217
Rubenstein, Artur, 177

Sainte-Beuve, C. A., 147
St. Matthew Passion (Bach), 36, 37

St. Simonians, 164n3
Salvation, 33, 42, 81, 297
Samson Agonistes (Milton), 245
Santayana, George, 130
Sartre, Jean Paul, 180
Schell, Jonathan, 13
Schelling, Friedrich, 41, 114, 182, 215, 217
Schiller, Friedrich, 52
Schleiermacher, Friedrich, 213–14, 215, 216, 222
Schmidt-Rottluff, Karl, 207
Schweitzer, Albert, 17, 77, 78, 90, 139, 234
Science(s), 38, 76, 88, 101, 117
Scofield Reference Bible, 12, 33
Secularism, 62, 113, 122–24, 147; Tillich on, 222
Secularization, 193
Secular philosophies, contemporary, 221–22
Segregation, 83, 252–53
Self-appraisal, 72
Self-determination, 121, 244, 245, 272
Self-will, 86–87
Separation of church and state, 132, 157, 258
Separation of Church and State, The (Troeltsch), 143
Separation of powers, 132, 136, 243
Sexism, 134
Sexuality, 296, 298–99
Shakespeare, William, 175, 244
Shalom, 70n4, 248, 304
Shelley, Percy Bysshe, 88
Shock of recognition, 3, 17, 274–80; in Greek tragedy, 276–77, 279
Sin, 124, 262–63, 269
Sleep, 233–38
Smith, Adam, 134
Social gospel, 94, 100
Socialist Decision, The (Tillich), 204, 210
Social protest, 231
Social struggle, 308
Social Teachings of the Christian Churches (Troeltsch), 38, 140
Société européenne de culture, 243, 245
Society, 79, 184, 185
Society for the Arts, Religion, and Contemporary Culture, 228
Sociology, 101, 173; of knowledge, 183; of religion, 119, 140, 148
Socrates, 48
Söderblom, Nathan, 36
South, Robert, 233
Sower, The (Millet), 36
Sperry, Willard, 38, 152, 252, 264
Spiritual and Anabaptist Writers (Williams), 71
Spirituality, 22, 55, 57, 68, 83, 178, 179; von Hügel on, 38, 62, 67